Understanding and Teaching
the Modern Middle East

The Harvey Goldberg Series
for Understanding and Teaching History

The Harvey Goldberg Series for Understanding and Teaching History gives college and secondary history instructors a deeper understanding of the past as well as the tools to help them teach it creatively and effectively. Named for Harvey Goldberg, a professor renowned for his history teaching at Oberlin College, Ohio State University, and the University of Wisconsin from the 1960s to the 1980s, the series reflects Goldberg's commitment to helping students think critically about the past with the goal of creating a better future. For more information, please visit www.GoldbergSeries.org.

Series Editors

John Day Tully is a professor of history at Central Connecticut State University and was the founding director of the Harvey Goldberg Center for Excellence in Teaching at Ohio State University. He has coordinated many Teaching American History grants and has received the Connecticut State University System's Board of Trustees Teaching Award.

Matthew Masur is a professor of history at Saint Anselm College, where he has served as codirector of the Father Guerin Center for Teaching Excellence. He has also been a member of the Teaching Committee of the Society for Historians of American Foreign Relations.

Brad Austin is a professor of history at Salem State University. He has served as chair of the American Historical Association's Teaching Prize Committee and has worked with hundreds of secondary school teachers as the academic coordinator of many Teaching American History grants.

Advisory Board

Leslie Alexander Associate Professor of History, University of Oregon
Kevin Boyle William Smith Mason Professor of American History, Northwestern University
Ross Dunn Professor Emeritus, San Diego State University
Leon Fink UIC Distinguished Professor of History, University of Illinois at Chicago
Kimberly Ibach Principal, Fort Washakie High School, Wyoming
Alfred W. McCoy J.R.W. Smail Professor of History, Director, Harvey Goldberg Center for the Study of Contemporary History, University of Wisconsin–Madison
David J. Staley Associate Professor of History, Director, Center for the Humanities in Practice, Ohio State University
Maggie Tran Chair of Social Studies, McLean High School, Virginia
Sam Wineburg Margaret Jacks Professor of Education and (by courtesy) of History, Director, Stanford History Education Group, Stanford University

Understanding and Teaching the Modern Middle East

Edited by

OMNIA EL SHAKRY

The University of Wisconsin Press

The University of Wisconsin Press
728 State Street, Suite 443
Madison, Wisconsin 53706
uwpress.wisc.edu

Gray's Inn House, 127 Clerkenwell Road
London EC1R 5DB, United Kingdom
eurospanbookstore.com

Printed in the United States of America
This book may be available in a digital edition.

Library of Congress Cataloging-in-Publication Data

Names: El Shakry, Omnia S., 1970– editor.
Title: Understanding and Teaching the Modern Middle East / edited by
Omnia El Shakry.
Other titles: Harvey Goldberg series for understanding and teaching
history.
Description: Madison, Wisconsin : The University of Wisconsin Press,
[2020] | Series: The Harvey Goldberg series for understanding and
teaching history | Includes bibliographical references and index.
Identifiers: LCCN 2020004270 | ISBN 9780299327606 (cloth)
Subjects: LCSH: Middle East—History—Study and teaching.
Classification: LCC DS61.8 .U53 2020 | DDC 956—dc23
LC record available at https://lccn.loc.gov/2020004270

For Nadeem, always

Contents

Contents

Contents

Preface

As I sit down to write this preface the world is currently in the throes of two world historical convulsions: one is the global pandemic known as COVID-19 and the other is the confrontation with anti-blackness, systemic racism, and police brutality all over the globe, and particularly in the United States.[1] The artwork that graces the cover of this book, *Shift* (2012) by Mona Hatoum (b. Beirut, Lebanon, 1952), aptly evokes the seismic shockwaves and topographical instabilities that reverberate across the globe, subtly indicating that what takes place in one part of the world can always be deeply felt, at a subterranean level, in other parts of the world as well.[2]

The Middle East has long been viewed as central to such seismicity, although perhaps not in the stereotypical manner that mainstream analysts have put forth. Not merely a zone of conflict and war, the Middle East has also been the source of profound cultural, social, and intellectual exchanges between east and west that belie the notion of distinct civilizational trajectories of "the West and the Rest." At the same time, it would be disingenuous, particularly in these "times of war and death," to pretend that the forces of European colonial violence, US military invasions and occupations, and Middle Eastern state sponsored repression have not profoundly shaped and reshaped the region in the current moment. At the present writing, Egypt's authoritarian crackdown on dissidents, Israel's annexation of the West Bank, Lebanon's massive economic crisis, the destabilization of Iraqi state and society, and the collapse of the health care system in Yemen loom large, to name but a few calamities.

As elsewhere in the world, COVID-19 has exposed the fault lines of decaying public health care systems, as well as the economic inequities apparent in the aftermath of the demise of state welfare systems and their replacement with the cruelty of neoliberal austerity. Regional, let alone global cooperation appears only in the realm of wishful thinking.

As Rochelle Davis demonstrates in this volume, humanitarian solutions remain, as they always have, a patchwork quilt that can never adequately address the deeper structural political change needed for a more just and equitable world in which life and death are not contingent upon the brute fact of one's geopolitical location and economic wellbeing.[3]

And yet it is precisely because the Middle East has been a zone of catastrophe (s. *nakba*, pl. *nakabat*) that we can contemplate resilience and repair in the modern world from its vantage point. Once again, we may take our cue from Middle Eastern artists. As Ali Cherri (b. Beirut, Lebanon, 1976) presciently enquired with respect to his film on geological fault lines in Lebanon, *The Disquiet* (2013), what might it mean to imagine the imminent disaster of our own ending? Or to imagine hope as survival in the aftermath of an ongoing catastrophe?[4] The *nakba* or catastrophe in this rendering, then, is neither a specific endpoint in historical time nor a past that can be overcome; it is, rather, an ongoing experience.[5] These are some of the lessons we might learn from the trajectories of catastrophe and care in the modern Middle East.

No less consequential than COVID-19 have been the sustained uprisings against anti-blackness, in the United States and elsewhere, that have followed the brutal murder of George Floyd at the hands of Minneapolis police. For scholars who work on the Middle East, there are transregional connections to be made with the United States—the militarization and quotidian violence of colonial policing and military occupations, as well as the suppression and repression of uprisings with the mass detention and criminalization of racialized populations. Such connections are not accidental; rather, they emerge directly from the histories of racial capitalism, colonialism, New World slavery, and its afterlife in the modern era. As Achille Mbembe has observed, any account of modern necropolitical power ("the power and the capacity to dictate who may live and who must die") must "address slavery, which could be considered one of the first instances of biopolitical experimentation."[6] Here, the longue durée perspective of the historian is useful, insofar as no history of colonial violence, whether in the Middle East or elsewhere, can neglect the antecedent foundational violence of chattel slavery as providing an exemplum for understandings of race, violence, and modernity.[7]

Indeed, the scholar who best theorized the connections between race and colonial violence was the Martinican philosopher and psychiatrist Frantz Fanon, who in describing colonial Algeria noted, "The colonial world is a world cut in two. The dividing line, the frontiers are shown by barracks and police stations. In the colonies it is the policeman and the soldier who are the official, instituted go-betweens, the spokesman of the settler and his rule of oppression."[8] Bringing this history closer to the contemporary geography of the US, scholars have made clear that patterns of global segregation have often explicitly modeled themselves on Jim Crow segregation in the United States. It was Woodrow Wilson, after all, who advocated so strongly for segregation in the US federal government, while helping to establish a nation-state system through the League of Nations. This was likewise a form of global racial segregation, as Andrew Zimmerman has outlined and as Sara Pursley reminds us in this volume.[9]

In more recent history, the scandals at Abu Ghraib prison in Iraq, as well as at US-sponsored rendition sites across the world, similarly inspire parallels.[10] Drawing on African American studies scholar Hazel V. Carby, Anne McClintock argues, "we need to see the historical continuities of torture that haunt US history from its inception: the torture of American Indians; slavery; lynching; torture in the Philippines, Vietnam, and Central America in the 1980s." To see these continuities, however, is not to trace a linear and commensurate history, but rather, she resumes, to render "visible the continuities of imperial torture with the carceral violence in the national prison system and the rituals of military training. In the Abu Ghraib photos, these circuits of violence are forgotten at the moment of their revelation."[11]

But there is another crucial way in which anti-blackness is relevant to the history of the modern Middle East, one which has gone far less remarked upon in the wider literature. This relates to the ways in which histories of race and slavery have been intimately linked to anti-blackness in the region. Pioneering scholars, such as Eve Troutt Powell, have decried the absence of slaves in the historiography of the modern Middle East, outlining what she terms "a different shade of colonialism" to describe Egyptian attitudes toward slavery, race, and the Sudan, in particular.[12] And yet, as the recent statement by the Board of the Middle East Studies Association of North America has pointed out, there is still much work to be done in grappling "with the long-marginalized history of Black slavery and its afterlives in the Middle East and North Africa." As they note, "this is a moment of reckoning with anti-Blackness and its entrenched history in our fields, classrooms, and communities in the region and diaspora. Now is the time to turn to anti-racist activists, as well as colleagues in Black Studies and Indigenous Studies for guidance on dismantling white supremacy."[13]

Returning to Fanon, we might productively read his writings on colonial violence in tandem with his earlier work in *Black Skin, White Masks*, in order to better understand that anti-blackness provided the template for colonial race prejudice and thus for global racial formations and relations in the modern era.[14] In David Marriott's phrasing "anti-blackness is the discourse through which a singular experience of the world is constituted. Such experience is not ineffable: anti-blackness is the thing against which the universal, the human, the ideal, etc., is enunciated and created; it is the means through which the racial discourse of being is articulated as spirit."[15] Or to repurpose Ali Cherri's metaphor, anti-blackness provides the geological fault lines, a *lapsus* or void, foundational to the sedimentation of race in the world—a foundational mythos that governs race in the world.[16]

As Marriott so lucidly argues, Fanon allows us to reflect upon the "persistent location of blackness as a necessary contamination of traditional political thinking," while simultaneously encouraging us to meditate on "the fall, the catastrophe, through which blackness has unfolded from its origin in the Middle Passage until its awaited arrival in the New World, an arrival for which we are still waiting, because such a possibility has to be invented if it is not to be missed."[17] It is, then, in the Fanonian "object of knowledge" where we may find the "unique singularity of blackness as the example of a *catastrophe that has already happened*."[18] By encountering anti-blackness as that through which the catastrophic itself can be anticipated, alongside the ongoing experiences of *nakabat* in the Middle East, we might better begin to contemplate our own disappearance.

Notes

1. I am grateful to Rajbir Singh Judge for helpful comments, suggestions, and edits on this preface.

2. This represents my own interpretation of Hatoum's artwork which is, of course, not necessarily how the artist intended the work to be read. I am grateful to Mona Hatoum and to Arter, Istanbul for permission to use this image on the cover. My thanks, as well, to Sophie Greig of Mona Hatoum Studio (London) for her assistance.

3. Rochelle Davis, "Refugees in and from the Middle East," in this volume.

4. Ali Cherri in conversation with Tarek El-Ariss, "Archives, Images, Memory" (conversation, at the conference "Unfixed Itineraries: Film and Visual Culture from Arab Worlds," University of California, Santa Cruz, October 26, 2013). See also https://www.alicherri.com/the-disquiet.

5. For a discussion of the catastrophic in relation to the Qur'anic notion of the ordeal (*ibtila*') understood as an encounter with the world and "a divine trial to which the subject is called to respond," see Stefania Pandolfo, *Knot of the Soul: Madness, Psychoanalysis, Islam* (Chicago: University of Chicago Press, 2019), 1–30, 225–26, 4.

6. Achille Mbembe, "Necropolitics," translated by Libby Meintjes, *Public Culture* 15, no. 1 (2003): 11–40, 11, 21.

7. The literature here is huge, but see, for example, Eric Williams, *Capitalism and Slavery* (Chapel Hill: University of North Carolina Press, 1944); C. L. R. James, *The Black Jacobins: Toussaint L'Ouverture and the San Domingo Revolution* (New York: Vintage Books, 1963); Hortense J. Spillers, "Mama's Baby, Papa's Maybe: An American Grammar Book," *Diacritics* 17, no. 2 (Summer 1987): 64–81; Saidiya V. Hartman, *Scenes of Subjection: Terror, Slavery, and Self- Making in Nineteenth-Century America* (Oxford: Oxford University Press, 1997); Robin Blackburn, *The Making of New World Slavery: From the Baroque to the Modern, 1492–1800* (London: Verso, 1997), to name but a few. For a foundational discussion of racial capitalism and the Black radical tradition, see Cedric J. Robinson, *Black Marxism: The Making of the Black Radical Tradition* (Chapel Hill: University of North Carolina Press, [1983] 2000).

8. Frantz Fanon, *The Wretched of the Earth*, translated by Constance Farrington (New York: Grove Press, [1961] 1963), 38.

9. Andrew Zimmerman, *Alabama in Africa: Booker T. Washington, the German Empire, and the Globalization of the New South* (Princeton: Princeton University Press, 2010), 201–2; Sara Pursley, "Colonialism, Empire, and Nationalist Movements," in this volume.

10. For colonial genealogies of counterinsurgency in the Middle East, see Derek Gregory, *The Colonial Present: Afghanistan, Iraq, Palestine* (Oxford: Blackwell, 2004); Laleh Khalili, *Time in the Shadows: Confinement in Counterinsurgencies* (Stanford, CA: Stanford University Press, 2013).

11. Hazel Carby, "A Strange and Bitter Crop: The Spectacle of Torture," *Open Democracy*, October 11, 2004, https://www.opendemocracy.net/en/article_2149jsp/. Quotation is from Anne McClintock, "Paranoid Empire: Specters from Guantanamo and Abu Ghraib," *Small Axe* 13, no. 1 (March 2009): 50–74, 64. In a somewhat related fashion, Nicholas Mirzoeff identifies "violence [as] the standard operating procedure of visuality," outlining three complexes of visuality: the plantation complex, from the seventeenth to the late nineteenth centuries; the imperial complex, from the late nineteenth to the mid-twentieth century;

and a military-industrial complex concerned with global counterinsurgency, from the mid-twentieth century to the present. Nicholas Mirzoeff, *The Right to Look: A Counterhistory of Visuality* (Durham, NC: Duke University Press, 2011), 10–22, 35–40, 292. On the historical singularity of slavery and its afterlife and its ontological and political incommensurability with Abu Ghraib, see Jared Sexton and Elizabeth Lee, "Figuring the Prison: Prerequisites of Torture at Abu Ghraib," *Antipode* 38, no. 5 (2006): 1005–22.

12. Eve Troutt Powell, *A Different Shade of Colonialism: Egypt, Great Britain and the Mastery of the Sudan* (Berkeley: University of California Press, 2003); Powell, *Tell This in My Memory: Stories of Enslavement in Egypt, Sudan and the Late Ottoman Empire* (Stanford, CA: Stanford University Press, 2012); Powell, "Will That Subaltern Ever Speak? Finding African Slaves in the Historiography of the Middle East," in *Narrating History: Histories and Historiographies of the Twentieth-Century Middle East*, ed. Israel Gershoni, Amy Singer, and Hakan Erdem (Seattle: University of Washington Press, 2006), 242–61; Powell and John Hunwick, eds., *The African Diaspora in the Mediterranean Lands of Islam* (Princeton, NJ: Markus Wiener Publishers, 2002). See also Terence Walz and Kenneth M. Cuno, eds., *Race and Slavery in the Middle East: Histories of Trans-Saharan Africans in Nineteenth-Century Egypt, Sudan, and the Ottoman Mediterranean* (Cairo: American University in Cairo Press, 2010).

13. https://mesana.org/advocacy/letters-from-the-board/2020/06/29/mesa -board-statement-in-solidarity-with-the-uprisings-against-systemic-racism-and -anti-blackness (posted June 29, 2020).

14. Frantz Fanon, *Black Skin, White Masks*, translated by Charles Lam Markmann (New York: Grove Press, [1952] 1967). This is not, of course, to imply that these racial formations are commensurable; they are ontologically and politically distinct.

15. David Marriott, *Whither Fanon? Studies in the Blackness of Being* (Stanford, CA: Stanford University Press, 2018), x.

16. On the *lapsus*, void, and abyss, see Marriott, *Whither Fanon?*

17. Marriott, *Whither Fanon?*, 5, xviii.

18. Marriott, *Whither Fanon?*, xviii, 114.

Acknowledgments

For many of us teaching is a collective practice—an ethical and intellectual vocation—and I owe my greatest debt to my undergraduate and graduate students at the University of California, Davis, who have taught me how to teach. All of the contributors here, talented scholars and teachers alike, deserve my immense gratitude. Many of them agreed to write chapters despite being overburdened by teaching, writing, and service obligations that can be extremely pressing for scholars who work on the modern and contemporary Middle East. They did so because they know not just that teaching matters, but that *how and why* we teach matters. Their skillful interweaving of content and pedagogy has made this a worthwhile and exciting volume.

This book would not be possible without the support of the Harvey Goldberg Series at the University of Wisconsin Press. I am indebted to the series editors—John Tully, Matthew Masur, and Brad Austin—in particular, and to the staff at the University of Wisconsin Press, more generally. Nathan MacBrien, Dennis Lloyd, Gwen Walker, Adam Mehring, Ivan Babanovski, and Jennifer Conn all provided helpful input at various stages of the book. Above all, my heartfelt thanks go to John Tully, who initially solicited me to work on the project and followed up with tremendous enthusiasm, support, and advice throughout every step of the process. He has been a wonderful sounding board for ideas, and I am grateful for his commitment to pedagogy and writing. The peer reviewers, too, provided useful feedback and criticism. I also thank Jane Curran for her skillful copyediting and Andrew Zonneveld for the index. I hope the book has been strengthened as a result of these combined efforts.

Andrea Lea Miller was with me from the very start of this project, helping with the book proposal, providing valuable feedback on the form and content of chapters, communicating with authors, working on permissions, and so much more. I simply could not have done this without her. Stephen Cox joined the project later and was instrumental in shaping the final product; beyond this, our work together in teaching The Middle East in the Twentieth Century has influenced my approach to pedagogy. I am grateful to both of them for their assistance, support, and friendship.

The history department, the History Project, and the Middle East/South Asia studies program at Davis have been wonderful environments conducive to writing, teaching, and pedagogical innovation. Research funding from the Dean's Office of the Division of Social Science and the Department of History at Davis helped support graduate student assistance that was indispensable to the completion of this book.

Much of the editing and writing for the book was done while I was in residence at the Stanford Humanities Center in 2018–2019. I am thankful to the staff and colleagues there for their warm intellectual engagement. I deeply value the friendships made over the course of that year, and a huge shout-out goes to Rachel Heiman, Karen Melvin, Adrien Zakar, Elizabeth Marcus, Lyndsey Hoh Copeland, Dominique Lestel, Jennifer Scappettone, and Nesrine Mbarek.

Going further back to 2013, the History Project and I received funding from the National Endowment for the Humanities for a Summer Institute for School Teachers at UC Davis on Roots of the Arab Spring, which was crucial for developing insights into teaching the modern Middle East. I was wonderfully assisted in this endeavor by Rajbir Singh Judge, Pam Tindall, Stacey Greer, and Phillip Barron; it was an inspiration for thinking about pedagogy generally and for becoming more attuned to the needs of K-12 teachers. Much of what I learned there from fellow UC Davis faculty, seminar participants, and History Project organizers has shaped the conceptualization of this book. Going back further still, my own mentors, especially Samira Haj, have deeply influenced my own understanding and teaching of the history of the modern Middle East.

At a more personal level, the completion of this book came during the most difficult of times in which Nadeem Haj, Stefania Pandolfo, and Diana Davis were always there for me. Dr. Gabrielle never gave up on me; she is a true healer. Dr. Isaac appeared just in time to save the day. Dr. Alex provided thoughtful and skillful care. Andrea Lea Miller, Nesa Azimi, Emily Wittman, Adam Thorpe, Susette Min, Benjamin Lawrance, Sherene Seikaly, Sally McKee, David and Susan Miller, as well as Rajbir and Abby Judge and the boys provided much needed love and support. My family has been a constant presence in my life despite the distance of living on two coasts and, often enough, several continents. I am extraordinarily thankful for their love and care.

Death, however painful, always reminds us that finitude is what makes life meaningful. Two deaths have overshadowed this book. In Monica Nelson's death there was much sorrow, but in remembrance there will be so much love. And I lost my little feline angel and writing muse, Fusto, who has been with us almost as long as we have been in Oakland, just before wrapping up this book. I send them both much love and quietude.

This book, like all of my other work, is for Nadeem, always.

Grateful acknowledgement is made for permission to reprint the following textual material:

One quarter of "Controversy in the Classroom: Lessons from the Modern Middle East" by Omnia El Shakry was originally published in *Perspectives in History: The Newsmagazine of the American Historical Association* 48, no. 5 (May 2010), https://www.historians.org/publications -and-directories/perspectives-on-history/may-2010/lessons-from-the -modern-middle-east.

"Understanding Sectarianism as a Global Problem" by Ussama Makdisi is derived from the introduction to *Age of Coexistence: The Ecumenical Frame and the Making of the Modern Arab World* (Oakland: University of California Press, 2019).

"America, Oil, and War in the Middle East" by Toby Craig Jones was originally published, in modified form, in the *Journal of American History* 99, no. 1 (2012): 208–18.

"Arab Uprisings in the Modern Middle East" by Asef Bayat draws heavily in information and analysis from *Revolution without Revolutionaries: Making Sense of the Arab Spring* (Palo Alto: Stanford University Press, 2017).

"The Armenian Genocide and the Politics of Knowledge" by Christine Philliou was originally published in *Public Books*, May 1, 2015, https://www.publicbooks.org/the-armenian-genocide-and-the-poli tics-of-knowledge/, and republished in *Jadaliyya* May 22, 2015, http:// www.jadaliyya.com/Details/32113.

Grateful acknowledgement is made for permission to reprint the following visual material:

Cover image: *Shift*, 2012, wool, 1.2 × 150 × 260 cm. (½ × 59 × 102¼ in.) by Mona Hatoum © Mona Hatoum. Courtesy of Arter, Istanbul (Photo: Murat Germen).

Jean-Léon Gérôme, *The Snake Charmer*, c. 1879, oil on canvas, 32⅜ × 47⅝ in. (82.2 × 121 cm). Courtesy of the Clark Art Institute, Williamstown, MA.

Lehnert & Landrock Studio, "Scenes and Types—Moorish Woman in Her Quarters," postcard. From The *Colonial Harem* by Malek Alloula, translated by Myrna Godzich and Wlad Godzich, introduction by Barbara Harlow (Minneapolis: University of Minnesota Press, 1986). Reprinted with the permission of the University of Minnesota.

"Napoleon's Campaign in Egypt, 1798," from William Shepherd, *Historical Atlas* (New York: Henry Holt and Company, 1911). Courtesy of the University of Texas Libraries, the University of Texas at Austin.

A young woman clutches Che Guevara whitebook and flower. *Tehran Musawwar*, January 1979. Courtesy of the Siagzar Berelian Collection, International Institute of Social History, Amsterdam, Netherlands.

Two women and a man, of the student defense guard at Tehran University, raise guns and V-for-victory fingers. Printed in a pamphlet by the London-based Iranian Women's Group in the spring of 1979. Courtesy of the Siagzar Berelian Collection, International Institute of Social History, Amsterdam, Netherlands.

US military patch, "If I tell you, I have to kill you." Trevor Paglen, detail of *Symbology*, volume 3, 2009. Courtesy of the artist and Altman Siegel, San Francisco.

Angel-winged, young revolutionaries fight attacks from the police and teargas. Street art by Ammar Abo Bakr, Luxor, Egypt, January 2012. Courtesy of the artist.

Poster from the film *The Battle of Algiers*, directed by Gillo Pontecorvo (Italy, Algeria: Casbah Film and Igor Film, 1966). Courtesy of Janus Films.

A resident of Tehran washes "Yankee Go Home" graffiti from a wall in the capital city of Iran, August 21, 1953. The newly installed prime minister Fazlollah Zahedi requested the cleanup after the coup d'etat that restored the shah of Iran to power. Image courtesy of the Associated Press.

Gamal Abdel Nasser cheered by supporters in Cairo, 1956.

Note on Transliteration

Arabic and Persian words and names have been transliterated into the Latin alphabet according to a simplified system based on the *International Journal of Middle East Studies*. To facilitate reading for the nonspecialist, all diacritical marks have been omitted except for the ʿayn (ʿ) and hamza (ʾ). Arabic and Persian names in common usage in English such as Saddam Hussein, Ayatollah Khomeini, Naguib Mahfouz, Mohammad Mossadegh, Hosni Mubarak, Gamal Abdel Nasser, and Muammar al-Qaddafi remain in the common form.

*Understanding and Teaching
the Modern Middle East*

Introduction

The Middle East in the World

OMNIA EL SHAKRY

A crowd of students huddled around the wiry figure of Egyptian author Sonallah Ibrahim as they clamored for his interpretation of the enigmatic and devastating final sentence of his 1981 novel, *The Committee*, a parable of state power and terror in which an unnamed protagonist stands before a shadowy tribunal.[1] We had spent the last two hours listening to his formative experiences in an Egyptian prison from 1959 to 1964, when he himself was not much older than the undergraduates in the audience.[2] His lecture perfectly complemented discussions in our course, The Middle East in the Twentieth Century, on the Faustian bargain struck under Gamal Abdel Nasser (r. 1954–1970)—the exchange of democratic political liberties for extensive social welfare programs—and on the dire socioeconomic consequences of Egypt's transition to *infitah*, the open-door economic policies inaugurated by Anwar al-Sadat in 1974. Students had become well aware of the stakes of political dissidence in the wider Middle East region in the postcolonial period, but also of the oftentimes ambiguous and ambivalent nature of artistic expression. Just the week prior, we had spent time analyzing ʿAbd al-Hadi al-Gazzar's paintings—anxious visions of techno-political utopias that traversed the early exuberance of anticolonial nationalism and a later pessimism toward the Nasserist project.[3]

When we returned to the classroom, we contemplated the meaning of decolonization in this context. Students were already familiar with Edward Said's definition of Orientalism "as a Western style for dominating, restructuring, and having authority over the Orient," one that

3

created an ontological and epistemological distinction between East and West.[4] But how were we to make sense of the internal dynamics of Middle Eastern societies, particularly in the period after independence, in a post-Orientalist fashion?

One might argue that, for us as historians, the principle challenge is to imagine the region outside of the commonplace assumptions about modern Middle Eastern societies, namely that they are best defined by a series of *absences* or *negations*—the lack of "authentic" nation-states, capitalism, democracy, secularism, human rights, and so forth. Against the hegemony of these Orientalist narratives, we can encourage students to understand history as a far more complex process of contingency and contradiction, for example, by grasping the contemporaneity of modernity and tradition. This style of thinking encourages students to move away from conceiving of history in terms of simple oppositions, such as capitalism *or* socialism, democracy *or* despotism, religion *or* secularism, and instead grasp historical processes in the elegance of their complexity. History emerges, then, as the unstable play of forces, rather than the unfolding of teleological logics. More concretely, this means viewing the Middle East as shaped by dynamic internal and external power relations—between elite and subaltern classes; between religious and secular groups; and between Middle Easterners, Europeans, and Americans.

Situating the Middle East within world history provides a way to break free from Orientalist thinking by emphasizing historical comparability. That is to say, when we study the Middle East we can study it in ways comparable to that of other regions. This means instead of emphasizing exceptionalism—the notion that the Middle East is different from other parts of the world—we may emphasize comparability. For example, we can focus on many of the themes that thread through world history more broadly by looking at histories of capitalism; colonialism; racial formations; the contours of cultural modernism, anticolonial nationalism, and postcolonial revolutionary movements; struggles around class and gender; and political contests over state power.[5]

Comparability does not, of course, mean sameness. No two societies or histories can be the same, and there is no need to homogenize the study of the Middle East in terms of an undifferentiated notion of culture or civilization. As such, teachers will notice that many of our contributors mobilize specific case studies—for example, Algeria and

Egypt—in order to highlight the heterogeneity of the various historical roads taken in the modern era. Both nations were past provinces of the Ottoman Empire, and in the nineteenth century the former became a French settler colony that was later marked by violent decolonization, while the latter was characterized by British indirect rule and negotiated decolonization. Indeed, we must study the social and political hetero-geneity of the Modern Middle East through the trajectories of distinct colonial and semicolonial encounters, anticolonial nationalist revolu-tions, and postcolonial national regimes.[6]

Thus, to provide a specific example, in discussing the postcolonial regime of Egypt under Gamal Abdel Nasser, we can pay careful atten-tion to how the regime was politically situated both globally and locally. The nationalization of the Suez Canal in 1956 drew France, the United Kingdom, Israel, and Egypt into armed conflict and the Americans and Soviets into negotiations. The Suez Crisis may thus be seen as a pinna-cle moment that brought together both the geopolitics of decoloniza-tion and the Cold War, as well as the particularity of Egyptian struggles over the sovereignty of the canal zone. It signaled larger Third World struggles over the control of natural resources, comparable to earlier events in Iran in 1951–1953 and later nationalization movements across the globe.[7] At the same time, it would be a mistake to define Nasserism solely in terms of the Suez Crisis.

We can explore the regime locally as simultaneously emancipatory and regulatory; land reform and social welfare programs aspired to make a better standard of living accessible to all, in tandem with an oftentimes ruthless repression of political initiatives from below. This combination of dominance and hegemony may be addressed through Partha Chatterjee's creative reformulation of Antonio Gramsci's insights on passive revolution as a general framework for thinking about postco-lonial transformations.[8] Students parse the socialist rhetoric embedded in Nasser's speeches in conjunction with clips from the documentary *Umm Kulthum: A Voice Like Egypt*, on Umm Kulthum, the iconic diva of modern Arabic music whose songs became intimately connected to Pan-Arabism in the 1950s and 1960s.[9] Such screenings provide a visual and acoustic sense of the cultural contours of postcolonial nationalism as we try to make sense of those heady days of the postwar era. In this way, students view the region as shaped by both exogenous and endog-enous political, social, and cultural forces.

*U*nderstanding and Teaching the Modern Middle East aims to help teachers and students navigate these multifaceted themes by presenting a variety of viewpoints on the modern history of the region. To facilitate ease of use the volume is divided into four parts. Part One focuses on the challenges that teachers face in the classroom. First and foremost is the challenge of actually demarcating what constitutes the Middle East. In "Why Can't You Find the Middle East on a Map?" Michael Gasper outlines the ambiguity involved in circumscribing the Middle East as stemming in part from the characteristics used to define it. He explains the genesis of the term *Middle East*, clarifying how its usage has changed over time. Is there such a thing, he asks, as a particular Middle Eastern religion, language, ethnicity, or politics, and if not, what gives the region its analytical coherence? Second, educators must be attuned to "Controversy in the Classroom." Omnia El Shakry walks teachers through a set of practical strategies for addressing controversial subject matter, such as examining paintings that present the Orient as a sexualized scene of fantasy, exploring media portrayals that routinely evoke the "backward" status of women and sexual minorities in Middle Eastern societies, and contemplating the graphic images that emerged from the torture and abuse scandal perpetrated by American personnel in Abu Ghraib prison in Iraq.

Part Two provides teachers with the necessary background for imparting historical content. Ovamir Anjum's magisterial survey, "The Legacy of Islam in the Modern Middle East," underscores the historical context of Islam's emergence, its subsequent conquests and expansion, mass conversions to Islam, its great imperial age (both Ottoman and Safavid), modern movements of reform and activism, and Wahhabism and Salafism. Anjum points out that while contemporary scholarship has stressed the need to de-essentialize Islam by emphasizing its diversity and variation, there remains a need to understand the central foundations of Islam. Such a perspective is brilliantly outlined by anthropologist Talal Asad in his groundbreaking article "The Idea of an Anthropology of Islam" in which he poses the central question of how to conceptualize Islam as an object of study, arguing that Islam is best understood as a discursive tradition "that relates itself to the founding texts of the Qur'an and the Hadith."[10] This framework emphasizes coherence while at the same time accounting for heterogeneity as well as continuities of agreement and disagreement within the Islamic tradition.[11]

The remaining essays in this section focus squarely on the modern period and range from synthetic accounts of colonialism and decolonization to more targeted discussions of knotted issues in modern Middle East history. In "Colonialism, Empire, and Nationalist Movements," Sara Pursley outlines the various forms of colonialism in the Middle East, ranging from settler colonies to the mandates of the interwar period, while situating them within the global history of empire, and she ends with a discussion of the transition from European colonialism to US empire. She takes us through various approaches to anticolonial nationalist movements and, crucially, criticizes narratives that view the nation-states of the region as "artificial." Muriam Haleh Davis grapples with "Decolonization and the Reconfiguration of the Global Order" by interrogating the form of territorial organization inaugurated by decolonization: the nation-state. How can we help our students, she asks, think about a unit of political organization that now seems natural, but whose victory was far from clear in the 1950s? Exploring decolonization as a process, she reflects on violence both as a strategy of imperial power and anticolonial struggle, as well as the cultural practices ushered in by decolonization, including the building of South to South solidarities, which crystallized around one event, the Suez Canal Crisis.

With incredible insight Sherene Seikaly delves into "The History of Israel/Palestine." She presents teachers with a number of guiding principles, such as decentering the notion of "conflict" and de-exceptionalizing Israel/Palestine, in order to help students engage Zionist and Palestinian historical claims, while addressing the question of objectivity as a philosophical-historical problem. In the process, she provides resources to help teachers recover silences in the historical record of Palestinians, address the history of anti-Semitism, explain the varieties of Zionist thought, and examine the debate around 1948. In "Understanding Sectarianism as a Global Problem," Ussama Makdisi explores a similar seemingly intractable issue. He encourages teachers to think broadly and comparatively in order to situate sectarian conflicts not within some primordial past but, rather, within a modern context of larger global histories of equality and inequality. Parsing the notion of an allegedly endemic sectarianism in the Middle East as an ideological invention of the West, Makdisi proposes a framework for thinking about sectarianism as a thoroughly nineteenth-century problem centered on the challenge of political inclusion that has plagued all modern states, including those in the West. Beyond that, he argues that the conjoined problem of sectarianism and coexistence cannot be understood outside of Western imperial intervention in the region.

Part Two concludes with Naghmeh Sohrabi and Arielle Gordon's "The Iranian Revolution: From Monarchy to the Islamic Republic," in which they ponder the complicated role of Shiʻi Islam as a historical factor in the 1979 revolution and emphasize the need to present a multiplicity of contributing factors. Examining the revolutionary period in Iran by drawing in the perspectives of the State, the Opposition, and the People, they reveal that Iran's 1979 revolution owes its roots to contending nationalist, anticolonial, Marxist, socialist, and Third Worldist discourses, as much it does to cultural and political Shiʻism.

In Part Three we turn to understanding the contemporary Middle East. Nathan Citino outlines "US Foreign Policy in the Modern Middle East" by providing teachers with a framework for understanding the relative importance of domestic politics, religion, strategy, and economic interests in American policy making. Arguing that an imperial framework situates America's changing role in the Middle East, Citino notes how thoroughly the US has replaced Britain as the Middle East's leading imperial power. In "America, Oil, and War in the Middle East," Toby Craig Jones looks at the role of Middle East oil in US foreign policy and war-making. Exploring why America has gone to war in the region, he encourages teachers to emphasize the political-economic aspects of oil and American policy. Despite the fact that preserving the security of allies in the Persian Gulf, most importantly Saudi Arabia, and of the flow of oil, were among the United States' chief objectives, security has been elusive. Since the late 1970s, the Gulf has been rocked by revolution, more direct forms of US intervention, and almost permanent war. In "Teaching the Global War on Terror," Darryl Li addresses *jihadism* as an analytically unhelpful concept that obscures more than it reveals. Rather than cover the many different kinds of groups (including states) in the world across history that purport to wage jihad, he instead focuses on transnational armed groups, such as al-Qaʻida, that have sought to engage in armed confrontation against the United States in the name of a global Muslim community and without geographical constraints. Placing transnational insurgencies alongside the globalized counterinsurgency of the War on Terror within the same analytical framework, this chapter will be essential reading for teachers who cover current events.

The next two chapters continue to discuss issues of ongoing contemporary relevance in the classroom from the perspective of Middle Eastern actors. Asef Bayat recaps the Arab uprisings that shook the Middle East beginning in December 2010, focusing on the nature of the revolts; their ideological orientations and aspirations, reformist or revolutionary; their causes, both proximate and distant; and outcomes. In "Refugees in and from the Middle East," Rochelle Davis introduces readers to the displacement of populations in the context of the international refugee regime. She contextualizes the widescale displacement of our era by analyzing the state-citizen model that defines contemporary political systems asking how refugees, as citizens outside their state, or stateless people, fit into that model; she explores the international refugee regime that provides humanitarian solutions for refugees and internally displaced populations; and she questions the framing of refugees as a crisis or political problem, encouraging us instead to emphasize the political and environmental forces that have displaced them.

In Part Four we explore a variety of specific methods and sources for teaching the region. Elliott Colla's "Literature as a Source for Teaching Modern Middle East History" asks us to think about Middle Eastern literature, and novels in particular, as allowing access to "structures of feeling." Encouraging teachers to identify the form, genre, frame, perspective, and voice of literary texts, he provides us with two illustrative themes, migration and national identity. Kamran Rastegar makes use of "Cinema as a Source for Teaching Modern Middle East History," not by using cinematic works as merely illustrative of historical or social events but, rather, by developing a critical literacy around films as historical documents. He does so by outlining the history of filmmaking in and about the Middle East, while reflecting on the various film cultures (both feature and documentary) "as a product of discrete cultural and historical conditions which must inform our understanding of their content and reception." In "Gender and Sexuality: Sources and Methods," Hanan Hammad focuses on enabling students in American classrooms to understand that gender and sexuality in Muslim communities, as everywhere else, result from historical, religious, cultural, social, economic, and political processes and require critical thinking and empathy, as well as close readings of primary sources.

Subsequent chapters address the so-called minority question in the region. In "Nuancing the Narrative," Alma Rachel Heckman asks how teachers can better integrate the Jewish modern Middle East into their historical narratives. "One cannot simply 'add Jews and stir' to the narrative of the Middle East," she states, "just as one cannot 'add women and stir' or any other population (incorrectly) deemed ancillary to major story lines and themes." Christine Philliou takes on the issue of the 1915–1917 Armenian genocide, a Gordian knot of late Ottoman studies, in her phrasing, surveying recent historiographical trends in light of the Turkish state's refusal to recognize the genocide. Drawing attention to the uncomfortable separation between the Armenian genocide and the rest of late Ottoman history, she attends to the politics of knowledge production while suggesting ways to integrate the two histories.

The concluding chapters of the volume are noteworthy in their hands-on approach to teaching. Kit Adam Wainer takes the document-based question as a central pedagogical strategy and homes in on two key events: the 1951–1953 Mossadegh project to nationalize oil in Iran and the 1956 Suez Canal Crisis in Egypt. By utilizing primary source documents on each he poses and contextualizes questions such as why did several non-Communist states in the region pursue nationalization, to what extent were the causes similar, and why were the outcomes in Iran and Egypt so different? Ziad Abu-Rish's "Keeping Current," ends our volume and will help teachers better navigate the rapid-fire pace of contemporary events within the Middle East, by examining specific examples, such as the Arab uprisings, of current and ongoing events while providing instructors with the necessary methods and sources for negotiating and adjudicating the plethora of digital, social, and other news media about the region.

While no single edited volume can do justice to the modern history of a region as vast and diverse as the Middle East, *Understanding and Teaching the Modern Middle East* aims to provide teachers with the foundational background knowledge, as well as concrete pedagogical strategies, for substantively addressing the region in the classroom. To address historical nuance and complexity, all of our authors synthesize and engage a wide historiography, while introducing a diverse range of sources, whether primary or secondary, written or audiovisual. Taken together, chapters encourage teachers to address the history of the region not as a "problem" or as a series of wars and conflicts but as a dynamic nexus of political, social, religious, and intellectual forces that have shaped the countries of the Middle East, a trend that we can only hope will continue.

NOTES

1. Sonallah Ibrahim, *The Committee*, trans. Mary St. Germain and Charlene Constable (Syracuse, NY: Syracuse University Press, 2001).

2. "Literature, Dissent and Revolution in Egypt: A Conversation with Egyptian Author Sonallah Ibrahim" (lecture, University of California, Davis, May 7, 2013).

3. On al-Gazzar see Alex Dika Seggerman, *Modernism on the Nile: Art in Egypt between the Islamic and the Contemporary* (Chapel Hill: University of North Carolina Press, 2019).

4. Orientalism was first discussed by Anouar Abdel-Malek in 1963 and then later famously elaborated by Edward Said in 1978 as the vast body of knowledge produced about the so-called Orient. Said offers three definitions of Orientalism: "anyone who teaches, writes about, or researches the Orient"; "a style of thought based upon an ontological and epistemological distinction made between 'the Orient' and . . . 'the Occident'"; and finally, beginning from the late eighteenth century, "the corporate institution for dealing with the Orient— dealing with it by making statements about it, authorizing views of it, describing it, by teaching it, settling it, ruling over it: in short, Orientalism as a Western style for dominating, restructuring, and having authority over the Orient." Said's central thesis is that Orientalism is "a *distribution* of geo-political awareness into aesthetic, scholarly, economic, sociological, historical, and philological texts . . . it *is* rather than expresses, a certain *will* or *intention* to understand, in some cases to control, manipulate, even to incorporate, what is a manifestly different (or alternative and novel) world; it is, above all, a discourse that is . . . produced and exists in an uneven exchange with various kinds of power . . . power political (as with a colonial or imperial establishment), power intellectual (as with reigning societies like comparative linguistics or anatomy, or any of the modern policy sciences), power cultural (as with orthodoxies and canons of taste, texts, values), power moral (as with ideas about what 'we' do and what 'they' cannot do or understand as 'we' do)." Edward Said, *Orientalism* (New York: Vintage, 1978), 2–3, 12, emphasis in original. See also Anouar Abdel-Malek, "Orientalism in Crisis," *Diogenes* 11, no. 44 (1963): 103–40; Zachary Lockman, *Contending Visions of the Middle East: The History and Politics of Orientalism* (Cambridge: Cambridge University Press, 2009), 182–214; Edmund Burke III and D. Prochaska, eds., *Genealogies of Orientalism: History, Theory, and Politics* (Lincoln: University of Nebraska Press, 2008).

5. Representative examples of this type of approach include Peter Gran, *Islamic Roots of Capitalism, 1760–1840* (Austin: University of Texas Press, 1979); Timothy Mitchell, *Colonising Egypt* (Berkeley: University of California Press, 1988); Eve Troutt Powell, *A Different Shade of Colonialism: Egypt, Great Britain, and the Mastery of the Sudan* (Berkeley: University of California Press, 2003); Omnia El Shakry, *The Great Social Laboratory: Subjects of Knowledge in Colonial*

and Postcolonial Egypt (Stanford, CA: Stanford University Press, 2007); Elizabeth Thompson, *Colonial Citizens: Republican Rights, Paternal Privilege, and Gender in French Syria and Lebanon* (New York: Columbia University Press, 2000); Beth Baron, *Egypt as a Woman: Nationalism, Gender, and Politics* (Berkeley: University of California Press, 2005); Joel Beinin and Zachary Lockman, *Workers on the Nile: Nationalism, Communism, Islam, and the Egyptian Working Class, 1882–1954* (Princeton, NJ: Princeton University Press, 1987); Hanna Batatu, *The Old Social Classes and the Revolutionary Movements of Iraq: A Study of Iraq's Old Landed and Commercial Classes and of Its Communists, Ba'thists and Free Officers* (London: Saqi Books, 2004).

6. We are greatly aided in our effort to understand the region as part of world history by the impressive array of translated primary source collections, such as Julia Clancy-Smith and Charles D. Smith, *The Modern Middle East and North Africa: A History in Documents* (Oxford: Oxford University Press, 2014); Akram Fouad Khater, *Sources in the History of the Modern Middle East* (Boston: Houghton Mifflin, 2004). In a related fashion, Edmund Burke III and D. Yaghoubian, eds., *Struggle and Survival in the Modern Middle East*, 2nd ed. (Berkeley: University of California Press, 2005) upends stereotypes and vividly demonstrates regional heterogeneity by bringing together the life stories of ordinary Middle Easterners—peasants, urban workers, Muslims and non-Muslims—across the region.

7. On nationalization in Iran see the chapters in this volume by Naghmeh Sohrabi and Arielle Gordon and by Kit Adam Wainer.

8. Antonio Gramsci, *Selections from the Prison Notebooks of Antonio Gramsci*, trans. and ed. Quintin Hoare and Geoffrey Nowell Smith (New York: International, 1971); 106–20; Partha Chatterjee, *The Nation and Its Fragments: Colonial and Postcolonial Histories* (Princeton, NJ: Princeton University Press, 1993), 200–219; El Shakry, *The Great Social Laboratory*, 197–218.

9. *Umm Kulthum: A Voice Like Egypt*, directed by Michal Goldman (Arab Film Distribution, 2007).

10. Talal Asad, "The Idea of an Anthropology of Islam," Occasional Paper Series (Washington, DC: Georgetown University, Center for Contemporary Arab Studies, 1986), 14. In this watershed paper, Asad develops the concept of an Islamic discursive tradition that orients itself to an Islamic past and future with reference to an Islamic practice in the present. He argues that religious traditions can embody their own forms of rationality, and although "Islamic traditions are not homogeneous, they do aspire to coherence, in a way that all discursive traditions do" (16–17).

11. For a sweeping history of Islamicate societies that challenged Orientalist narratives *avant la lettre*, see Marshall Hodgson, *The Venture of Islam: Conscience and History in a World Civilization*, vols. 1–3 (Chicago: University of Chicago Press, 1974), and Hodgson, *Rethinking World History: Essays on Europe, Islam, and World History*, ed. Edmund Burke III (Cambridge: Cambridge University Press, 1993); and Edmund Burke III and Robert J. Mankin, *Islam and World History: The Ventures of Marshall Hodgson* (Chicago: University of Chicago Press, 2018).

PART ONE

The Middle East in the Classroom

Why Can't You Find the Middle East on a Map?

MICHAEL GASPER

Some define the Middle East as the Arab states of the Eastern Mediterranean and Persian Gulf plus Iran, Turkey, and Israel. Others include Morocco, Algeria, Tunisia, Libya, Mauritania, Sudan, and Somalia. There are those, however, who leave out the North African states of Morocco, Algeria, Tunisia, Libya, and still others who place Kazakhstan, Turkmenistan, Tajikistan, Uzbekistan, Kirgizstan, and Afghanistan in their Middle East. So, we may be forgiven for being perplexed when asked to name the countries of the Middle East. To complicate matters more, the older term "Near East" and the more recent "Middle East" are sometimes still used interchangeably. For example, despite the fact that since Harry S. Truman US presidents have spoken about the "Middle East," the US State Department's section dedicated to the area continues to be known as the Bureau of Near Eastern Affairs (NEA) and the Defense Department (DoD), too, employs this term in its Near East and South Asia Center (NESA). However, neither agency understands the region in the same way; the State Department's NEA covers the area from the Atlantic coast of Morocco to Iran, while the DoD's NESA is responsible for the area from Morocco to the Eastern Mediterranean across India and then to Sri Lanka and Nepal.

So, if even various branches of the US government differ about where to draw the boundaries of the Middle East, should we be surprised that the nonspecialist might be a bit flummoxed when asked to pinpoint the region on a map? In these pages I want to offer an alternative way to approach this question by interrogating how the Middle East has been represented in the modern geopolitical imagination. I suggest that the ambiguity in enumerating the contours of the region stems, at least in part, from the characteristics used to define it.

While usage of both the "Middle East" and the "Near East" continues today, over the course of the twentieth century the newer term "Middle East" became more common in everyday speech and in media. So where did the newer term come from? American naval officer, maritime strategist, and one-time president of the American Historical Association Alfred T. Mahan claimed to have coined the term in an influential 1902 essay about the future of British naval operations in the Indian Ocean.[1] However, the term that Mahan purportedly invented was already in use by British officials and commentators such as Lord Curzon and General Sir Thomas Gordon.[2] British officialdom had adopted "Middle East" to distinguish the Far East of China from British interests in the "Near East" (i.e., the Balkans, Anatolia, and the Eastern Mediterranean). But the British Middle East of the late nineteenth and early twentieth centuries would be unrecognizable to the contemporary reader because it referred almost exclusively to the Indian subcontinent and adjacent areas. The British understanding of the term, however, evolved along with their strategic considerations. For instance, when the British navy switched from coal to oil in the first decade of the twentieth century, their interests gravitated westward to petroleum-producing areas in Persia and the Ottoman Empire.[3] British officialdom then began to refer to the Middle East in ways more familiar to us today—centered around the Persian Gulf and the Eastern Mediterranean or the Levant. In any case, what is abundantly clear here is that military strategists and diplomats, rather than geographers and mapmakers, have historically defined the region.

Later, institutions reflecting American strategic concerns helped establish the term "Middle East" in the English-speaking world from around the time of the Second World War. During the war the Allies set up an agency charged with regulating all production, consumption, and shipping across a number of Allied-held colonial possessions, territories, and vassal states to organize and rationalize civilian commerce for the war effort. Based in Cairo, the Middle East Supply Centre (MESC), as it was known, was quite successful, and Egypt and the Eastern Mediterranean saw a dramatic rise in economic production and expansion during the war years.[4] Indeed, there were even proposals to transform the MESC into a permanent regional development institution after the war. Eventually the United States backed away from the project because of the British distaste for the idea. Perhaps the primary legacy of the MESC is that it cemented the term "Middle East" into American public consciousness, even if the boundaries of the region remained (and remain) an open question.[5]

II.

Now, let's take some of what was already said, add some new elements, and then mold this admixture into three caveats to keep in mind as we forge ahead. First, in thinking about the meaning of the "Middle East" (or indeed any such geographic abstraction) we should continually bear in mind that they are subject to the technological parameters of an era and reflect the worldviews and political and cultural horizons of the people who create them. In other words, we should remain cognizant of the "history-ness" (or historicity) of the organizing logic that people from different eras use to describe their world. What does this mean? Let's look at a simple example to illuminate this point. We learn in school that the Strait of Gibraltar separates the continents of Africa and Europe, and for us this often means it draws a sharp boundary between the cultures, societies, and political-economic histories of the peoples on either side of this nine-mile divide. For us, in the twenty-first century, this is an unassailable fact. Or is it?[6] Let us for a moment try to imagine this nine-mile expanse of water through the eyes of someone living in the twelfth-century Iberian Peninsula. Given the ease of short-range sea travel (not to mention the comparative difficulty of crossing certain mountain ranges, such as the Pyrenees[7]), the notion that Europe and Africa are separate continents composed of (opposing?) ensembles of peoples, cultures, and societies would not have occurred to our twelfth-century observer. Indeed, in the times of the Almohad Caliphate (1121–1269) and its successors, whose influence and power ran from what is now Mauritania to central Spain, drawing such a stark distinction between these two coasts would have made no sense at all.[8] The strait was a relatively easily navigated body of water within the Almohad domain, and certainly not the dividing line between incommensurable cultural-geographic, sociopolitical economic formations, and even civilizations.

Second, we should stay attentive to the fact that, while there are advantages for using abstractions such as the "Middle East" to help us organize our geographical knowledge, they can also mislead us into imbuing the actual places that they represent with greater coherence than is warranted. The appellation "Middle Eastern" often shapes outsiders' perceptions about the entire panoply of human experience within the region. Consequently, it is not unusual to encounter the phrase: "The people of the Middle East are . . ."[9] This sort of construction should give us pause, and we should make every effort to avoid the inverted logic trap where our terms and our analytical concepts—rather than the histories and cultures of lived reality on the ground—determine how we portray the region.

Finally, a third, but related point. In the history of writing and thinking about the region there are a set of recurring, putatively unique characteristics cited to exemplify the "East" (or the "Orient"). Nearly sixty years ago this observation inspired a reappraisal about the ways that Europeans came to learn and think about the "East." In a 1963 article the sociologist Anouar Abdel-Malek suggested that Europeans had come to regard the region in terms of "otherness" to Europe.[10] This insight was later elaborated upon by Edward Said in his seminal work *Orientalism* in 1978 and by many others since.[11] As Europe emerged from the internecine religious wars of the early modern era, European thinkers, weary from decades of sectarian strife, sought to build a collective identity that de-emphasized the idea of Europe-as-Christendom. The notion of the "Orient" (or "East") played a crucial role in this process. The "East" in this formulation was not so much a particular place, but rather a conceptual antithesis for everything these Europeans hoped "Europe" (and later the "West") would become—rational, dynamic, productive, and civilized. As a consequence, the "Orient" came to stand for everything that this newly imagined Europe was said not to be: irrational, static, backward, uncivilized, and so forth.

Along with colonial rule and global dominance Europe gained the power to impose its knowledge, analytical concepts, and epistemic logic on the rest of the world, and as such, the Orientalist imaginary was indelibly and inextricably sutured onto the ideas of the East, the Near East, and the Middle East throughout the entire world.[12]

III.

With those three caveats in mind, let's examine the vague sociological/political paradigms most often adduced to define the Middle East.

Perhaps the most common assumption is that Islam is the linchpin for understanding the Middle East.[13] Do we gain any useful insight by describing Middle Easterners as Muslims? No. First, the region contains significant minorities of non-Muslims such as Christians, Jews, Bahi'is, Zoroastrians, and so on. Second, the Muslim world and the Middle East are in no way equivalent terms. In fact, the vast majority of Muslims live outside the region, residing instead in Southeast Asia, South Asia, and Africa.[14] Therefore, the term "Muslim world" might very well better describe other parts of the world.[15] In addition, Muslims within the region do not constitute a single homogeneous group; there are the Sunnis and the Shi'ites and a host of other traditions whose adherents connect them to Islam in some manner—such as the Alawites and Druze of the Levant, the Alevis of Turkey and the Caucuses, the Zaydis of Yemen, Yazidis in Iraq, and the Ibadis in Oman and North Africa. Even if we ignore all the above, there remains the much more vexing question about the practice and meaning of Islam to Muslims in innumerably diverse cultural, social, and historical settings and contexts within the region, to say nothing of the differences between classes, genders, and ages. In addition, how could the blunt analytical instrument "Islam" account for transformations in the practice of Islam that resulted from evolving technologies and expanding capacities of the modern state, all of which are deeply contextual? Ultimately, in holding onto "Islam" as the primary critical rubric with which to view the region's peoples and societies, we necessarily exclude from analysis millions of people, and we erase dense historical economies of faiths, practice, and identity.

Even if the foregoing were not true, we could even question the utility of taking "Muslim" as an analytical category. After all, what sort of coherent cultural, social, or political knowledge can one gain about a "group," if that group comprises a fifth of the world's population and lives in every corner of the globe? What sort of group is this? One need only ask what one could learn about the history, politics, culture, and lived experience of the peoples of Russia, Italy, the Philippines, Mexico, Brazil, the Republic of the Congo, Ethiopia, Colombia, Argentina, South Africa, France, Poland, Ukraine, and Kenya by grouping them all together as Christians? That many Russians or Filipinos self-identify as Christian would tell us very little about those individual countries or the regions in which they live. Neither would it afford us a valuable comparative instrument for study.

Nevertheless, in almost any library one can find stacks of dusty books arguing for the centrality of Islam to "Middle Eastern" society, politics, and history.[16] No single paradigm has informed much of this literature apart from a vague, if unyielding assumption that Islam is the key for understanding a region and its peoples. For example, during the Cold War authors were quick to reassure their readers that Middle Easterners were averse to communism, radical politics, and revolution because of the quietist nature of Islam.[17] That Islam mollified its adherents into fatalistically acquiescing to this world as it is and waiting for salvation in the next was for many years the orthodox canon in European and American scholarship and public discourse. After the 1979 Iranian Revolution, however, a rash of warnings about the "revolutionary" (and even warlike or violent) nature of Islamic political activism began to appear.[18] We saw the same thing happen with the upsurge of militant extremism (itself, in part, a product of decades of US-led military operations in the region) when Islam and violent radicalism became all but synonymous to many commentators.[19] We will almost certainly continue to see Islam haphazardly attached to every political, social, or cultural development and upheaval in the region. That a range of commentators have described "Islam" as quietist, revolutionary, violent, moderate, and anti- or pro-Western points to the fact that such a signifier is simply far too broad to provide any useful insight into the lived and historical experience of any region—whether we are talking about North Africa, Southwest Asia, or Southeast Asia.

If religion fails to help us distinguish what is Middle Eastern about the Middle East perhaps language (Arabic) or ethnicity (Arab) can. The sheer diversity of the region belies the notion that a homogeneous ethnicity, "Arab," speaking a single language, "Arabic," predominates. While Arabic is widely spoken in the region, one will also find it spoken in areas not usually included in the Middle East, such as in the Sahel region of Africa. Even within the area commonly thought of as the Middle East, however, there are more than a hundred and fifty million speakers of other languages, from Turkish to Farsi to Kurdish to Hebrew and many, many more. In fact, the magnitude of linguistic diversity in the region is astonishing. For example, in so-called Farsi-speaking Iran only about half the population speak Farsi as its mother tongue. In addition, even within majority-Arabic countries there are significant differences between dialects used on a day-to day basis even if there does exist a single formal lingua franca with which educated speakers are very familiar.

Ethnicity? Don't some people use the terms "Middle East" and the "Arab world" interchangeably?[20] Yes, but in doing so they are mistaken. There exists great diversity among the peoples of the region: from Turks to Persians to Amazigh (Berbers) to Nubians to Kurds to say nothing of the Mazandarani, Greeks, Turkmen, Armenians, Azeris, Circassians, Mhallamis, Assyrians, Qawliya, Lurs, Mandaeans, Balochis, Georgians, Laz, Bosnians, and the various Romany peoples of the region. In any case, one ought to be very cautious about thinking of "Arab" as an ethnic archetype. Just as the Arabic language has many dialects, Arabic speakers come in all shapes, sizes, and colors. Indeed, like most ethnicities, the term "Arab" has, at best, a very imprecise relationship to any physical or cultural attributes. This can lead to much confusion. For example, one sometimes reads that the conflicts in Sudan (in Darfur or that between Northern and Southern Sudan) pitted "Africans" against "Arabs" as if these were racial or ethnic conflicts.[21] Since both Northern Sudanese and Southern Sudanese live in Africa, they are all Africans. But more importantly, those on all sides of the conflict in Sudan do not differ significantly from one another with regard to physical appearance.[22] Thus, a "black" versus "brown" frame for understanding these conflicts simply does not pass muster.

Just as there exists no characteristic Middle Eastern religion, language, or ethnicity, there is no unique "Middle Eastern" political system either. While it is true that the region contains a variety of authoritarian regimes, including the absolute monarchies of the Arab Persian Gulf and beyond (almost without exception dependent on British, French, and most recently American military protection), the region has no monopoly on authoritarian governments. There are also semi-democratic systems operating from Tunisia to Lebanon, and from Israel to Turkey to Iran. One would be hard-pressed to identify a single political structure or ideological orientation in the Middle East that does not appear in other parts of the globe.

Institutionally, Middle Eastern states are organized in ways familiar to any political scientist. Liberal, social-democratic, statist, corporatist, and socialist ideologies exist alongside Islam-inspired political movements and organizations that themselves have equivalents and even branches throughout the wider Muslim world and beyond. Likewise, there are no "Middle Eastern" ideologies, unless one counts the official nationalisms of individual states that in any case bear a close family resemblance to their counterparts throughout the world.[23] This is not to deny that there have been powerful ideological currents that have transcended the region's national borders over the last century and a half—such as socialism, pan-Arabism, and Pan-Islamism—and that for periods these have been genuinely important.[24] However, if we examine the case of pan-Arabism (an ideology that argues that the Arabs are a single national group), we find that even this idea that would appear to be very specific and unique to the Middle East was shaped by the same populist, Third-Worldist, and anticolonial ideas that drove social movements and revolutionary organizations from Oakland to Algiers and from Hanoi to Havana. Nevertheless, whatever currency these political philosophies achieved, none have been able to overcome the centrifugal political, economic, and social forces at play in the Middle East. In the region and beyond, the nation-state and its modern form of nationalist ideology reign supreme.

IV.

We have argued so far that no Middle Eastern religion, language, ethnicity, or politics exists. So, can we use climate or natural resources to develop a coherent schema for our Middle East instead? While one might be forgiven for thinking that the region is defined by wide semiarid expanses and deserts, the inhabitants of the forested and snow-peaked mountains of Lebanon, Turkey, and Morocco might find that odd at best. While deserts define parts of Northern Africa, the Syrian and Iraqi interiors, and some areas around the Persian Gulf, one will also find marshlands and coastal regions with a humid Mediterranean climate, cool and rainy highlands, lush river deltas, and rolling agricultural plains.[25]

What about oil and natural gas? While there are several of the world's largest oil and gas exporters in the region, such as Saudi Arabia, Iraq, Iran, Qatar, and Algeria, possession of vast petroleum and gas reserves is not unique to the Middle East. The United States and Russia are among the largest oil and gas producers in the world while China and Canada regularly rank among the top five. In fact, one finds important producers in nearly every corner of the world.[26] At the end of the day, apart from the extraction process itself, petroleum- and gas-producing countries have little in common. Even in the Middle East these states run the gamut from small, sparsely populated countries, such as the United Arab Emirates, to large, densely populated urbanized states, such as Algeria.[27]

One sometimes reads that the wealth derived from oil and gas insulates the entire region from forces of globalization.[28] This could not be further from the truth. The centrality of these fossil fuels to the functioning of the world economy necessarily means that the region is profoundly integrated into the international economic order since it is quite literally *fueling* it. In addition, that these regimes are some of the largest importers of Western military hardware and expertise in the world underscores their importance to the functioning of the global political economy.[29]

Even if they accept some of the arguments above, many commentators and influential media figures insist on seeing the region through the lens of "exceptionalism." The basic idea of exceptionalism is that the social, political, and economic life of Middle Eastern societies operates according to unique criteria that have no parallels anywhere else in the world. There is a long history of the production of "Middle Eastern exceptionalism" in Western academia and media.[30] This often gets translated into familiar clichés such as "the people in the Middle East have been killing one another since the beginning of time" or that political problems in the region are "unresolvable" because they are ultimately expressions of irrational "tribal" or "primordial" hatreds, or that "fundamentalist" obscurantism has produced whole populations of benighted and misguided youth.[31] Like all such hackneyed clichés, rather than deepening our understanding, they reflect not only the ignorance but also the political *and* cultural power of those who repeat them.

Unfortunately, however, refuting these clichés can be difficult, because: (1) their banal simplicity appeals to those lacking in knowledge of the region and who have no interest in acquiring it; and (2) they conform to the muddled consensus about the region that serves as conventional wisdom. In other words, it is a case of confirmation bias— one accepts an idea because it conforms to one's preexisting beliefs. The effect, regrettably, is to create a Middle East-as-exception by substituting history and politics (both realms of human action or agency), with a fabulist amalgam of geopolitical folklore and almost seemingly satirical mythology. Seen from this perspective, the Middle East stands outside the rules of history and rationality. Its peoples are said to reject "modernity," and many of them are "fundamentalists" who putatively hate such things as "freedom of speech, a multi-party-political system . . . women's rights, pluralism, secularism, short skirts, dancing, [and] beardlessness."[32]

This sort of reasoning is scarcely a harmless—albeit slightly amusing—example of intellectual laziness. Indeed, one finds it reflected in media commentary and in policy-making circles, and as such, without putting too fine a point on it, "Middle East exceptionalism" serves the imperial aims of the West. For instance, since the 9/11 attacks some influential opinion makers and public figures have backed their calls for US intervention in the region with "exceptionalist" narratives that speak of "contagion" or "metastasizing disorder" emanating from the "medieval religious" orientations among Middle Easterners.[33] Because this endangers the entire world, so the reasoning goes, the United States and its allies are compelled to undertake military action as an antidote. This sort of thinking should concern all of us because not only has it has been at the heart of the many ill-considered military interventions into the region since the 1970s, but it also continues to frustrate our ability to come to grips with the local consequences of those actions.

If the Middle East possesses any unifying characteristic, this exceptionalist model clearly fails to identity it. Far from being isolated from developments around the world, a cursory glance at events in the Middle East clearly demonstrate that changes there run in synch with parallel developments across the globe. For example, beginning in the mid-twentieth century a number of states in the region created welfare states that were modeled to some extent on those being developed in Western Europe at the time. These welfare states were so successful that the Arab Mediterranean region outperformed southern Europe and the rest of the non-Arab world in increasing life expectancy and education levels for over three decades, between 1970 and 2007.[34]

V.

Despite the fact that there is a Saudi-owned pan-Arab daily with the name *The Middle East*, one rarely sees the term used in the region. In the previous sections we examined some of the leitmotifs or themes that outsiders believe characterize the Middle East. But what about the locals? Does the term "Middle East" mean anything to them?

If one were to consider overarching identities that have existed in the region's past, one finds that these were most often reflections of political or religious circumstances rather than products of regional or cultural identification. So that terms such as "Dar al-Islam" (the Abode of Islam) or "al-Ummah" (community of Muslims) would have had far more resonance than a sense of sharing some kind of regional identity. Dar al-Islam was simply any place in the world where Muslims formed a significant population, while al-Ummah encompassed all Muslims wherever they dwelled. Likewise, in the Ottoman (1300–1923) or Safavid/Qajar (1500–1923) worlds in Persia, the idea of being subjects of the sultan or the shah would have also had greater meaning than any kind of particular regional identification.

Is there some common history that impels us to accept the Middle East as a single analytical unit? Nearly fifty years ago the esteemed historian of the Middle East Nikki Keddie took up this question in her essay "Is There a Middle East?"[35] She concluded that from about the time of the emergence of Islam in the seventh century until the emergence of the Sunni/Shi'a divide in the sixteenth century the term "Middle East" might have had some kind of internal coherence. After 1500, however, this logic no longer held as the (Sunni) Ottoman and the (Shi'a) Safavid Empires took increasingly divergent paths, and as a consequence whatever historical justification for thinking of the region as a single unit evaporated.[36] But subsequent scholarship raised questions about Keddie's provisional thesis. Looking beyond the Middle East, scholars uncovered a range of alternative geographies that for centuries marked the imaginative frontiers for peoples in the region and beyond.[37] For example, one recent historian describes in vivid detail the "cosmopolitan Islamic Eurasia" of the eighteenth century that consisted of a vibrant "arena of circulation and exchange" incorporating the lands around the Indian Ocean.[38] Beginning in the seventeenth century, however, as economic and military clout shifted from the Mediterranean to Northern Europe, so too did Europe's power to impose its conceptual apparatus on other parts of the world.

With the inescapable power of the European imaginary, the peoples of the Middle East were faced with an unprecedented epistemic reckoning. European hegemony overflowed the economic and military realms and streamed into the conceptual. European knowledge supplanted local forms of knowing and learning in all fields and, in so doing, interjected itself into the local geographical imagination. For example, as

Ottoman and Qajar officials adapted to the new reality of European power, they were also obliged to recast the ways that they conceived of their increasingly precarious sovereignty.[39] This can be seen in the way that local cartographers represented these new strategic challenges by adopting European visions of world geography.[40] In the process, alternative geographic-historical imaginaries were displaced by Eurocentric notions of the Near and Middle East that were themselves ideational expressions of the considerable military, economic, and ideological power of the West.[41]

While one should be cautious in generalizing too much, it is not a stretch to say that, since the late eighteenth century, the peoples of the Middle East understood the primary factor defining their relationship to each other and to "their" region to be the extent to which they, their lands, and their resources have been an object of the imperial gaze and on the receiving end of frequent Euro-American interventions.[42] Over the centuries, a host of geopolitical paradigms have informed the imagining of a variety of "Middle Easts." The exigencies of colonial/ imperial projects, the imperatives of the Cold War, and, more recently, the so-called war on terror have all produced contingent incarnations of the region. Indeed, the idea of the Middle East cannot be separated from the West's power to create and impose categories of knowledge on the rest of the world. The Middle East exists because the West possesses sufficient power to give this idea the capacity to produce effects on people in the region and the lives they lead. In this way, the colonial past and the imperial present both number among the elements that make the Middle East "real."

The term "Middle East" evokes a set of questions, or often a set of problems, more than it does a clearly delineated geographical location. That there is a Middle East we can scarcely deny; at the same time, we should not lose sight of the fact that the Middle East is best thought of, not as a place on a map, but rather as an example of the imaginative power of the West. The concept of the Middle East was born out of strategic concerns for the United States and its closest allies in Europe and elsewhere. It follows that its provisional boundaries shift according to these outsiders' geostrategic perspectives. Therefore, instead of looking at maps to find the region, it makes more sense to regard the Middle East as a set of suppositions—of Europeans and Americans—that ultimately shapes and fills it with conceptual and moral attributes. Accordingly, we should remain assiduous in searching out and exposing the links between the production of knowledge about the Middle East and its impact on the lives of the people in the region.[43]

In sum, as we have said above, the ways in which the region that we now call the "Middle East" has been defined do little more than reflect a range of sociological/political paradigms imposed by people from outside the region. The Middle East in that sense is less a specific place and much more an unstable and shifting political idea. As we have seen, none of the frameworks said to organize the essential characteristics of the region stand up to analysis. There exist no overall cultural, ethnic, religious, political, or economic features that exemplify, and that are specific to, the entire region. Thus the "Middle East," as it is usually understood, is an idea devoid of much expository value for the scholar or researcher. Therefore, it should come as little surprise that people in the Middle East often don't even recognize themselves as part of a coherent region and only infrequently use the term. Nevertheless, even if historically estranged from the notion, they cannot simply think the Middle East into oblivion. Even as they come to regard the idea for what it is—an equivocal political term with an imperial pedigree—they do not have the luxury to reject it. The Middle East is an inescapable reality for those living in the countries of the eastern and southern Mediterranean and southwest Asia even if the provenance of the mental map on which it depends has a long history outside of the region. There is far too much political, military, economic, and cultural infrastructure invested in the idea for them to escape its conclusions and consequences.

So, then, what about those of us outside the region? How do we come to grips with the fact that in studying the Middle East we may be unwittingly accepting and promoting the very same ideological assemblages that have resulted in so much misery there? While there is no easy answer to that question, I suggest an ethical response. In an analogous way to how some study history with the expectation of learning about the past in order to change the future, perhaps we can study the Middle East with the hope of imagining a different relationship between the peoples of the region and the West.

NOTES

I would like to thank Agne Jomantaite and Joshua Schreier for their careful and generous readings of this chapter. Any misstatements or factual errors in these pages are the author's sole responsibility.

1. A. T. Mahan, "The Persian Gulf and International Relations," *National Review*, September 1902, 27–45.

2. Sir George Nathaniel Curzon (1859–1925) was a British member of parliament and statesman who served as viceroy of India and foreign secretary in a career that spanned from 1884 to 1924. Sir Thomas Edward Gordon (1832–1914) was a British Army officer, diplomat, and author. He served in India, Persia, and Central Asia.

3. See Timothy Mitchell, *Carbon Democracy: Political Power in the Age of Oil* (New York: Verso, 2011).

4. The MESC included "Egypt, the Sudan, [Libya], Eritrea, Ethiopia, British and French Somali land, [Yemen], Palestine, Syria, the Lebanon, [Jordan], Saudi Arabia, the Arab Sheikdoms [of the Persian Gulf], Iraq, [Iran], and Cyprus. Malta also was at one time included." D. P. E., "The Middle East Supply Centre: I—Organization and Functions," *Bulletin of International News* 21, no. 16 (1944): 619–25, 620.

5. Martin W. Wilmington, *The Middle East Supply Centre* (Albany: State University of New York Press, 1971).

6. Martin W. Lewis and Kären Wigen, *The Myth of Continents: A Critique of Metageography* (Berkeley: University of California Press, 1997).

7. Indeed, the historian Fernand Braudel noted that to medieval observers, the Pyrenees were a more formidable geographical boundary than the Mediterranean.

8. Amira Bennison, *The Almoravid and Almohad Empires* (Edinburgh: Edinburgh University Press, 2016).

9. The phrase is found in many media reports about the region, from "high quality" online and print publications to those aimed at policy makers. See, for example, Aaron David Miller, "Does Obama Have Any Regrets about His Middle East Policy? Probably Not. But If I Were Him I Would," *Foreign Policy*, September 29, 2015, https://foreignpolicy.com/2015/09/29/does-obama-regrets-middle-east-policy-syria-iraq-islamic-state/; Daniel Halper, "McCain Offers Support to Middle East Protesters," *Weekly Standard*, March 1, 2011, https://www.weeklystandard.com/daniel-halper/mccain-offers-support-to-middle-east-protesters; and Bernard Lewis, "The Revolt of Islam: When Did the Conflict with the West Begin, and How Could It End?," *New Yorker*, November 11, 2001, https://www.newyorker.com/magazine/2001/11/19/the-revolt-of-islam.

10. Anouar Abdel-Malek, "Orientalism in Crisis," *Diogenes* 11, no. 44 (1963): 103–40.

11. Edward W. Said, *Orientalism* (New York: Pantheon Books, 1978); see also A. L. Macfie, *Orientalism: A Reader* (New York: New York University Press, 2000).

12. Zachary Lockman, *Contending Visions of the Middle East: The History and Politics of Orientalism*, 2nd ed. (Cambridge: Cambridge University Press: 2009), 66–148.

13. Thus, one should not be surprised to come across a phrase such as "the general and vivid pattern that unifies . . . the Middle East is, of course, Islam." Yahya Armajani, *Middle East: Past and Present* (Englewood Cliffs, NJ: Prentice-Hall, 1970), 19.

14. The four countries with the largest Muslim populations in the world are Indonesia, Pakistan, India, and Bangladesh.

15. We should also remind ourselves that to some extent the idea of a singular "Muslim world" is itself an artifact of imperialism and then modern ideologies of Pan-Islamism. See Cemil Aydin, *The Idea of the Muslim World: A Global Intellectual History* (Cambridge, MA: Harvard University Press, 2017).

16. While many older books make these sorts of claims explicit, more recent books continue to do so implicitly by placing an emphasis on the putative connections between politics and Islam in the Arab world and the Middle East, generally. See, for example, Robert D. Lee, *Religion and Politics in the Middle East: Identity, Ideology, Institutions, and Attitudes*, 2nd ed. (London: Taylor and Francis, 2018); Mark A. Tessler, *Islam and Politics in the Middle East: Explaining the Views of Ordinary Citizens* (Bloomington: Indiana University Press, 2015); Avi Max Spiegel, *Young Islam: The New Politics of Religion in Morocco and the Arab World* (Princeton, NJ: Princeton University Press, 2015); Lawrence Rubin, *Islam in the Balance: Ideational Threats in Arab Politics* (Stanford, CA: Stanford University Press, 2014); Jorgen Nielsen, *Religion, Ethnicity and Contested Nationhood in the Former Ottoman Space* (Leiden: Brill, 2012); Bernard Lewis, *Faith and Power: Religion and Politics in the Middle East* (New York: Oxford University Press, 2010); Nathan J. Brown and Amr Hamzawy, *Between Religion and Politics* (Washington, DC: Carnegie Endowment for International Peace, 2010); Nelly Lahoud and Anthony Johns London, eds., *Islam in World Politics* (London: Routledge, 2005); Larry Diamond, Marc F. Plattner, and Daniel Brumberg, *Islam and Democracy in the Middle East* (Baltimore: Johns Hopkins University Press, 2003); Fred Halliday, *Nation and Religion in the Middle East* (Boulder, CO: Lynne Rienner, 2000); Tamara Sonn, *Between Qur'an and Crown: The Challenge of Political Legitimacy in the Arab World* (Boulder, CO: Westview Press, 1990); Alan R. Taylor, *The Islamic Question in Middle East Politics* (Boulder, CO: Westview Press, 1988); Metin Heper and Raphael Israeli, eds., *Islam and Politics in the Modern Middle East* (New York: St. Martin's Press, 1984); Michael Curtis, *Religion and Politics in the Middle East* (Boulder, CO: Westview Press, 1981).

17. For a sampling, see Nissim Rejwan, "Left on the Defensive in Egypt," *Jerusalem Post*, March 2, 1976, 8; Khalifa Abdul Hakim, *Islam and Communism*, 2nd ed. (Lahore, Pakistan: Institute of Islamic Culture, 1976); Hafeez Malik, "The Spirit of Capitalism and Pakistani Islam," in *Contributions to Asian Studies*, 2nd ed., ed. Aziz Ahmad (Leiden: E. J. Brill, 1971), 59; Nissim Rejwan, "Egyptian Minds in Revolt: Failure of Indoctrination," *Jerusalem Post*, January 3, 1969, A4; Kenneth Cragg, "The Intellectual Impact of Communism upon Contemporary

Islam," *Middle East Journal* 8 (January 1954): 127; Bernard Lewis, "Communism and Islam," *International Affairs* 30, no. 1 (1954): 1–12; Sayed El Hashimi, "Islam and Communism in the Middle East," *Contemporary Review* 183 (January 1953): 84; Robert T. Hartmann, "150 Million Moslems Get the Word on Communism," *Los Angeles Times*, December 17, 1952, A5; Manfred Halpern, "Implications of Communism for Islam," *Muslim World* 43, no. 1 (January 1953): 28–41; A. W. Battersbey and Ṭufail S. Muḥammad, *The Problem Which Concerns You: A Study of Islam and Communism* (Lahore, Pakistan: Ahmadiyya Anjuman Ishaat-i-Islam, 1951).

18. See, for example, Michael Axworthy, *Revolutionary Iran: A History of the Islamic Republic* (Oxford: Oxford University Press, 2013); Thomas Pierret, *Religion and State in Syria: The Sunni Ulama from Coup to Revolution* (Cambridge: Cambridge University Press, 2013); Millard Burr, *Revolutionary Sudan: Hasan al-Turabi and the Islamist State, 1989–2000* (Leiden: Brill, 2003); Eric Hooglund, ed., *Twenty Years of Islamic Revolution: Political and Social Transition in Iran since 1979* (Syracuse, NY: Syracuse University Press, 2002); David Menashri, *The Iranian Revolution and the Muslim World* (Boulder, CO: Westview Press, 1990); Dilip Hiro, *Holy Wars: The Rise of Islamic Fundamentalism* (New York: Routledge, 1989); Henry Munson, *Islam and Revolution in the Middle East* (New Haven, CT: Yale University Press, 1988); John Laffin, *Holy War, Islam Fights* (London: Grafton Books, 1988); Amir Arjomand Said, ed., *From Nationalism to Revolutionary Islam* (Albany: State University of New York Press, 1984); Shaul Bakhash, *The Reign of the Ayatollahs: Iran and the Islamic Revolution* (New York: Basic Books, 1984); William Griffith, "The Middle East, 1982: Politics, Revolutionary Islam, and American Policy," working paper no. 82-1 (Cambridge: Center for International Studies, Massachusetts Institute of Technology, 1982).

19. Reuel Marc Gerecht, "Sandstorm: The Middle East in Chaos," *Weekly Standard* 20, no. 5 (October 13, 2014): 22–28; M. Steven Fish, Francesca R. Jensenius, and Katherine E. Michel, "Islam and Large-Scale Political Violence: Is There a Connection?" *Comparative Political Studies* 43, no. 11 (November 2010): 1327–62; Gerard Donnadieu, "Islam, Islamism and Violence," *Futuribles* 269 (November 2001): 73–84; Steven Emerson, "Unholy War," *New Republic* 219, no. 11/12 (September 14–21, 1998): 22–23; Martin Kramer, "Ballots and Bullets," *Harvard International Review* 19, no. 2 (Spring 1997): 16; Daniel Pipes, "An Islamic Internationale?," *Forward*, July 22, 1994, 7; Judith Miller, "The Challenge of Radical Islam," *Foreign Affairs* 72, no. 2 (Spring 1993): 43; Haim Gerber, *Islam, Guerrilla War, and Revolution: A Study in Comparative Social History* (Boulder, CO: Lynne Rienner, 1988); Robin B. Wright, *Sacred Rage: The Crusade of Modern Islam* (London: A. Deutsch, 1986); "Islam the Militant Revival," *Time*, April 16, 1979.

20. This is a common misconception and one with a long tradition in the writing on the region. Many books on the "Arab world" view the Arab world as somewhat more homogeneous than it is. See, for example, Margaret K. Nydell,

Understanding Arabs: A Guide for Westerners (Yarmouth, ME: Intercultural Press, 1996); M. Moughrabi Fouad, "The Arab Basic Personality: A Critical Survey of the Literature," *International Journal of Middle East Studies* 9, no. 1 (January 1978): 99–112; and the "classic work" on the topic, Raphael Patai, *The Arab Mind* (New York: Scribner, 1973); new editions of Patai's work were published in 1983, 2002, 2007, and 2014.

21. See, for example, Jasmin Bauomy, "In the World's Youngest Country, Skin Whitening and the Issue of Colourism Is Linked to a Complex History," Al Jazeera, December 9, 2018; Makau Mutua, "Racism at Root of Sudan's Darfur Crisis," *Christian Science Monitor*, July 14, 2004; Douglas H. Johnson, *The Root Causes of Sudan's Civil Wars* (Bloomington: Indiana University Press, 2003); Francis M. Deng, "Sudan—Civil War and Genocide: Disappearing Christians of the Middle East," *Middle East Quarterly* 8, no. 1 (Winter 2001): 13–21.

22. See Jok Madut Jok, *Sudan: Race, Religion, and Violence* (Oxford: Oneworld, 2007); Somini Sengupta, "In Sudan, No Clear Difference between Arab and African," *New York Times*, October 3, 2004.

23. On the question of the family resemblances between nationalisms across the world, see Benedict Anderson's classic, *Imagined Communities: Reflections on the Origin and Spread of Nationalism* (New York: Verso, 2016 [1983]).

24. Here are a sampling of books on these phenomena: Tareq Y. Ismael, *The Rise and Fall of the Communist Party of Iraq* (Cambridge: Cambridge University Press, 2008); Hanna Batatu, *The Old Social Classes and the Revolutionary Movements of Iraq* (Princeton, NJ: Princeton University Press, 1978); Malik Mufti, *Sovereign Creations: Pan-Arabism and Political Order in Syria and Iraq* (Ithaca, NY: Cornell University Press, 1996); Cemil Aydin, *The Idea of the Muslim World: A Global Intellectual History* (Cambridge, MA: Harvard University Press, 2017); Carrie Rosefsky Wickham, *The Muslim Brotherhood: Evolution of an Islamist Movement* (Princeton, NJ: Princeton University Press, 2015); James P. Jankowski, *Nasser's Egypt, Arab Nationalism, and the United Arab Republic* (Boulder, CO: Lynne Rienner, 2002).

25. A typical elaboration of this argument reads thusly: "The term 'Middle East' . . . designate[s] an area with an unmistakable character and identity, a distinctive—and familiar—personality shaped by strong geographical features." Bernard Lewis, *The Shaping of the Modern Middle East* (New York: Oxford University Press 1994), 4.

26. On oil producers see CIA, *World Factbook*, https://www.cia.gov/library/publications/the-world-factbook/fields/261rank.html (August 29, 2019); see the same source for gas producers: https://www.cia.gov/library/publications/the-world-factbook/fields/261rank.html (August 29, 2019).

27. Some 72.6 percent of Algeria's forty million inhabitants live in urban areas. CIA, *World Factbook*, https://www.cia.gov/library/publications/the-world-factbook/geos/ag.html (July 28, 2019).

28. For example, see Rolf Schwarz, "Introduction: Resistance to Globalization in the Arab Middle East," *Review of International Political Economy* 15, no. 4 (2008): 590–98. For a critique of these arguments, see Waleed Hazbun, "The Middle East through the Lens of Critical Geopolitics: Globalization, Terrorism, and the Iraq War," in *Is There a Middle East? The Evolution of a Geopolitical Concept*, ed. Michael E. Bonine, Abbas Amanat, and Michael Ezekiel Gasper (Stanford, CA: Stanford University Press, 2012), 207–30.

29. Saeed Kamali Dehghan, "Nearly Half of US Arms Exports Go to the Middle East," *Guardian*, March 3, 2018, https://www.theguardian.com/world/2018/mar/12/nearly-half-of-us-arms-exports-go-to-the-middle-east; Louis Uchitelle, "The US Still Leans on the Military-Industrial Complex," *New York Times*, September 22, 2017, https://www.nytimes.com/2017/09/22/business/economy/military-industrial-complex.html.

30. Hazbun, "Middle East through the Lens."

31. For a typical rendering of such views, see Thomas L. Friedman, "Tribes with Flags," *New York Times*, March 22, 2011, https://www.nytimes.com/2011/03/23/opinion/23friedman.html. Friedman took the name of his column from one of the best-known works popularizing this view, Charles Glass, *Tribes with Flags: A Journey Curtailed* (London: Picodor, 1992). For a critique of the analytical value of so-called primordial hatreds to explain current political developments, see Jonathan Viger, "The Tribalist Trap," *Jacobin*, June 18, 2018, https://www.jacobinmag.com/2018/06/syria-bashar-al-assad-religion-identity-patronage. For a general account of the colonial provenance of the idea of a "tribe," see Mahmood Mamdani, "What Is a Tribe," *London Review of Books* 34, no.17 (September 13, 2012): 20–22.

32. As quoted in Charles Hirschkind and Saba Mahmood, "Feminism, the Taliban, and Politics of Counter-Insurgency," *Anthropological Quarterly* 75, no. 2 (Spring 2002): 349; Salman Rushdie, "Fighting the Forces of Invisibility," *Washington Post*, October 2, 2001.

33. Graeme Wood, "What ISIS Really Wants," *Atlantic Monthly* 315, no. 2 (March 2015): 78–90, 92, 94.

34. Omar S. Dahi, "Understanding the Political Economy of the Arab Revolts," *Middle East Reports* (*MERIP*) 41, no. 259 (Summer 2011).

35. Nikki Keddie, "Is There a Middle East," *International Journal of Middle East Studies* 4, no. 3 (July 1973): 255–71.

36. Even within its boundaries, because of its vast expanse lying across three continents, day-to-day life in the Ottoman Empire differed greatly from place to place and from one era to another. The Ottomans were well known for incorporating local laws, customs, and elites in their system of rule. As such, there were multiple ideas of sovereignty and juridical institutions and practices simultaneously operating across the empire. Thus, to a large extent there was not a particular historical coherence even to the Ottoman world before the nineteenth

century. Molly Greene, "The Ottoman Experience," *Daedalus* 134, no. 2 (Spring 2005): 88–99.

37. This reappraisal goes back to, at least, Janet L. Abu-Lughod, *Before European Hegemony: The World System, A.D. 1250–1350* (Oxford: Oxford University Press; 1989). Some interesting works on this topic are Giancarlo Casale, *The Ottoman Age of Exploration* (Oxford: Oxford University, 2010); and Engseng Ho, *The Graves of Tarim: Genealogy and Mobility across the Indian Ocean* (Berkeley: University of California Press, 2006). One of the more accessible and charmingly written accounts is Amitav Ghosh, *In an Antique Land: History in the Guise of a Traveler's Tale* (London: Granta Books, 1992).

38. Gagan D. S. Sood, *India and the Islamic Heartlands: An Eighteenth-Century World of Circulation and Exchange* (New York: Cambridge University Press, 2016).

39. The Ottoman state was established in the thirteenth century, spreading from western Anatolia to Central Europe, the Eastern Mediterranean, North Africa, Persian Gulf, and Indian Ocean. It was dissolved in 1923. The Qajar state inherited much of the old Safavid realm and reunited Persia from 1794 to 1925.

40. Arash Khazeni, *Tribes and Empire on the Margins of Nineteenth-Century Iran* (Seattle: University of Washington Press, 2010).

41. Lockman, *Contending Visions*.

42. Of course, this observation holds true for almost every region of the world outside of Western Europe, whether or not that area was ever colonized directly. On North Africa's fraught relationship with "Middle Easternness," see "Why Are There No Middle Easterners in the Maghrib?" in *Is There a Middle East?*, 100–116.

43. Maria Todorova in her *Imagining the Balkans* (New York: Oxford University Press, 1997) has described something quite similar occurring in the Balkans. Building on the work of Edward Said, she argues that the accumulation of knowledge about the Balkans gave birth to a discourse she calls "Balkanism." Subsequently, this discourse has had significant repercussions on the politics and society on the nations of the peninsula as well as on how the rest of the world has conceived of, and interacts with, the area. Thus, whether an idea is a fair representation of reality may be of secondary importance to the *effects* the idea has on the lived experience of human beings.

KEY RESOURCES

Bonine, Michael, Abbas Amanat, and Michael Ezekiel Gasper, eds. *Is There a Middle East? The Evolution of a Geopolitical Concept.* Stanford, CA: Stanford University Press, 2011.

Burke, Edmund, III, and David Yaghoubian, eds. *Struggle and Survival in the Modern Middle East.* 2nd ed. Berkeley: University of California Press, 2005.

Ghosh, Amitav. *In an Antique Land: History in the Guise of a Traveler's Tale.* London: Granta Books, 1992.

Hirschkind, Charles. "What Is Political Islam?" *Middle East Reports (MERIP)* 27, no. 205 (Winter 1997): 12–14.

Perry-Castañeda Library Map Collection, University of Texas at Austin, Libraries, https://legacy.lib.utexas.edu/maps/middle_east.html.

Controversy in the Classroom

Lessons from the Modern Middle East

OMNIA EL SHAKRY

Orientalism, Islamic revival, Israel/Palestine, the gendered discourse of the veil, the Iranian revolution, the politics of oil, torture and terror—could there be a more controversial list? Yet these are precisely some of the thematic topics that I routinely cover when I teach my Middle East in the Twentieth Century course. To complicate matters even further, not only do scholars of the modern Middle East deal with inherently politicized subject matter (in addition to widespread cultural stereotypes), but we also have to deal with the messy and delicate issue of how students perceive our own cultural, ethnic, political, and religious identification with the region. Despite (and perhaps because of) all of these nettlesome issues I have found teaching the modern Middle East a profoundly rewarding experience, in large part because areas of controversy arose precisely where I least expected it, and students responded to such controversies in ways that I would not have imagined possible. In what follows, I focus on three themes: visual representations of "the Orient," gender and sexuality, and torture and terror. At the same time, I try to suggest productive strategies for engaging, and not quashing, controversy in the classroom.

One of the first issues I address in the classroom is the question of the diversity of student interest in and connection to the region. I begin with a simple and, crucially, anonymous task. Distributing index cards to the students, I ask them to free-associate the very first things that come to mind when they hear the terms "Middle East" and "Islam." On the other side of the card, I have students list the reasons for their interest in the course. I can then use these anonymous responses to explore all of the things that have brought us together in the classroom, which range widely—such as Middle Eastern heritage, a love for Middle East cuisine, or military deployment in the region. Teachers can easily collate all responses and create a Wordle that will visually demonstrate the variety and frequency of answers. Elucidating this type of diversity for students helps them see that as a group we are as diverse in our origins as in our interests.

Anonymity serves a further purpose in that oftentimes students may be too timid to voice opinions or make statements that they feel may be perceived as stereotypical in any way—for example, that they are interested in the relationship between Islam and violence. Such timidity often inhibits the open discussion of stereotypes that need to be discussed, rather than dismissed out of hand. I have found that it is important to set the tone for the course in this way—so that students feel that they may discuss any issue, so long as it is done respectfully and opens up the classroom to a broad range of viewpoints.

The Imaginary Orient

One of the best strategies for engaging controversy productively in my experience has been the use of thought-provoking, and at times controversial, visual material. Thus, for instance, Sut Jhally's 1998 documentary *Edward Said on Orientalism*, in which the director relates the question of Orientalism to contemporary processes of racialization, has spawned the most vibrant and extended classroom discussions.[1] In point of fact, it is Jhally's linking of historical discourses of Orientalism to present-day racial prejudices that enables students to relate the question of Orientalism to contemporary questions and experiences (in some instances, quite personal experiences) of race, difference, and identity.

In 1978 comparative literature scholar Edward Said defined Orientalism as an ontological (referring to ways of being) and epistemological (referring to ways of knowing) distinction between East and West that serves to further political and economic asymmetries between the Middle East and the West. For example, the notion that the West is rational and self-controlled while the East is mystical and sensual would be characterized as Orientalist. Such Orientalist depictions are common in contemporary visual culture; just think of *Raiders of the Lost Ark* (1981), *Aladdin* (1992), or *The Mummy* (1999). In fact, the dust jacket of Said's 1978 book was the visually arresting *The Snake Charmer*, painted by Jean-Léon Gérôme (1824–1904) sometime in the last third of the nineteenth century. The painting depicts a naked boy handling a python while an old man plays a flute as a group of men watch intently. Erotically charged, like many other nineteenth-century depictions of the Middle East, the painting can be gainfully used to launch a discussion of representation, reality, and fantasy in European visual illustrations of the Middle East region.

A valuable resource for this is the groundbreaking article "The Imaginary Orient" by the late feminist art historian Linda Nochlin.[2] Nochlin draws our attention to several facets of the painting, namely the fact that it might be more aptly called *The Snake Charmer and His Audience*, as the viewer's gaze is meant to fixate on the lethargic and unseemly audience gaping at the nude boy. The painting is remarkable for its aspiration to realism and its staggering detail: tile work, carpet, calligraphy—although

Jean-Léon Gérôme, *The Snake Charmer*, c. 1879, oil on canvas, 32⅜ × 47⅝ in. (82.2 × 121 cm). Courtesy of the Clark Art Institute, Williamstown, MA.

37

anyone familiar with the Middle East can instantly recognize its lack of correspondence to reality. Its pastiche of disparate, disconnected elements is drawn from a mythic past of the Orient as imagined by a European traveler. Nochlin ingeniously analyses the painting through a series of absences that belie its verisimilitude: history, temporal change, and European presence. In so doing, she demonstrates how paintings, much like the literary and political works that Said analyzed, helped define the presumed cultural inferiority of the Islamic Orient while hiding the colonial presence designed to justify and perpetuate European dominance.

Students may find late nineteenth-century painting quite distant from their own everyday lives, and it is often helpful to think with them about contemporary instances of Orientalism. Two examples are from music videos: Lady Gaga's "Aura" (*Artpop*, 2013), initially titled and leaked as "Burqa" in 2012, and Katy Perry's "Dark Horse" (*Prism*, 2013).[3] While the former is far more problematic than the latter, both demonstrate the continued salience of Orientalism and enable teachers and students alike to think about the Orient as a scene of fantasy and desire that simultaneously enables the political and economic domination of the region.

Gender and Sexuality

The representation of the Orient in music videos as a playful scene of fantasy and desire ("Dark Horse") or as a scene of violence and oppression ("Aura") highlights the significance of gender and sexuality to Western understandings and representations of the region. The specter of Islam often looms large over these debates, whether in the headscarf controversies across Paris and Istanbul, or in American neoconservative discussions of shari'a law. Mainstream media and popular scholarly portrayals routinely evoke the "backward" status of women and sexual minorities in Middle Eastern societies, such as Egypt and Iran, in order to mark the alleged difference between the West and the non-West.[4] Such representations of Islam as a backward and oppressive social system antithetical to gender and sexual equality have garnered a range of scholarly responses. Numerous scholars have linked discourses on gender and sexuality to justifications for the war on terror and its attendant rhetoric of civilization and barbarism.[5] Thus, for example, in response to Western claims to save Afghan women from the Taliban as a pretext for war in Afghanistan, Lila Abu-Lughod has posed the provocative question: "Do Muslim women really need saving?"[6]

Central to the rhetoric of salvation has been the fetishization of the veil—simultaneously an object of desire (a symbol or cipher of the mysterious East, inaccessible and alluring) as well as a marker of "backward" and oppressive social traditions. Indeed, the veiled woman figures prominently in nineteenth- and twentieth-century representations, both in painting and photography. Malek Alloula's *The Colonial Harem* (discussed more extensively in Sara Pursley's chapter) contains a collection of French colonial postcards of North African women erotically staged to appear in their "harems" or in other confined spaces.[7] Renowned psychiatrist and philosopher Frantz Fanon in his "Algeria Unveiled" provides us with a discussion of the veil; its cultural, historical, and psychological significance, as well as its overdetermined role in both the violent colonization of Algeria and the Algerian war of independence (1954–1962).[8] Often criticized for its essentialization of both culture and gender, the article nonetheless conveys the eroticized, racialized, and politicized nature of the colonial gaze and its anticolonial retort.

Such highly charged representations of Middle Eastern women continue into the postcolonial era and perhaps nowhere more so than in contemporary discussions of Iran. As brilliantly explored in Naghmeh Sohrabi and Arielle Gordon's chapter on the 1979 revolution, the challenge of lecturing on the Iranian revolution is to present compelling historical narratives that are not reductive stories of autocratic modernizers, religious zealots, and radical Marxists while simultaneously including students in the conversation who have very little preconceived notions about Iran prior to the revolution. Once again, the introduction of complex visual material may help, and here I use Shirin Neshat's visually arresting, albeit problematic, series of photos entitled *Women of Allah* (1993–1997) in which she juxtaposes the feminist poetry of Forough Farrokhzad to images of women in chadors in a meditation on the nature of spirituality and martyrdom in contemporary Iran.[9] The debates sparked are wide ranging, unsettling notions of gender and veiled docility but also call into question the artist's visual use of the chador.

A particularly startling discussion of the veil can be found in Ellen McLarney's "The Burqa in Vogue: Fashioning Afghanistan," which charts the burqa's rise from "shock to chic" amidst the "supposed liberation of Afghanistan" by American forces.[10] Initially viewed as a symbol of oppression and as "Afghanistan's veil of terror" in the prelude to war and the immediate aftermath of 9/11, the burqa slowly evolved into a commodified emblem of haute couture on the Western runway, featured in spring 2006 designs by John Galliano (for Christian Dior) and Jun Takahashi's fall 2006 Undercover collection of "burqa punk."[11] As McLarney notes,

> The post-9/11 era ushered in the burqa's most recent incarnation, fetishized and ritualized as a shibboleth. Conflict [has] helped produce the burqa as ideology . . . when the burqa is used as it has been in the Western media: as tool of imperial domination, justification for warfare, disguise for violence, erasure of history, and method of reifying hierarchies of class and race. . . . This is perhaps the secret of the burqa's association with repression, as masking the violence of the liberation. The couturiers interpret the burqa in this vein: as an emblem of conflicts fabricated by the West, as a product of the West's own design. Onto the burqa are projected relationships of domination simultaneously infused with sexual content and the politics of capitalism's global expansion. Through a mode of neoliberal emancipation, the burqa has been incorporated into the dominant culture of signs and accordingly redeemed through a culture of consumption.[12]

We should pause, alongside our students, to think about the gravity of the appropriation of the burqa as fashion in the midst of the longest-running US war in history. Marking the simultaneous destruction of a country and peoples at the very moment of their commodification and exoticization, it evokes the poignant poem by Samih al-Qasim, "How I Became an Article," composed of only two simple lines: "They killed me once / Then wore my face many times."[13]

Torture and Terror

The role of the burqa in justifying military involvement in the region brings us to yet another controversial topic of classroom debate and discussion, namely counterinsurgency wars in the Middle East and their relationship to torture and terror. Although the war in Afghanistan is the longest-running war in US history, students may be more familiar with the war in Iraq due to its extensive representation in popular media, and they may well have family members who have served in either or both wars. Despite the heated nature that such discussions will inevitably provoke, it is arguably our ethical obligation to discuss the Iraq invasion and war of 2003 to the best of our knowledge while paying attention to the perspective of its Iraqi victims. Here, I focus on the question of torture and terror (for a broader view of US involvement in Iraq and the Persian Gulf, see Toby Craig Jones's chapter).

A major flashpoint in the US invasion of Iraq in 2003 was the prisoner abuse scandal that took place at the Abu Ghraib prison complex. The vast majority of our students will be completely unfamiliar with the scandal and the leaked photos, and there are several ways to approach this. First, the evidentiary basis of the scandal must be outlined for students. Historians have a wide base of evidence for documenting the torture that took place: extensive investigative journalism, as well as leaked reports by the International Committee of the Red Cross (ICRC) and leaked investigations by high-ranking US military officers.[14] Second, the scandal may be productively approached by linking the Abu Ghraib torture and abuse (much of it sexualized in nature) to longer histories of warfare and counterinsurgency practices. It is useful here to introduce students to the concept of unconventional or asymmetrical warfare, namely warfare that does not take place between the conventional standing armies of nation-states, but that often involves guerilla warfare or other modes of irregular, mobile warfare.[15]

Once placed in this context, the Iraq war can be fruitfully compared to Vietnam or to the Algerian war of independence (1954–1962). Colonial Algeria was a French colony from 1830 to 1962 characterized by a large European settler population, extensive expropriation of native lands, and an apartheid-like segregation of natives and settlers through spatial segregation and a tiered legal system.[16] Its war of independence was one of the bloodiest ever fought (for more, see Muriam Haleh Davis's chapter on decolonization). I screen Gillo Pontecorvo's powerful *Battle of Algiers* to help students visualize the anticolonial nationalist struggle through the perspective of anticolonial agitprop.[17] It is a riveting film that students find openly ideological and surprisingly engaging. To connect it to Iraq, I pair it up with a reading by Michael T. Kaufman, "What Does the Pentagon See in 'Battle of Algiers'?," exploring some of the reasons behind the 2003 screening of the film.[18] The film sparks a broad-ranging debate on the nature of insurgency and the supposed necessity of torture, and inevitably, the students draw their own connections, much as did the Pentagon, to the contemporary war in Iraq. Laleh Khalili's *Time in the Shadows* also traces genealogical connections between torture, terror, and counterinsurgency campaigns from Algeria to Iraq. But educators should also be prepared to discuss the differences between more "classical forms" of asymmetrical warfare, such as in Algeria and Vietnam, and the more decentered forms of warfare that characterize the most current stage of imperial warfare in the Global War on Terror (see Darryl Li's chapter in this volume).

A final point must be taken into consideration, the complex question of whether or not to show the graphic images from Abu Ghraib in the classroom. This is a question that educators should agonize over, not because the images are "too graphic" but rather because of the ethical implications of showing the images. I am quite clear with my students about my own ethical decision to *not* show the photographs, and in my PowerPoint I include an empty blank slide without any images or text that affords me the opportunity to explain why I do not show the images. I also ask students to refrain from looking at the images on their phones, at least until they have heard me out. Why? First, the reproduction of the images was a crucial component of the torture of Iraqi detainees; prisoners were threatened with the circulation of the graphic Abu Ghraib photos to their families and friends in an attempt to get them to confess to crimes that they had not committed or to coerce them into becoming informants. This means that being photographed in this way while threatening *to show* the photos was itself a form of psychological torture.[19] Second, and more broadly, as Nicholas Mirzoeff puts it, "Violence is the standard operating procedure of visuality."[20] Mirzoeff argues that "visuality's first domains were the slave plantation, monitored by the surveillance of the overseer, operating as the surrogate of the sovereign. . . . To coin a phrase, visuality is not war by other means: it is war. This war was constituted first by the experience of plantation slavery, the foundational moment of visuality and the right to look."[21] In other words, the power to see and "the right to look," that is to say, visuality, has always been implicated with dominant and racialized regimes of power. What might it mean to ask our students *not to look* in this particular instance? It is a question worth pondering collectively, and educators will be pleasantly surprised by the profundity of our students' grasp of such questions given their upbringing in an era where the visual reigns supreme.[22]

But in contravening the type of narratives that wish to present the torture at Abu Ghraib as an aberration or the work of a few "bad apples," do I lack balance in my presentation? I would argue that the question might be something of a red herring. If, indeed, our task as educators is to do "more than merely summarize contemporary debates," then it behooves us to complicate such *public* debates, which so often truncate historical evidence, for the sake of political arguments.[23]

42

I must point out that these discussions can be tense. Clearly, it would be easier as educators to shy away from controversial topics, or to present more reconciled and less complex views on certain subjects, and we might find ourselves better liked by our students if we did so. But, in the end, we would be doing them a disservice if we did not foster disagreement and challenge their thinking in ways that led them to question received ideas, accepted narratives, and easy generalizations. Regardless of their endpoints, we must hope that our students leave the classroom emboldened by the Fanonian injunction "make of me always a [person] who questions!"[24]

NOTES

This chapter draws some material from "Engaging Controversy: Lessons from the Modern Middle East," *Perspectives in History: The Newsmagazine of the American Historical Association* 48, no. 5 (May 2010), https://www.historians.org/publications-and-directories/perspectives-on-history/may-2010/lessons-from-the-modern-middle-east.

1. *Edward Said on Orientalism*, directed by Sut Jhally (Media Education Foundation, 1998). The film is subdivided into several sections and may be used either in its entirety or in part, depending on classroom time constraints.

2. Linda Nochlin, "The Imaginary Orient," in *The Politics of Vision: Essays on Nineteenth Century Art and Society* (New York: Harper and Row, 1989), 33–59.

3. "Katy Perry—Dark Horse (Official) ft. Juicy J," YouTube video, 3:45, posted by Katy Perry, February 20, 2014, https://www.youtube.com/watch?v=oKSOMA3QBUo; "Lady Gaga—Machete Kills—Aura (Lyric Video)," YouTube video, 3:41, posted by Lady Gaga, October 9, 2013. There is a "Lady Gaga—Burqa (2012 Demo Leak)," YouTube video, 4:34, posted by Azelf550TV, June 9, 2017, https://www.youtube.com/watch?v=zxZxIhwpylg.

4. See, for example, Nicholas Kristoff and Sheryl WuDunn, "Is Islam Misogynistic?," in *Half the Sky: Turning Oppression into Opportunity for Women Worldwide* (New York: Vintage Books, 2009), 149–65; Ayaan Hirsi Ali, *The Caged Virgin: An Emancipation Proclamation for Women and Islam* (New York: Simon and Schuster, 2006). Both of these texts are riddled with false arguments and blatant misrepresentations, none of which have lessened their popularity. On Hirsi Ali see Max Blumenthal, "Exposing Anti-Islam Author Ayaan Hirsi Ali's Latest Deception," alternet.org, March 26, 2015, http://www.alternet.org/media/anti-islam-author-ayaan-hirsi-alis-latest-deception.

5. Charles Hirschkind and Saba Mahmood, "Feminism, the Taliban, and Politics of Counter-Insurgency," *Anthropological Quarterly* 75, no. 2 (2002): 339–54;

Jasbir Puar and Amit Rai, "Monster, Terrorist, Fag: The War on Terrorism and the Production of Docile Patriots," *Social Text* 20, no. 3 (2002): 117–48; Inderpal Grewal, "Outsourcing Patriarchy: Feminist Encounters, Transnational Mediations and the Crime of 'Honour Killings,'" *International Feminist Journal of Politics* 15, no. 1 (2013): 1–19.

6. Lila Abu-Lughod, "Do Muslim Women Really Need Saving? Anthropological Reflections on Cultural Relativism and Its Others," *American Anthropologist* 104, no. 3 (2002): 783–90.

7. Malek Alloula, *The Colonial Harem* (Minneapolis: University of Minnesota Press, 1986).

8. Frantz Fanon, "Algeria Unveiled," in *A Dying Colonialism* (New York: Grove Press, 1965), 35–67.

9. For an artist's statement, see http://signsjournal.org/shirin-neshat/.

10. Ellen McLarney, "The Burqa in Vogue: Fashioning Afghanistan," *Journal of Middle East Women's Studies* 5, no.1 (2009): 1–20.

11. As Meyda Yeğenoğlu notes, "the figure of 'veiled Oriental woman' has a particular place in these texts, not only as signifying Oriental woman as mysterious and exotic but also as signifying the Orient as feminine, always veiled, seductive, and dangerous." Yeğenoğlu, *Colonial Fantasies: Towards a Feminist Reading of Orientalism* (Cambridge: Cambridge University Press, 1998), 11.

12. McLarney, "Burqa in Vogue," 19–20.

13. Samih al-Qasim, "How I Became an Article," in *Victims of a Map: A Bilingual Anthology of Arabic Poetry*, ed. Abdullah al-Udhari (London: Saqi, 2005).

14. Laleh Khalili, "Banal Procedures of Detention: Abu Ghraib and Its Ancestors," in *Time in the Shadows: Confinement in Counterinsurgencies* (Stanford, CA: Stanford University Press, 2013), 141; *Standard Operating Procedure*, directed by Errol Morris (Participant Media, 2008). For other documentation of torture, see the following: Human Rights Watch, "Torture in Iraq," *New York Review of Books* 52, no.17 (November 3, 2005), http://www.nybooks.com/articles/18414; Eric Schmitt and Carolyn Marshall, "TASK FORCE 6–26: Inside Camp Nama; In Secret Unit's 'Black Room,' a Grim Portrait of US Abuse," *New York Times*, March 19, 2006, http://query.nytimes.com/gst/fullpage.html?res=9C0CE6DD1F 31F93AA25750C0A9609C8B63&pagewanted=all; Lisa Hajjar, "The CIA Didn't Just Torture, It Experimented on Human Beings," *Nation*, December 16, 2014; and Jon Wiener, "Why the Torture Report Won't Change Anything," *Nation*, December 16, 2014.

15. Khalili, *Time in the Shadows*, 11.

16. John Ruedy, *Modern Algeria: The Origins and Development of a Nation* (Bloomington: Indiana University Press, 2005).

17. *Battle of Algiers*, directed by Gillo Pontecorvo (Rialto Pictures, 1966).

18. Michael T. Kaufman, "The World: Film Studies; What Does the Pentagon See in 'Battle of Algiers'?," *New York Times*, September 7, 2003, http://www

.nytimes.com/2003/09/07/weekinreview/the-world-film-studies-what-does-the-pentagon-see-in-battle-of-algiers.html.

19. Anne McClintock, "Paranoid Empire: Specters from Guantanamo and Abu Ghraib," *Small Axe 28* 13, no. 1 (March 2009): 50–74.

20. Nicholas Mirzoeff, *The Right to Look: A Counterhistory of Visuality* (Durham, NC: Duke University Press 2011), 292.

21. Mirzoeff, *The Right to Look*, 2, 6. See the preface to this volume for a discussion of the complex yet incommensurable relationship between slavery, its afterlife, and Abu Ghraib.

22. Susan Sontag discusses the nature of the torture photographs and their relation to our troubled times, "Regarding the Torture of Others," *New York Times Magazine*, May 23, 2004, https://www.nytimes.com/2004/05/23/magazine/regarding-the-torture-of-others.html. For a critique of Sontag, see Hazel Carby, "A Strange and Bitter Crop: The Spectacle of Torture," *Open Democracy*, October 11, 2004, https://www.opendemocracy.net/en/article_2149jsp/. Students can also engage in discussions of contemporary films such as *Zero Dark Thirty*, so long as their role in the justification of torture is clarified: Patrice Taddonio, "WATCH: How the CIA Helped Make 'Zero Dark Thirty,'" *Frontline*, May 15, 2015, PBS, https://www.pbs.org/wgbh/frontline/article/watch-how-the-cia-helped-make-zero-dark-thirty/. Likewise, a film such as *American Sniper* can be juxtaposed to the leaked footage in "Collateral Murder," YouTube, April 3, 2010, http://www.youtube.com/watch?v=5rXPrfnU3Go.

23. Committee A on Academic Freedom and Tenure, AAUP, "Freedom in the Classroom," June 2007, http://www.aaup.org/AAUP/comm/rep/A/class.htm.

24. Frantz Fanon, *Black Skin, White Masks* (New York: Grove Press, 1967), 232.

KEY RESOURCES

Abu Lughod, Lila. *Do Muslim Women Need Saving?* Cambridge, MA: Harvard University Press, 2015.

Alloula, Malek. *The Colonial Harem.* Minneapolis: University of Minnesota Press, 1986.

Jhally, Sut, dir. *Edward Said on Orientalism.* Media Education Foundation, 1998.

Khalili, Laleh. *Time in the Shadows: Confinement in Counterinsurgencies.* Stanford, CA: Stanford University Press, 2013.

McLarney, Ellen. "The Burqa in Vogue: Fashioning Afghanistan." *Journal of Middle East Women's Studies* 5, no.1 (2009): 1–20.

Morris, Errol, dir. *Standard Operating Procedure.* Participant Media, 2008.

Nochlin, Linda. "The Imaginary Orient." In *The Politics of Vision: Essays on Nineteenth-Century Art and Society*, 33–59. Boulder, CO: Westview Press, 1989.

Pontecorvo, Gillo, dir. *The Battle of Algiers.* Rialto Pictures, 1966.

Said, Edward. *Orientalism.* New York: Vintage, 1978.

PART TWO

Understanding and Teaching Historical Content

The Legacy of Islam in the Modern Middle East

OVAMIR ANJUM

Telling the story of a major world civilization spanning three continents and a millennium and a half is a complex task if there ever was one. The teacher must come up with simplifications, generalizations, and, most importantly, illustrative stories that try to capture deeper insights that are truthful or at least helpful and defensible. Learning Islam poses an additional challenge, because apart from being foreign to most students, it is a living religion (or, as often said, it is a "way of life") for one-fifth of the world's population. Modern scholars often and rightly emphasize the need to de-essentialize Islam, challenge false stereotypes in both popular culture and Orientalist scholarship, and present its diverse manifestations and interpretations. Yet, for students who may come with greatly varying preconceived notions, ranging from Islam as the religion of violence and Muslims as worshipers of the "moon god," to the hope that good Muslims are indistinguishable from good liberal Protestants, that method of presentation is not always satisfying. Although it is important to burst the bubbles of myths teach diversity and variation in time and place in the world of Islam, there is a need to identify central pillars to help the learners begin building their own edifice of understanding. This essay, I should note at the outset, is focused on the Middle East, and not the whole of the Muslim world.

Origins

To Muslims, Islam is humankind's original religion, or orientation to reality. "Islam" is a self-chosen label frequently mentioned

49

in the Qur'an and signifies the act of *islam* (lit. peaceful surrender) that is at the heart of the religion. The Arabic word for peace, *salam*, is a related word with the same root, and the greeting *al-salam 'alaykum*—"peace be upon you"—is the most ubiquitous phrase one hears around Muslims.

Historically, Islam emerged out of developments within the Abrahamic family of faiths, and theologically learned Christians, Jews, and Muslims have generally taken for granted the fact that they worshipped the same Creator-God, even when they have disputed divine attributes. I have found it useful in teaching to dwell on this historical consensus to dispel the notion, entertained by some Muslims as well as others, that Islam was sui generis. Muhammad, the prophet of Islam, presented himself not as Islam's "founder" but as the last link in a long line of prophets, who, according to the Qur'an, were all men whom God had chosen to convey His message (Q 21:7). The Qur'an places itself squarely within the Abrahamic tradition, speaking of Abraham, Ishmael, Isaac, Moses, Jesus, and many other biblical prophets as being part of the same monotheistic teaching: submission to one true God, Allah. Before Islam, the word "Allah" had been used to refer to Abraham's and his progeny's God, not only by Arabic-speaking Jews and Christians but also the Arabian pagans, in particular, the Meccans, whose city housed the Ka'ba (literally, cubicle) in a sanctuary known as the "House of Allah." Although the sanctuary housed many other deities, reportedly including even a representation of Jesus and Mary, the Meccans believed that Allah was the only Creator-God who controlled the world and their destinies, whereas lesser, local or tribal deities, represented by idols, functioned as intermediaries. As such, teachers should find the concept of the "Abrahamic tradition" a useful pedagogical tool.

Muhammad was born in the city of Mecca on the western edge of the Arabian Peninsula in "the Year of the Elephant," which corresponds to 570 CE.[1] Largely unlettered, without a commonly accepted dating system, and without a political power to impose one, the Arabs referred to years in reference to memorable events, and Muhammad's birth year was so-called because it was marked by the invasion of Abraha, the Christian Abyssian governor of Yemen who had sought to destroy the Ka'ba with his army, reinforced by charging elephants, but he was frustrated by a divine intervention in which, the Qur'an reports, Allah sent little birds with stones that destroyed the army and thus refreshed in the memory of the Arabs the power of Allah and His care for His house. The Qur'an recounted the incident in a short chapter called "The Elephant" (Surah 105). Thus, being not the first but the last prophet of Islam, Muhammad began preaching at forty when the Archangel Gabriel brought God's messages to him piecemeal as rhythmic recitations delivered in sleep or a wakeful state over his twenty-three-year mission. The first thirteen years of his mission were spent in Mecca, and the last ten in Medina, a small oasis town to the north of Mecca that gave him refuge when his own city rejected him. The leaders of Quraysh — the tribe that occupied Mecca as the keepers of its ancient sanctuary — rejected his mission, but Mecca had already given its best to Muhammad's mission: men and women who became the backbone of the new religion, and who arrived in Medina with Muhammad as immigrants (*muhajirun*), welcomed by the new Medinan converts, the helpers (*ansar*).

To reiterate the aforementioned pedagogical theme, I note how Muslim commentators have observed that if Muhammad in Mecca was like Jesus, persecuted and almost assassinated for his uncompromising mission, he was in Medina like Moses, the leader, judge, and lawgiver of his community. Muhammad's own sayings, known as "hadiths" (preserved for the first century orally, in contrast with the Qur'an, which was immediately written down), frequently show him interpreting his mission in the Abrahamic heritage: he called himself the prayer of his father Abraham, who had settled his wife (or, according to the biblical tradition, concubine) Hagar and son Ishmael many (by biblical account, some twenty-five) centuries earlier in the barren valley of Mecca surrounded by hills of volcanic rock. With Ishmael, he built the Ka'ba and prayed to God for a messenger in his progeny: "Our Lord! And raise up in their midst a messenger from among them who shall recite unto them Thy revelations, and shall instruct them in the Scripture and in wisdom and shall make them grow in purity. Lo! Thou, only Thou, art the Mighty, Wise" (Q 2:129). As history unfolded under Muslim rule, these genealogical connections to the biblical teachings were crucial in not only accommodating but also incorporating Jewish and Christian communities and traditions into the fabric of Muslim societies as well as Islamic tradition. Unlike medieval Christendom, which had no significant minorities of other faiths in its midst to contend with or tolerate, Islamdom was populated by the "People of the Book" (Jews and Christians) both theologically and demographically.

Modern scholarship has shed much new light on the context in which Islam emerged, even though the field of Western scholarship on early Islam remains deeply divided about how much to trust the early Islamic literary sources. The most common approaches range between, to use Fred Donner's classification, source-critical (approaches that see the outline of the traditional narrative as more or less correct, but particular reports to be subject of critique) and tradition-critical (critical of the entire narrative).[2] The radical skepticism of the latter approach, which appeared in the 1970s and speculated that even the Qur'anic text may have remained unsettled as late as the third/ninth century, has been allayed by the carbon dating of portions of the Qur'anic text to the first/seventh century.[3] The older, source-critical approach, which is now once again predominant and the more relevant one, has generally granted the authentic attribution of the Qur'an to Muhammad but has been more skeptical of the hadiths and other materials; recent research in this domain too has moderated the critics' claims, bringing modern scholarship into conversation with the traditional Muslim science of hadith criticism.[4]

Pedagogically, another important theme among scholars is that of the continuities and changes that Islam brought to the Middle East of Late Antiquity. Much recent research activity has turned to deepening the conversation with the scholarship of Late Antiquity, exploring the religious landscape to which Islam would respond and in conversation with which it was born. This period was itself preceded by the so-called Axial Age, the roughly thousand-year-long period starting in 800 BCE during which all the major world religious traditions, including Lao-Tzu, Buddha, Greek philosophy, the Hebrew prophets, and the Upanishads in India, originated. Islam, in this list, is a latecomer, for Islam itself claimed to be a God-given reformation of the earlier Abrahamic messages, and in many ways, a continuity. The Qur'an declared that all human communities had been sent God's prophets with the same essential message of monotheism in different languages; neither Arabs, nor Jews, nor any other race or tribe has any particular claim on God. Yet, remarkably, the Qur'an singled out for engagement and partial endorsement only one of these various traditions, the Abrahamic, in its Hebrew and Christian versions; all other traditions are categorically ignored, classified under the general error of *shirk* (lit., associating partners to God)—the antonym for monotheism.

Modern studies have also suggested that in contrast to earlier stereotypes and perhaps later Muslims' own impression, the Islamic civilization in its social and political institutions was continuous with that of its predecessors, although the distinctiveness of Islamic civilization is nontrivial. One may, therefore, accept with caution the assumption that "the institutional patterns characteristic of Islamic societies had their origin in ancient Mesopotamia in the third millennium BC."[5] Other scholars have characterized this civilizational heritage as the "Irano-semitic" complex.[6] Attempts to show direct borrowing have seen mixed results. The argument that Islamic law was a continuation of Roman provincial law has not been successful.[7] Even an extra- Qur'anic institution such as the endowment (*waqf*), which has its closest parallel in earlier Sasanian institutions, is best explained as a creative result of internal dynamics spawned by Qur'anic law rather than a simple borrowing.[8] The institution of *dhimma*, the granting of legal status to non-Muslim communities in return for a poll tax, had parallels in the earlier empires, although in its details it too is Qur'anic.[9] Most significantly, studies show early Muslims' deliberate break from the general Near Eastern imperial heritage, inasmuch as they saw themselves as an egalitarian community ruled by a commander (*amir*), a first-among-equals who shall not be given the title used for kings (*sultan* or *malik*).[10] Although this resistance gave way to regional patterns within a century, religious ideals continued to preserve a strong egalitarian undercurrent.[11]

Conquests and Expansion

In the three decades following the death of the Prophet Muhammad (in 632 CE), Muslim armies had unified the Arabian Peninsula, captured Persia, taken Mesopotamia, Egypt, and North Africa, and made forays into the Iberian Peninsula. Eventually, distance from the center, exhaustion, and internal political divisions enervated the armies: in the west, the Muslim armies composed of Arabs and Berbers crossed Iberia eventually to Gaul (France) but were finally repelled; the fortification of Constantinople frustrated the Arabs' attempts to secure that prized capital of the Byzantines, allowing that empire to survive another seven centuries until the Ottomans took it in 1453; in the east, Central Asian and northern Indian regions offered continual resistance until about the tenth century. Within a century, a huge new Islamic empire (known to Muslims as *Dar al-Islam*, the Abode of Islam) had arisen in the middle of the Eurasian continent. Yet, the conquests were never complete: resistance as well as new aggression continually challenged the Middle East from the west by the Byzantine Empire and beyond, leading up to the Crusades in the eleventh century, and especially from the Steppe in the northeast, leading to the Mongol onslaught in the thirteenth century. Nor were the conquests one-way, and the more complete the conquest had been, as in the case of Persia, the more thorough the internalization of the conquered civilization.

The early Islamic conquests have lent themselves comparison with other great nomadic conquests and empire building on the one hand and religious movements on the other. The rapidity of the conquests, the reasons for their spectacular success, and the combination of religious and secular motivations behind them have long captured scholarly attention.

The initial conquests had taken place under the Rashidun, the first four caliphs (i.e., successors) of the Prophet.[12] Note that Sunni Muslim majority has come to consider the thirty-year reign of these four to be a normative continuation of the Prophet Muhammad's life, whereas the Shi'a, a protest movement built around the memory of the Prophet's son-in-law and cousin 'Ali, ultimately came to consider him and his progeny the only legitimate rulers. A civil war tore apart the caliphate after the assassination of the third caliph, 'Uthman. The Umayyad dynasty that followed succeeded in maintaining unity and continuing expansion, but at the expense of the egalitarianism and religious ideals of the early period. The supporters (Shi'a) of 'Ali, a broad and often eclectic political alliance during the seventh century, mounted many failed rebellions in order to regain power for the Prophet's lineage, rebellions that were fueled by the high-handedness of the Umayyad rule. Based in part on the resentment against the Umayyad treatment of non-Arab converts to Islam and in part on the Alid sentiment, a successful rebellion in 750 brought to power the Abbasids, a dynasty that fully admitted non-Arab Muslims into the Ummah (the Muslim community), but also transformed the caliphate into an absolute monarchy after the pre-Islamic Sassanid pattern.[13] The two ensuing centuries are considered the golden period of Islamic material civilization, science, wealth, and influence. By 945, Abbasid Baghdad was overrun by local Shi'a warlords, the Buyids, and Abbasid power was reduced to symbolic authority that nonetheless lasted for another three centuries.

Shi'a-Sunni Split

As the Abbasids consolidated their rule along the lines established by the Umayyads, now accepting non-Arab, Persian Muslims as equal to other Arabs, and all as subjects of an imperial caliphate, the revolutionary zeal as well as Alid support was spent. With the rising wave of mass conversion to Islam over the course of the eighth and ninth centuries, the demographics began to change, and the new majority was more attracted to pious social life lived by scriptural standards, explained and embodied by scholars ('ulama), rather than political idealism or messianic justice. Moderate Alid supporters too were assimilated into the mainstream; the Shi'a that remained were, as a result, hardened.[14] It is at this point, from the eighth to tenth centuries, that Shi'ism developed as a distinct theology and split not only from the mainstream but further subdivided into at least three major groups: the Zaydis, who continued to uphold the duty to resist but remained theologically moderate, the Imamis (or Twelvers) who embraced moderately messianic beliefs along with political quietism, and the Seveners (Isma'ilis), who embraced radical messianic and esoteric beliefs, earning the label *ghulat* (extremists) from the other Shi'a as well as the mainstream.[15] The last two groups accorded infallibility and eschatological significance to selected scions of Alid lineage, who alone could be legitimate rulers, or imams. The majority that willy-nilly accepted the Abbasid rule, seeing the proverbial glass as half full, came to be known as the Ahl al-Sunna wa-l-Jama'a: namely, those who adhere to the normative tradition and the mainstream community or, in short, Sunni. The backbone of this new majority was the urbanized Arab and non-Arab Muslims who saw little point in old disputes.[16]

Sunni Islam, however, did not emerge only in response to radical religious sects, but in equal part to *kalam*, the rationalist theological discourse inspired by Islam's polemical encounter with preexisting Hellenized theologies of the Middle East. Perhaps the best contemporary description of the Sunnis comes from the matchless prose of their archenemy from this camp, the essayist al-Jāḥiẓ (d. 869), who labeled them as *al-nābita*, literally, the rootless leaders of the masses, the demagogues. He describes the Sunni movement as a consolidation of various groups opposed to *kalam*, and whose supporters, he writes, included "worshippers, jurists, hadith people, and ascetics." These figures had been closing ranks against advocates of rationalist *kalam*, "accusing them of sedition, innovation, disbelief, and calling them 'the people of heresies!'"[17] By the fourth/tenth century, many Sunnis as well as Shi'a were beginning to accept their own versions of *kalam* dedicated to defending their respective orthodoxies, recasting their disagreements in rationalistic terms.

Pedagogically, I find it useful to emphasize the evolving nature of the Sunni-Shi'a split, in which at first political differences were theologized. Despite the hardening over time, significant theological change remains possible until today: Iran, a stronghold of Sunni Islam, was converted by force to Twelver Shi'ism only in 1500 by the Safavids; the Zaydi Shi'a of Yemen drew notably closer to Sunnism as a result of hadith studies during the eighteenth century, and the adamantly nonpolitical Twelvers became recently politicized only due to certain twentieth-century theological innovations.

Conversions to Islam

Perhaps one of the most valuable things a course on the history of Islam can do is to help students navigate between the popular notions that "Islam spread by the sword" and that "Islam spread peacefully." Historians agree that the mass conversion to Islam of the conquered regions outside the Arabian Peninsula did not take place immediately following the conquests; the best estimates place it between the mid-eighth and tenth centuries.[18] This lays to rest the myth that Islam spread by the sword; the conversions were a prolonged social process, which is not to deny that without the conquering armies first having changed the power dynamics, such conversions could not have been conceived. The conquests of the first half century resulted in an array of ad hoc treaties with the people who not infrequently welcomed their new imperial masters for collecting fair taxes and leaving their religions alone.[19] For the first century or two, therefore, the Arab-Muslims constituted a small elite ruling over non-Muslims. This elite, we learn from measures attributed to the second caliph, 'Umar, wished to protect itself from the corrosive effects of the decadent but far more sophisticated cultures it had conquered; the limits on assimilation must have also limited meaningful contact. The Umayyads at least occasionally discouraged conversion in order to protect their privileges.

In a situation that can only be called exceptional in the long history of ancient Near Eastern empires, the conquering religion had been stronger than the conquering elite, and the universalizing message of the religion allowed the conquered people to claim religious authority; within a century many of the great authorities of Islam were now non-Arabs drawn from the conquered peoples. The Abbasid revolt of 750 (whose military might derived from Persian converts in Khurasan), and the simultaneous emergence of a new kind of egalitarian Islam (Sunni-ism) were primarily results of this factor. Islam had spawned a civilization that survived the conquest movement that had brought it thanks to three powerful factors, the religion (centered on a strict monotheism), the Arabic language, and the law.

Muslim traders and mariners carried goods and ideas from the Middle East to Southeast Asia and China, spreading their religion, culture, and the Arabic and Persian languages from East Africa to Indonesia. In the ninth century, for instance, over a hundred thousand Arabs, Persians, and Jews had taken up residence in the south China city of Guangzhou.[20] The Abbasid power disintegrated over the next two centuries, but the caliphate lived on, now separated from mundane power and transformed into a theological symbol of Sunni Islam representing the unity of politically fragmented Muslims and continuity with the sacred past.

In 1258, though, Mongol forces captured and destroyed Baghdad, killing the last Baghdadi caliphs and severely disrupting the established Islamic world.[21] The Abbasid caliphate was nominally reestablished in Cairo three years later, but the former glory of the caliphate never recovered. After a hiatus during the tenth through fourteenth centuries (late middle period) when horse-warrior invaders from northern regions continually invaded and ruled over the caliphate as well as the expanding Islamic societies, three new groups rose to become great empires: first the Ottomans, who inherited much of the western part of the Islamic world; then in the early 1500s the Safavids, who established their rule over Persia, converting by force its largely Sunni population to Twelver Shiʿism; and the Mughals, who conquered most of India.[22]

Pedagogically, useful comparisons can be made between the spread of Islam and other phases of globalization through conquest and trade in world history. The significance of the spread of Islam for the course of world history was profound. First and foremost, it created a realm of common language and custom covering much of the Old World within which trade, ideas, and culture could develop. Fortunately for the rest of the world, the Islamic world loved books and libraries; indeed, the largest libraries in the world during the eighth to the fifteenth centuries were in Islamic lands, the most famous perhaps being the library at Alexandria in Egypt. In these libraries were stored not just the treasures of the Islamic world, but the classics from ancient Greece and Rome as well. The expansion of Islamic empires along the Mediterranean Sea, moreover, cut

Europe off for centuries from the Indian Ocean, the dynamic center of world trade. It was said that as long as Muslims dominated the Mediterranean, Europeans "couldn't even float a plank on it."[23]

The Second Imperial Age:
The Ottomans and the Safavids

As noted earlier, in the period designated as early modern in European history, nearly the entire Muslim world came to be reconsolidated, after centuries of dispersion into smaller kingdoms, into three large empires: the Ottomans (who ruled from Istanbul over the Balkans in the west and the Arabic-speaking Middle East and parts of North Africa in the east and south), Safavid (Persia), and Mughal (the Indian subcontinent). Although on the intellectual plane and in administrative practices there is little that was drastically new, each of the empires erected strong centralized bureaucratic institutions unprecedented in their coherence since the High Abbasid times, and the general populace achieved a considerable level of prosperity.

Pedagogically, the change from the Mamluk period "warrior-on-the-horseback" to the Ottoman era "gunpowder empires" lends itself to a lesson in the decisive significance of military technology. I often make the point by showing or discussing Hollywood's *The Last Samuri* (2003) in class.

The Ottomans, the largest and most successful of the three, were Sunni but moderately religious, interested in empire building through perfecting institutions rather than theocracy. The Safavids, in contrast, were a formidable theocracy.[24] Although the Safavids had their origins in a Sunni Sufi order, the radical army that brought them to power were *ghulat* (extremist Shi'a), who attributed divine powers to their shah (king). The shah, upon consolidating his grip on power, wanted neither the messianic militarism of his army nor any obligation to submit to the neighboring Sunni Ottomans, thus choosing quietist Twelver Shi'ism for his realm. He imported Imami ulama into Iran and forced the conversion of the largely Sunni population to Twelver Shi'ism. The two empires clashed militarily, first in the Battle of Chaldiran in 1514 and then intermittently for the next two hundred years, after which the Safavids lost power.

Teachers may find it useful to point out the interconnectedness of religious and socioeconomic history by examining the relative difference between the status of the Sunni versus Shiʿa ulama in the modern world and its roots in the respective Ottoman and Safavid policies. The Twelver Shiʿī ulama were empowered by the religious ideology of the Safavid realm, and after the founding dynasty lost its sway, the ulama's power, based in secure economic endowments and religious taxes peculiar to Shiʿism, only increased in time. The Ottoman ulama, by contrast, had become state functionaries and had no independent institutional base. An Ottoman qadi (judge) administered not only the divine law, Shariʿa, to Muslims but also the sultan's *qanun* law to all subjects.[25] Furthermore, this may have diminished the traditional role of socioreligious leadership the Arab ulama had played since their rise in the early centuries of Islam and that had allowed them to act as a check against political tyranny.

The Modern Period

"In the sixteenth century of our era," writes the foremost twentieth-century American historian of the Islamic world, "a visitor from Mars might well have supposed that the human world was on the verge of becoming Muslim."[26] Hodgson's insightful observation is a great pedagogical tool to help students think through common presentist and anachronistic biases. An education in history fails to be anything other than a confirmation of our current prejudices unless it is accompanied by an effort to step into the shoes of our historical actors.

The world, of course, did not become Muslim. While the three Muslim empires continued to slowly improve the old pattern of agrarianate empires, Western Europe, hitherto an obscure and small corner of the world, with a dazzling combination of luck (the encounter with a whole new resource-rich continent), colonial violence, institutional legacy, and ideas, transformed the path of history. By the nineteenth century, the invincible Ottomans of a century earlier had given way to a weakened empire, struggling to transform their decentralized, diverse, and tolerant conglomeration of numerous ethnicities and religions into a modern nation-state. The process of state building, as elsewhere in Europe, was nonlinear, bloody, and disruptive, leading to the loss of the Mediterranean Muslim empire's earlier, flexible character and legal and ethnic pluralism. The other Muslim empires fared worse; the Indian Mughal Empire fell to the British East India trading company already by the middle of the eighteenth century, becoming a formal colony a century later; in Persia, the weak Qajar dynasty began losing territories to Imperial Russia.

During the nineteenth century the emerging modern Arabic culture, in particular, in Egypt—the semiautonomous Ottoman province under an Albanian Ottoman general and autocratic modernizer, Mehmed 'Ali—articulated notions of nationhood and citizenship through a creative synthesis of medieval Islamic and European ideas. In Egypt, as in the central Ottoman regions, modernization was primarily top-down state building. The invasion and short-lived occupation of Egypt by Napoleon in 1798, the first modern invasion of an Arabic-speaking people, led to intensive and expensive modernization efforts that ultimately culminated in the British colonial occupation in 1882.[27] Three decades later, the Ottomans decided to back the Axis Powers in the First World War, driven by their rivalry with the Russians and aggressive British involvement in the Arab provinces, particularly in inciting the Arabs to revolt against them. Even as the Ottomans lost the war and the empire, a century's worth of modernization bore fruit as the Turkish army fought back the attempts to parcel out its base in Anatolia, while also abolishing the caliphate in 1924, ending the institution that had lasted thirteen centuries; the region has never recovered stability, identity, or balance ever since.[28]

Reformism and Activism

Islamic modernist reformers tried to bridge the gap between tradition and modernity by declaring a need for the reinterpretation of Islam. Perhaps the most renowned early modernizer was the Egyptian scholar and educationalist Rifaʿa al-Tahtawi (d. 1873), whose view of Islam's fundamental compatibility to the emerging European civilization is evident: "All the deductions that civilized nations (*al-umam al-mutamaddina*) have reached by reason, and that they have made the foundations of their laws and civilization rarely deviate from the principles underpinning the branches of Islamic jurisprudence that concern human interaction. What we call the principles of Islamic jurisprudence is similar to what they call natural rights or natural laws."[29]

After the disillusionment that accompanied the colonial experience and the First World War, an alternative response became dominant. The modernization attempts of the nineteenth century, in particular the printing press, rise of literacy, and public schooling, created a new class of secularly educated but devout Muslims who were neither the ulama of old nor their trusting followers. This "intellectual middle class" peopled modern Islamic activist movements—the Muslim Brotherhood in the Middle East and Jamaat-i-Islami in South Asia.[30] These movements neither rejected modernity nor embraced it all. In the context of the Cold War, they rejected both Western capitalism and Soviet communism/socialism and stressed that Islam offers an alternative path to modernity. These early activist movements influenced the development of many other movements across the Muslim world, both mainstream and radical, that continue to be significant forces in modern Islam.

The British and the French had drawn the current boundaries of the Middle Eastern nation-states after the First World War, and by the end of the Second World War they were unable to hold any territories. After the ostensible independence of the mid-twentieth century, the Muslim rulers who took power were often military dictators or, in a few cases, kings who had risen to power riding the wave of anticolonial nationalism. The older Islamic sociopolitical institutions having been decimated by colonialism, Muslim masses now had little defense against the autocratic rulers they had inherited, whom they had not and perhaps would not have chosen.

As the two emerging super powers, the United States and the USSR, became locked in a cold war that replaced the old colonial powers, the new Muslim states, now part of the "Third World," were little more than pieces on the chess board to the geostrategists on either side. In response to the perceived socialist threat in the Arab and Muslim world, the United States oversaw operations involving overt attacks and covert operations including regime change, staged coups, assassinations, or other forms of political intrigue in nearly every one of the fledgling Muslim majority states.

In my undergraduate classroom, against the perception of a timeless hostility between Islam and the United States, I have found it helpful to underscore the unpredictable evolution of this relationship. During the late 1960s and 1970s, Islam enjoyed a growing profile in personal and public life. Although it might seem ironic in hindsight, the United States actively encouraged and supported traditional Islamic movements as well as jihad against the Soviets and the local leftist movements. "We see the Islamic resurgence as terribly important," National Security Advisor Brzezinski wrote to King Hussein of Jordan. "It marks the rebirth of Arab vitality, which is the best bulwark against communism."[31]

By the 1980s and 1990s it was clear that a quiet revolution had occurred. From North Africa to Southeast Asia, Islam played a stronger role than it ever had since the collapse of the Ottoman caliphate in the religious, socioeconomic, and political life of society. The longest-lasting ally of the United States in the region against the "godless Soviets" has been the oil-rich desert kingdom of Saudi Arabia, to which we now turn.

Wahhabism and Salafism

The Kingdom of Saudi Arabia was founded as a result of the religious call of a Ḥanbali preacher, Muḥammad b. ʿAbd al-Wahhāb (1703–1787) in central Arabia, on the periphery of the Ottoman Empire.[32] The first religio-political uprising was suppressed by the Egyptian ruler Mehmed ʿAli at the behest of the Ottoman sultan in 1812, but the movement's religious call was successfully revived and utilized by ʿat al-ʿAzīz b. Saʿūd who, in 1902, proclaimed himself imam of the Wahhabis and restored the Saudi kingdom, taking control of the Hijaz and the holy places. The family of the original religious reformer, Āl al-Shaykh, maintained close alliance with the Saudi royal elite, Āl Saʿūd, strengthened by bonds of intermarriage and mutual need. The kingdom's religious character, not to mention economic prosperity, is doubtless anchored by the fact that it is land of the prophet of Islam and houses the two holy cities of Mecca and Medina. Since the discovery of oil in 1933, the Saudis have maintained cooperation with the United States and in particular American oil companies.[33] For much of the middle part of the twentieth century, Saudi Arabia, along with the shah's Iran, led the pro-American and anticommunist block in the "Arab Cold War" against Egypt and its allies. Like other oil-producing countries, Saudi Arabia saw its heyday of economic boom with the oil crisis of 1973 and has seen declining wealth since the 1980s. The kingdom has used its petro-dollars liberally for its religio-political agenda of promoting a strict monotheism against both syncretic, folk, intellectual, and mystical religious practices in Muslim communities around the world, on the one hand, and leftist and socialist tendencies on the other.

Most of all, the Shiʿite theocracy of Iran since the Islamic revolution of 1979, led by the powerful ulama base referred to earlier, has emerged as the Saudis' single greatest rival. This rivalry continues to animate the geopolitics of the Middle East today.[34]

Salafism, a modern rekindling of back-to-basics Islamic revivalism so common in Islamic history, is often conflated with Wahhabism. It is a response in equal part to European modernity and late medieval syncretic Sunniism. Like many revival Muslim movements in history, it seeks to restore what it believes to be the true Islam of the early golden age. "Salafism," in the words of a historian, "is first and foremost a label that Sunni purists use to designate their approach to Islam," one that is marked by "a rigorist creed and religious methodology that share a 'family resemblance' (to use Wittgenstein's expression) to Wahhabism or are intimately linked to the religious establishment of Saudi Arabia."[35]

Salafism can be understood in two ways. Structurally, it is a kind of restorationist movement. That restoration could be interpreted in a modernizing or conservative vein. This ambiguity has historically allowed that label to include modernizing reformists as well as ultraconservatives. This is how the late nineteenth-century modernizers such as Jamal al-Din al-Afghani (d. 1897) and Muhammad Abduh (1849–1905) and their associates can be labeled as Salafi alongside the late twentieth-century ultraconservatives such as 'Abd al-'Aziz Bin Bāz (d. 1999) and Nāṣir al-Dīn al-Albānī, the former a Wahhabi-Hanbali scholar and the latter the great champion of ahl al-ḥadīth. But if understood strictly through its theology, a genealogy of certain recurring ideas can be constructed. Salafi theology "articulate[s] a very demanding interpretation of monotheism, which has the consequence of making unbelief more likely" and "an expansive definition of innovation (bid'a), which narrows the scope of acceptable Islamic practice."[36] Another scholar sums it up aptly, "Islam is an inherently iconoclastic faith, and claims to authority or institutional stability outside of the Quran and Muḥammad's authoritative precedent (Sunnah) rarely go uncontested. . . . Always present in Islamic thought, this iconoclastic movement burgeoned in the early 1300s in the scholarly centers of Damascus, Jerusalem, and Cairo. In particular, the prolific writings of the Damascene firebrand Ibn Taymiyya (d. 1328) and his compatriot al-Dhahabi (d. 1348) epitomized this Salafi ethos."[37] But a form of Salafism could emerge even at the heart of the Ottoman Empire, a Hanafi milieu quite foreign to the hadith-centered Hanbali leanings of Damascene Salafism: "When temporal power shifted to the Ottoman capital of Istanbul, manifestations of conservative iconoclasm and reform gained popular support there as well in the form of the Kadızadeli movement in the first half of the seventeenth century."[38]

The worldwide diffusion of Salafism during the twentieth and twenty-first centuries, therefore, is not entirely exceptional.

The Arab Uprisings of 2011

The specter of the 2011 Arab uprisings (sometimes dubbed "the Arab Spring") has forced us to think again about the complexity and depth of Islamic commitments in the Arab World. What began as an apparently secular, pro-democracy, and peaceful uprising of young, cosmopolitan, ostensibly secular, Facebooked youth, on the one hand, and disenfranchised workers and labor movements, on the other, saw a variety of Islamists get involved and compete in democratic elections that followed. At first, the results looked promising; life-long presidents were compelled to stepped down in Tunisia and Egypt, violently removed with international assistance in Libya, and seriously threatened in Syria and Yemen. The conservative, antidemocracy forces in the region, namely, the ousted elite bankrolled by the Gulf monarchies and the blessing of Western powers, were successful in reversing the democratic gains. In Egypt, the democratically elected president Morsi of the Muslim Brotherhood was deposed and imprisoned until his premature death, and bloody civil wars ensued in Libya, Syria, and Yemen. The three civil wars, in which the regional and world powers were intimately involved, as well as the increasing inequality, mistrust, and lack of transparency, have rendered the region more unstable than it has been in a century. Tunisia remains the only successful, if still troubled, transition to democracy. Even though the uprisings did not achieve their goals, they have permanently transformed the region. Over the last decade, the regional geopolitics has seen tremendous shifts, and three hostile blocks have emerged: Saudi Arabia, United Arab Emirates (UAE), Egypt, and allies form the antidemocratic, conservative Sunni block allied with the right-wing governments in the United States and Israel; Turkey and Qatar form the Sunni reformist, populist block; and Iran and the ruling parties in Syria and Iraq form the Shi'a block.

Conclusion

A word must be said in closing on the Muslim attitude toward history. Islam has doubtless produced great historians, including the first philosopher of history, Ibn Khaldun (d. 1406). Yet, unlike the science of jurisprudence and ethical and mystical discourses, history apart from hadith sciences has had little place in the central curricula of Islamic lands in the recent centuries. To most Muslims, the story of Islam is the cultural memory of the twenty-three-year mission of the Prophet Muhammad and stories of the great ascetics, conquerors, liberators, scholars, philosophers, mystics, and saints that followed. On this traditional Muslim view of the world, whenever Muslims fail in their duty to God and become mutually divided, God sends reminders, trials, reformers, and revivers. The great upheavals of the world, the rise and fall of colonialism and modernity, the unsettling discoveries of natural and social sciences, are all mere footnotes to this covenant of God with his people. With the exception of the preservation of hadith, traditional Muslim scholarship has not been committed to a concerted study of the history of the community, trusting the overall rectitude of the community that has preserved and delivered down to our time the fonts of divine guidance, the Qur'an and the hadith. This attitude is changing; emergent in contemporary Muslim scholarship is a renewed interest in critical historiography, as much an imperative of modern historicist, revivalist, and progressivist pressures as a renewal of indigenous historical Muslim consciousness evident in traditional hadith criticism.

NOTES

1. W. Montgomery Watt and M. V. McDonald, *The History of al-Tabari*, vol. 6, *Muhammad at Mecca* (New York: State University of New York Press, 1998), xiii.

2. Fred Donner, *Narratives of Islamic Origins* (Princeton, NJ: Darwin Press, 1998).

3. For an iconic instance of radical skepticism, see Patricia Crone and Michael Cook, *Hagarism: The Making of the Islamic World* (Cambridge: Cambridge University Press, 1977); for Crone's final views where she acknowledges the authenticity of the Qur'an, see Crone, *The Qur'anic Pagans and Related Matters: Collected Studies in Three Volumes*, vol. 1, ed. Hanna Siurua (Leiden: Brill, 2016), xiv.

4. Jonathan A. C. Brown, *Hadith: Muhammad's Legacy in the Medieval and Modern World*, rev. ed. (London: Oneworld, 2018); Harald Motzki, *Hadith: Origins and Developments* (New York: Routledge, 2016).

5. Ira Lapidus, *A History of Islamic Societies*, 2nd ed. (Cambridge: Cambridge University Press, 2002), xix.

6. Marshall Hodgson, *Venture of Islam: Conscience and History in a World Civilization*, 3 vols. (Chicago: University of Chicago Press, 1974).

7. See review of Patricia Crone's *Roman, Provincial, and Islamic Law* by Wael B. Hallaq, "The Use and Abuse of Evidence: The Question of Provincial and Roman Influences on Early Islamic Law," in *Journal of the American Oriental Society* 110, no. 1 (1990): 79–91, where he argues that certain institutions of Islamic law, as Muslim scholars well knew, are based on the pre-Islamic heritage of the Arabs and the Semitic peoples in general.

8. Peter C. Henningan, *The Birth of a Legal Institution: The Formation of the Waqf in Third-Century A. H. Hanafi Legal Discourse* (Leiden, The Netherlands: Brill, 2004).

9. Milka Levy-Rubin, *Non-Muslims in the Early Islamic Empire: From Surrender to Coexistence* (Cambridge: Cambridge University Press, 2011).

10. Aram Shahin, "Arabian Political Thought in the Great Century of Change" (PhD diss., University of Chicago, 2009).

11. Louise Marlow, *Hierarchy and Egalitarianism in Islamic Thought* (Cambridge: Cambridge University Press, 2002).

12. Hugh Kennedy, *The Prophet and the Age of the Caliphates: The Islamic Near East from the Sixth to the Eleventh Century* (London: Pearson Education, 1989).

13. Hodgson, *Venture of Islam*, 1:280.

14. For various theories of the origins of Shi'i ideas, see Robert Gleave, "Shi'ism," in *A Companion to the History of the Middle East*, ed. Youssef M. Choueiri (Oxford: Wiley-Blackwell, 2008), 89–90.

15. Hodgson, *Venture of Islam*, 1:265–66.

16. Lapidus, *History of Islamic Societies*, 81–82.

17. Wadād al-Qāḍī, "The Earliest 'Nābita' and the Paradigmatic 'Nawābiṭ,'" *Studia Islamica* 78 (1993): 53.

18. Richard Bulliet, *Conversion to Islam in the Medieval Period: An Essay in Quantitative History* (Cambridge, MA: Harvard University Press, 1979).

19. Kennedy, *Prophet and the Age*, 60–64; Hodgson, *Venture of Islam*, 1:200–209.

20. Robert B. Marks, *The Origins of the Modern World: A Global and Ecological Narrative*, 2nd ed. (Lanham, MD: Rowman and Littlefield, 2007), 49.

21. On Mongols, see David Morgan, *The Mongols* (Malden, MA: Blackwell, 1986); on the history of the caliphate and its loss, see Mona Hassan, *Longing for the Lost Caliphate: A Transregional History* (Princeton, NJ: Princeton University Press, 2018).

22. See Rula Jurdi Abisaab, *Converting Persia* (London: I. B. Tauris, 2015).

23. Marks, *Origins of the Modern World*, 53.

24. Metin Kunt, "Ottomans and Safavids: States, Statecraft, and Societies, 1500–1800," in Choueiri, *Companion to the History of the Middle East*.

25. Kunt, "Ottomans and Safavids," 197.

26. Marshall Hodgson, *Rethinking World History* (Cambridge: Cambridge University Press, 1993), 97.

27. Lapidus, *History of Islamic Societies*, 513–15.

28. David Fromkin, *A Peace to End All Peace: The Fall of the Ottoman Empire and the Creation of the Modern Middle East* (New York: Henry Holt, 2001); James Gelvin, *The Modern Middle East: A History*, 4th ed. (New York: Oxford University Press, 2015).

29. Rifaʿa al-Tahtawi, *al-Murshid al-Amin li-l-Banat wa-l-Banin* (Cairo: Maktabat al-Adab, 2008), 124.

30. Lapidus, *History of Islamic Societies*, 529.

31. Lloyd C. Gardner, *The Long Road to Baghdad: A History of U.S. Foreign Policy from the 1970s to the Present* (New York: The New Press, 2008), 55–56; Rashid Khalidi, *Sowing Crisis: The Cold War and American Dominance in the Middle East* (Boston: Beacon, 2010).

32. Natana Delong-Bas, *Wahhabi Islam: From Revival and Reform to Global Jihad* (Oxford: Oxford University Press, 2008).

33. Robert Vitalis, *America's Kingdom: Mythmaking on the Saudi Oil Frontier* (London: Verso, 2009).

34. Simon Mabon, *Saudi Arabia and Iran: Power and Rivalry in the Middle East* (London: I. B. Tauris, 2015).

35. Henri Lauzière, "The Construction of Salafiyya: Reconsidering Salafism from the Perspective of Conceptual History," *International Journal of Middle East Studies* 42 (2010): 370.

36. Lauzière, "Construction of Salafiyya," 370.

37. J. A. C. Brown, "From Quietism to Parliamentary Giant: Salafism in Egypt and the Nour Party of Alexandria," presentation at "Islam in the New Middle East," University of Michigan, Ann Arbor, March 20, 2012.

38. Brown, "From Quietism to Parliamentary Giant."

KEY RESOURCES

Brown, Jonathan A. C. *Hadith: Muhammad's Legacy in the Medieval and Modern World*. Rev. ed. London: Oneworld, 2018.

Donner, Fred. *Narratives of Islamic Origins*. Princeton, NJ: Darwin Press, 1998.

Hodgson, Marshall. *Rethinking World History*. Cambridge: Cambridge University Press, 1993.

Hodgson, Marshall. *Venture of Islam: Conscience and History in a World Civilization*. 3 vols. Chicago: University of Chicago Press, 1974.

Lapidus, Ira. *A History of Islamic Societies*. 2nd ed. Cambridge: Cambridge University Press, 2002.

Colonialism, Empire, and Nationalist Movements

SARA PURSLEY

The question of definitions is crucial. What do we mean by "colonialism," "settler colonialism," "empire," "imperialism"? Was the Ottoman Empire an empire in the sense we mean when we speak of European empires? Was the mandate system established after World War I a new form of imperial power, or a transitional phase from colonialism to independence? Is Israel a settler colonial state? Can US power in the post–World War II Middle East be described as imperialist? Without engaging these questions in the classroom, the tendency will be to narrate this history through the experience of countries, such as Egypt and Algeria, that fit most closely the expectation that colonialism describes a particular form of rule with a clear beginning and, most importantly, an end. A celebratory narrative of progress will be hard to avoid, no matter how much we insist that colonial power in these places was both violent and modern. I do not deal with all of these topics in what follows, since some are covered in other essays in this volume, but they call for exploration when teaching this theme in the classroom.

Relatedly, I have found it critical when teaching the history of colonialism in the region to grapple explicitly with the notions of progress, modernization, and linear time that accompanied the expansion of European colonialism and its "civilizing mission." Otherwise, it is too easy for students to locate colonialism itself within that conception of time, narrating it as an unfortunate but overcome episode of the past. The opportunity is missed to explore both the enduring legacies of European colonial rule in the Middle East and the ways in which similar

68

conceptions of progressive time are invoked to justify ongoing Western military interventions in the region. Even apparently cogent critiques of European colonialism can work to justify recent US interventions. An example is the "artificial state" narrative, a familiar version of which posits that the European colonial powers created all the troubles of the present-day Middle East by drawing arbitrary borders and producing impossible states. The United States thus does not need to be held accountable for destroying a state such as Iraq, which according to this narrative never authentically existed in the first place.

Orientalism and the Making of the West

The expansion of European empires from the sixteenth through the eighteenth centuries did not involve lasting conquests of territory in what is today known as the Middle East. But it did have significant effects on that region. It could hardly have done otherwise, since a key motive for European expansion was to bypass the merchants of the early modern Islamic empires in trade between Europe and the Far East. The European conquest of the Americas was a byproduct of this quest to cut out the Ottoman and other predominantly Muslim middlemen from European profits in trade with India, China, and Southeast Asia. In the end, of course, these conquests had enormous effects on the region, since the massive wealth extracted by Europeans from the natural resources of the Americas and the exploitation of African and Native American slave labor helped spark the economic transformations that fueled the rise of the Western European states as global powers. This would eventually contribute to the demise of the Ottoman Empire and the creation of the nation-state system in the region. Thus, this period of European expansion is relevant to understanding the history of the modern Middle East, though not necessarily in ways that students might assume.

Moreover, it was during the period from 1500 to 1800 that "the West" was constructed as a geographical and cultural entity, in relation to those who became the "others" of that construction. As Zachary Lockman writes: "The concepts of Europe and of the West in their modern senses emerged just as a new global order centered on Europe was coming into being, and the two processes were intimately and inextricably interwoven."[1] Scholarship has shown how "much of what we are accustomed to thinking of as quintessentially modern, European, and/or

Western actually originated in interactions between those who, as an outcome of those very same interactions, would come to be categorized as either Westerners or non-Westerners."[2] Despite this now significant body of literature on the emergence of "modernity" in interactions between Europeans and the people they encountered abroad, the belief that "the West" shot ahead of "the Rest" in this period due to internal factors—cultural superiority, technological cleverness, democratic political values, and so on—remains incredibly persistent.

It was in the long nineteenth century that European colonial powers began directly conquering the lands of what we now call the Middle East. Edward Said's classic *Orientalism* focuses mainly on this period, exploring how "the Orient has helped to define Europe (or the West) as its contrasting image, idea, personality, experience."[3] It can be read by undergraduates, and sections can be assigned to high school students. Said's later *Culture and Imperialism* is also useful; it covers some of the same territory as the earlier book, and responds to some critiques of it, but attends more carefully to resistance to colonial power and forms of knowledge. The introduction also lays out more explicitly Said's understanding of "culture" as a category of analysis that can help trace how the European "idea and practice" of empire acquired "the consistency and density of continuous enterprise, which it did by the latter part of the nineteenth century."[4]

Said's work can easily be supplemented with primary sources deploying European Orientalist imaginaries, since it focuses on artistic productions, especially novels. Orientalist paintings, easy to find online, are productive to explore once students have become familiar with the basic tropes. For the early twentieth century, Malek Alloula's *The Colonial Harem* provides a powerful critical analysis of Orientalist images: French colonial postcards of Algerian women posed to appear in their "harems," many in various states of undress. As Alloula writes, to track "the colonial representations of Algerian women—the figures of a phantasm—is to attempt a double operation: first, to uncover the nature and the meaning of the colonialist gaze; then, to subvert the stereotype that is so tenaciously attached to the bodies of women."[5] The work is explicitly framed as itself a form of resistance to European colonial power, an attempt "to return this immense postcard to its sender."[6] It can be productively and provocatively read along with Frantz Fanon's well-known essay "Algeria Unveiled."[7]

70

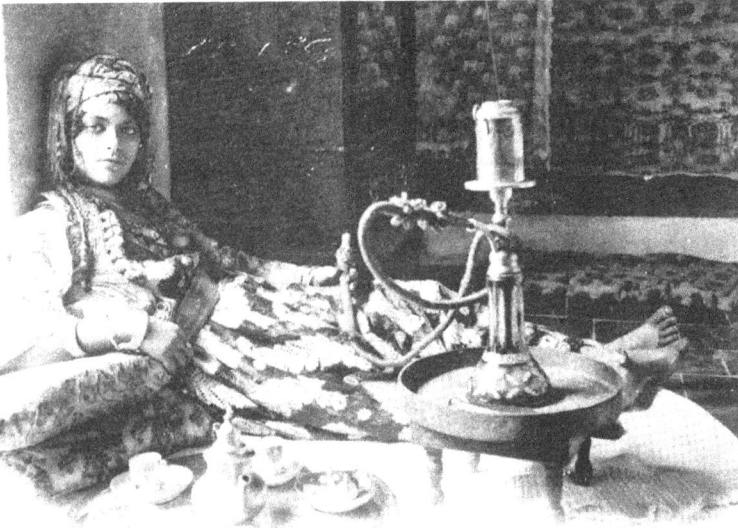

SCÈNES ET TYPES. — Mauresque dans son Intérieur. — LL

Lehnert & Landrock Studio, "Scenes and Types—Moorish Woman in Her Quarters," postcard. From *The Colonial Harem* by Malek Alloula, translated by Myrna Godzich and Wlad Godzich, introduction by Barbara Harlow (Minneapolis: University of Minnesota Press, 1986). Reprinted with the permission of the University of Minnesota.

Conscripts of Western Civilization?

The global expansion of colonial power in the nineteenth century need not be seen only as the direct expansion of European rule over native populations. Numerous scholars have connected colonialism to the expansion of modern forms of knowledge and the modern state more generally. Talal Asad's article "Conscripts of Western Civilization," which insists that the world we live in was "brought into being by European conquest," is a provocative launching pad for discussing connections between modernity (especially the modern state) and European colonial expansion.[8] I have assigned the article to undergraduates, even in survey courses, though they may need to be walked carefully through the argument. According to Asad, modern state governance is characterized by its coercion of subjects to "become 'better than they were,'" which "required in the first place the destruction of all those conditions in which practices belonging to a 'lower civilization' were

71

both possible and desired."[9] The argument can open up discussions of whether certain modernizing projects of the Ottoman and Egyptian states in the nineteenth century can be framed as Orientalizing or colonizing in relation to their own or neighboring populations.[10]

Another way to explore the arguable "conscription" of subjects into European/colonial forms of knowledge is to examine perceptions of Europe and Europeans in Middle Eastern texts or artworks. A generative primary source is Rifaʿa al-Tahtawi's reflections on his trip to Paris in the 1820s.[11] Students may be startled by what seem to be counterintuitive discoveries, such as al-Tahtawi's praise of the Europeans for their condemnation of male homosexuality and his criticism of his own society for purportedly accepting it. These reactions can be used to explore how understandings of what counts as "modern" have changed considerably from the nineteenth century to our own time, sometimes to the point of complete inversion, even while the spatiotemporal classification of the West as modern and the East as backward has remained consistent. Similarly useful in this regard is the work of Afsaneh Najmabadi on nineteenth- and early twentieth-century Iran; many of her primary sources are Qajar images that can be examined during lectures or by students independently.[12]

European Military Conquests in the Long Nineteenth Century

In 1798, Napoleon's army invaded Ottoman Egypt. While the occupation only lasted three years, it had long-term effects on the Egyptian state as well as on the expansion of European knowledge of the region. There are rich primary sources in English translation from both sides, including an account by the Egyptian historian ʿAbd al-Rahman al-Jabarti and the *Description de L'Egypte* produced by Napoleon's vast team of scholarly experts.[13] A helpful recent history is Juan Cole's *Napoleon's Egypt: Invading the Middle East*.[14]

Two other events of the nineteenth century had more lasting colonial effects: the French colonization of Algeria starting in 1830, which can be studied to explore settler colonialism as a form of imperial rule, and the British occupation of Egypt in 1882, which has long been the subject of debate as to whether it marks some kind of historical transition in the workings of British imperial rule globally. Here I focus on the second event.

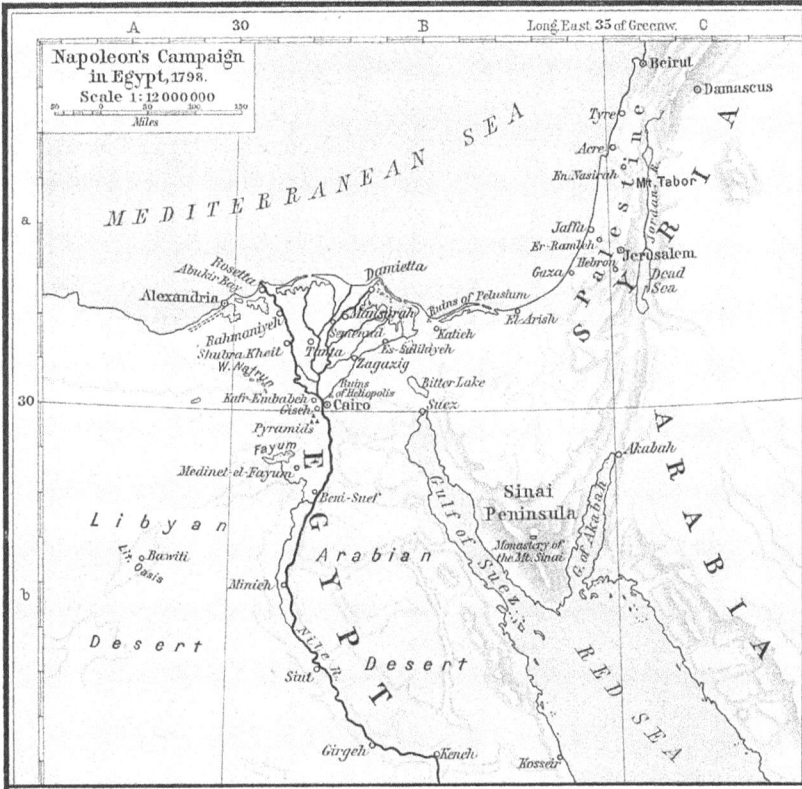

"Napoleon's Campaign in Egypt, 1798," from William Shepherd, *Historical Atlas* (New York: Henry Holt and Company, 1911). Courtesy of the University of Texas Libraries, the University of Texas at Austin.

In 1875, the Egyptian government declared bankruptcy, a result of decades of increasing subordination to European economic structures and, more immediately, of an inability to repay massive loans acquired from European lenders. Britain and France responded to the bankruptcy by asserting control over Egypt's finances on behalf of private lenders from those countries and out of concern for protecting the Suez Canal, Britain's vital passageway to India. The intervention led to the 'Urabi revolt protesting European control over Egypt's affairs, which in turn was used to justify Britain's devastating naval bombardment of Alexandria in 1882 and subsequent military occupation.

The invasion marked the beginning of effective British rule over Egypt, though the territory was still officially subject to Ottoman rule until World War I. Even after Britain terminated nominal Ottoman control during the war, it declined to call Egypt a "colony," preferring terms such as "protectorate." The British model of rule in Egypt was quite different from the French model in Algeria. Egypt was not a settler colony, and although British military forces did not leave Egypt until 1956, during most of this period it relied on various forms of indirect or informal rule. There was a king, who was required to remain loyal to Britain, and after 1922 Britain held publicly that Egypt was "independent," though it retained significant control over much of the country's administrative and military apparatus. The period from 1922 to 1952 (or 1956) is often described as a form of semicolonial rule.

Roger Owen's 1994 article "Egypt and Europe: From French Expedition to British Occupation" provides a useful historical background to the 1882 invasion.[15] It focuses especially on socioeconomic issues, including the government's massive borrowing from private European lenders to pay for modernization projects and the Suez Canal as well as the growing reliance on a single export crop, cotton, which made it difficult to disentangle the economy from dependence on Europe. Owen also attends to changes on the European side of things, especially the emergence of a new institution, the finance company, which sought "speculative outlets" for capital abroad.[16] Finally, the article is valuable in bringing together two strands of the story that are often kept separate: increasing European intervention in Egypt's finances, on the one hand, and the emerging national movement, on the other. By looking at the interaction between these factors, Owen is able to bring to the fore the role of Egyptian social groups often ignored in both of the other approaches.

The article also encourages us to step back and consider the larger shifts in the global history of empire during this period, including the new ways empire was being theorized at the time. As Owen points out, the 1882 British invasion of Egypt "occupies a central role in the genesis of theories of capitalist imperialism," and it came to be seen "not merely as just another example of European expansion but as one of its classic cases."[17] Specifically, it was recognized as the first time that British financial agents, rather than colonial officials, were "held to be chiefly responsible for an act of imperial expansion."[18] It inspired a wave of

European critiques of imperialism, including J. A. Hobson's well-known *Imperialism: A Study* in 1902 and Henry Brailsford's *The War of Steel and Gold* in 1914. The latter viewed the British occupation of Egypt as leading to the scramble for Africa among the European powers and as a contributing factor in the conflicts that produced World War I (which Brailsford predicted just before its outbreak).[19] Chapter 4 of Hobson and chapter 3 of Brailsford can be assigned to undergraduates to explore contemporary critiques of the British empire, and of its connection to finance capital, that were sparked by the occupation of Egypt.

World War I and Its Aftermath

In 1914, on the eve of World War I, "the Ottoman East had been the object of British, French, and Russian imperialist expansion for more than a century."[20] Incorporation into the global, European-centered capitalist economy had some effects similar to what happened in Egypt, for example as the Ottoman state began borrowing from European lenders on unfavorable terms. Repeated wars with Russia throughout the nineteenth century required massive military funding and resulted in lost territory and disruptive migrations. The intervention of the European powers into Ottoman affairs on behalf of Christian and other minorities exacerbated growing sectarian tensions and independence movements, which by 1914 had resulted in the loss of most of the European provinces of the empire.

While World War I is often narrated as an insular (and rather incoherent) internal European affair that occasionally used other regions as battlegrounds, it might be more cogently understood within the context of global European colonial contestation and of European struggles over the Ottoman Empire in particular. Indeed, the oftentimes incoherent narration of the war can be a useful pedagogical tool; I sometimes begin by asking students what they think they know about World War I and use this discussion as a way to think about how the incoherence might be related to the insularity of the narrative. World War I started in the Balkans, as is well known, but what is less often considered is how it was in some ways a continuation of the Balkan Wars of 1912–1913, during which the Ottoman Empire lost most of its territory in Europe to local nationalist movements and the machinations of the Western European states. The war was also linked to increasing battles among the European powers over access to colonial and other territories overseas, including in Ottoman lands, such as conflicts between Britain and Germany over railway and oil concessions in Mesopotamia.[21]

Another challenge of teaching World War I in the Middle East is that there is a well-known narrative according to which all of today's problems in the region are explained by reference to what happened after the war. Even if students can relate few actual events of this period, many are attached to the basic narrative: the European powers divvied up the region among themselves and created "artificial states" by drawing arbitrary borders that failed to correspond to cultural, ethnic, or religious identities. This led to the creation of unstable and essentially impossible states, hopeless ethnic and sectarian conflicts, and deep resentments against the West rooted in a time now past.

The basic historical narrative is not entirely false. But there are reasons to regard some of its assumptions with suspicion and to push students to question these. The narrative's very repetition across the political spectrum for more than a century should itself raise a few red flags. What interests has this narrative served historically and what interests does it serve today? The notion of "artificial states" is closely linked to that of "weak states" and has been widely used to justify recent US military interventions in the region. Another disturbing aspect of the narrative is its implication that states founded on some notion of religious or ethnic identity are more "authentic" (non-artificial), ignoring the uncomfortable fact that such states often turn out to have been created through foundational acts of ethnic cleansing.[22]

Another powerful narrative that has been difficult to dislodge, in spite of a fair amount of critical scholarship, is that European colonialism contended with a "Wilsonian ideal" of self-determination after World War I. Assumptions related to both sides of the binary in this narrative—the colonial and the Wilsonian—are questionable. European colonial thought was not stuck in a traditional groove but was searching creatively for new ways to secure European economic and strategic interests. For many colonial thinkers, this meant supporting some form of self-determination. As for President Wilson, he discovered his "ideal" of self-determination only after Lenin had proclaimed a more radical version and British prime minister Lloyd George a very similar version of the same ideal. One way to rethink the Wilsonian legacy is to consider the president's now well-known support for racial resegregation in the United States in relation to his supposedly more idealistic support for the creation of self-determining nation-states abroad. Rather than view Wilson's domestic and international policies as contradictory, we could see the nation-state system as itself a form of global racial segregation, a solution to the challenges to empire posed by anticolonial movements that would help immobilize formerly colonized populations (within newly created borders) while continuing to ensure Western access to natural resources in those territories.[23]

The League of Nations mandate system came out of the postwar negotiations, as a solution to the problem of the former Ottoman territories now under Allied occupation and of German colonial territories. In the Ottoman lands, Britain was given the mandate to govern Iraq, Transjordan, and Palestine, and France received the mandates of what would become Syria and Lebanon. Article 22 of the 1919 Covenant of the League of Nations, which established the mandate system, is a key primary source on this period. Students might explore the concept of "stage of development" as it appears in this text, which introduced the concept into international law.[24] Other critical primary sources on the postwar settlements are Wilson's Fourteen Points (which, it will be noted, did not use the term "self-determination") and the Treaty of Lausanne, which established the basic laws of the former Ottoman states and introduced the concept of "majority race" into international law.[25] How this concept relates to tragic events such as the compulsory 1923 Greek-Turkish population exchange and the 1948 expulsion of Palestinians from their homes and land might be explored as a counterpoint and challenge to the critique of "artificial" states.

Colonial Rule in the Interwar Period

In the interwar period, the European colonial powers governed large swathes of the region. In addition to the occupied mandate territories, Britain retained significant control over Egypt and the Gulf states; the French directly ruled Algeria, Tunisia, and Morocco; and Libya was an Italian colony.

The scholarship on Egypt during the British protectorate and semi-colonial periods is more expansive than that on most other Arab states. One especially important analytical framework in recent decades has been that of "colonial modernity," which posits that colonialism was not an aberration in the history of modernization in Egypt, or anywhere else. Rather, colonialism is what produces some people as "modern" and others as "nonmodern"; thus, "modernity" itself only makes sense within the history of colonial relations of power. This insight has been enormously productive in Middle East studies, especially in works on late nineteenth-century and interwar Egypt.[26]

Much of the scholarship on colonial modernity, often influenced by Foucauldian frameworks of biopolitics and governmentality, has focused on the spheres of education, law, and the family. How colonial practices of direct corporeal violence fit into these frameworks has been less clear. Moreover, understandings of colonial rule are still shaped by often unchallenged assumptions about such violent practices, such as the idea that French colonialism was more violent than British colonialism in the region; that British "indirect rule" was less violent than "direct rule"; and that the direct violence of colonial rule diminished over time. Yet in the interwar period, the mandate states all saw extreme levels of colonial violence, despite their short durations and transitional nature. In other words, these states were not, as they are sometimes portrayed, some kind of "colonialism lite."

The history of air bombardment as a technique of imperial rule is intertwined with the history of European mandate governance in the Middle East, nowhere more than Iraq. The Iraq mandate served as Britain's laboratory for "rule from the air," which British colonial officials also referred to as "control without occupation." From 1921 to 1932, the British Royal Air Force carried out 130 air bombing raids in Iraq, or an average of almost one per month for twelve years in official peace time, some of which dropped "ten tons of bombs, not infrequently resulting in villages being 'practically destroyed . . . the debris being completely burnt up by incendiary bombs.'"[27] A hundred casualties were not unusual in a single operation, not to mention those lost to starvation after the burning of villages. Whether for attacking British communications, refusing to pay taxes at crushing rates, or harboring rebels, many villages were bombed into submission. Rather than simply a transitional phase between "traditional" colonial rule and national independence, aspects of European mandate rule in the Middle East can be seen as a harbinger of later twentieth-century forms of imperial intervention, including by the United States.

While the British use of Iraq as a laboratory for rule from the air has been explored by several scholars, other aspects of the violence of British and French mandate rule have remained understudied. Recent scholarly works have begun to address this problem.[28] In a work on the

Syria mandate, Daniel Neep explores the French use of airpower as well as other forms of coercive power and collective punishment. Neep argues that scholarship on the Middle East (and in postcolonial studies generally) has failed to critically analyze colonial violence and asks "why Postcolonial scholars have preferred to direct their critical scrutiny to areas such as sexuality, education, law, the family and urban planning, rather than military force."[29]

Anticolonial and Nationalist Movements

For the nineteenth century, giving students a sense of the diversity of forms of anticolonial resistance to European domination serves several purposes. It shows that colonized people were not passive, much less willing, subjects of European domination, thereby countering colonial narratives that Europeans brought civilization to the region. It can also help challenge the notion that nationalist movements were expressions of unified national essences, thus countering elite nationalist narratives that suppress class and other conflicts within national memory as well as narratives that simply turn colonial historiography on its head without disrupting the linear narrative of progress that undergirds it.

One strategy for challenging retrospective nationalism is to explore forms of resistance to nineteenth-century state-building projects implemented by local (non-European) rulers. If colonial forms of governance were not necessarily European, and might be integral to the modern state itself, then resistance to such powers did not always target Europeans. For example, Khaled Fahmy has shown how the state-building projects of the Ottoman Egyptian khedive Mehmed Ali, including the creation of a modern military, did not inculcate nationalist loyalty among conscripts but on the contrary were resisted through often desperate acts such as self-mutilation.[30]

Forms of nonelite anticolonial resistance can be explored in ways that do not reduce such movements to a "prepolitical" or "protopolitical" status, a reduction that reinscribes them within a teleological or retrospective view of linear national becoming.[31] Numerous scholarly works look at populist anticolonial organizations, labor uprisings, and cultural expressions of resistance in vernacular songs and theater.[32] Although many of these frame such forms of resistance within a national frame (e.g., Syria or Egypt), their focus on popular expressions of resistance and on fissures within national formations can help decenter narratives of elite nationalist movements leading to unified states.

So too can attending to fissures, conflicts, and productions of difference within the future boundaries of nation-states. The literature on gender and nationalism is extensive and one of the most theoretically generative subfields in Middle East studies.[33] Engaging with scholarship on constructions of racial, ethnic, and sectarian identities within Middle Eastern nationalist movements can help decenter triumphalist linear narratives leading to unified nationalist states or, especially in the case of states deemed "artificial," can disrupt the idea that pluralistic identities necessarily inhibit the formation of national identities.[34]

If exploring difference within future nation-states is one way to challenge both colonial and nationalist narratives, another is to look at alliances across those future boundaries. Michael Provence argues that the various uprisings against the European colonial powers in the post-Ottoman states after World War I are best understood not as separate nationalist movements (Turkish, Syrian, Palestinian, etc.), even though they were often expressed that way. Rather, they can be seen as a single phenomenon of resistance to European colonial rule, led mainly by former Ottoman officers and soldiers with shared experiences and worldviews.[35]

These recent transregional or transnational histories go beyond an older preoccupation with tensions between Arab nationalism and the "territorial" nationalisms—for example, by focusing on similarities and alliances between Turkish and Arab nationalist movements. Meanwhile, studies of Arab nationalism have moved beyond the linear tale of an entity called "Arab nationalism" that is born, develops, and ultimately dies. Some scholars have explored how Arab nationalism could be used not only to promote a differently bounded nation-state but also to challenge the nation-state model itself, while others have turned to ways in which Arab nationalism (or Arabism) was often highly productive for the formation of territorial nation-states.[36]

From European Colonialism to US Empire

In teaching the history of colonialism in the region, I strive to avoid narratives that posit a sharp divide between European colonial rule up to the middle of the twentieth century and US imperial power after it. Many narratives of colonialism—including at times the very notion of a "postcolonial era" — suggest just such a divide. I am not advocating the sorts of facile comparisons that, for example, ask how US policy makers can avoid the tactical "mistakes" that British officials supposedly made in Iraq in the 1920s. Such questions often assume that the British failed on their own terms in mandate Iraq, which is not at all clear.

But more rigorous analytical comparisons can be made that encourage students to think about the historical significance of recent projections of US power in the region. For example, discussions of the use of armed drones by the US military since the attacks of 9/11 can benefit from comparisons with the British use of Iraq as a laboratory for imperial "rule from the air" in the 1920s. Such comparisons can help bring to the fore what is truly new — as well as not new — about drones as a form of asymmetrical warfare. Similarly, there are photographs of French colonial soldiers posing with naked Algerian women — whom they have presumably raped — that have shocking similarities to the Abu Ghraib photos taken by US soldiers in Iraq. While both sets of images must be introduced to students with great care, and there are arguments to be made for not showing them directly, discussions of their existence can open up important conversations about the imbrication of gender, sexuality, and imperial power, and at the very least should pose some challenges to familiar narratives that Western interventions have liberating effects on Middle Eastern women.

NOTES

1. Zachary Lockman, *Contending Visions of the Middle East: The History and Politics of Orientalism* (Cambridge: Cambridge University Press, 2009), 61.

2. Lockman, *Contending Visions*, 61. For the period 1500–1800, see especially chapter 2, "Islam, the West, and the Rest." Chapter 3, "Orientalism and Empire," looks at changing Western perceptions of the region and of Islam during the long nineteenth century.

3. Edward Said, *Orientalism* (New York: Vintage, 1978), 1–2.

4. Edward Said, *Culture and Imperialism* (New York: Vintage, 1994), 10.

5. Malek Alloula, *The Colonial Harem* (Minneapolis: University of Minnesota Press, 1986), 5.

6. Alloula, *Colonial Harem*, 5.

7. Frantz Fanon, "Algeria Unveiled," in *A Dying Colonialism* (New York: Grove Press, 1965).

8. Talal Asad, "Conscripts of Western Civilization," in *Civilization in Crisis: Anthropological Perspectives*, ed. Christine Ward Gailey, Dialectical Anthropology, vol. 1 (Gainesville: University Press of Florida, 1992), 334.

9. Asad, "Conscripts of Western Civilization," 338.

10. Asad's article might be supplemented with the work of scholars who have made related arguments for specific Middle East historical contexts, such as Ussama Makdisi, "Ottoman Orientalism," *American Historical Review* 107 (2002): 768–96; Timothy Mitchell, *Colonising Egypt* (Berkeley: University of California Press, 1991); Khaled Fahmy, *All the Pasha's Men: Mehmed Ali, His Army and the Making of Modern Egypt* (Cairo: American University in Cairo Press, 2002); Eve M. Troutt Powell, *A Different Shade of Colonialism: Egypt, Great Britain, and the Mastery of the Sudan* (Berkeley: University of California Press, 2003).

11. Rifa'a al-Tahtawi, in Akram Khater, ed., *Sources in the History of the Modern Middle East*, 2nd ed. (Belmont, CA: Wadsworth, 2011), 58–60.

12. Afsaneh Najmabadi, *Women with Mustaches and Men without Beards: Gender and Sexual Anxieties of Iranian Modernity* (Berkeley: University of California Press, 2005), esp. chapters 1 and 2. See also Afsaneh Najmabadi, "Veiled Discourse–Unveiled Bodies," *Feminist Studies* 19, no. 3 (1993): 487–518.

13. Abd al-Rahman al-Jabarti, *Napoleon in Egypt*, trans. Shmuel Moreh (Princeton, NJ: Markus Wiener, 2003).

14. Juan Cole, *Napoleon's Egypt: Invading the Middle East* (New York: St. Martin's Griffin, 2008).

15. Roger Owen, "Egypt and Europe: From French Expedition to British Occupation," in *The Modern Middle East: A Reader*, ed. A. Hourani, P. Khoury, and M. Wilson (Berkeley: University of California Press, 1994), 111–23.

16. Owen, "Egypt and Europe," 116.

17. Owen, "Egypt and Europe," 112.

18. Owen, "Egypt and Europe," 111.

19. See Timothy Mitchell, *Carbon Democracy: Political Power in the Age of Oil* (London: Verso, 2011), 74.

20. Michael Provence, *The Last Ottoman Generation and the Making of the Modern Middle East* (Cambridge: Cambridge University Press, 2017), 59.

21. See Mitchell, *Carbon Democracy*, 55–65.

22. I elaborate on these critiques in Sara Pursley, "'Lines Drawn on an Empty Map': Iraq's Borders and the Legend of the Artificial State," *Jadaliyya*, June 2, 2015, Part I (http://www.jadaliyya.com/Details/32140) and Part II (http://www.jadaliyya.com/Details/32153).

23. For an argument about Wilson as a leader of the "Segregationist International" after World War I, see Andrew Zimmerman, *Alabama in Africa: Booker T. Washington, the German Empire, and the Globalization of the New South* (Princeton, NJ: Princeton University Press, 2010), esp. chapter 4.

24. Gilbert Rist, *The History of Development: From Western Origins to Global Faith* (London: Zed Books, 2002), 61. See also Antony Anghie, *Imperialism, Sovereignty and the Making of International Law* (Cambridge: Cambridge University Press, 2007).

25. On the Treaty of Lausanne, see Eric Weitz, "From the Vienna to the Paris System: International Politics and the Entangled Histories of Human Rights, Forced Deportations, and Civilizing Missions," *American Historical Review* 113, no. 5 (2008): 1313–43.

26. Important works that fit into this genre include Mitchell, *Colonising Egypt*; Omnia El Shakry, *The Great Social Laboratory: Subjects of Knowledge in Colonial and Postcolonial Egypt* (Stanford, CA: Stanford University Press, 2007); Wilson Chacko Jacob, *Working Out Egypt: Effendi Masculinity and Subject Formation in Colonial Modernity, 1870–1940* (Durham, NC: Duke University Press, 2011); Samera Esmeir, *Juridical Humanity: A Colonial History* (Stanford, CA: Stanford University Press, 2012).

27. Mohammad Tarbush, *The Role of the Military in Politics: A Case Study of Iraq to 1941* (London: Kegan Paul International, 1982), 17.

28. On the use of airpower in Iraq, see Priya Satia, "The Defense of Inhumanity: Air Control and the British Idea of Arabia," *American Historical Review* 111, no. 1 (2006): 16–51; Jafna Cox, "A Splendid Training Ground: The Importance to the Royal Air Force of Its Role in Iraq, 1919–32," *Journal of Imperial and Commonwealth History* 13, no. 2 (1985): 157–84; Toby Dodge, *Inventing Iraq: The Failure of Nation Building and a History Denied* (New York: Columbia University Press, 2005); David E. Omissi, *Air Power and Colonial Control: The Royal Air Force, 1919–1939* (Manchester: Manchester University Press, 1990).

29. Daniel Neep, *Occupying Syria under the French Mandate: Insurgency, Space and State Formation* (Cambridge: Cambridge University Press, 2012), 6. On British mandate violence in Iraq, including but not limited to airpower, see also Sara Pursley, *Familiar Futures: Time, Selfhood, and Sovereignty in Iraq* (Stanford, CA: Stanford University Press, 2019), chap. 1.

30. Khaled Fahmy, "The Nation and Its Deserters: Conscription in Mehmed Ali's Army," *International Review of Social History* 43 (1998): 421–36.

31. For the Maghrib, studies of "rural jihads and millenarian protest . . . have come to similar conclusions: these supposedly pre-political movements were in fact eminently political." Edmund Burke III, "Theorizing the Histories of Colonialism and Nationalism in the Arab Maghrib," *Arab Studies Quarterly* 20, no. 2 (1998): 25. See Ali Abdullatif Ahmida, introduction to *Beyond Colonialism and Nationalism in the Maghrib: History, Culture, and Politics*, ed. Ahmida (New York: Palgrave Macmillan, 2000), 7.

32. James Gelvin, "The Social Origins of Popular Nationalism in Syria: Evidence for a New Framework," *International Journal of Middle East Studies* 26 (1994): 645–61; Joel Beinin and Zachary Lockman, "1919: Labor Upsurge and National Revolution," in Hourani, Khoury, and Wilson, *Modern Middle East*, 395–428; Ziad Fahmy, *Ordinary Egyptians: Creating the Modern Nation through Popular Culture* (Stanford, CA: Stanford University Press, 2011).

33. Examples include Beth Baron, *Egypt as a Woman: Nationalism, Gender, and Politics* (Berkeley: University of California Press, 2005); Lisa Pollard, *Nurturing the Nation: The Family Politics of Modernizing, Colonizing, and Liberating Egypt, 1805–1923* (Berkeley: University of California Press, 2005); Lila Abu-Lughod, *Remaking Women: Feminism and Modernity in the Middle East* (Princeton, NJ: Princeton University Press, 1998).

34. An example of the former is Omnia El Shakry, "Anthropology's Indigenous Interlocutors: Race and Egyptian Nationalism," in *Great Social Laboratory*, 55–86; for the latter, see Sami Zubaida, "The Fragments Imagine the Nation: The Case of Iraq," *International Journal of Middle East Studies* 34, no. 2 (2002): 205–15.

35. Provence, *Last Ottoman Generation*, 6. See also Michael Provence, "Ottoman Modernity, Colonialism, and Insurgency in the Interwar Arab East," *International Journal of Middle East Studies* 43 (2011): 205–25.

36. For challenges to the model, see Joseph Massad, *Colonial Effects: The Making of National Identity in Jordan* (New York: Columbia University Press, 2001). For explorations of the productivity of Arab nationalism for territorial state formation, see the special issue "Relocating Arab Nationalisms," *International Journal of Middle East Studies* 43, no. 2 (May 2011).

KEY RESOURCES

Alloula, Malek. *The Colonial Harem*. Minneapolis: University of Minnesota Press, 1986.

Asad, Talal. "Conscripts of Western Civilization." In *Civilization in Crisis: Anthropological Perspectives*, ed. Christine War Gailey, Dialectical Anthropology, vol. 1. Gainesville: University Press of Florida, 1992.

Djebar, Assia. *Fantasia: An Algerian Cavalcade*. Portsmouth, NH: Heinemann, 2003.

Fanon, Frantz. *A Dying Colonialism*. New York: Grove Press, 1965.

al-Jabarti, Abd al-Rahman. *Napoleon in Egypt*. Trans. Shmuel Moreh. Princeton, NJ: Markus Wiener, 2003.

Khalili, Laleh. "Banal Procedures of Detention: Abu Ghraib and Its Ancestors." In *Time in the Shadows: Confinement in Counterinsurgencies*. Stanford, CA: Stanford University Press, 2013.

Pontecorvo, Gillo, dir. *The Battle of Algiers*. Rialto Pictures, 1966.

Provence, Michael. "Ottoman Modernity, Colonialism, and Insurgency in the Interwar Arab East." *International Journal of Middle East Studies* 43 (2011): 205–25.

Said, Edward. *Orientalism*. New York: Vintage, 1978.

Satia, Priya. "The Defense of Inhumanity: Air Control and the British Idea of Arabia." *American Historical Review* 111, no. 1 (2006): 16–51.

Decolonization and the Reconfiguration of the Global Order

M URIAM H ALEH D AVIS

When asked about decolonization in the Middle East and North Africa, some scholars might echo Mahatma Gandhi's comments about Western Civilization when he said, "I think it would be a good idea." Despite this cynical (if not inaccurate) view on a period that is commonly touted as the "end of colonization," decolonization profoundly restructured global politics, national identity, and economic structures. Yet scholars tend to view this phenomenon through a lens that foregrounds a formal change in sovereignty; Prasenjit Duara defines decolonization as "the process whereby colonial powers transferred institutional and legal control over their territories and dependencies to indigenously based, formally sovereign, nation-states."[1] Yet luckily for those teaching the subject, the dynamics and processes engendered by decolonization are considerably richer than this procedural definition would have us believe.

In addition to the problems inherent in defining decolonization, historians of the region must confront the question of periodization. When focusing on Africa and Asia, decolonization seems to have been one of the defining features of the period following the Second World War; this temporal framework also encompasses the three French colonies of North Africa, known as the Maghreb. Yet including the Mashreq in this narrative—which encompasses Egypt and the Arab countries to its east—offers a different set of historical issues. For example, it necessitates a study of the First World War and the mandate system set up by Western powers in its aftermath. Sovereignty was officially granted to Iraq in 1932, with Syria achieving tentative independence in 1936, though both Syria and Lebanon would have to wait until the end of the Second World War for the formal abolishment of the mandate system.

However, as with many diplomatic negotiations, the devil was in the details. As Susan Pederson has argued for the Iraqi case, formal independence was often a farce deliberately concocted by colonial powers in order to maintain their foothold in the region. Britain's support for Iraqi independence at the League of Nations was a kind of trial run to see if this new, heavily conditional form of sovereignty would be acceptable to the international community.[2] Unfortunately for the inhabitants of the region who dreamed of controlling their own resources, defense strategies, or foreign policy, it was. We are thus left with the question: did Iraq "decolonize" with formal independence, or in 1958 with the overthrow of the British-backed monarchy? Similarly, for Egypt, while formal sovereignty was granted in 1922, and a revolution occurred in 1952, it was Gamal Abdel Nasser's nationalization of the Suez Canal in 1956 that represented the high point of demands for economic and political autonomy.

All sovereignties, then, were not created equal. Moreover, they were attained with different degrees of violence and came after discrepant forms of revolt. This variegated terrain presents a number of challenges in teaching decolonization as both a global movement and a series of events rooted in national specificities. Moreover, as Frederick Cooper has pointed out, we have trouble understanding the full range of motivations and visions that drove anticolonial activists because we know how the story ended.[3] For historians of the Middle East, framing decolonization as part of the "tide of history" has the effect of erasing the considerable sacrifices made by individuals who resisted colonization. It also propagates colonial ideologies that sought to portray colonial powers as having voluntarily supported independence.[4] The current political situation in the region also presents certain challenges in teaching the inheritances of decolonization. For example, presenting students with the secular commitments of parties such as the Ba'th party, or leaders such as Tunisian president Habib Bourguiba, can be jarring for students who view the region through the intractable lens of Islamism and terrorism.

This chapter identifies four themes that can help students understand the complexities inherent in the study of decolonization. Many of them focus on two cases that, I would argue, are revelatory because of their extreme nature: Algeria, a settler colony, and Egypt, an indirect colony that became the center of Pan-Arab sentiment under Gamal Abdel Nasser. First, the chapter interrogates the form of territorial organization inaugurated by decolonization: the nation-state. What does it mean to identify with such an entity, and what were its chances for existence after a long experience with colonial rule? In other terms, how can we help our students think about a unit of political organization that now seems natural, but whose victory was far from clear in the 1950s? Second, the chapter reflects on how to help students make sense of violence both as a strategy of imperial power and anticolonial struggle. In addition to the military tactics adopted by colonial and nationalist armies during decolonization, this period also gave rise to important cultural practices: decolonization ushered in the building of south to south solidarities that encouraged revolutionary subjectivities that were demonstrated in dress, cinema, and even sports.[5] Indeed, much of this Pan-Arab ferment crystallized around one event, the Suez Crisis, which is discussed in the fourth section of the chapter. The Suez Crisis introduced two relatively new actors to the world stage of decolonization, Israel and the United States, both of which became central actors in the region.

Which Traditions to Invent?
Making Sense of Nation-States

One of the most important products of decolonization was the introduction of a system of nation-states in the Middle East and North Africa. While this may seem unsurprising from our current vantage point, there was nothing inevitable about the nation-state as a political form. To convey this point, I often start the semester by showing students a map of the Middle East and North Africa with no borders drawn in. I ask them to circle certain regions: where is the "Arab world" for example? What about "North Africa"? I make it clear that there are no wrong answers to this exercise and use their maps to pose certain questions: Why is Egypt often left out of definitions of North Africa? How should we make sense of the considerable Berber populations in Morocco and Algeria, or other minorities in the Mashreq? I follow this discussion by showing students various maps—that of the Ottoman Empire and of the British and French mandates, for example. In my experience, these representations of space encourage students to think about different forms of territorial organization and the myriad bonds that might connect people to one another.

I then ask the class about the nation-state as a form: How do we know we live in a nation-state and what defines this attachment? Students will inevitably bring up language, religion, and holidays. I try to encourage them to think about historical myths that conceal longer histories of violence—Columbus Day, for example. I might also bring in the national section of a newspaper, observing that the news also gives us a sense of belonging to an "imagined community."[6] This discussion allows me to introduce the role of historiography (specifically nationalist historiography) as well as print capitalism. At the same time, I highlight the other terms that anticolonial thinkers employed in constructing collective identities that were opposed to empire. For example, one might address the question of translation; the Arabic terms *qawmiyya* and *wataniyya* denote different understandings of belonging and roughly correspond to the notions of nationalism and patriotism. Other terms that might be helpful are the Ba'th party's emphasis on the region (*qutr*), and the notion of the *ummah* in the Islamic worldview. All of these terms help students reflect on the spatial scales and cultural or political ties that did not necessarily foresee a straight line to the nation-state. Other geographical imaginaries, such as that of the nationalist Moroccan leader Allal al-Fassi, who advocated for a "Greater Morocco" that stretched from Northern Morocco to Mauritania, can also be highlighted. Collectively, these visions show that regional aspirations were not only strategies for economic survival; they also reflected a struggle for power among leaders in the Middle East and North Africa.

After exploring this range of possibilities, the task then remains to explain why the nation-state emerged victorious. Part of the answer inevitably involves the international context of the "Wilsonian moment" that recognized nations, not federations, as deserving of rights on the world stage, along with imposing the constraints of the nation-state system on the Middle East (see Sara Pursley's chapter).[7] Two primary sources that can be useful in this regard are Article 22 of the Convent of the League of Nations, which speaks of "peoples not yet able to stand by themselves under the strenuous conditions of the modern world," and the 1941 Atlantic Charter, which promised self-determination for colonized peoples, envisioned as a "society of nation states."[8]

It is also important to underscore the central role played by the Cold War in decolonization, a discussion that also elucidates the inclusion of socialist or even communist ideals in many Arab countries. Nasser's speeches, available with subtitles on YouTube, are wonderful to show students the relationship between socialism and Islam, especially when coupled with an explanation of Ahmed Ben Bella's ideas regarding a "specifically Algerian socialism."[9] Despite its quirky nature, Muammar al-Qaddafi's "Green Book" might also be a useful text to assign. The question of how to reconcile Islam and socialism was at the heart of decolonization and also presents an opportunity to discuss the fault lines between socialism, Arabness (al-ʿuruba), and Islam, including why the Baʿth party's emphasis on Arabness would have been less effective in a North African context marked by significant Berber populations. The Berbers, the original inhabitants of the region prior to the Arab invasion that began in the mid-seventh century, did convert to Islam but retained a distinctive cultural and linguistic identity.

While these conceptual discussions are important, it can also be useful to encourage students to think about decolonization in concrete terms. For example, following the lectures on colonial structures and the failure of interwar reform, I divide students into groups and assign each group a country. I ask the students to complete a kind of "balance sheet" of the country immediately following independence. Students are given specific categories to analyze, such as education and literacy, land holdings, trade patterns, indigenous authority structures, and national cohesion. I then have students draft a "five-year plan" that aims to make the country a prosperous nation-state, an assignment that requires a detailed set of proposals. For example, they must grapple with the need to create national cohesion among a polity that may be fractured for various historical reasons linked to the colonial strategy of divide and rule.

This exercise also encourages students to think about how decolonization required the invention of new customs that used the cloak of tradition to do the fundamentally modern work of creating a nation-state. For this, one of my favorite clips to show is that of the Moroccan king re-creating an allegedly "traditional" ceremony, the bayʿah, a yearly ritual where dignitaries from Morocco pay tribute to the king, which can be found on YouTube.[10] While this ceremony dates to the times of the Prophet Muhammad, it takes on a different meaning in the Moroccan context where the Sultan became king largely thanks to French support; in other words, his authority has both traditional and colonial roots. The ceremony itself is rich with symbolism—the king sits under an umbrella, representing the central pole around which the celestial canopy turns.

Other examples of inventing traditions might draw on fashion or the military, drawing on Joseph Massad's book on Jordan, which argues that "the colonial state, through its institutions, is, in fact, instrumental in the production of national culture."[11]

One example that I find useful (this is particularly successful in years where the World Cup is being played) in teaching decolonization is the development of national consciousness through the creation of national sports teams, particularly soccer. Algeria and Palestine provide two excellent parallel examples: the Algerian nationalist FLN (National Liberation Front) had a soccer team long before they had won an independent nation-state.[12] Its star player, Rachid Mekhloufi, often spoke about his decision to play for Algeria rather than France as well as how the performance of independence—on and off the pitch—preceded the official achievement of sovereignty.[13] The question of sports also underscores how revolutionary states encouraged certain forms of masculinity and physical praxis to strengthen the national body.

To contrast this with a story of incomplete decolonization, one might speak about the recent controversy surrounding FIFA and the Palestinian soccer team. In October 2017 FIFA refused to intervene against Israeli soccer clubs that were based in the West Bank, despite the fact that these settlements are illegal according to international law.[14] The Palestinian soccer federation was challenging FIFA at the Court of Arbitration for Sport at the time of writing this chapter. Yet regardless of how this issue is resolved it points to how international symbols of legitimacy have played a key role in decolonization.

Violence and Counterinsurgency

Decolonization did not rely solely on diplomatic or symbolic strategies to gain the recognition of the international community. The use of violence was central in wrestling away sovereignty from European powers that often clung to empire with murderous tenacity. This was most famously the case in Algeria, where the National Liberation Front (FLN) waged a bloody war of independence from 1954 to 1962 that killed at least 400,000—and up to 1.5 million—people.[15] Yet even in cases such as Tunisia, where sovereignty was achieved relatively peacefully in 1956, the nationalist party, Neo-Destour, found it important for "blood to flow" to rally people to their cause, viewing violence as a tool that would polarize the population and create a zero-sum game in their favor.[16] In the Mashreq, the violence came earlier with unrest in Iraq in 1920, Syria in 1927, and Palestine in 1936–1939. The bombing of the King David hotel by the Irgun, a militant Zionist association, targeted a prominent symbol of the British presence in Palestine in 1946, killing ninety-one people. These episodes of violence were central not only to the process of decolonization but also to the national polities that would emerge in its wake.

Before debating the use of violence during decolonization, it is important for students to have a good understanding of the failure of reform in the interwar period. Without an appreciation of the structural blockages that made equality impossible through normal political channels (especially in the framework of settler colonialism), it is difficult to grasp why nationalist leaders drew on violent tactics. I often tackle this aspect by looking at the Algerian case and having students study the Blum-Viollette proposal of 1936, a failed and relatively modest attempt at reforming the colonial system under the Popular Front government. I divide students into groups and ask each group to comment on the proposal from the perspective of an Algerian nationalist, a European settler, or a French metropolitan politician. Each group is responsible for choosing one person to speak in front of the class for three to four minutes and is expected to communicate the high passions that risked flaring at this hopeful but volatile moment. While these roles are of course oversimplified, it does allow students to see how the situation of the settler colony is triangulated among three different perspectives. Moreover, it elucidates how the entrenched privilege of the settlers served as a brake on any meaningful changes to the system.

A classic work for understanding revolutionary violence, hailed as the "bible of decolonization," is Frantz Fanon's *Wretched of the Earth*, particularly his chapter "On Violence." Students often find this text exciting due to its centrality to other revolutionary movements—from the Black Panthers in the United States to the Dalit Panthers in India. For those who follow contemporary politics, Fanon's claim that colonized individuals revolted because they are not able to breathe also has important echoes in the Black Lives Matter movement. Another insight in this essay, that the "colonial world is a world divided in two," helps make sense of what it felt like to live in a settler colony by invoking the physical landscape of the city.[17]

Both of these aspects are masterfully communicated in the 1966 film directed by Gillo Pontecorvo, the *Battle of Algiers*. I often show the film

in class after students have read Fanon and reflected on Fanon's observations regarding the Manichean aspects of the settler colony. Certain
scenes warrant a more careful analysis; for example, I usually pause
the film during the scene where the FLN fighter and hero of the historical
Battle of Algiers, Ali La Pointe, runs across the pristine downtown streets
of Algiers and is tripped by a European settler. While in the narrative of
the film this scene mainly communicates the petty crimes in which La
Pointe was involved before his activities with the FLN, the scene sym-
bolizes a key aspect of living in a settler colony: certain zones are clearly
designated for "white" Europeans. La Pointe has committed a grave act
of trespassing in straying from the Casbah, the section of the city that
was designated for the Muslim populations. These insights from Fanon
and Portecorvo can be fruitfully coupled with discussions on urban
planning in colonial contexts as well as the politics of colonial monu-
ments, as they are both attentive to the production of colonial space.

A second scene that I find pedagogically useful in the film is when
the FLN officiates marriages, thereby taking on the functions of a state,
while also making sure these ceremonies correspond to Islamic custom. Lastly, the classic scene in which the FLN uses female operatives
to plant bombs at a European café shows how European notions of
race and gender allowed Algerian women to subvert the rules of circulation, as well as how women enjoyed relative moments of freedom
during the war, even as they remained under the watchful masculine
gaze of their revolutionary male superiors. Indeed, a scene that often
resonates with students is when the Algerian nationalist Larbi Ben
M'hidi gives a press conference. In response to a question by a French
journalist that questions the morality of the FLN's attack on civilians
and use of women fighters who use their shopping baskets to conceal
weapons, Ben M'hidi answers: "Give us your bombers and you can
have our baskets" (Donnez-nous vos bombardiers monsieur, et on vous
donnera nos couffins). This dialogue presents an opportunity to describe asymmetric warfare and highlight the difference between wars
of decolonization and the more traditional violence of the two world
wars, where there was a clear distinction between combatants and civilians, and military strategy focused on gaining territory rather than "winning over" the population of a territory.

Strategies of violence were not only a concern for anticolonial nationalists, but also for colonial powers who fought them. The particular
strain of "pacification" that came to the fore during the Algerian War

drew on the postwar tools of behavioral psychology that were first developed in Vietnam and came to be known as "Counterinsurgency warfare."[18] It was outlined in the 1964 manual of the French military officer David Galula, *Counterinsurgency Warfare: Theory and Practice*. This strategy built on the observation that armed conflict no longer involved only combatants but also civilian actors who provided shelter for fighters and whose "hearts and minds" needed to be conquered. Another axiom stated that showing a population the material benefits that Western powers could provide—often in the guise of economic and social development initiatives—would help sway opinion in their favor.

Galula's influence did not end with decolonization, as evidenced by the US Army's screening of the *Battle of Algiers* in 2003, during the Iraq War.[19] In order to pull out the continued relevance of these tactics, it might be interesting to read portions of David Galula's text or secondary works on the continued use of these techniques by Emmanuel Blanchard and Neil MacMaster.[20] As Derek Gregory has argued in his insightful book on Palestine, Iraq, and Afghanistan, ways of seeing inherited from colonialism and decolonization also inform the present.[21] Indeed, discussions of colonial and anticolonial violence can also provide a useful way of thinking about historical memory and the continued influence of decolonization for postcolonial immigration and policing strategies.

South to South Ties

Films such as the *Battle of Algiers* did not merely communicate the dramatic reordering of politics and society for which decolonization hoped; they were also a medium for introducing that change. Third Cinema, a movement that emerged in Latin America, rejected bourgeois norms that focused on individual stories. It instead sought to capture the aspirations of the masses and serve as a platform for creating revolutionary solidarity. The *Battle of Algiers* is a model of this in many ways; it was shot on the streets of Algiers and, with one exception, used nonprofessional actors to create a sense of realism. There are parallels here with cultural production under Nasser, many examples of which can be found in Joel Gordon's book *Revolutionary Melodrama: Popular Film and Civic Identity in Nasser's Egypt*.

Film was just one facet of a larger project to encourage ties among countries in the Global South during decolonization, whether they were cultural, political, or economic. Creating new solidarities was a strategy to replace the bilateral ties with the ex-colonial powers with multilateral exchanges. The so-called Third World, a term coined by the French demographer Alfred Sauvy in 1952, refused to be aligned with either the First (capitalist) or Second (communist) Worlds and was a term that was directly inspired by the Third Estate. As a cultural and political block, the Bandung Conference that met in Indonesia in 1955 is often seen as the inauguration of the era of Third Worldism, a movement that included the Middle Eastern countries of Algeria, Egypt, Palestine, Iraq (after 1958), and Syria.

Cultural ties were fostered through a piece of technology that revolutionized how news and information were experienced during the Cold War: the radio. *Sawt Al-Arab*, an Egyptian program, aimed to foster nationalist sentiments across the region and unite Arabs into one singular entity. This is a great moment to reflect, once again, on how the tools of modernity were appropriated by the Third World. Here I might give students two very different texts on the radio: Frantz Fanon's essay "This Is the Voice of Algeria" and Daniel Lerner's *The Passing of Traditional Society*.[22] While Lerner argued that exposure to media messages would facilitate the transition of Muslim societies from tradition to modernity, Fanon showed how this medium worked as a tool in the fight for liberation. Although these texts worked toward opposite political ends, they both realized that technology was changing people's engagement with the colonial (and later postcolonial) state in fundamental ways. The link between media, Pan-Arabism, and decolonization could also be highlighted by playing "Walla Zaman Ya Selahy," the song by Umm Kulthum that was performed during the Suez Crisis and that Egyptians would have heard frequently on the radio at the time.[23]

This song went on to be the anthem for the United Arab Republic (UAR), a union between Egypt and Syria that lasted from 1958 to 1961. This entity was short-lived, largely because of the jockeying for power between the two nations. Moreover, not all Arab countries looked favorably on the revolutionary fervor that swept through the region; the Hashemite monarchy in Jordan, for example, considered *Sawt Al-Arab* to be a subversive force. Historians have argued that these conflicts constituted an "Arab Cold War," which divided nationalist from pro-Western Arab states, symbolized in the Baghdad Pact or the Syrian crisis of 1957. Yet even among comrades, tensions emerged. While Algerian president Ben Bella was largely indebted to Nasser for ideological and financial support, he was also wary of the latter's revolutionary stature—a mantle he himself wanted to adopt. Yet regardless of these complications, important strategic and military links were forged among countries in the Global South, such as Algerian hospitality and assistance for various revolutionary groups from Palestine to South Africa to Mozambique.

In addition to these military and diplomatic contacts, Third Worldism attempted to craft revolutionary subjects and introduce a social and economic program characterized by land reform, industrialization, support for the military, and campaigns to increase literacy. The domain of education was particularly fraught and also raised the question of language; Modern Standard Arabic was an important tool of Pan-Arabism, developing a single literary medium for inhabitants of the region stretching from Morocco to the Persian Gulf, whose dialects were sometimes mutually incomprehensible. The formal Arabization of the state also came up against tensions with minorities who fought for official recognition of their own languages—such as Amazigh or Kurdish. Lastly, Arabization initiated a process whereby older elites, often more comfortable in the language of the colonizers, found themselves challenged by opponents within the state who tended to be of a more conservative religious stripe, particularly in North Africa.

Decolonization also encouraged greater economic solidarity and a changed global context, as evidenced by organizations such as the UNCTAD (The United Nations Conference on Trade and Development) initiated in 1964 in order to address the concerns of developing countries. As Giulino Garavini has argued, the UNCTAD slogan "trade, not aid" reflected the active role the Third World would play in highlighting "competing visions of modernity and models of internationalism."[24] Thus, from cultural production to economic and military policy, decolonization empowered a block of countries that had formerly been colonized to collectively express a more hopeful vision for the future.

The Suez Crisis and the Nasserist Moment, 1956–1967

In the decolonization of the British Empire, no single moment augured the end of empire and the vision of Third Worldism as poignantly as Nasser's nationalization of the Suez Canal in July 1956. His decision was motivated by several factors that pointed to the continuation of colonial influence in the region such as the presence of

British troops on Egyptian soil and Egyptian dependence on funding from the United States and the UK. This prompted Israel to invade the Sinai in October of the same year, with British and French troops arriving the following month. The coordination among these three powers led observers in the Arab World to refer to these events as the "Tripartite Aggression." The crisis was resolved largely through American and Soviet diplomatic pressure, signaling the more prominent role that the United States would play as the British and French empires waned in the 1950s and 1960s and the United States introduced the Eisenhower Doctrine in January 1957.

One way to introduce students to the Suez Crisis is to show clips from Nasser's speech nationalizing the Suez Canal on July 26, 1956. Coverage of the speech by the BBC is available online and stresses that Nasser's decision was explained by recourse to the "centuries of humiliation" that Egypt had experienced at the hands of the West.[25] Yet before delving into the heady year of 1956, there are other teachable moments that emerge from Nasser's speech. For example, Nasser names the Frenchman who had built the canal, Ferdinand de Lesseps, at least thirteen times. Not only was this a way to invoke the long imperial history of the canal, but the Frenchman's name also served as a code word that alerted the Egyptian army to begin the seizure and nationalization of the canal. Ferdinand de Lesseps, a dissident Saint-Simonian, obtained a concession from Said Pasha to create a company to construct a canal in the 1850s.[26] In recounting the events that led to the construction, de Lesseps mentioned his own ruminations about "Oriental questions," reminding us that his father had represented France in Egypt after the peace of Amiens at the very beginning of the nineteenth century, which ended the hostilities between France and Britain after the revolutionary wars. At that time, the French were looking for a Pasha that could break down the power of the Mamluks who were hostile to French policies. Thus, the very engineering feat that created the canal is tied to a long history of French geopolitical designs in Egypt.

The Saint-Simonians help bring up another link that would be crucial for the Suez Crisis: Egypt's relationship with Algeria. Although the Saint Simonians left Egypt for Algeria in the nineteenth century, Nasser's strategic and logistical help for the Algerian nationalists was well known and helps explain France's decision to invade Egypt. Moreover, Algerian nationalists looked to the Suez "affair" as a model for anti-imperial practice.

In short, the Suez Crisis exemplifies the hopes and disappointments associated with decolonization in the Middle East and North Africa in three ways. First, seen from the vision of Western nations, it demonstrated how the humiliation of Britain and France at the hands of the Soviet Union and the United States signaled the changing geopolitical configuration in the region. Secondly, it illustrated the desire of Third World countries to regain full autonomy, including control over their own economic resources and the withdrawal of foreign troops from their territory. Thirdly, it indicated that the only institution that had the power to organize such audacious unilateral policies in these countries was the military, a fact that had clear repercussions on the political regimes that formed in Nasser's wake.

Egypt's dramatic defeat during the 1967 Arab-Israeli war was a decisive blow to this vision of independence and economic justice; when Nasser died in 1970 in the midst of a conference dedicated to finding a solution for Palestine, it was a major event in the region, in many ways ending an era where a comprehensive vision for an alternative form of global politics remained a possibility.

Conclusion

As David Scott has written of revolutions more broadly, decolonization has given rise to a number of attempts to understand the legacy of unfulfilled hopes and disappointments in the Middle East and North Africa.[27] Yet the narrative of "revolutionary romance," however wrongheaded, continues to be a major political touchstone in the region, as demonstrated by (not unproblematic) nostalgia for figures such as Houari Boumediène in Algeria or Nasser in Egypt.[28] Indeed, the Hirak movement in Algeria, a massive protest movement that began in February 2019, has creatively invoked Algeria's revolutionary heritage. Yet despite these warnings, uncovering the utopias embedded in the Third Worldist vision can be exciting for students who are otherwise bombarded with stories of a pathological, violent, or extremist Middle East. Indeed, a study of decolonization invites comparisons with the so-called Arab Spring, which points to the dramatic changes in the forms of political engagement and organization that have occurred in the region in the last sixty years. As David Scott reminds us, the labeling of the present as "tragic" has the effect of erasing the ways that the future might hold solutions that remain unscripted. This radical hope of creating something fundamentally new from the ashes of structural violence remains vital for those studying the Middle East and North Africa at the present time.

NOTES

1. Prasenjit Duara, ed., *Decolonization: Perspectives from Now and Then* (New York: Routledge, 2004), 2.

2. Susan Pederson, "Getting Out of Iraq—in 1932: The League of Nations and the Road to Normative Statehood," *American Historical Review* 4 (2010): 975–1000.

3. Frederick Cooper, *Colonialism in Question: Theory, Knowledge, History* (Berkeley: University of California Press, 2005).

4. Todd Shepard, *The Invention of Decolonization: The Algerian War and the Remaking of France* (Ithaca, NY: Cornell University Press, 2006).

5. For works on cinema and decolonization in Egypt see Joel Gordon, *Revolutionary Melodrama: Popular Film and Civic Identity in Nasser's Egypt* (Chicago: University of Chicago Press, 2002). Many of the techniques involved in film production in postcolonial nations have been discussed in terms of "Third Cinema," as explored in Anthony R. Guneratne and Wimal Dissanayake, eds., *Rethinking Third Cinema* (New York: Routledge, 2003). *The Battle of Algiers* is the most famous of these examples and has received a good deal of analysis, such as the recent publication by Suhail Daulatzai, *Fifty Years of "The Battle of Algiers": Past as Prologue* (Minneapolis: University of Minnesota Press, 2016). For a recent work on sports and identity in the region see Danyel Reiche and Tamir Sorek, eds., *Sports, Politics and Society in the Middle East* (Oxford: Oxford University Press, 2019).

6. Benedict Anderson, *Imagined Communities: Reflections on the Spread of Nationalism* (London: Verso, 2006).

7. Erez Mandela, *The Wilsonian Moment: Self-Determination and the International Origins of Anticolonial Nationalism* (Oxford: Oxford University Press, 2007).

8. Daniel J. Sargent, *A Superpower Transformed: The Remaking of American Foreign Relations in the 1970s* (Oxford: Oxford University Press, 2015), 23.

9. For Nasser speaking about his definition of socialism see "Jamal Abdel Nasser Defines Socialism in His Own Words," https://www.youtube.com/watch?v=ExaonayiLQs (accessed August 29, 2018). Ben Bella's nebulous ideas regarding Islam and socialism are described in Raymond Vallin's "Muslim Socialism in Algeria," in *Man, State, and Society in the Contemporary Maghrib*, ed. William Zartman (New York: Praeger, 1973), 50–65.

10. This ceremony can be found at "Mohamed 6: La cérémonie d'allégeance," https://www.youtube.com/watch?v=vrLccOItOCs (accessed August 29, 2018).

11. Joseph Massad, *Colonial Effects: The Making of National Identity in Jordan* (New York: Columbia University Press, 2001), 7.

12. "Mekhloufi and the FLN Team," Al Jazeera English, July 9, 2014, https://www.aljazeera.com/programmes/footballrebels/2013/03/201336102359464263.html (accessed August 29, 2018). For more audiovisual sources on this topic in English see "FLN Football Team—Front de Liberation Nationale," https://www.youtube.com/watch?v=lKS9soP9oao (accessed September 29, 2018).

13. Matthew Connelly, *A Diplomatic Revolution: Algeria's Fight for Independence and the Origins of the Post–Cold War Era* (Oxford: Oxford University Press, 2003).

14. Al Jazeera English News Agency, "FIFA Delays Stand on Israel Settlement Football Teams," May 9, 2017, https://www.aljazeera.com/news/2017/05/fifa-delays-stand-israeli-settlement-football-teams-170510040009344.html (accessed April 1, 2018).

15. These numbers continue to be the subject of a heated debate in the Algerian and French historiography on the War of Independence.

16. Kenneth Perkins, *A History of Modern Tunisia* (Cambridge: Cambridge University Press, 2004), 102.

17. Frantz Fanon, *The Wretched of the Earth*, trans. Richard Philcox (New York: Grove Press, [1961] 2004), 3.

18. Muriam Haleh Davis, "Between the Cold War and Decolonization: The American Social Sciences and French Planning in Algeria, 1958–1962," *Journal of Contemporary History* 52, no. 1 (2017): 73–94.

19. See Michael T. Kaufman, "What Does the Pentagon See in 'Battle of Algiers'?," *New York Times*, September 7, 2003, https://www.nytimes.com/2003/09/07/weekinreview/the-world-film-studies-what-does-the-pentagon-see-in-battle-of-algiers.html?module=ArrowsNav&contentCollection=Week%20in%20Review&action=keypress&region=FixedLeft&pgtype=article (accessed August 29, 2018).

20. David Galula, *Counterinsurgency Warfare: Theory and Practice* (Westport, CT: Praeger Security International, [1964] 2006); Emmanuel Blanchard and Neil MacMaster, "David Galula and Maurice Papon: A Watershed in COIN Strategy in de Gaulle's Paris," in *Decolonization and Conflict: Colonial Comparisons and Legacies*, ed. Martin Thomas and Gareth Curless (London: Bloomsbury Academic, 2017) 213–28.

21. Derek Gregory, *The Colonial Present: Afghanistan, Palestine, Iraq* (Malden, MA: Blackwell, 2004).

22. Frantz Fanon, "This Is the Voice of Algeria," in *A Dying Colonialism*, trans. Haakon Chevalier and Adolfo Gilly (New York: Grove Press, [1959] 1965).

23. The song "Walla Zaman Ya Selahy" can be found on YouTube, https://www.youtube.com/watch?v=jSSy6Xl2VGA (accessed April 4, 2020).

24. Giuliano Garavini, *After Empires: European Integration, Decolonization, and the Challenge from the Global South, 1957–1986*, trans. Richard R. Nybakken (Oxford: Oxford University Press, 2012), 7.

25. The BBC documentary "The Other Side of Suez" is available online at https://www.youtube.com/watch?v=ETOUALw2EIs&t=107s (accessed August 29, 2018).

26. Original documents pertaining to the history of the canal, as well as de Lesseps's involvement can be found in Barbara Harlow and Mia Carter, eds., *Archives of Empire*, vol. 1, *From the East India Company to the Suez Canal* (Durham, NC: Duke University Press, 2003).

27. David Scott, *Conscripts of Modernity: The Tragedy of the Colonial Enlightenment* (Durham, NC: Duke University Press, 2004).

28. Amr Adly, "The Problematic Continuation of Nasserism," *Jadaliyya*, March 31, 2014, http://www.jadaliyya.com/Details/30469/The-Problematic-Continuity-of-Nasserism (accessed April 1, 2018); Ed McAllister, "Reimagining the Belle Epoque: Remembering Nation-Building in an Algiers Neighborhood," *Jadaliyya*, November 3, 2013, http://www.jadaliyya.com/Details/29728/Reimagining-the-Belle-Epoque-Remembering-Nation-Building-in-an-Algiers-Neighborhood (accessed April 1, 2018).

KEY RESOURCES

Belli, Meriam. *An Incurable Past: Nasser's Egypt Then and Now*. Gainesville: University Press of Florida, 2013.

Connelly, Mathew. *A Diplomatic Revolution: Algeria's Fight for Independence and the Origins of the Post–Cold War Era*, 2003. Oxford: Oxford University Press.

Fanon, Frantz. *The Wretched of the Earth*. Trans. Richard Philcox. New York: Grove Press, (1961) 2004.

Jansen, Jan, and Jürgen Osterhammel. *Decolonization*. Trans. Jeremiah Riemer. Princeton, NJ: Princeton University Press,

Louis, Wm. Roger. *Ends of British Imperialism: The Scramble for Empire, Suez, and Decolonization*. London: I. B. Tauris, 2006.

Said, Edward. *Culture and Imperialism*. New York: Alfred A. Knopf, 1993.

Shepard, Todd, ed. *Voices of Decolonization: A Brief History with Documents*. Boston: Bedford/St. Martin's, 2015.

Shipway, Martin. *Decolonization and Its Impact: A Comparative Approach to the End of Colonial Empires*. Oxford: Blackwell, 2008.

Prasenjit, Duara. *Decolonization: Perspectives from Then and Now*. London: Routledge, 2004.

Young, Robert. *Postcolonialism: A Historical Introduction*. Oxford: Blackwell, 2001.

The History of Israel/Palestine

S H E R E N E   S E I K A L Y

Teaching Israel/Palestine can be one of the most rewarding experiences for any instructor invested in link-
ing history to the lived present. Students will have historic, religious,
national, or familial ties to the place. Some may be involved in intense
debate just outside the classroom. The challenge is to build an inclusive
and critical space for collective learning. Welcoming questions, disagreement, and debate while rejecting racism in all its forms (including
antisemitism, Islamophobia, Orientalism, antiblackness) is an effective
framework to anchor student participation. Students are often intimi-
dated to speak their mind in class. Making sure the instructor's door is
open to conversation will go a long way to understanding subjective
links and concerns as well as dismantling assumptions. Weekly writing
assignments are an effective way to track student opinion and compre-
hension. Teaching Israel/Palestine can be a rich opportunity to allow
students to direct their learning. Teachers should be most of all ready to
learn from their students.[1]

Guiding Principles

There are five guiding principles that facilitate spaces of
collective learning on Israel/Palestine. One is to decenter "conflict" as the
only way to understand people's experiences, histories, and claims. The
simple suggestion that students will be learning about the history of
Israel/Palestine as opposed to the history of the Israel/Palestine *conflict*
is crucial. Conflict alone cannot capture the spectrum of experiences,

narratives, and expressions of Israelis and Palestinians over the last one hundred years. Incorporating music, film, and art in each unit allows students to move beyond ahistorical narratives of a supposedly two-thousand-year conflict. Such an approach also allows students to grasp the texture of everyday life. A second principle is to insist to students that they will be learning not just about other people but also about themselves. This makes Israel/Palestine less exceptional. The history of Israel/Palestine is part of Middle East and Arab history, race, colonialism, Third Worldism, the struggle for decolonization, as well as the promises and limits of the Enlightenment, the trajectories and exclusionary power of European nationalism, the history of antisemitism that gave birth to the political movement of Zionism, and the rise of US hegemony. Giving a sense of these intersections from the outset moves students beyond simplified depictions of Israel/Palestine in popular US media. A third principle is to insist on radical empathy. The history of the genocide of the Jewish people in Europe, the Holocaust or the Shoah ("catastrophe" in Hebrew), and the history of the dispossession of the Palestinians in 1948, or the Nakba ("catastrophe" in Arabic), are often posed as oppositional. The Shoah and the Nakba are not oppositional. We must teach them together. This is not to say that the Shoah and the Nakba are similar or comparable. Such a claim would be shallow and ahistorical. This is to say that engaging the significance of the Shoah and the Nakba together reveals the centrality of catastrophe in Jewish and Palestinian histories.

In the last sentence, I have used "Jewish" and not "Israeli." This brings me to a fourth guiding principle: language is itself a product of history. The terms we use to understand the history of Israel/Palestine are themselves objects we have to dismantle on multiple levels. On the first level, it is important to challenge how pundits discuss the history of Israel/Palestine as one of "two sides." This depiction flattens Israelis and Palestinians into homogenous and mutually exclusive categories. There are more than "two sides"; there are internal divisions and differences of class, race, gender, sexuality, and ability among and between Israelis and Palestinians. Moreover, the "two sides" narrative equates the Israeli state with the Palestinian people. Such an equation elides the power differential between a state and an occupied people.

On a second level, there are several pairings that appear synonymous or antonymous in the history of Israel/Palestine. One such pairing is Jewish and Zionist. "Jewish" and "Zionist" are not synonymous.

102

Judaism is the world's first monotheistic religion. It is four thousand years old. Zionism is a political nationalist movement that began in the late nineteenth century. Not all Jewish people are Zionists. Not all Zionists are Jewish. Another pairing is that of Arab and Jew. "Arabs" and "Jews" are not antonyms. Indeed, the majority of Jewish people lived under Arab or Muslim rule until the twelfth century, when many began migrating to Europe. Moreover, up until the 1950s substantial numbers of Arab Jews lived throughout the Arab world: from North Africa to Iraq. Zionism and Arab nationalism made the category of the Arab Jew impossible. This is a good place to remind students that Arabs are an ethnic group. Arabs can be Jewish, Muslim, Christian, or any other religion. The categories of Arab and Jew became national political markers in the late nineteenth and early twentieth centuries. The seemingly oppositional relationship between Arab and Jew did not cause the Zionist-Palestinian conflict. The Zionist-Palestinian conflict produced this opposition. These five principles: decentering conflict, de-exceptionalizing Israel/Palestine; insisting on radical empathy; dismantling the "two sides" narrative; and transgressing seemingly self-evident pairings provide students with tools to approach the themes below.

Getting History Wrong

It is important to engage Zionist and Palestinian historical claims. Zionism is a nationalist movement that sought to provide refuge for Jews from centuries of European persecution, extermination, and ultimately genocide. It was born of the European Enlightenment and as such is based on an understanding of Europe as a superior and civilizing force. Zionists claim a direct link to Abraham, who immigrated to Palestine from Ur (Mesopotamia) in the second millennium BCE. In 1000 BCE, King David led the Jews to victory over the Canaanites and established the Kingdom of Israel. The kingdom existed as a unified entity for seventy years. The northern kingdom, called Israel, lasted until 722 BCE, when Assyrians conquered it. The southern kingdom, Judah, lasted until 586 BCE, when it fell to the Babylonians. The Judeans returned to the land of Israel in 535 BCE and remained there until the Roman conquests destroyed the second temple in 70 CE. *Eretz yisra'il* or "the land of Israel" is a central symbolic site in Jewish faith and practice.

Palestinians have resided on the land of Palestine continuously for seven hundred years. They claim to be the descendants of Canaanites, the people whom Abraham encountered in the second millennium BCE. The term "Palestine" first appears in the work of the Greek historian Herodotus (484–425 BCE), to denote both space (the coastal land between Phoenicia and Egypt) and an ethnic group (people distinct from Phoenicians and Egyptians). The Romans adopted the term in the second century CE, and Arab geographers have used it since the seventh century CE. Neither Zionism nor Palestinian nationalism are unique in claiming that their territorialized concept of political identity has existed since the ancient period. It all depends on when you choose to begin the story.[2]

It is useful to pose the question, "Where do we begin the history of modern Palestine?"[3] Palestinian narrations of the modern can begin with Napoleon's arrival in Palestine in 1799. Some point to the period 1831–1840, when Ibrahim Ali, the son of the Albanian Ottoman officer who branched off to become the "father" of modern Egypt, Mehmed Ali, temporarily dislodged Ottoman rule and conquered Palestine. Ibrahim Ali instituted shifts in agriculture, taxation, conscription, and infrastructure, as well as overseeing a constitutional system that included representations of Christians and Jews alongside the majority Muslim inhabitants of Palestine. Still others point to the administrative and governing reforms, or Tanzimat, that the Ottomans instituted in the mid-nineteenth century throughout their empire including in Palestine, which they ruled from 1517 to 1918. Zionist narratives of modern Israel date the emergence of the modern with the first wave of Zionist immigration to Palestine in the 1880s. In these narratives, Israel is an extension of Europe amid an Eastern wilderness, or what the Zionist thinker Theodor Herzl would call "a rampart of Europe against Asia, an outpost of civilization as opposed to barbarism."[4] It is crucial to remind students that the national is not eternal. It is a product of human invention.

Objectivity as a Problem

What is said about Israel/Palestine is a policed matter. The charges of "bias" are persistent. This persistence can be a productive for asking, "Can history tell us the truth?" Teaching Israel/Palestine with readings on philosophy destabilizes conflict as an analytical lens. It also flattens differences of knowledge and familiarity; reading philosophy is difficult for everyone. Michel Rolph-Trouillot's *Silencing the Past* is an accessible and powerful text to inspire students to think differently about history and objectivity.[5]

It is useful to first provide students with a review of philosophy and its branches by summarizing first-order knowledge (philosophy that aims to describe the "real" state of things, such as ontology and cosmology) and second order knowledge (philosophy that is based on the first order and attempts to describe what is "good" for people, such as ethics and politics). The instructor can then describe two approaches to historical writing: objectivism and constructivism. Objectivism contends that reality exists independently of consciousness; individuals are in direct contact with reality through sensory perception. Constructivism posits that people generate knowledge and meaning from their experiences. In *Critique of Pure Reason* (1781), Immanuel Kant, suggested that although the world was fixed, our perceptions of the world were constantly changing.[6] For him, knowledge was the nature of things as we perceive them. Almost two hundred years later in *The Structure of Scientific Revolutions* (1962), Thomas Kuhn suggested that the world was constantly changing.[7] He went further to posit that how we perceive the world changes it.

Having surveyed these canonical figures, the next step is to address how philosophy and the claims to truth are themselves sites of power. Is it a coincidence that the canonical philosophers we study are Western European or North American? How do colonialism and racism shift our understandings of truth? The intellectual Frantz Fanon, in analyzing the decolonization struggle in Algeria, explained "for the native, objectivity is always directed against him."[8] Does this mean that historical writing is a narrative or a representation? Trouillot has the best answer to this question. Exploring the history of Haiti, Trouillot insists that the historical narrative is distinct from fiction. We are not prisoners of history, but it is not whatever we make of it either. History is the fruit of power, but power is never transparent; the challenge is to expose its roots. We have to ask, he suggests, not who has power but how does power work. In addition, history is produced outside of academia, through museums, textbooks, and cultural products. What does it mean, Trouillot asks, to write a history of the United States in a world where little boys prefer playing as the cowboy and not the "Indian"?

It means that history is a social process. People are involved in this process at several different stages. They are agents (occupying structural positions); actors (interacting with their contexts); and subjects (voices). We are all doubly historical because we take part in both the historical process and narrating that process. The production of history is full of silences. Silences happen in the creation of facts (documents), in the assembly of facts (archives), in retrieving facts (narratives), and in determining retrospective significance. These lessons allow students to distinguish between history and historiography; to recognize the links between subjectivity, power, and the production of history; and to be alert to the bottomless silences in both history and historiography.

Recovering Silences

One such resounding silence in the history of Israel/Palestine is everyday life and political economy in eighteenth-century Palestine. Even today in the twenty-first century what Edward Said called the Palestinians' "remembered presence" is more than ever subject to erasure.[9] Engaging Palestinian history is the best exit for these erasures.

Beshara Doumani's *Rediscovering Palestine* gives students the chance to explore the relationship between history and historiography.[10] Doumani responds to several historiographies: Zionist and European historiographies that erase any history before European arrival; Ottoman historiography that credits the government of Istanbul as the source of ideas, politics, and policies; and Arab and Palestinian nationalist historiographies that maintain that five hundred years of Ottoman rule were a period of stasis. Doumani details the social life of textiles, cotton, and olive oil in Jabal Nablus to explore the history of peasants and merchants over a two-hundred-year period. By revealing patterns of taxation, moneylending, and speculative financial tools, such as advance money contracts, Doumani shows how eighteenth-century Palestinian merchants and peasants set the stage for further transformation through political centralization, the commoditization of land, the urban domination of the countryside, and the transformation of a notable elite into an embryonic class. There was a commercial land market in Palestine before Zionist immigration in the 1880s and European domination thereafter. It was not the Ottomans who introduced this land market. In conventional historiography, the privatization of property begins with the Ottoman Land Code of 1858, which many argue was yet another case of European mimesis. Doumani shows that the Land Code was a response to, not an introduction of, private property. Palestinians are a heterogenous group comprised of different locales, classes, and interests. It was not simply Palestinian elites, such as the Jarrar or Abdulhadi families, who had a stake in this process. Peasants used the new courts that the Ottoman government introduced as part of the Tanzimat. Palestinian peasants used and adapted Ottoman citizenship to demand political and economic rights. Palestinian merchants and peasants are *subjects* not *objects* of history.

What was this Ottoman citizenship? Some have argued that it constituted a sort of "civic religion": an imperial identity that overlapped with emerging national identities. Here, drawing on James Gelvin's *The Israel-Palestine Conflict*, we can trace how "cultures of nationalism" and the rise of the state as a force administering social power were central shifts in the nineteenth and twentieth centuries. States in the early modern period became invested in the control of subjects through legal codes, educational systems, armies, and economic planning. The idea that people are naturally divided into unified groups based on the territories in which they live further empowered this form of social power. In late nineteenth- and early twentieth-century Palestine, various forms of belonging overlapped, intersected, and sometimes contradicted one another. Michelle Campos details the "civic religion" of Ottomanism. A major turning point that enabled this "civic religion" was the Ottoman Constitutional Revolution of 1908, a turning point for people in Palestine and throughout the Arab territories of the Ottoman Empire. Through figures such as Shlomo Yellin, Campos reveals a forgotten moment when imperial, national (Zionist and Arab), and territorial identities were not necessarily mutually exclusive. Yellin was the quintessential Ottoman subject who spoke Yiddish, Arabic with his Iraqi mother, Hebrew, and Judeo-Spanish. He was also involved with the Beirut branch of the Committee of Union and Progress, the party that initiated the Constitutional Revolution of 1908. Through detailing these figures and ideas, Campos evidences that the "separation in Palestine between Jews and Arabs came about as the result of the Zionist-Palestinian conflict—it was not the cause."[11]

In this period, there were new global formations of a "public" that changed the rhythms of everyday life. In Palestine and throughout the Middle East alongside China, Japan, Russia, and Mexico, constitutionalism was the ideological framework to which people flocked. It rested on the idea that the government should be legally limited in its powers, and that the government's authority depends on how it observes these legal limitations. In Western Europe and North America, the mass movements that took shape included communism, trade unionism, and anarchism. Throughout Europe another ideological framework began to consolidate: antisemitism.

The History of Antisemitism

Understanding the historical trajectory of antisemitism is a crucial component of teaching Israel/Palestine. The Israeli state and its supporters have used the charge of antisemitism to contain critique of Zionism or Israel. As a result, many avoid engaging the history of antisemitism. This is a mistake. The history of antisemitism is a central pillar of the Jewish experience, the history of Israel/Palestine, and the modern experience more broadly.

One text that gives a glimpse of this history is Stephen Eric Bronner's *A Rumor about the Jews*, which is a social history of the antisemitic pamphlet *The Protocols of the Elders of Zion*.[12] The secret police of Imperial Russia, the Okhrana, drafted and published this crude forgery in 1903. The pamphlet lives well into the twenty-first century; it bridges the discourses of nineteenth-century reactionaries and twentieth-century Nazis. Bronner traces the old right of the aristocracy and landed elites and the new right of conservatives and military reactionaries. *The Protocols* express these old and new right forces' failures in the face of a rapidly changing world. To stem their vulnerability, these right-wing figures and institutions embraced a politics of hate. They represented Jewish people as subjects who stand outside history, as the source of capitalism *and* communism, as the motive force of economy *and* its downfall, and as the explanation of all the ills of the modern era. But this hatred has a deeper history. Bronner details religious Judeophobia in the ancient period. He shows how the Christian charge of deicide grew with the institutional dominance of the Catholic Church in the fifteenth century. He turns to the social persecution of Jews following the period of Emancipation in the eighteenth century, when Jews' emergence from the ghetto fueled charges of their visibility and historical distortions of economic power. It was the category of race that caused the final shift to a state-led antisemitism, which would ultimately lead to the genocide of the Holocaust or Shoah. For Bronner, antisemitism is a squarely European phenomenon that shatters the illusion of Judeo-Christian heritage.

Zionism was a reaction to the consolidation of antisemitism in the late nineteenth and early twentieth centuries. Pogroms, or state-sanctioned attacks on Jewish people that included murder, rape, and looting, were triggers for migration to Palestine. One such pogrom took place in Kishinev in the Russian Empire in 1903 and again in 1905. However, Zionism was neither the only nor the most popular reaction to the oppression of Jewish people in Europe. Other reactions included socialism, communism, and immigration. Zionism did not become a popular option for Jews fleeing persecution until the rise of Nazi power in Germany in 1933. At that point, countries such as the United States and the United Kingdom had closed their doors to Jewish refugees. Palestine witnessed an upsurge of Jewish immigration. The Zionist movement became the preeminent solution to the Jewish question. From its very inception in the late nineteenth century, Zionism was never one thing. Comparing two early primary sources is one way to indicate debates and difference in Zionist thought.

Zionism's Many Houses

Perhaps the most known of early Zionist intellectuals is the Viennese journalist Theodore Herzl (1860–1904). In works such as *The Jewish State* (1896), Herzl posited that the Jewish question in Europe was neither social nor religious; it was national and political.[13] The solution he proposed was a Jewish state in Palestine that would be an extension of Europe and "a rampart of civilization in a sea of barbarism." It is useful to contrast Herzl's thinking with another Zionist thinker, Asher Ginsberg, or as he was known, Ahad Haʾam (1856–1927). Haʾam came from a Hasidic family in what is today known as Ukraine. In his piece "The Truth from Eretz Yisrael," he drew on his visit to Palestine to posit a cultural vision of Zionism.[14] He hoped for an intellectual center that did not have political or military importance. To highlight the variety of Zionist thought, it is useful for students to draw on excerpts from these primary sources and to compare how Herzl and Haʾam discuss Jews, Arabs, the land, and Europe. Whereas Herzl understood the land of Palestine as empty of a unified people, Haʾam predicted that the natives of Palestine would not easily yield their place. While Herzl insisted that Palestine was an uncultivated desert, Haʾam reported that it was hard to find land that was not already tilled. Herzl was primarily concerned with what was good for Jews, but Haʾam cared most about what was good for Judaism. Ha'am's experience with antisemitism and Pan-Slavic movements led him to deeply mistrust Europe. Herzl was invested in Europe and the Enlightenment and believed in imperialism as a civilizational force. It was Herzl's approach of embracing and embodying European notions of superiority that largely triumphed. In both accounts, the Palestinian is by and large absent.

Back to Palestine

About two decades after Herzl and Ha'am would pen their visions, British colonial rule granted the Zionist movement hegemonic power in Palestine. British colonial rule sought to erase Palestinians as subjects with political rights. This is most clear in the Balfour Declaration of 1917, which would become the legal foundation of the British Mandate government in Palestine. This declaration announced the British colonial government's intent to facilitate a Jewish national home while safeguarding the civil and religious right of the "non-Jewish" people in Palestine. The Balfour Declaration categorized the Palestinians by what they were not: that is, "non-Jews." It denied the very possibility of Palestinian political rights. At this time, in 1917, Jewish people constituted about 8 percent of the people living in Palestine.

Twentieth-century Palestine was a place of dynamism and innovation. Detailing Palestinian political demands as well as the cultural, political, and social texture of everyday life is crucial. The lively and rapidly shifting social landscape included labor organizing, a women's movement, a Pan-Arabist political party, a nascent capitalist class, and unprecedented youth organizing. Most importantly, Palestinians like many colonized people in Africa and Asia in the 1930s, mobilized a broad-ranging national uprising against British colonialism and Zionist settlement. In 1936, Palestinians successfully led a national strike for six months. For three years after this strike, Palestinians waged an armed uprising against British colonial rule called the Great Revolt (1936–1939). In response, the British colonial government innovated techniques of deportation, torture, targeted assassination, and collective punishment that continue to mark Palestinian experience and would be used throughout the colonial world in the twentieth and twenty-first centuries. Palestinian political and social life emerged devastated.

At the same time, British forces in the Middle East now faced the onset of World War II. By 1942, people began to learn of the massive scale of the Nazi genocide of six million Jews and an additional five to nine million Roma, communists, socialists, Catholics, Jehovah's Witnesses, ethnic Poles, Soviets, people with disabilities, and people charged with homosexuality and sexual dissidence. In the throes of this global catastrophe, the Zionist movement seized its opportunity to realize the Jewish state. The war of 1948 witnessed the birth of the Israeli state and the death of a contiguous Palestine. It gave birth to the Palestinian refugee condition. For the Palestinians, the exodus and its aftermath were a full-fledged catastrophe, or Nakba. The denial of self-determination and basic rights, as well as dispossession and displacement, did not end in 1948; it is ongoing. This is why Palestinians call their condition an ongoing Nakba.

The Debate about 1948

What happened in 1948? Nothing illustrates the constitutive absence of the Palestinian condition in Israeli historiography as well as the debate on 1948. Avi Shlaim summarizes the findings of an important group of Israeli scholars known as the "new historians."[15] Two crucial historical developments influenced these historians. One was the Israeli state's release of documents in 1978, due to a liberal archive law. The second was the Israeli invasion of and war with Lebanon in 1982. This war rattled many Israelis because it was in public perception, the state's first "war of choice." Until this time, the public depiction of Israel in North America and Western Europe was that of a righteous David facing the ugly Goliath of the surrounding Arab nations. The war of 1948 was an important stage on which Israelis would retroactively build this mythology.

This mythical story goes something like this: In 1947, the United Nations proposed a partition plan; the Arab League, an organization of Arab nations, rejected the plan out of intolerance. Great Britain in turn frustrated the Jewish state, and seven Arab states attacked the fledgling nation. The smaller Jewish military triumphed miraculously. The Palestinians who became refugees were simply responding to Arab state orders; they fled instead of demonstrating "coexistence." After the war, Israel strove tirelessly for peace with its neighbors and found no partner among them. Historians such as Morris, Pappe, and Shlaim began dismantling six pillars of this mythology, at least in Israeli eyes. They showed that the British did not in fact frustrate the Jewish state. The

Yishuv was better prepared, mobilized, organized, and centralized than the Arab armies; by the second stage of the war, the Yishuv was also better armed. Rather than the impenetrable wall of hatred and animosity typically depicted, the Yishuv had an intimate ally across the Jordan river. King Abdullah and the Jewish Agency enjoyed and nourished a thirty-year strategic partnership. Moreover, while the Arab armies used the rhetoric of "throwing the Jews into the sea," they cared less about the Palestinians and were too preoccupied with their own national interest to coordinate militarily or diplomatically. The narrative of an "elusive peace" was similarly flawed: it was postwar Israel that was intransigent. Egyptian, Jordanian, and Syrian governments each offered deals that David Ben-Gurion, prime minister of Israel in 1948, rejected. There is a political economy of knowledge production at stake here. Palestinian, Middle Eastern, and Western scholars such as Walid Khalidi, Nur Masalha, and Maxine Rodinson had made the same arguments for decades before. It was only when Israeli scholars using Israeli archives made these arguments that they became legitimate.

The final myth Shlaim summarizes is the birth of the Palestinian refugee condition. Morris found no Arab state orders for the Palestinians to flee. Similarly, Shlaim suggests that Morris similarly did not find any blanket Israeli orders to expel the Palestinians. However, Morris had evidenced "Plan Dalet," which was a military blueprint that the nascent Israeli army prepared in March 1948 in anticipation of the Arab countries' attack in May. The plan had two main goals: the taking of any installation evacuated by British forces and "the clearing of hostile and potentially hostile forces out of the interior" of the future Jewish state, thus the removal of as many Palestinians as possible.[16] Each military brigade received a list of villages, and as a result 470 to 500 villages were destroyed. Despite these historical facts, some continue to insist that this condition was born of circumstance not design. But this question of "design versus circumstance" is to a large extent the framework of the perpetrator; it is about Israeli ethics, history, and memory. The Palestinians need not wonder about Israeli intentions; they have lived the consequences of those intentions historically. They live them in the present. In 1948, approximately 750,000 Palestinians became stateless refugees.[17] The remaining 150,000 would become second-class citizens living under military rule in Israel; they were now strangers in their own home.

Zionism from the Standpoints of Its Victims

Zionism and the state of Israel clearly mean different things to different people. Exposing students to the ideas and visions of Zionist thought is crucial. Exposing them to the critique of that thought is just as crucial. There are two pieces that open important windows onto this critique, especially when read together. In "Zionism from the Standpoint of Its Victims," Edward Said explicates how European understandings of Eastern culture, politics, and social life as inferior were bases for Zionist thought and practice. The juridical foundations of Zionist claims were made by a European power about a non-European territory in "flat disregard of both the presence and the wishes of the native majority." There was not a place in the new state of Israel, Said explains, that did not have a former Arab population. In a prescient nod to the debate about the Palestinian condition, he insists "the dispersion for the Palestinians was not a fact of nature but a result of specific force and strategies."[18] Said explains that Zionism was a form of imperialism, which sought to civilize those black, brown, and yellow people as part of white racial and cultural hegemony. Like various other imperialist enterprises, Zionism sought to transform what its intellectuals understood as uselessly occupied territories into a useful extension of Europe. Said explains that just as Zionism has touched every Jewish life in the last one hundred years, it has also marked every Palestinian life.

But Zionism did not have only one victim. In her "Sephardim in Israel: Zionism from the Standpoint of Its Jewish Victims," Ella Shohat shows how the Ashkenazi (European) Israeli took on the mantles of civilization, rationality, and racial superiority in contradistinction to the aberrance, underdevelopment, and inferiority that the Mizrahim (Eastern) came to symbolize.[19] Zionism required the European Jew to create a racialized and inferior other. Zionism narrated Jewish history as primordially European. Shohat traces the erasure of centuries of Judeo-Islamic history and symbiosis. She delineates Arab Jews' ambiguous relationship to Zionism. She indicts Zionism and Arab nationalism's collusion in making the "Arab-Jew" an impossible category. Finally, she traces the experiences of Mizrahim in Israel through transit camps and dispersion as well as systematic and structural social, political, and economic exclusion in Israel. For Shohat, the Mizrahim are Zionism's Jewish victims.

These two pieces together constitute an important framing device for teaching Israel/Palestine. The history of Israel/Palestine reveals the failures and limitations of nationalism and in particular its European variant. In the case of Zionism, a people who were promised entry into the category of the "European" only if and when they left Europe would be led by a movement that embraced the very nationalist and civilizational hierarchies from which it sought refuge. The ongoing dispossession, displacement, and denial of basic rights that Palestinians suffer under Zionism is a direct outcome of nationalism's exclusionary force.

NOTES

1. In 2009, Joel Beinin shared with me the syllabus from which I draw here and which has become a school for me and all of the students I have taught.

2. See James Gelvin, *The Israel–Palestine Conflict: One Hundred Years of War*, 3rd ed. (Cambridge: Cambridge University Press, 2014).

3. Ilan Pappe, *A History of Modern Palestine* (Cambridge: Cambridge University Press, 2004), and Rashid Khalidi, *Palestinian Identity: The Construction of Modern National Consciousness* (New York: Columbia University Press, 1997).

4. Theodor Herzl, *The Jewish State: An Attempt at a Modern Solution of the Jewish Question*, trans. Sylive D'Avigdor, Jacob M. Alkow, and Alex Bein (New York: American Zionist Emergency Council, 1946), 15.

5. Michel-Rolph Trouillot, *Silencing the Past: Power and the Reproduction of History* (Boston: Beacon Press, 1995).

6. Immanuel Kant, *Critique of Pure Reason* (Cambridge: Cambridge University Press, 1998).

7. Thomas Kuhn, *The Structure of Scientific Revolutions* (Chicago: University of Chicago Press, 1962).

8. Frantz Fanon, *The Wretched of the Earth*, trans. Richard Philcox (New York: Grove Press, [1961] 2004), 77.

9. Edward Said, "Invention, Memory, and Place," *Critical Inquiry* 26, no. 2 (Winter 2000), 175–92; 184.

10. Beshara Doumani, *Rediscovering Palestine: Merchants and Peasants in Jabal Nablus, 1700–1900* (Berkeley: University of California Press, 1995).

11. Michelle Campos, *Ottoman Brothers: Muslims, Christians, and Jews in Early Twentieth-Century Palestine* (Stanford, CA: Stanford University Press, 2011), 19.

12. Stephen Eric Bronner, *A Rumor about the Jews: Reflections on Antisemitism and the Protocols of the Elders of Zion* (Oxford: Oxford University Press, 2000).

13. Theodor Herzl, *The Jewish State* (New York: Dover, 1988).

14. Ahad Ha'am, "The Truth from Eretz Israel," trans. Alan Dowty, in *Prophets Outcast: A Century of Dissident Writing about Zionism and Israel*, ed. Adam

Shatz (New York: Nation Books, 2004); Ha'am, "Much Ado about Little: Ahad ha-Am's 'Truth from Eretz Yisrael,' Zionism, and the Arabs," trans. Alan Dowty, *Israel Studies* 5, no. 2 (2000): 161–78.

15. Avi Shlaim, "The Debate about 1948," *International Journal of Middle East Studies* 27, no. 3 (August 1995): 287–304.

16. Benny Morris, *The Birth of the Palestinian Refugee Problem: 1947–1949* (Cambridge: Cambridge University Press, 1987), 62.

17. See the United Nations Relief and Works Agency for Palestine Refugees in the Near East, "Palestine Refugees," https://www.unrwa.org/palestine-refugees.

18. Edward Said, "Zionism from the Standpoint of Its Victims," *Social Text* 1 (Winter 1979): 7–58; 9–10, 11.

19. Ella Shohat, "Sephardim in Israel: Zionism from the Standpoint of Its Jewish Victims," *Social Text* 19/20 (Autumn 1988): 1–35.

KEY RESOURCES

Bronner, Stephen Eric. *A Rumor about the Jews: Reflections on Antisemitism and the Protocols of the Elders of Zion*. Oxford: Oxford University Press, 2000.

Campos, Michelle. *Ottoman Brothers: Muslims, Christians, and Jews in Early Twentieth-Century Palestine*. Stanford, CA: Stanford University Press, 2011.

Doumani, Beshara. *Rediscovering Palestine: Merchants and Peasants in Jabal Nablus, 1700–1900*. Berkeley: University of California Press, 1995.

Fanon, Frantz. *The Wretched of the Earth*. Trans. Richard Philcox. New York: Grove Press, (1961) 2004.

Gelvin, James. *The Israel-Palestine Conflict: One Hundred Years of War*, 3rd ed. Cambridge: Cambridge University Press, 2014.

Ha'am, Ahad. "Much Ado about Little: Ahad ha-Am's 'Truth from Eretz Yisrael,' Zionism, and the Arabs." Trans. Alan Dowty. *Israel Studies* 5, no. 2 (2000): 161–78.

Ha'am, Ahad. "The Truth from Eretz Israel." In Adam Shatz, ed., *Prophets Outcast: A Century of Dissident Writing about Zionism and Israel*. Trans. Alan Dowty. New York: Nation Books, 2004.

Khalidi, Rashid. *Palestinian Identity: The Construction of Modern National Consciousness*. New York: Columbia University Press, 1997.

Morris, Benny. *The Birth of the Palestinian Refugee Problem: 1947–1949*. Cambridge: Cambridge University Press, 1987.

Pappe, Ilan. *A History of Modern Palestine*. Cambridge: Cambridge University Press, 2004.

Said, Edward. "Invention, Memory, and Place." *Critical Inquiry* 26, no. 2 (Winter 2000): 175–92.

Said, Edward. "Zionism from the Standpoint of Its Victims." *Social Text* 1 (Winter 1979): 7–58.

Shlaim, Avi. "The Debate about 1948." *International Journal of Middle East Studies* 27, no. 3 (August 1995): 287–304.

Shohat, Ella. "Sephardim in Israel: Zionism from the Standpoint of Its Jewish Victims." *Social Text* 19/20 (Autumn 1988): 1–35.

Trouillot, Michel-Rolph. *Silencing the Past: Power and the Reproduction of History.* Boston: Beacon Press, 1995.

Understanding Sectarianism as a Global Problem

USSAMA MAKDISI

To understand the problem of sectarianism in the Middle East one should think about the term critically and comparatively. Different political cultures around the world have grappled with what is essentially a similar problem, namely how to reconcile meaningful equality of citizens with diversity and how to balance this reconciliation with effective sovereignty. Think for a moment about how the United States has struggled, and still struggles, with racial politics and racism. Think about how modern France and Britain have grappled with nationalism, anti-Semitism, and Islamophobia. Think about how South Asia struggles with caste racism and communalism. Then think about how the diverse countries in the Middle East have been burdened with the problem of sectarianism. The sooner one puts the problem of sectarianism in its modern and global context, the sooner one will understand that its significance lays not in its allegedly medieval past but in profoundly and quintessentially modern conundrums over sovereignty, political equality, unequal access to resources, employment, the extent of secular law, and cultural autonomy. The claims of modern sectarianism emerge within a world of nation-states with nominally equal citizens. They are, therefore, part of a contentious, global history of equality that applies as much to a great power such as the United States as it does to a tiny country like Lebanon.

In the quotidian, journalistic, and academic usage, to be sure, sectarianism is typically evoked as an adjective akin to racism, so that one can talk about sectarian outlooks, actions, and thoughts in a similar manner to how one would talk about racist outlooks, actions, and thoughts. The term "sectarianism" often denotes pervasive forms of prejudice against religious or ethnic others; it also implies the identification with one's own religious or ethnic community as if it were a political party. It can also mean the mobilization through which political, economic, and social claims are made, and sectarian patronage networks are built, in multireligious and multiethnic societies. It can also refer to a solidarity that insists on equality in one domain only to deny it or obscure it in another, similar in this sense to what the scholar David Roediger, borrowing from W. E. B. DuBois, famously described as the "wages of whiteness," that is to say the psychological compensation for poor whites in a manifestly inegalitarian capitalist order that nevertheless overtly and blatantly discriminates against blacks.[1] "Sectarianism" can also indicate the workings of a political order, or what political scientist Arend Lijphart famously described as "consociational democracy" to refer to the ability of elites to create seemingly stable political bargains across sectarian or confessional or ethnic lines such as the National Pact in Lebanon of 1943, or in the Netherlands.[2] But the term "sectarianism" can just as easily be used to denote outright communal mobilizations and intercommunal warfare: the Damascus riots of 1860 when Christian subjects of the Ottoman Empire were killed, the Farhud in Baghdad in 1941 that targeted Jewish citizens of Iraq, the Gujarat genocide in 2001 when Indian Muslims were slaughtered, and the terrible aftermath of the US invasion of Iraq in 2003.

Sectarianism as an Ideological Invention

The term "sectarianism" is clearly analytically imprecise. It is also supremely ideological insofar as it endows the very idea of communities and communal relations in the Middle East with an alleged solidity that obscures relations of power, violence and hierarchy. No group openly identifies itself or its goals as "sectarian" in the modern world. Instead, the label "sectarian" is often invoked as a way to stigmatize or tarnish the legitimacy of individuals or groups with whom one disagrees. Communists such as Lenin were alert to the ideological power of the term when he vehemently denied in any way that he or his party were sectarian.[3] Within the Arab world too, sectarianism has often been a term of opprobrium. More to the point, directly and indirectly, deliberately and inadvertently, the invocation of sectarianism usually overlooks the work—the "sectcraft" (to adapt Barbara and Karen Fields's understanding of what they describe as "racecraft")—that goes into making communal identities and mobilizations in the region appear inherent and outside of history.[4] The normalization of the term "sectarianism" elides the fact that the very concept of political sectarianism in Arabic emerged recently in the context of debates about the viability of secular republicanism in Lebanon.[5] In the Middle East, therefore, "sectarianism" incorrectly assumes that age-old religious mentalities and habits guide contemporary political behavior in the region. Sectarian identities thus *appear* to trump all other forms of affiliation among the diverse people in different cities, regions, classes, families, and environments. Far from actually explaining why specific events unfold in a particular time and place, the term "sectarianism" suggests that what happens in the Middle East has *always* been happening over there. Empires rise and fall; new geopolitics emerge; history changes, but we are led to believe that sectarianism in the Middle East does not change. Sectarianism and its victims, therefore, are assumed to belong apart from the "civilized" world that is presumed to be "secular" and, of course, Western.

Although a voluminous self-critical literature in Arabic has developed over the course of the twentieth century, Western views of sectarianism in the Middle East have often Orientalized it as a problem of *others* that allegedly has little relevance for the modern world.[6] Many American politicians and pundits, therefore, like many British and French colonial officials who ruled the Middle East before them, describe the Arab world as if it were trapped within its own sectarian prison. Most of all, these observers understand sectarianism to be a one-dimensional and immutable social reality that allegedly corresponds neatly to the religious and ethnic diversity in the Middle East. In April 1991, for example, President George H. W. Bush declined to "interfere" in Iraq—this after demolishing Iraq's infrastructure in the previous months and encouraging Iraqis to overthrow then president Saddam Hussein—by claiming that "internal conflicts have been raging in Iraq for many years, and we're helping out, and we're going to continue to help these refugees."[7] Two decades later, President Barak Obama evoked a similar canard in his April 2016 interview in the *Atlantic* magazine. Expressing his disappointment with the Middle East, Obama declared, "You've got countries that have very few civic traditions, so that as autocratic regimes start fraying, the only organizing principles are sectarian."[8] There is little irony in the fact that Obama's message about an inherently sectarian

Middle East tallies precisely with the paternalism of L. Paul Bremer III, the US administrator of the Coalition Provisional Authority in Iraq. Bremer, who knew no Arabic and had very little understanding of Iraqi society or history, was placed in supreme authority over occupied Iraq in 2003. Bremer insisted that Iraqis only "vaguely understand the concept of freedom" and pleaded for US guidance. In his view, sectarianism in the region was endemic, so much so that Bremer described parts of Iraq as "the Sunni homeland."[9]

The emphasis on the allegedly endemic sectarian problem of the Middle East by Bush, Bremer, and Obama serves to obscure Western military, economic, and political domination over the inhabitants of the region. It also reinforces the notion that the Middle East, and Muslims more broadly, are more insidiously religious than the secular West. This notion of the age-old, "medieval" religiosity of the Middle East and its inhabitants underscores a fundamental problem in the broader journalistic coverage of the region — what the late scholar Edward Said referred to as "covering" Islam in such a manner that routinely emphasizes differences rather than commonalities and the abstractions of allegedly canonical religious texts over the richness, variability, and contradictions of human context. In a word, Orientalism is privileged over secular humanism.[10] In its coverage of the bombing in Pakistan in February 2013, for example, Reuters informed its readers that the "the schism between Sunnis and Shi'ites developed after the Prophet Muhammad died in 632 when his followers could not agree on a successor."[11] Yet Reuters would not presumably commence an article on the infamous Branch Davidian cult fiasco in Waco, Texas, or the actions of any other of the innumerable sects that proliferate within the United States, by referring to the sects of ancient Christianity. In the United States and the "West" more broadly, there is, it seems, a religious past and a secular present. In the Middle East, apparently, there is only a religious past and present. The orientalist Bernard Lewis, who was a medievalist by training and became one of the most influential interpreters of Islam in the United States, made a career out of comparing a stereotype of the enlightened and secular West with an equally caricatured stereotype of the "Muslim" and the Islamic world.[12] Even the venerable Middle East correspondent for the BBC Jeremy Bowen, for instance, slips into this lazy Orientalism when he describes in 2013 how the "weight of a millennium and a half of sectarian rivalry is crushing hopes of a better future." Bowen thus describes Saddam Hussein as "a Sunni strongman who fought against Shia Iran."[13] Bowen ignores other important facts that Saddam Hussein was also Tiqriti, Ba'thi, Iraqi, and Arab. Saddam Hussein, after all, also killed Sunni Kurds and Arabs and communists and anyone else who threatened his rule. He also invaded "Sunni" Kuwait—all inconvenient facts that complicate Bowen's highly misleading one-dimensional sectarian narrative. Think, most of all, about how Western journalism and scholarship about the Middle East routinely identify individuals in the Middle East as being either "Sunni" or "Shi'i" or "Christian," although these individuals almost rarely identify themselves as such, whereas this same journalism refuses (understandably) to refer constantly to the "black" Barack Obama or the "white" Clinton or the "Latina" Sonia Sotomayor.

Stop Medievalizing the Middle East

There is little point in denying that sectarian conflicts raged within the Byzantine Empire between different Christian groups over the nature of Jesus Christ, or in the early Muslim community over the question of succession to the Prophet Muhammad that led eventually to the emergence of Shi'i Islam. It would be crucial, nevertheless, to appreciate how even in this early period terms such as "Sunni" and "Shi'i" are not self-explanatory: they are often retrospective labels applied by chroniclers and scholars to individuals who may not have understood or accepted such labels. The anachronistic usage of sectarianism assumes that a transhistorical sectarian identity—rather than politics, economics, empire, or power—motivates and provokes change over time. The Ottoman Empire, for example, is often discussed as a "Sunni" empire that was at war with the "Shi'i" Persian Safavids. Yet the Ottomans also invaded the "Sunni" Mamluks of Egypt. More importantly, the Ottomans also often venerated "Shi'i" figures such as the Caliph Ali and the grandson of the Prophet Husayn (killed at Karbala in 680 by fellow Muslims). To assume that being a "Sunni" empire dictates a certain kind of sectarian agency is what must be questioned.

To teach about sectarianism in the modern world, therefore, requires first and foremost a disruption of notions of stable and agentic religiosity or the idea that there is one kind of sectarianism that operates across the history of the Middle East. Insofar as sectarianism constitutes a genuine political problem identified by the people of the Middle East in the modern era, it is not primarily about religion, but about politics. It is not about splitting off from a universal church, which is how Ernest Trolesch and Max Weber understood the emergence of sects as part of the sociology of religion, but about competition and mobilization within and across communities in what is almost always formally secular national political sovereignty. To go back in time in search of a religious explanation for modern problems is not only misleading; it misses the degree to which the emergence and identification of sectarianism reflect global rather than simply Middle Eastern concerns.

Thinking about Sectarianism and Racism as Nineteenth-Century Problems

If there is indeed a beginning point to the story of modern sectarianism, it surely lies in the nineteenth century where questions of citizenship, nationalism, diversity, equality, and sovereignty were raised in many different locales. The Ottoman Empire, of which most of today's Middle East was then a part, contributed its distinctive part to a much larger global problem of citizenship and equality that pulled in several different and often deeply contradictory directions. Under enormous European military, political, and economic pressure, and in the face of internal rebellions, the Ottoman rulers realized by the mid-nineteenth century that the old regime, whereby Ottoman Muslims were privileged over non-Muslims ideologically and legally, had to be transformed. They implemented a major overhaul of Ottoman administration known as the Tanzimat, whose principal slogan was nondiscrimination between Ottoman subjects of different faiths. A vast multilinguistic, multiethnic, and multireligious Islamic empire with non-Muslim subjects rapidly sought to become an empire of all its citizens. It was a momentous and controversial shift that occurred amid war and bankruptcy. This last throw of the dice to create a viable modern Ottoman sovereignty was also predicated on increased conscription of its Muslim subjects and, under European pressure, the concession to uphold the allegedly "ancient" privileges granted by Ottoman sultans to non-Muslim communities. This shift was controversial and occasioned discontent and even episodes of anti-Christian violence in cities such as Aleppo in 1850 and Damascus in 1860, when in July the largest single anti-Christian riot in the city's modern history occurred. Churches were ransacked, homes were pillaged, and hundreds of Christian subjects were wounded or killed.

This shocking episode was certainly, at one level, sectarian insofar as the victims were clearly singled out because they were Christian. Jewish subjects in Damascus, however, were not attacked. Many Muslims in the city protected their Christian neighbors. Traditionally, this episode has been interpreted in the Orientalist literature as an example of Muslim resistance to the spirit of equality allegedly inherent in the Tanzimat. More recently, scholars have explored the economic, political, and material bases for these sectarian riots.[14] Yet almost no scholar has thought to situate the "sectarian" crisis of 1860 alongside other midcentury crises that illustrate how difficult and vexed any transition from a formally discriminatory culture toward an allegedly emancipatory one is in any part of the world. To do so is to transform a lurid, Orientalized sectarian moment into a global one from which one can learn about the human condition. The United States, after all, endured its Civil War and many bouts of antiblack race rioting at roughly the same time as the Ottoman Empire witnessed unprecedented fragmentation and sectarian mobilizations and massacres involving the emancipation of non-Muslims.[15]

The point of any juxtaposition is inherently heuristic. Simply comparing the recognized multiethnic empires (the Ottomans and Russians, for instance) obfuscates not only the fact that European empires such as Britain and France were also multiethnic and multireligious, but also that the United States itself constituted a vast multiethnic, multilinguistic, and multireligious "continental empire" in this same period.[16] It also obscures the fact that the challenge of political inclusion has plagued every secular state in the modern era—whether democratic republics or nominal empires. The conjoined problem of coexistence and sectarianism in the modern Middle East emerged at roughly the same time as those of nationalism and racial anti-Semitism in modern Europe and those of emancipation and segregation in postbellum United States. These cases might well be juxtaposed to emphasize their coevalness. They each refracted older discourses and practices of discrimination through a radically new lens of equality and citizenship.

The point is to not to pretend that non-Muslims in the Ottoman case had the same economic, social, racial, or political status as black slaves in America, or Jews in European ghettoes. Islamic imperial rule that legitimated Muslim ideological, legal, and cultural privilege over non-Muslims (while guaranteeing them protection and religious autonomy) is not the same thing as the hateful ideology of white supremacy that posited the innate, biological, and perpetual supremacy of one group over all others and that was elaborated in the context of chattel slavery and settler colonialism in the United States. Rather my point is to suggest that what race has been to America, religion has been to the Middle East—perceived as stable and obvious categories but whose political implications, in fact, changed radically across a century. In other words, if in America the question of race defined, undergirded, contradicted, and rendered ambivalent the meaning of US citizenship, in the Ottoman Middle East the question of religious difference haunted an incomplete, paradoxical, and often contradictory nineteenth-century project of equal citizenship.

The difference between the Middle East and the United States (and the West more generally), however, is that the inhabitants of the Middle East have hardly affected, intervened, and transformed the nature of modern Europe or the United States to the degree that Europeans and Americans have transformed, and still transform, the Middle East. Western powers went from being increasingly important factors, players, and agents in what remained a sovereign Ottoman polity to being the *hegemonic* architects of the post-Ottoman Arab world. There is a brute reality of Western involvement that simply cannot be denied, nor should it for a moment be obscured or obfuscated as secondary to the "self-inflicted wounds" that allegedly really "matter," as Fouad Ajami tendentiously put it.[17]

Colonialism, Nationalism, and Sectarianism

The nineteenth century intensified the competition between rival imperial European powers to control the Middle East, a competition known as the Eastern Question. One of the most significant aspects of the Eastern Question was how various European powers—Britain, France, and Russia primarily—justified their imperial interventions in the Ottoman domains in the name of religious freedom and of protecting one or another non-Muslim community. Rather than encouraging the transformation of the Ottoman Muslim empire into a state of secular citizens, the European powers encouraged the end of Ottoman Muslim rule over the Christian Balkans, opened up Ottoman markets to "free trade," insisted on the extraterritoriality of their own European subjects, and protected Western Catholic and Protestant missionary movements that proselytized across the Ottoman Empire. The fact that

European powers insisted on the secularization of Ottoman law and administration and aggressively intervened on behalf of specific Christian communities in the empire profoundly undermined the meaning and implications of secular equality in the Middle East. France, Britain, and Russia insisted that their tutelage was utterly necessary to shepherd the Ottoman Empire into "civilization." The British consul in the Ottoman Empire James Brant, who was stationed in an eastern Anatolian town, described this diminishment of Ottoman sovereignty candidly in 1856. "Reform," he wrote, "is a necessary condition of the existence of Turkey as an independent nation; and her existence as such, being indispensable to the peace of Europe . . . she must be reformed, and her positive independence will have to be placed in abeyance until she has learned to administer her own government on an enlightened and equitable system."[18]

This paternalism was not simply hypocritical or cynical. It was also supremely consequential in the sense that Western interventionism on behalf of non-Muslims in the Ottoman and post-Ottoman Middle East encouraged the transformation of non-Muslim religious communities into so-called politicized, and often racialized or national, "minorities" that were set against the will of the Muslim "majority." Suppose, therefore, a situation in which a foreign power removed the federal government in the United States, abolished the US Army, and encouraged the division of the United States along racial lines, much as the United States has done in Iraq since 2003, the race problem in America would inevitably be exacerbated and its implications changed. This is not because the racial problem in America is unchanging or "age-old," but rather because the meaning and transformation of racial identities, like sectarian ones, are so clearly dynamic products of specific historical, material, and geopolitical contexts. If in the United States the term "minority," and the associated calls for freedom for these minorities, designate groups that need basic protection of constitutional rights of equality, in almost no sense do they imply the need for foreign intervention. Indeed, American discussions about minorities presume a powerful US sovereign. Yet in the Middle Eastern case, the term "minority" often went—and still goes—hand in hand with the limitation or the abrogation of sovereignty. The 1856 Treaty of Paris, which ended the Crimean War, included specific safeguards to protect Christian, as opposed to Muslim, communities in the Ottoman Empire. Following the defeat of the Ottomans in the First World War, the rump empire was forced to concede the educational, linguistic, and cultural autonomy of various racialized "minorities." According to the harsh Treaty of Sèvres of 1920, these minorities had the right to appeal to colonial European powers whose authority was final. In addition, when Egypt was unilaterally declared "independent" by Britain in 1922, the latter controlled foreign relations and the Suez Canal and guaranteed the protection of minorities. As scholar Benjamin Thomas White has noted, while Europeans insisted on the applicability of "minority" clauses for less powerful nations, they utterly rejected the notion that such clauses were applicable to areas under their own juris-diction.[19] Scholar Georges G. Corm pointed out decades ago that the upshot of this was far less to reinforce a sense of commonality with fellow citizens of different faiths than to reinforce basic sectarian dif-ferences that neither satisfied minority communities nor the Muslim majority in either Turkey or the post-Ottoman Arab world.[20]

The Anglo-French partition of the Ottoman Empire in 1920 destroyed the unitary, if fragile, Ottoman sovereignty. Direct European colonial-ism nevertheless forced different Arabs to confront questions of sover-eignty, religious diversity, and secular citizenship with an urgency that they had not before. This was the moment, in other words, when every former Ottoman subject suddenly had to affiliate to the new structures of colonial power and new borders that invariably sectarianized the landscape of the Arab East or Mashriq, denied the possibility of an over-arching common nationalism in the region, and worked relentlessly to segregate and separate. There was a massive difference, after all, between thinking of oneself as a Christian Arab or as a Christian "minority" in the Muslim-majority Arab world; between being an Arab Jew or a Zion-ist Jew who desired to build a separate and exclusive Jewish state; between being a Muslim Arab who identified with his non-Muslim compatriots or a member of the Muslim Brotherhood who believed that "Islam" was the solution to political, economic, and social problems.

It was the colonial period that opened the door wide for communal politics that was expressed most clearly in the emerging Maronite-dominated sectarian state of Lebanon established in 1920. It was the colonial period that also, paradoxically and perhaps even inevitably, pro-vided the impetus for the elaboration of overtly anticolonial nationalist politics that came to dominate Egyptian, Syrian, and Iraqi politics during the mandate era. Tellingly, I think, the post-Ottoman era most clearly invented sectarianism—al-ta'ifiyya—as a negative trope of antimodernity and antinationalism in Syria, Egypt, Iraq, and Lebanon. Radical and

nationalist antisectarian groups and social movements opposed colonial rule, and that drew cadres from nearly all religious communities—
whether the Soviet-inspired Communist parties in Lebanon, Palestine,
Egypt, and Iraq, trade unions, or the secular Pan-Arabist Ba'th party
in Syria. To be antisectarian in the post-Ottoman era clearly did not
suggest a simple commitment to secularism, let alone to radical politics
of land reform, democracy, or gender equality. But it did suggest an
awareness of the inescapable pluralism of the region shared by a panoply of competing and contending political, religious, and cultural Arab
identifications.

For many, if not most, Arab intellectuals of the twentieth century,
the modernist anticolonial projects of nationalism held the key to combating what they often regard as an archaic sectarianism. They believed
that they, as critical Arab thinkers and policy makers, held the key to
their own salvation, for just as much as there was a local problem of
sectarianism, there was also a local antidote of antisectarian consciousness and mobilization. The émigré author Khalil Gibran captured this
antisectarian sensibility in the 1934 *Garden of the Prophet*. "Pity the nation
divided into fragments," he wrote, "each fragment deeming itself a
nation."[21] By the 1950s, the secular nationalists such as Sati al-Husari,
Constantine Zurayk, Edmond Rabbath, and Michel Aflaq described "sectarian fanaticism" in evocatively modernist terms. Zurayk, for example, regarded sectarianism to be a problem "cascading from the past
into the present," and thus an anachronism "in the age of nationalisms,
and indeed in the age of the atom and space."[22] For these men, sectarianism reflected a problem akin to other anachronisms they identified as "feudalism" and "colonialism." They defined sectarianism not
against secularism but against the aspirations for modern postcolonial
sovereignty. At stake was not the persistence of religious identities, for
religious identity, and especially Islamic symbols and motifs, were an
integral part of Arab nationalist imagination. Rather, the problem was
the alleged manipulation and subversion of religious pluralism by ret-
rograde domestic and foreign interests. Sectarianism was not the intrusion of religion into the public and political realm, but the intrusion
of the wrong kind of religiosity: supposedly backward, separatist, and
subversive of the putative common national community.

The problem for these secular nationalists was that European powers held ultimate military power, and as long as this was the case, the
modern Arab imagination of antisectarianism remained consistently

oppositional and disadvantaged by a nominal or beleaguered sovereignty. There was no Arab equivalent to the independence enjoyed by Kemalism in Turkey—at least not until the mid-1950s when revolutions swept away monarchies in Egypt and Iraq. This era of decolonization inaugurated a new chapter in the story of the antisectarian mobilization and ideology—a story simultaneously full of hope and at the same time carrying within it the seeds of tragedy. Whether in Iraq, Syria, or most famously Nasser's Egypt, the commitment to antisectarianism became an ineluctable aspect of revolutionary mobilization whose history—at a deep level—we barely know. At the same time, however, this same era witnessed the beginnings of the consistent deployment of the allied tropes of antisectarianism and anticolonialism as part of the arsenal of the despotism of national-security states that today so disfigure the modern Middle East. What may have begun as genuine ecumenical commitments to combating sectarianism have often degenerated into a debased language of antisectarianism that consolidates brutal state power: in the name of national unity, dissidents were and continue to be suppressed, opposition banned, and political freedoms abolished. The implications of these "internal" failings have been augmented and exacerbated by the US project to "contain" and roll back the secular and anticolonial dimensions of Arab nationalism in the Middle East—especially since 1967. The United States has chosen to support the self-proclaimed Jewish state of Israel no matter how oppressive it is to the indigenous Palestinians and to uphold Wahhabist Saudi Arabia as a key cog in the post–World War II petroleum order of the region. There is no way to meaningfully separate these fateful US policy decisions from the contemporary sectarianization of the region, especially after the disastrous US invasion of Iraq in 2003.[23]

Antisectarianism

To reduce modern sectarian problems to a question of only colonial "divide and rule" shunts aside the agency of Arabs, Turks, Armenians, Kurds, and others who were most invested in these problems. By the same token, to pretend that these sectarian problems are not themselves produced in the modern era that has been continually dominated and shaped by Western imperialism is to ignore what is most obvious about them: that sectarian identifications and mobilizations occur within specific geopolitical contexts in which the inhabitants of the Middle East are rarely the major players. Yet just like racial politics in the United States, where racial sentiments change and are part of a spectrum of political activism that ranges from the openly racist and conservative to the most liberal, so too in the Middle East are communal sentiments diverse. Every sectarian act, like every antisectarian act, is a product of will and investment. Communities do not cohere magically or naturally in any part of the world. To understand this basic point is to understand how the struggle to free oneself from what the English radical poet William Blake once called the "mind-forg'd manacles" is constant and ongoing in every part of the world. And just as important, it is also to be prepared to recognize the meaning and implications of those moments in the past, present, and future that betray the persistence of such manacles. What is clear, above all, is that for the story of sectarianism to be told as history rather than as prophecy, we need to historicize sectarianism and antisectarianism. We need to underscore over and over again the profound instability, contradictions, and paradoxes that make up the substance and drama of how history actually unfolds: not as an inevitable path to anything but as a series of contingent, constrained, and fateful choices, moments, and turning points that create particular realities.

NOTES

This essay is derived from the introduction to *Age of Coexistence: The Ecumenical Frame and the Making of the Modern Arab World* (Oakland: University of California Press, 2019).

1. David R. Roediger, *Wages of Whiteness: Race and the Making of the American Working Class* (London: Verso, 1991).

2. Arend Lijphardt, "Consociational Democracy" (1969), reprinted in Lijphardt, *Thinking about Democracy: Power Sharing and Majority Rule in Theory and Practice* (London: Routledge, 2008), 25–42.

3. Vladimir Ilyich Lenin, "The Three Sources and Three Component Parts of Marxism," reproduced at https://www.marxists.org/archive/lenin/works/1913/mar/x01.htm.

4. I am adapting here the term "racecraft" used by scholars Karen E. Fields and Barbara J. Fields, *Racecraft: The Soul of Inequality in American Life* (London: Verso, 2012), which builds on Barbara Jeanne Fields's classic essay, "Slavery, Race and Ideology in the United States," *New Left Review* 181 (1990): 95–118.

5. I expand upon this point in my book *Age of Coexistence*. Mahdi ʿAmil exposed the ideological underpinnings of sectarianism in the "sectarian state" in Lebanon in *Fi al-dawla al-taʾifiyya* (Beirut: Dar al-Farabi, [1986] 2003).

6. For a useful review of Arabic literature on sectarianism, see Fanar Haddad, "Sectarianism and Its Discontents in the Study of the Middle East," *Middle East Journal* 71 (2017): 363–82.

7. Maureen Dowd, "After the War; Bush Stands Firm on Military Policy in Iraqi Civil War," *New York Times*, April 14, 1991.

8. See Karla Adam, "Obama Ridiculed for Saying Conflicts in the Middle East 'Date Back Millennia': Some Don't Date Back a Decade," *Washington Post*, January 13, 2016, https://www.washingtonpost.com/news/worldviews/wp/2016/01/13/obama-ridiculed-for-saying-conflicts-in-the-middle-east-date-back-millennia-some-dont-date-back-a-decade/ (accessed September 8, 2016); Jeffrey Goldberg, "The Obama Doctrine," *Atlantic*, April 2016, http://www.theatlantic.com/magazine/archive/2016/04/the-obama-doctrine/471525 (accessed September 8, 2016).

9. L. Paul Bremer III, with Malcolm McConnell, *My Year in Iraq: The Struggle to Build a Future of Hope* (New York: Simon and Schuster, 2006), 71.

10. Edward W. Said, *Covering Islam: How the Media and the Experts Determine How We See the Rest of the World* (New York: Vintage, [1981] 1997). See too Edward W. Said, *Orientalism* (New York: Pantheon Books, 1978).

11. "Bomb Kills 64 in Pakistan's Quetta," Reuters, February 17, 2013.

12. Bernard Lewis's most infamous piece remains "The Roots of Muslim Rage," *Atlantic*, September 1990; but see also Lewis, *What Went Wrong: Western Impact and Middle Eastern Response* (Oxford: Oxford University Press, 2002).

13. Jeremy Bowen, "Sharpening Sunni-Shia Schism Bodes Ill for the Middle East," BBC News, December 20, 2013, https://www.bbc.com/news/world-middle-east-25458755 (accessed February 2, 2014).

14. See Leila Tarazi Fawaz, *An Occasion for War: Civil Conflict in Lebanon and Damascus in 1860* (Berkeley: University of California Press, 1994); Bruce Masters, *Christians and Jews in the Ottoman Arab World: The Roots of Sectarianism* (Cambridge: Cambridge University Press, 2001); and Ussama Makdisi, *The Culture of Sectarianism: Community, History and Violence in the Nineteenth-Century Ottoman Empire* (Berkeley: University of California Press, 2000).

15. For antiblack violence in the United States, see W. Fitzhugh Brundage, *Lynching in the New South: Georgia and Virginia, 1880–1930* (Urbana: University of Illinois Press, 1993); Steven Hahn, *A Nation under Our Feet: Black Political Struggles in the Rural South from Slavery to the Great Migration* (Cambridge, MA: Belknap Press of Harvard University Press, 2003); David W. Blight, *Race and Reunion: The Civil War in American Memory* (Cambridge, MA: Belknap Press of Harvard University Press, 2001).

16. For the comparison with Russia, see Michael Reynolds, *Shattering Empires: The Clash and Collapse of the Ottoman and Russian Empire, 1908–1918* (Cambridge: Cambridge University Press, 2011). For a comparison with Austria, see Omar Bartov and Eric D. Weitz, eds., *Shatterzone of Empires: Coexistence and Violence in*

the German, Habsburg, Russian and Ottoman Borderlands (Bloomington: Indiana University Press, 2013). For continental empire see William Earl Weeks, Building the Continental Empire: American Expansion from the Revolution to the Civil War (Chicago: Ivan R. Dee, 1996); and Bradford Perkins, The Cambridge History of American Foreign Relations, vol. 1, The Creation of a Republican Empire, 1776–1865 (Cambridge: Cambridge University Press, 1993).

17. Fouad Ajami, The Arab Predicament: Arab Political Thought and Practice since 1967 (Cambridge: Cambridge University Press, 1981), 3.

18. James Brant, "Memorandum on Reform," reprinted in David Gillard, ed., The Ottoman Empire in the Balkans, 1856–1875, part 1, series B, vol. 1 of British Documents on Foreign Affairs: Reports and Papers from the Foreign Office Confidential Print (Fredrick, MD, 1984), 8.

19. Benjamin Thomas White, The Emergence of Minorities in the Middle East: The Politics of Community in French Mandate Syria (Edinburgh: Edinburgh University Press, 2011).

20. Georges G. Corm, Contribution a l'étude des sociétés multi-confessionnelles (Paris: Librarie Générale de droit et de jurisprudence, 1971), 237.

21. The Garden of the Prophet, reproduced in Khalil Gibran, The Complete Works: The Original Texts in English and Arabic, ed. Tony P. Naufal (Beirut: Naufal, 2010), 369.

22. Constantine Zurayq, Nahnu wa-l-tarikh (Beirut: Dar al-'ilm lil-malayin, 1959), 213.

23. Nader Hashemi and Danny Postel, eds., Sectarianization (London: Hurst, 2017).

KEY RESOURCES

Fields, Karen E., and Barbara J. Fields. Racecraft: The Soul of Inequality in American Life. London: Verso, 2012.

Haddad, Fanar. "Sectarianism and Its Discontents in the Study of the Middle East." Middle East Journal 71 (2017): 363–82.

Makdisi, Ussama. Age of Coexistence: The Ecumenical Frame and the Making of the Modern Arab World. Oakland: University of California Press, 2019.

Makdisi, Ussama. "The Mythology of the Sectarian Middle East." Center for the Middle East, Rice University's Baker Institute for Public Policy, February 2017.

Said, Edward W. Orientalism. New York: Pantheon Books, 1978.

The Iranian Revolution

From Monarchy to the Islamic Republic

NAGHMEH SOHRABI AND ARIELLE GORDON

One of the most important "sticking points" in studying and teaching the 1979 revolution in Iran is how Islam, as a factor of the revolution and the postrevolutionary state, predetermines students' and educators' (and even scholars') evaluation of the revolution itself. The persistent image of the Islamic Republic of Iran as a turbaned/veiled theocracy, combined with the difficulty of teaching revolutions as the contingent events they truly are, works to minimize the contradictory processes and complex ideologies that came together in the fall of 1978 and eventually led to the victory of the revolution in February 1979.

It is, of course, impossible to study and teach the Iranian Revolution without acknowledging the deep-rooted influence of Shiʻi Islam on Iranian culture and the discourses, imageries, and rhythms of uprising between 1978 and 1979. As a language of revolutionary dissidence and as an organizing social force, Shiʻism shaped the Iranian Revolution. Scholars have produced extensive examinations of the role of Shiʻism on the mobilization, networks, and idioms of the revolution, particularly the ways in which the Karbala paradigm—the story of the martyrdom of Imam Husayn and his supporters at the hands of the unjust ruler Yezid—framed revolutionary sensibilities across the ideological spectrum. It gave shape to the protests in the streets and articulated a language of revolution that was legible to all social strata, from merchants in the bazar to rural-to-urban migrants, radical clergy to intelligentsia, university students to oil workers. Shiʻism was a "'language,' used in

132

different ways by different actors in order to persuade their fellows, to manipulate situations, and to achieve mastery, control, or political position."[1] Many sectors of the anti-shah alliance who in fact did not subscribe to religious theology in their ideology—such as leftist students and urban guerrilla groups—found themselves under the umbrella of "Shiism as an ideology of protest . . . under which divergent groups came together and destabilized the government."[2]

However, a problem arises when we emphasize Islam as the sole historical factor, particularly in the political atmosphere of the twenty-first century. It reduces the many competing and varying lineages of social and cultural transformation to one essentialist category. The visible shape of the Islamic Republic of Iran (where women are veiled, "Death to America" is chanted, and turbaned clerics seemingly run the country) and the ultimate influence of Ayatollah Khomeini on the direction of the postrevolutionary state, have seduced many casual observers and even analysts into viewing the event that was the 1979 Iranian Revolution as one that was guided at its core by the dicta and desires of Shi'ism—ultimately leading many to term it an "Islamic" Revolution. A historical examination of the revolutionary period in Iran, however, reveals that the events of 1979 owe their roots as much to competing nationalist, anticolonial, Marxist, socialist, and Third Worldist influences, as they do to cultural and political Shi'ism.

One way to present a more complex picture is to focus the discussion of the revolution around three "actors": the Pahlavi State, the Opposition, and the People. In doing so, we suggest emphasis be placed on how each of these actors creates a different periodization and framework of analysis for the revolution, even though they all intersected in the lead-up to 1979. This division can also fit onto an imperfect timeline that moves from the 1950s to the 1970s as demonstrated below. By shifting the beginning point of the revolution, and by presenting multiple explanations for the events leading to it, educators can simultaneously stress the unpredictable nature of this revolution (and revolutions in general), acknowledge how an event as forceful as a revolution can simultaneously be many things to many people, and probe with students the degree to which their current ideas about politics, religion, culture, and even revolution determine their views of the past. To facilitate this, in each section we introduce mainly primary sources that embody the complexities this essay highlights. There is, of course, a rich body of scholarship focusing on the political, economic, cultural, ideological, and social causes of the revolution, a few of which we have referenced below but many of which can be found in online searches of libraries or syllabi on modern Iran or the Middle East.

The State

By beginning our story with the Pahlavi state, we can focus on the longer-term processes that allow for revolutionary sentiments to arise. Two moments stand out as the most common points of entry: the 1953 CIA-led coup against the premiership of Mohammad Mossadegh and the 1963 White Revolution. The nationalization of oil in 1951 in Iran triggered a sequence of events that eventually led to a CIA-led and British-backed coup, ousting the popular Mossadegh and bringing the young Muhammad Reza Shah Pahlavi back into power. The effects of the coup were several, including the end of a brief period of political pluralization in Iran, the start of the United States as the principal foreign power in Iranian politics, a realignment of Iran's regional role in the Cold War, and a popular perception that linked the United States to the demise of Iran's democratic nationalist movement. The 1953 coup has been written about extensively from both the US and the Iranian perspectives and within the context of the 1979 revolution. There are a number of English-language primary sources on the conception and planning of the coup available for students to examine and with which to critically engage.[3]

One way to get at this complexity is to have students read the CIA's 1954 history of the event, along with the shah's perspective outlined in *Mission for My Country*, and Mossadegh's detailed response to the shah in his memoirs.[4] This trio of perspectives is a useful starting point for emphasizing how a single event can look completely different from multiple actors. It also establishes a base of longer-term factors shaping political discontent and discourse, including why the anti-imperialism of the global 1960s and the armed struggles of the 1970s resonated so strongly with Iranians.

In 1963, the shah launched a six-point program, known as "The White Revolution," that included land reform, nationalization of state forests, sale of state factories, the creation of a literacy corps, a program of profit-sharing for industrial workers, and the granting of voting rights to women. Lauded by the monarchy as "the revolution of the Shah and the people," these reforms were expected to modernize Iran, while simultaneously co-opting key platforms, such as land reform, from the agenda of the leftist opposition (in the hopes of diluting its political influence).

In retrospect, the gap between what the White Revolution was to accomplish and what actually occurred stands as one of the chief contributing factors toward the buildup of revolutionary momentum. As noted by Ali M. Ansari, "the *White Revolution* not only undermined the structural foundations of the Pahlavi monarchy, but also crucially contributed to its ideological destabilization."[5] In theory, agrarian reforms were intended to do three things: eliminate the power of landed aristocracy, whom the shah had come to see as a threat to his power in the aftermath of the 1953 coup (Mossadegh, after all, belonged to that strata of society); give land to the landless, thus creating a new class of citizens with a stake in the system; and develop the agricultural sector as one means to "modernize" Iran. Instead, the shah managed to alienate the aristocracy and eliminate them as a mediating class. What is more, due to the uneven nature of the program's implementation, many landless peasants remained that way. Of those who became new landowners, most did not get the proper support to develop their land. What followed was a drop in agricultural production and a significant increase in urban migration. Instead of the support base for which the shah had hoped, this "new class of citizens," by the late 1970s, made up a significant portion of the discontented revolutionary masses.

The White Revolution is a great place to introduce two concepts: unmet expectations as a long-term factor in the creation of revolutionary sentiments, and unintended consequences in history. One can begin with the name: Why "revolution?" Why "white" as opposed to another color? And why "the revolution of the Shah and the people?" To answer these questions, instructors can bring in broader regional and global points of comparison, noting, for example, the importance of land reform to Egypt, Syria, Iraq, Bolivia, Cuba, and Chile from the 1950s into the 1960s. In doing so, one can brainstorm with students as to how the monarchy co-opted both the term "revolution" and specific platforms characteristic of socialist movements, as a way to counteract leftist agendas at the time (thus "white" as opposed to "red"). "Revolution from above" was a way of avoiding what the shah had witnessed happening elsewhere, in other "red" liberation movements throughout the globe. Additionally, considering the White Revolution allows us to expand the geography of revolutionary sentiments to those in rural areas.[6]

The Opposition

It was against the White Revolution that Ayatollah Ruhullah Khomeini burst onto the national political scene. The brewing tensions between Khomeini and the shah came to a boil in 1963, when Khomeini gave a fiery sermon in Qum, directly addressing the shah and calling him a "miserable wretch."[7] When young seminarians demonstrated in his support, many were killed or wounded by government troops.

After Khomeini delivered another scathing speech that October, against Iran's granting of capitulation rights to the United States, he was exiled to Turkey, then to Iraq, and, by October 1978, to France. Both these speeches and their aftermath established Khomeini as a bold critic of the shah and daring defender of Iranian sovereignty. A translation of the "capitulations" speech is a great tool in the classroom to begin a conversation about the complexity of the revolutionary discourse and alliance.[8] Educators can ask students to read parts of the speech out loud as it was meant to be heard, and to then parse out its nationalist, religious, and anticolonial components. It is useful to point out, for example, that the issue at the heart of this important speech is that of national sovereignty, and not religion (even as it is given by a religious figure in a city of revered religious men). In doing so, one can better understand the sweeping appeal of Khomeini's rhetoric, as one that spoke to a layered range of discontents.

Just as Khomeini's speech disrupts commonplace divisions between nationalist versus religious sensibilities, the bifurcated line drawn between "leftist" and "Islamist" also fails to accurately represent the spirit of the revolutionary movement. Conventional narratives have often grouped the anti-shah opposition into two: the "secularist" groups such as the communist Tudeh party, the National Front, and the Marxist guerrilla groups such as the Fadaiyan-i Khalq, and the "Islamists" that included the "radical clergy" led by Khomeini. This bipolar narrative often presents the Iranian Revolution as a struggle instigated by nationalists, socialists, and guerrillas; which, after they were driven underground or decimated by the monarchy's repression, left space in the mid-1970s for the radical clergy to come in and "hijack" the revolution.

In reality, the revolutionary movement was not so orderly. For example, some of the people who were later termed "Islamists" in the early

postrevolutionary period (such as Sadegh Qotbzadeh, Khomeini's unofficial spokesman while in exile, or Mustafa Chamran, the Islamic
Republic's first defense minister, a Berkeley-trained physicist who in his
travels to Cuba and Lebanon and his support of the PLO was a 1960s
revolutionary par excellence) came out of the Liberation Movement
of Iran (LMI), a group that subscribed to "hybrid" ideologies of Islamic
socialism, constitutionalism, and Iranian nationalism. The founding
members of the Mujahedin-i Khalq (MKO), an Islamic-Marxist guerrilla
group that was the first to "develop systematically a modern revolutionary interpretation of Islam" also came from the LMI.[9] Not all Islami-
cally oriented groups were Khomeinists, just as not all clergy supported
Khomeini in his belief that the clerical class should be involved in politics. The presence of all of these groups in the decades leading up to the
revolution was extremely significant in disproving the state's carefully
cultivated "myth of omniscience," the pervasive notion that the state
was all-knowing and all-powerful (due to its vast network of informants and infamous reputation for torture)—proving to the public that
the monarchy was not invincible, and that opposition to it was in fact
possible.

Two of the most influential thinkers of the 1960s and 1970s, Jalal Al-e
Ahmad and Ali Shari'ati, also defy binary categorizations. The former's
conceptualization of *gharbzadegi* (literally: West-struck-ness) as a disease that had hollowed out Iranian identity by enslaving it to the West
and the latter's articulation of a revolutionary Shi'ism neither beholden
to reactionary clerics nor inauthentic Marxism permeated prerevolutionary thought—particularly among the younger generation. Though they
died before 1979, both (Shari'ati in particular) were upheld as heroes in
the mass protests of late 1978. In other words, in the lead-up to the revolution, there was an entire "color-wheel" of ideologies that bled into
each other and made the final revolutionary alliance possible.[10]

In thinking about the Iranian Revolution, which is so often taught
as a historical outlier (i.e., not a "revolution" but an "Islamic" one), it is
imperative that we remember that Iranian revolutionaries of all stripes
placed themselves in a dialogue with global traditions of revolutionary
thought, toeing a delicate line between regional and international politics. As discussed earlier, even the shah more than a decade previously
understood that the language of dissent in Iran was in conversation
with the liberation movements of the broader globe. The grasp of Third
Worldism and a politics of socialist revolution affected not only the

intellectual thought produced by theorists of the era, but by the 1960s provided a tangible model for anti-shah organizations to turn to armed struggle against the regime. As one guerilla fighter proclaimed: "We advocate armed struggle because we have examined carefully both the revolutionary experiences of other countries . . . What is more, the revolutionary experiences of Vietnam, Cuba, Algeria, and the Palestinians have shown us the new road . . . We have two choices: victory or martyrdom."[11] Such statements remind us that those who imagined what revolution would look like, in the decades beforehand, intimately located it in the anticolonial and socialist traditions of an international and Third Worldist sphere.

As such, in teaching the revolutionary period, it is crucial to step out of the anachronistic categories of "left versus right" and "secular versus religious" and rather pay attention to the ways in which political identities and revolutionary ideologies were amalgamations of multiple cultural currents that defined the times. It is clear that much of the "revolutionary consciousness"—the mythologies and imaginations of anti-shah uprising—in the decades leading up to the events of 1979 was not formulated by just the radical clergy but by a diverse cast of characters that included guerrilla organizations such as the Fadaiyan and the Mujahedin, revolutionary theorists both within and outside Iran from the likes of Al-e Ahmad to Shari'ati to Frantz Fanon to Che Guevara, and nationalist movements such as the LMI, not to mention Iranian youth who embodied the cultural and intellectual pull of these ideas.

Samad Behrangi's 1963 *Little Black Fish* is an allegory about a small fish's journey from home, ultimately to his death in the mouth of a pelican. It is widely considered to be one of the most popular critiques of the shah's authoritarian regime, even though it was published by the Institute for the Development of Children and Young Adults, an organization set up by the Empress Farah in 1965 to promote cultural literacy among youth. The little black fish sacrifices himself to kill the pelican that had swallowed him and others, thus causing the pelican to open his mouth and allow others to escape. His sacrifice becomes a source of inspiration for later generations of fish. In asking students how the allegory argues for political action and how this language would work in the context of revolutionary history, educators can begin to illuminate the palimpsest of the revolution's ideas laid out earlier in this essay.[12]

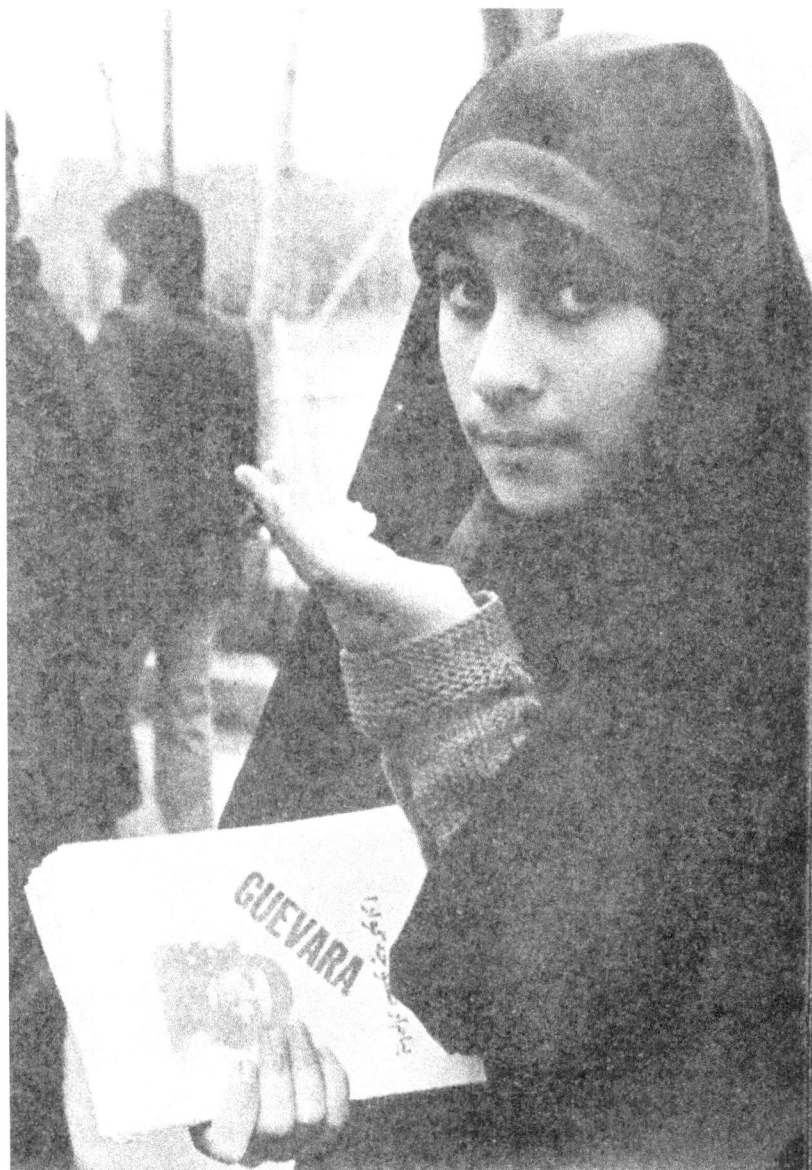

A young woman clutches Che Guevara whitebook and flower. *Tehran Musawwar*, January 1979. Courtesy of the Siagzar Berelian Collection, International Institute of Social History, Amsterdam, Netherlands.

Roy Mottahedeh's *Mantle of the Prophet* is an excellent work of narrative nonfiction that follows the education and politicization of Ali Hashemi, a young man from Qum, while simultaneously providing a deep historical account of modern Iranian education, religion, politics, and culture.[13] Intertwining micro and macro histories, *Mantle* allows the students to see how ideas that may seem contradictory to us are seen as harmonious in another era. In doing so, he also brings to life the ways in which revolutions are comfortable with and even thrive on ambiguities. In teaching this book, educators might ask students to identify the different social bases and cultural amalgamations of different characters: Have they recently migrated to the city due to the agrarian reforms of the 1960s? Are they a member of the intelligentsia, or part of the rapidly growing demographic of educated youth radicalized by the political texts of urban intellectual circles? In which spaces do different ideologies comingle? How does religious language or identity enter discourse about revolutionary action? And what, if anything, does the absence of women in this story reflect? Just as this essay has emphasized how historical categories can be malleable, Mottahadeh demonstrates how a character can embody multiple "demographics," and how "revolutionary consciousness" is hardly static, but rather can shift over time. The diversity of geography, characters, and cultural symbolisms within this text make it an excellent teaching source to capture the development and formation of identity in modern Iranian history.

The People

How did the "movement," which was mainly youth based, become, by 1978, a multigenerational "revolution"?

The period between 1978 and 1979 marked a shift away from structures and discourse to *action*. Photographs and footage of the mass protests that came to define the winter of 1978–1979 show the faces of middle-aged and elderly women and men spread throughout the crowd. Voices of discontent were vast and varied. *This* — the moment in which dissent transcends class, gender, and generation — becomes the revolution. What brings people from a wide swath of society out into the streets so defiantly?

The answer requires us to move our focus from the long-term processes of revolution laid out in previous sections to ones of short term in 1978. A combination of external factors, such as Jimmy Carter's "human

rights" foreign policy that pressured the shah into more political openness, and domestic ones, such as the burning of Cinema Rex in the southern city of Abadan in August 1978 and the shooting into the crowd in
Jaleh Square in Tehran that September, produced a concomitant sense
that "enough was enough" and that revolutionary potential was now,
more than ever, "viable."[14] The rhythm of protests in 1978 perfectly
captures how the various strands of political thought, which had ebbed
and flowed in the previous decades, came together in the last year of
the Pahlavi dynasty's rule: The first half of the year was defined primarily by mobilizations set to the forty-day cycles of Shi'i mourning (Ashura)
while the second half saw the entry of general strikes, defiance of military curfews, and, by December 1978, sustained anti-shah mass protests. By the fall of 1978, Khomeini, by then in France, was considered
the undisputed leader of the revolution. On January 16, 1979, the shah
and his family fled Iran, never to return. On February 1, 1979, after fifteen years in exile, Khomeini returned. Oceans of people came to greet
him. And on February 11, 1979, after days of street fighting, the revolution was declared victorious. A provisional government headed by
Mehdi Bazargan (of the LMI), formed only a week earlier by Khomeini's decree, officially took over.

For this period, visual texts such as posters, paintings, pamphlets,
and moving images offer a fantastic window into the sensibilities of the
revolution—how it *looked*, how it *sounded*, how it *felt*. The Iranian revolution was truly televised; even a cursory YouTube search would reveal
scores of reportages that convey the scale of uprising in late 1978. There
are also several accessible visual sources that can be used in the classroom. Peter Chelkowski and Hamid Dabashi's book *Staging a Revolution: The Art of Persuasion in the Islamic Republic of Iran* is a comprehensive
collection of poster art, government-commissioned art, street murals,
stamps, photographs, pamphlets, and so forth spanning from the prerevolutionary period well into the final years of the Iran-Iraq War.[15] The
book offers an important window into the aesthetics of the revolutionary period that flavored the revolution's anticolonial, nationalist, Third
Worldist, socialist, and Islamic dispositions. The University of Chicago
hosts a digital archive titled "Middle Eastern Posters Collection," which
contains dozens of poster imagery produced between the 1970s and
1980s.[16] In addition, the digital archive "Nashriyeh," a rich collection of
Iranian newspapers and magazines, is an excellent source, as it helpfully
divides its holdings chronologically and provides a useful description

for each publication. While the written text of these holdings are in Persian, the complex cover art and photographs within magazines such as *Tehran Musawwar* and *Firdawsi* offers students an invaluable window into the visuals of the revolutionary period.[17]

While the aforementioned resources can aid in developing a vibrant array of primary texts for students and educators, they can also be used comparatively with the imageries of other revolutions. Many recurring motifs and tropes of the iconography of 1979 reveal the notable influence of Russian, Mexican, Cuban, and Chinese revolutionary aesthetics. (As one painter who produced political art in the revolution stated regarding the founders of Mexican muralism: "We knew them better than [we knew] Picasso.")[18]

If we take the visual medium seriously as a mode of historical analysis, it can offer us access and insight to political actors that we might otherwise miss—namely women as active participants and as revolutionary symbols. Most of the available speeches, ideological texts, and secondary accounts feature men's revolutionary activism as the central (and often sole) force of the opposition movement. The photographs and political posters of the period, however, tell a different story: one in which women were not only present in the streets but crucial to the production of revolutionary mythologies and to the incitement of political vigor and spirit.

Let us examine a photograph of two young revolutionary women alongside a male comrade, taken outside of Tehran University in early 1979 and reprinted in a pamphlet of a leftist women's group that May.[19] The women raise V-for-victory fingers in the air, a symbol that proliferated globally in student protests of 1968 and in the liberation struggles of Latin America and the Middle East. This gesture (along with the clenched fist) became a favored one in Iran to relate anti-Pahlavi sentiment to international eyes and a message of solidarity to other anti-imperial and anticolonial movements. Furthermore, the women in this image wear baggy clothing and some sort of loose head covering as they pose alongside their male comrade. Women in leftist circles were expected to dress modestly and obscure their bodies in loose clothing. The concept of "politicized chastity," in which sexual modesty was considered a requirement for women's participation in the movement, echoed Al-e Ahmad's *gharbzadigi* critique. Al-e Ahmad not only identified this "disease of the West" in the "effeminate man" with no personality, but also

WOMEN IN IRAN:
The Part they played in the Revolution

Two women and a man, of the student defense guard at Tehran University, raise guns and V-for-victory fingers. Printed in a pamphlet by the London-based Iranian Women's Group in the spring of 1979. Courtesy of the Siagzar Berelian Collection, International Institute of Social History, Amsterdam, Netherlands.

in *arusak farangi*, or "Western doll," the bourgeois women who painted their faces with makeup and spent money on miniskirts.[20] The concerns over women's bodies designated them as a site upon which the religious and the leftist discourse found common ground: the chaste woman was also the authentic Iranian woman, and as such "chastity" (loose clothing, covered hair), became a revolutionary requirement. The fervid debates over the *hejab* (and ultimately its total imposition) is one of the most notable manifestations of this sentiment in the postrevolutionary state.[21] The photo's reprinting by an Iranian Women's Group in May, in the midst of these debates that began in March 1979, also reflects a particular political aim to assert the centrality of women in the revolution, during a period when their social rights seemed increasingly tenuous.

Interrogating imageries allows students to parcel out central concepts of Iran's revolutionary discourses—such as the movement's anticolonial ancestry, the contemporary intellectual critique of *gharbzadegi*, and religious imagery—as demonstrated above. We often use photographs to serve a *documentary* purpose (in this case, they show us that women were indeed there, front and center in the history of a revolutionary movement that often omits their presence). Yet the use of images can prove to be most fruitful if used *interactively*, by engaging in a textual analysis of the visual source. Students should pay attention to the pose and gestures of the subject, the symbolic objects depicted, and the aesthetic composition. What assumptions does this image challenge? For whom was this image intended? Where, and why, was it reproduced (if at all)? Who, in the moment of publication, saw this image? How might the contemporaneous viewer have been influenced by its symbolism?

The Aftermath

With the fall of the Pahlavi dynasty, the glue that had held the revolution together became undone. On March 8, 1979, thousands of women, both veiled and not veiled, took to the streets of Tehran, protesting a speech by Khomeini that stated women should be covered when entering government buildings. By the end of March in a referendum on the nature of the postrevolutionary state, 98 percent voted "yes" to "Islamic Republic"—even though what exactly that meant was unclear to many who voted for it. By the summer, elections were held for an Assembly of Experts tasked with drafting a constitution. The complex character of the ensuing document, borne out of the revolutionary alliance between seculars, leftists, religious nationalists, Islamist-Marxists, and clerics, haunts the Islamic Republic to this day.

On November 4, a group of students climbed up the US embassy wall and took Americans hostage for 444 days, leading to the fall of the Provisional Government. It also led to the breaking of relations with the United States, the implications of which continue to this day. With the implementation of the constitution in December, the concept of *vilayat-i faqih* ("rule of the jurisprudent"), which had been articulated by Khomeini in a series of lectures in the 1960s, became manifest. Khomeini, the undisputed leader of the last great revolution of the twentieth century, became the Islamic Republic's first "supreme leader." In the summer of 1980, the eight-year war between Iran and Iraq, one of the twentieth century's bloodiest conventional wars, began. Starting in 1981, a wave of brutal repression by Khomeinist factions eliminated the leftist, secular, nationalist members of the original revolutionary coalition, imprisoning, killing, or driving them into exile.

The Iranian Revolution had done what revolutions tend to do: it had simmered, boiled, and then come to a head swiftly. Like other revolutions before it, neither the shape it took before its declared victory nor what it spawned afterward was predictable.

One of the lesser-discussed aspects of this revolution is the postrevolutionary tensions (and violence) between an empowered and mobilized population and revolutionary elite who task themselves with building a new society. This story is no less complicated than the story of the revolution itself. While we have devoted the majority of this essay to the revolution, we end with three texts that capture this immediate tension between the people and the newly born state. Asef Bayat's *Street Politics: Poor People's Movement in Iran*, which focuses on everyday practices of the urban poor and delinks their historical trajectory from that of the revolution's, complicates the oft-repeated trope of the poor and the rural migrant's story to the revolution and beyond.[22] One productive way of talking about this book is to ask students to think about the revolutionary crowds they have seen and heard and to ask them: Where do people go once a revolution is over? What happens to their lives and to their demands?

Carrying forth the story of youth and women is one of the most popular memoirs of the first years of the Islamic Republic: Marjane Satrapi's *Persepolis* (initially written as a series of graphic novels and later adapted into an Oscar-nominated animated film).[23] *Persepolis* presents us with a vision of postrevolutionary violence, war, and displacement, as Satrapi takes the reader from her childhood in the prerevolutionary period to her young adulthood in diaspora. Without sensationalizing her experience, she complicates the Western imagination of Iran as that of hostage takers and ayatollahs issuing *fatwas* against acclaimed writers, instead permitting us a bird's-eye view of the revolution and its aftermath through the eyes of a young girl.[24] But in teaching this wonderful text, it is crucial to analyze the author's subjectivity, while still affirming the work's validity as one legitimate perspective among many. Satrapi's story is that of many secular, nationalist, middle-class families who quickly after the revolution felt they were the true losers of history. By contrast, Farhad Khosrokhavar's "Attitudes of Teenage Girls to the Iranian Revolution" features two teenage girls from the holy city of Qum, who are vocal in their belief that the revolution, the *Islamic* revolution, had delivered them its promise of freedom.[25] Though their aspirations are seemingly quite different, the girls of both texts share more than first meets the eye. The spirit of youthful rebellion imbues their ideas. But their varying subjectivities—based on class, family background, geography—allow them to articulate different relationships to the revolution and the postrevolutionary state. These differences are all part and parcel of the complicated story of the 1979 revolution in Iran.[26]

NOTES

1. Michael M. J. Fischer, *Iran: From Religious Dispute to Revolution* (Madison: University of Wisconsin Press, 1980), 4.

2. Mohsen M. Milani, *The Making of Iran's Islamic Revolution*, 2nd ed. (Boulder, CO: Westview Press, 1994), 112.

3. See Iran-related foreign relations documentation at "Iran 1953: State Department Finally Releases Updated Official History of Mosaddeq Coup," National Security Archive, https://nsarchive.gwu.edu/briefing-book/iran/2017-06-15/iran-1953-state-department-finally-releases-updated-official-history.

4. Donald Wilber, "CIA Clandestine Service History: Overthrow of Premier Mossadegh of Iran, November 1952–August 1953," 1954, https://archive.org/details/CIA-Mossadeq-Iran-1953/page/n24/mode/2up; Mohammad Reza Pahlavi, *Mission for My Country* (London: Hutchinson, 1961); Mohammad Mosaddeq, *Musaddiq's Memoirs*, ed. Homa Katouzian (London: JEBHE, National Movement of Iran, 1988), 422–81.

5. Ali M. Ansari, "The Myth of the White Revolution: Mohammad Reza Shah, 'Modernization,' and the Consolidation of Power," *Middle Eastern Studies* 37, no. 3 (July 2001): 2.

6. Mary Elaine Hegland, *Days of Revolution: Political Unrest in an Iranian Village* (Stanford: Stanford University Press, 2014); Eric J. Hooglund, *Land and Revolution in Iran, 1960–1980* (Austin: University of Texas Press, 1982).

7. Speech delivered in Qum on June 3, 1963, in Ruhullah Khomeini, *Islam and Revolution: Writings and Declarations of Imam Khomeini*, trans. Hamid Algar (Berkeley, CA: Mizan Press, 1981), 177–80.

8. Ruhullah Khomeini, "The Granting of Capitulatory Rights to the US," October 27, 1964, in Khomeini, *Islam and Revolution*, 181–94.

9. Ervand Abrahamian, *The Iranian Mojahedin* (New Haven, CT: Yale University Press, 1989), 1.

10. Many thanks to the students of History 135B: The Middle East and its Revolutions at Brandeis University for coming up with this metaphor.

11. Testimony of Sa'id Mohsen, 1972, in Abrahamian, *Iranian Mojahedin*, 134.

12. A free version of Samad Behrangi's "The Little Black Fish" is available at Iran Chamber Society, http://www.iranchamber.com/literature/sbehrangi/works/the_little_black_fish.php. For an article that places Behrangi, Al-e Ahmad, and Shari'ati in conversation with each other, see Brad Hanson, "The 'Westoxication' of Iran," *International Journal of Middle Eastern Studies* 15, no. 1 (1983): 1–23.

13. Roy Mottahedeh, *The Mantle of the Prophet: Religion and Politics in Iran* (1985; repr., Oxford: Oneworld, 2000).

14. Charles Kurzman raises the "viability" factor as the main reason for the formation of revolutionary masses in the fall of 1978 in *The Unthinkable Revolution* (Cambridge, MA: Harvard University Press, 2004). For university students, Kurzman's shorter essay from 1996 works very well both as a summary of social movement theories and for his introduction of "perceived opportunity" as a causal explanation for the creation of the mass movement in 1978 Iran. See Kurzman, "Structural Opportunity and Perceived Opportunity in Social-Movement Theory: The Iranian Revolution of 1979," *American Sociological Review* 61, no. 1 (February 1996): 153–70.

15. Peter Chelkowski and Hamid Dabashi, *Staging a Revolution: The Art of Persuasion in the Islamic Republic of Iran* (New York: New York University Press, 1999). Also see Hamid Dabashi, *In Search of Lost Causes: Fragmented Allegories of an Iranian Revolution* (Asheville, NC: Black Mountain Press, 2014).

16. "Middle Eastern Posters Collection, 1970s–1990s," University of Chicago Library, 2010, https://www.lib.uchicago.edu/e/scrc/findingaids/view.php?eadid=ICU.SPCL.MEPOSTERS.

17. "Nashriyah: Digital Iranian History," University of Manchester Library, https://luna.manchester.ac.uk/luna/servlet/Manchester~18~18.

18. Nicky Nodjoumi, interview with Talinn Grigor, January 2010, quoted in Talinn Grigor, *Contemporary Iranian Art: From the Street to the Studio* (Chicago: University of Chicago Press, 2014), 33.

19. Photograph printed in leftist pamphlet, n.d., Siagzar Berelian Collection, Box 14, International Institute of Social History, Amsterdam, Netherlands.

20. Afsaneh Najmabadi, "Hazards of Modernity and Morality: Women, State, and Ideology in Contemporary Iran," in *Women, Islam, and the State*, ed. Denis Kandiyoti (London: Palgrave Macmillan, 1991), 48–77.

21. Arielle Gordon, "The Woman with a Gun: A History of the Iranian Revolution's Most Famous Icon" (bachelor's thesis, Brandeis University, 2016).

22. Asef Bayat, *Street Politics: Poor People's Movements in Iran* (New York: Columbia University Press, 1997).

23. Marjane Satrapi, *Persepolis* (New York: Pantheon, 2004).

24. Amy Malek, "Memoir as Iranian Exile Cultural Production: A Case Study of Marjane Satrapi's *Persepolis* Series," *Iranian Studies* 39, no. 3 (2006).

25. Farhad Khosrokhavar, "Attitudes of Teenage Girls to the Iranian Revolution," in *Children in the Muslim Middle East*, ed. Elizabeth Warnock Fernea (Austin: University of Texas Press, 1995), 392–409.

26. We recommend the titles listed below in addition to the resources discussed in the chapter.

KEY RESOURCES

Abrahamian, Ervand. *A History of Modern Iran*. New York: Cambridge University Press, 2008.

Abrhamian, Ervand. "Structural Causes of the Iranian Revolution." *MERIP Reports* 87 (May 1980): 21–26.

Ansari, Ali M. *Modern Iran: The Pahlavis and After*. London: Pearson Education, 2003.

Ghamari-Tabrizi, Behrooz. *Foucault in Iran: Islamic Revolution after the Enlightenment*. Minneapolis: University of Minnesota Press, 2016.

Milani, Mohsen. *The Making of Iran's Islamic Revolution: From Monarchy to Islamic Republic*. 2nd ed. Boulder, CO: Westview Press, 1994.

Nabavi, Negin. *Modern Iran: A History in Documents*. Princeton, NJ: Markus Wiener, 2016.

Paidar, Parvin. *Women and the Political Process in Twentieth-Century Iran*. Cambridge: Cambridge University Press, 1995.

Sreberny-Mohammadi, Annabelle, and Ali Mohammadi. *Small Media, Big Revolution: Communication, Culture, and the Iranian Revolution*. Minneapolis: University of Minnesota Press, 1994.

PART THREE

Understanding and Teaching the Contemporary Middle East

US Foreign Policy in the Middle East

NATHAN J. CITINO

At the beginning, I ask students: "What comes to mind when I say 'the United States and the Middle East'?" They typically respond with a series of stock images: the biblical Holy Land; the desert; oil; the Israeli-Palestinian conflict; Islam; and "terrorism." Such responses provide an opportunity for analyzing student preconceptions. These include a tendency to reduce the US encounter with the Middle East to stereotypes about Arabs and Muslims and to seemingly age-old religious conflicts. Historians have debated whether such stereotypes have influenced US policy. Some have even cited representations of the Middle East in popular culture, from the Disney film *Aladdin* to TV series such as *Homeland* and video games such as *Call of Duty*.[1] A useful activity is discussing how stereotypical images of the Middle East might be related to the US role there. Your discussion can set the stage for later debates about the relative importance of domestic politics, religion, strategy, and economic interests in American policy making. This chapter explains how empire can be used as a framework for studying US relations with the Middle East. As a pedagogical approach, it recommends asking students to analyze particular primary historical sources in order to understand the changing nature of US imperial power and the ways in which American elites have sought to legitimize that power.

Empire as a Framework

Empire provides a useful framework for teaching about the US encounter with the Middle East since the nineteenth century.

The geographic expression "Middle East" was popularized by American naval strategist Alfred Thayer Mahan to describe the place of the region in Britain's empire.[2] The first advantage of an imperial framework is that many students will recognize it. Campaigns by elites to project their power across distances and to impose control over territories, resources, and other peoples, who usually resisted, constitute universal historical themes. In modern history, empires have been the predominant global actors. The United States was born in a revolution against the British Empire, and students who have studied world history will likely have encountered imperialism, whether in Europe, the Americas, Africa, or Asia. Empire therefore offers teachers a way to consider US policies in the Middle East as part of global history and to transcend the particular stereotypes associated with this part of the world.

Empire likewise helps to explain America's changing role within the Middle East. Many different empires have attempted to rule over the diverse societies found in the region encompassing North Africa, the Levant, Arabian Peninsula, Mesopotamia, and western Asia. From the early modern period until the twentieth century, much of this region was governed by the Ottoman Empire, the longest-lived Islamic empire, whose institutions incorporated various Christian, Jewish, and other communities. Initial American encounters during the nineteenth century consisted mainly of trade and missionary enterprises. Religious pilgrims, and even Americans who had never visited, portrayed the Middle East using exotic and biblical imagery. Protestant Christian missionaries made few converts among Ottoman subjects but interacted with intellectuals who were engaged in debates about how to reform the empire. Around the turn of the twentieth century, these reformers associated the US presence with the modern educational institutions that missionaries had established in Ottoman cities such as Istanbul and Beirut. One important US religious community in the Ottoman Empire was the American Colony in Jerusalem. Ask students to review documents and photos about this community available from the Library of Congress.[3] How did Americans describe Ottoman Palestine and imagine their role there? How did that role change with the coming of World War I?

Wilson and Self-Determination

The United States first exercised significant influence in the Middle East following World War I, as the British and French claimed

Ottoman territories according to secret wartime agreements and partitioned this multiethnic, religiously diverse empire into nation-states. At the Paris Peace Conference, President Woodrow Wilson portrayed the United States as an anti-imperial power and promoted self-determination and "autonomous development" for peoples living under Ottoman rule.[4] In 1919, a commission led by Wilson's associates Henry King and Charles Crane toured Ottoman territories claimed by the Europeans. The commission met numerous local petitioners, most of whom called for independence and expressed opposition to Zionism, or the campaign led by European Jews to establish a Jewish state in Palestine. By tracing the commission's route through Ottoman Syria using the interactive map provided by the Oberlin College Library, students can learn more about the commission's work.[5] With whom did the commissioners meet? How did they understand the concept of "self-determination"? Students should appreciate the diversity of this part of the Ottoman Empire and the many parties that contended over its political future. They can also assess the recommendations made in the commission's report.[6]

Leaders such as Egyptian statesman Saʻd Zaghlul sought to capitalize on Wilson's support for self-determination to free Egypt from Britain's control, but the president never intended this principle to apply to non-Europeans. The British and French also opposed self-determination. The British had endorsed Zionism in the 1917 Balfour Declaration, which promoted a "national home" for the Jewish people. This commitment would be enshrined in the mandate for Palestine awarded to Britain by the League of Nations. Mandates were league-sanctioned colonial states, which the European powers claimed to administer for the benefit of their populations. In addition to Palestine, Britain received mandates for Transjordan and Iraq. France governed mandates in Syria and Lebanon. Although they represented the height of European imperialism, mandates as institutions also paid a certain respect to the ideal of self-determination by requiring European powers to show that they were preparing subject peoples for eventual independence. Wilson therefore influenced postwar diplomacy and earned some support for the United States among Middle Eastern leaders, but only because Wilsonianism appeared to promote democratic self-rule.

As the United States developed imperial interests of its own, Americans' attempts at exercising control over the Middle East would increasingly contradict their stated democratic principles. The United States became a major power at a time when anticolonial movements around the world were successfully beginning to challenge imperial authorities. US influence expanded into many places where European empires were in retreat, but this set of circumstances created a challenge in terms of justifying American power. During the twentieth century, that power increased within a world system that came to be made up of ostensibly sovereign, but in reality highly unequal states. Ironically, America grew into the most formidable imperial power ever seen in the Middle East just when empires as political institutions were rapidly losing legitimacy.

Oil, War, and Zionism

The most important US economic interests in the region grew out of the investments American companies made to develop oil resources in the Gulf. Those companies came late to the competition over the region's oil, which Europeans had dominated. In 1928, American firms including Jersey Standard and Standard Oil Company of New York took a minority stake in the Iraq Petroleum Company together with British, French, Dutch, and other stakeholders. Five years later, Standard Oil of California signed an agreement with King 'Abd al-'Aziz ibn Sa'ud of Saudi Arabia. Ibn Sa'ud had been a client of the British Empire and was simultaneously courting British oil interests. His agreement with California was the origin of what would become the Arabian American Oil Company (Aramco), the all-American firm that developed the richest petroleum fields in the world. While Aramco portrayed its role as modernizing rather than colonizing Saudi Arabia, its commitments to training and promoting local labor forces lagged behind those of Anglo-Iranian, the British-owned firm in Iran. The US government nevertheless supported Aramco and even considered acquiring a stake in it during World War II, when petroleum grew in strategic value. Following the war, a sister company to Aramco constructed Tapline, a massive pipeline for transporting oil from eastern Saudi Arabia to the Mediterranean coast. Petroleum from the Gulf became crucial to postwar plans for rebuilding Western Europe and to sustaining US military forces from Europe to East Asia.

World War II made the United States into a global military power and represented a turning point in relations with the Middle East. Not only did the war increase American interest in Saudi oil, but it also brought US influence into other historically British imperial spheres such as Iran, Egypt, and Palestine. After Britain deposed Reza Shah in favor of his pro-Allied son Muhammad Reza Shah, US officials established close ties with Iran's government. Iran became the conduit for transporting American Lend-Lease aid to the Soviet Union. In cooperation with Britain, the United States helped administer the Middle East Supply Centre, which coordinated wartime economic planning from Tehran to Cairo. The politics around Zionism also changed dramatically. Concerned about relations with Arab countries, British officials curtailed Jewish immigration to Palestine. Zionist leaders consequently shifted their diplomatic efforts toward the United States and in 1942 held a conference at New York's Biltmore Hotel calling for the establishment of a Jewish commonwealth in Palestine.[7] The destruction of Europe's Jewish communities by the Nazis put moral force behind this campaign. Both major US political parties endorsed it during the presidential election year 1944. The war therefore increased US interest both in developing Saudi oil and in supporting Zionism. President Franklin D. Roosevelt confronted the contradiction in US policy when he met Ibn Sa'ud in February 1945. The king rejected Roosevelt's appeal to accept further Jewish immigration to Palestine. Roosevelt pledged not to do anything that would prove hostile to the Arabs and to consult both Arabs and Jews before making decisions about Palestine. Translating for FDR was William A. Eddy, a Marine colonel who had a missionary background and worked in wartime intelligence. He also served in the State Department and consulted for Aramco and the CIA. Eddy later published his account of Roosevelt's encounter with Ibn Sa'ud.[8] Ask students to read Eddy's account of the famous meeting. How did FDR appeal to the king? What was Ibn Sa'ud's response? According to Eddy, what happened after FDR's death? Why?

In the Middle East, the United States emerged after the war as the leading power. Officials faced the predicament of legitimizing American influence in an intensely anti-imperial climate. Roosevelt's successor, Harry Truman, and his advisers confronted this challenge as they shaped policies toward America's wartime allies. Britain admitted that it had failed to reconcile Arab and Jewish political claims within its Palestine mandate. The British appealed to Truman to establish a commission to study the issue of Jewish immigration into Palestine, which resulted in a recommendation to admit a hundred thousand Jewish refugees. Britain announced its intention to withdraw from the mandate and to hand the issue to the new United Nations Organization. Truman's administration displayed support for anti-imperialism by pressuring France to withdraw its forces from Syria and Lebanon, even as Washington backed the restoration of the French empire in Indochina. But it was in relations with the Soviet Union that the United States defined the justification for its own postwar empire. The United States assumed Britain's longstanding role contesting Russian influence in Iran. When Soviet leader Josef Stalin refused to withdraw troops from Iran and pressured the shah into granting an oil concession, Truman's administration confronted the Soviets at the UN. Britain also announced that it could no longer subsidize governments in Greece, where the government faced internal communist resistance, and Turkey, which was under pressure from Moscow. In a 1947 speech, Truman convinced Congress to contribute hundreds of millions of dollars to those two governments by stating that it should be US policy "to support free peoples who are resisting attempted subjugation by armed minorities or by outside pressures."[9] Ask students to analyze the language Truman used in his speech. Why did he describe his foreign policy in this way? The Iranian, Greek, and Turkish cases fit into an emerging pattern of confrontation with the Soviet Union, in which US officials portrayed the expansion of American power in defensive terms as the "containment" of communism.

The changing politics and costs of empire in the twentieth century help account for American policies, rather than any fundamental difference between the United States and other powers. In fact, many US policies resembled those that Britain and France had previously developed to govern their mandates. By requiring those powers to demonstrate that they were developing mandates economically while preparing them for independence, the League of Nations raised the costs associated with having an empire. In response, Britain granted independence to Iraq in 1932 but sought to maintain access to Iraq's oil through private companies and kept control over its military bases. The United States employed a similar approach toward Saudi Arabia by supporting Aramco and maintaining an airbase at Dhahran. Like Britain, whose Palestine mandate fostered a Jewish Homeland, the Truman administration sought political and strategic advantages by supporting Zionism while also trying to cooperate with Arab governments. France justified control over its mandates on the basis of a civilizing mission to impart universal republican values. The United States would similarly associate American

influence with economic development and modernization. This promise to improve poor societies replaced an explicit ideology of white
supremacy (the "white man's burden"), which had previously been used
to justify Western imperialism before falling into disrepute. Officials
and development experts promoted the United States as the exemplar
of modernity, a claim that Arab travelers and other observers of American society accepted selectively and frequently disputed.[10] American
officials did resort to military intervention whenever they felt it necessary. Yet global circumstances after 1945 tended to act as a check on the
use of American military power. These circumstances included the growing number of postcolonial states, which wielded influence through
the UN to eliminate the vestiges of colonialism. Just as importantly, the
Soviet Union served as an economic and ideological rival to the United
States, one that possessed nuclear weapons.

America's foreign policy elite disagreed over how to define the country's interests even as they shared a belief in the necessity of projecting
US power. An intense debate pitted the desire to preserve access to oil
and military bases in Arab countries against the commitment of some
Americans to Zionism. Politicians from both major parties, Zionist organizations, labor movements, and certain Christian churches supported
Zionism out of a humanitarian impulse to create a haven for Jews following the Holocaust. Some cited Jews' biblical claim to the Holy Land or
argued that Israel could serve as a strategic ally. Opponents, including
oil company executives and diplomats, insisted that recognizing Israel
would jeopardize access to oil in Arab countries. Others argued that
given the Arab majority in Palestine, a Jewish state could be created
only through violence and that supporting Zionism therefore contradicted stated American respect for self-determination. Despite Roosevelt's assurances to Ibn Saʿud, President Truman first approved a UN
proposal to divide Palestine into an Arab and a Jewish state, and then
recognized Israel in 1948. Diplomats such as Ambassador Loy Hender-
son and Secretary of State George C. Marshall had lobbied Truman
against recognition. But in an election year, when the president was
concerned with securing Jewish American votes in key states such as
New York, Truman sided with his political advisers Clark Clifford and
David Niles. Students can participate in this consequential debate using
documents and oral histories made available by the Truman Library.[11]
Following recognition, American leaders never seriously reconsidered
supporting Israel, which became a bipartisan commitment backed by

effective political lobbying. As one historian notes, Israel received about $65 billion between 1948 and 1996, "making it the largest recipient of US foreign aid."[12]

The United States would broker negotiations following Arab-Israeli military conflicts in 1948, 1956, 1967, and 1973. These negotiations sought to replace the ceasefires established between Israel and the Arab states following the 1948 war with more permanent agreements. They also unsuccessfully tried to resolve the status of some 750,000 Palestinian Arab refugees who had fled or were driven from their homes during Israel's establishment. Many refugees and their descendants settled in camps located in neighboring Arab countries. In June 1967, Israel occupied additional territories including East Jerusalem, the Gaza Strip, Sinai Peninsula, the West Bank of the Jordan, and the Golan Heights. As a result, the focus of US diplomacy changed from addressing the issues raised by Israel's establishment in 1948, including Palestinian dispossession, to negotiating the status of the territories that Israel occupied in 1967. The debate over US interests shifted further in 1973 after Saudi Arabia and other Arab petroleum-exporting states embargoed oil going to the United States in retaliation for American military aid to Israel. The increase in oil prices created economic problems in the United States and other countries. Successive rounds of negotiations sought to reconcile firm support for Israel with American interests among the Arab states. This "peace process" may therefore be understood not primarily as the pursuit of peace for its own sake, but instead as a long-term effort at managing contending interpretations of American interests in the Middle East. The effect has been to perpetuate the Israeli-Palestinian conflict rather than resolve it.

Decolonization and the Cold War

The intersection between anticolonialism and the Cold War meant that the United States could not be seen to act in the conspicuously aggressive ways that had characterized previous imperial strategies. For instance, the United States could not seek to annex overseas territories as it had done a half century earlier in the Philippines. After 1945 anticolonial leaders in the Middle East and North Africa, as in other regions, led movements against Western imperialism and sought to establish sovereign states, a process known as decolonization. In the Middle East, popular anti-imperial leaders included Iranian prime minister Mohammad Mossadegh and Egyptian president Gamal Abdel Nasser. American and British intelligence agents secretly engineered Mossadegh's overthrow after the prime minister nationalized British oil interests in Iran. Students can learn about this operation from the CIA's report.[13] Beginning with the 1955 Meeting of Afro-Asian States at Bandung, Indonesia, Nasser forged ties with leaders in other decolonizing regions. He defied the United States and its allies the following year first by nationalizing the Suez Canal after the United States withdrew its support for Egypt's Aswan High Dam project, and then by surviving an invasion of Egypt by Britain, France, and Israel. Students can hear Nasser's perspective about the Arab-Israeli conflict and the role of the United States in a later interview conducted in English.[14] The French fought a bloody war against the Front de Libération Nationale (FLN), an anticolonial movement in Algeria that eventually won independence. The FLN owed its success partly to the recognition it won at the UN for the legitimacy of its struggle. Though France was an ally, the American delegation at the UN withheld its full support out of concern the United States would be associated with imperialism. The strength of anticolonialism influenced the forms that American power assumed in the Middle East.

Like the United States, the USSR claimed to be an anti-imperial power and offered military and economic aid to postcolonial states. The Soviets similarly tried to benefit from the retreat of European empires but promoted a communist development model that directly clashed with American capitalism. In this context, acting like a traditional imperial power created serious political liabilities. So did overtly supporting imperialism by other countries. Such policies would contradict US claims to promote democracy and would alienate newly independent states, which might then become Soviet clients. It was for this reason that the United States opposed the tripartite invasion of Egypt described above and forced Britain, France, and Israel—all US allies—to withdraw. During the conflict, the Soviet leader Nikita Khrushchev threatened to use nuclear weapons against the aggressors. Afterward, Nasser forged closer ties with Moscow and partnered with the Soviets to build the Aswan High Dam. Regional actors who accepted aid from the Soviet Union and communist China tended to voice the greatest support for anticolonialism while opposing US cooperation with Israel. Those actors included Egypt, Syria, Iraq, Algeria, South Yemen, Libya, and the Palestine Liberation Organization (PLO). For its part, the United States pursued strategic alliances such as the Central Treaty Organization, maintained military bases with cooperation from pro-US governments, and provided them with military and economic assistance. Washington portrayed these policies as defensive measures to help weaker states resist Soviet communism, rather than as self-interested assertions of US power. In 1957, President Dwight D. Eisenhower proclaimed that the United States would assist Middle Eastern states resist "International Communism."[15] When he sent marines to Lebanon the following year and coordinated this action with British intervention in Jordan, he characterized the operation as helping Lebanon defend its independence. As the Mossadegh example illustrates, American officials also deployed covert operations to destabilize or replace unfriendly leaders. Officials resorted to such tactics throughout the Third World, because they seemed to offer the United States a way of controlling governments without being labeled an imperial power.[16] But these operations seldom remained secret and often had negative long-term consequences, which could take the form of an anti-American backlash, as occurred in Iran.

Toward an Empire in the Gulf

In retrospect, it appears that the forces acting to restrain US imperialism in the Middle East diminished in the later years of the twentieth century. These changes made it possible for American officials to adopt more interventionist strategies. One reason is that the "peace process" marginalized the Soviet Union in the Middle East while reducing the negative political consequences for the United States of supporting Israel. By the 1970s, the United States regarded Israel, which possessed nuclear weapons, as an important Cold War ally. Secretary of State Henry Kissinger largely excluded the Soviets from peace talks following the 1973 Arab-Israeli war. President Jimmy Carter later negotiated the Camp David Accords between Israeli prime minister Menachem Begin and Egyptian president Anwar Sadat. The ensuing peace treaty retired Egypt, the largest Arab state, from the conflict with Israel. By providing Egypt with billions of dollars in assistance, the United States further drew Egypt away from the Soviets. But these developments had serious regional consequences. Documents from the Jimmy Carter Presidential Library can help students understand the implications of the Accords. Note especially their achievement of peace between Egypt and Israel while leaving the Palestinian issue unresolved.[17]

What political pressures were placed on Carter (Document 3)? What were Sadat's concerns (Document 6)? How did the envisioned Framework for Peace signed at Camp David[18] differ from the treaty concluded between Egypt and Israel?[19]

The Persian Gulf, a last bastion of Britain's Middle East empire, became the focus of American interventions. The end of America's war in Vietnam, where the United States had inherited France's imperial role, made it practical for officials to contemplate military operations elsewhere. After Britain withdrew from the Gulf in the early 1970s, Presidents Richard Nixon, Gerald Ford, and Jimmy Carter relied principally on the shah of Iran to sustain order. In 1979, the shah was overthrown in a revolution led by Ayatollah Khomeini, a serious challenge to US power dramatized by the taking of hostages at the American embassy in Tehran.[20] The Soviet Union also invaded Afghanistan, which Carter interpreted as a threat to oil resources. He issued the Carter Doctrine, proclaiming that "any attempt by an outside force to gain control of the Persian Gulf region will be regarded as an assault on the vital interests of the United States" and "will be repelled by the use of any means necessary including military force."[21] His advisers discussed expanding US military aid and bases in the Gulf and western Asia in the way that previous administrations had done in Europe and East Asia.

These events led to the consolidation of America's empire in the Middle East. First, the Iranian Revolution and the Iran-Iraq war led the US to increase its presence in the Gulf. The United States supported Iraq's leader, Saddam Hussein, although Ronald Reagan's administration also illegally sold arms to Iran in an effort to gain the release of US hostages held in Lebanon by pro-Iranian groups. Students can study this episode using documents compiled by the National Security Archive.[22] The US Navy began patrolling the Gulf as part of a mission to protect oil tankers. In 1987, an American frigate was attacked by Iraqi aircraft, and the following year, missiles from the USS *Vincennes* shot down an Iranian civilian airliner. Second, the United States cooperated with Saudi Arabia and Pakistan to funnel billions of dollars to insurgents fighting against the Soviet forces occupying Afghanistan. This policy contributed to an Afghan civil war and to the rise of Islamist militants who would turn against US interests once the Soviets withdrew. Following a devastating war against Iran, Saddam Hussein resented the unwillingness of other Gulf Arab states to help defray Iraq's costs. He therefore claimed Kuwait as an Iraqi province and sent his forces to occupy it. This led to the largest US military operation since the Vietnam War, in which President George H. W. Bush dispatched hundreds of thousands of US troops to defend Saudi Arabia and eject Iraqi forces from Kuwait. The Soviet Union, heading toward collapse, was not in any position to object. An American-sponsored resolution at the UN authorized the war.

The century ended with the illusion of a "pax Americana." "Victory" in the Cold War appeared to signal the universal triumph of liberal capitalism, with Democrats and Republicans similarly embracing globalization sustained by American military power. In the Middle East, President Bill Clinton promoted the Oslo agreements, the most far-reaching attempt yet to address the Israeli-Palestinian conflict and mitigate the contradictions in US policy. With Clinton presiding, PLO leader Yasir Arafat and Israeli prime minister Yitzhak Rabin shook hands on the White House lawn in 1993. But their mutual recognition did not lead to peace. Oslo never promised Palestinians a fully sovereign state, and Israel only accelerated the building of settlements in the occupied territories. Rabin was assassinated two years later, while Palestinian terrorist attacks turned the Israeli public against Oslo and in favor of politicians such as Benjamin Netanyahu, who opposed compromise. In the Gulf, both Iran and Iraq were under US economic sanctions. American aircraft patrolled a "no-fly" zone in northern Iraq, enabling a Kurdish quasi-state to emerge. Officials portrayed US policies as responses to so-called rogue states such as Iran, Iraq, and Libya, as well as to the threat of "terrorism." Americans had applied the latter term to a range of militant activities since the 1960s, including airline hijackings by secular Palestinian revolutionaries and attacks on civilians such as the killing of Israeli athletes at the 1972 Munich Olympics. They also applied this term to Iranian-supported Islamist groups in Lebanon that opposed the 1982 Israeli invasion and that took hostages and bombed US targets in Beirut.[23] Attacks on aviation and "soft" targets associated with Americans continued during the 1980s. In 1998, two US embassies in east Africa were the target of bomb attacks carried out by terrorists with backgrounds in the Afghan anti-Soviet resistance. Ad hoc alignments between rogue states and terrorist groups appeared to threaten American personnel and assets but did not represent any serious challenge to US imperial power.

The attacks of September 11, 2001, when terrorists crashed hijacked planes into the World Trade Center in New York, the Pentagon, and a field in Pennsylvania, killing almost three thousand people, are often portrayed as a historic watershed. They were in the sense that they turned the inchoate threat of terrorism into the rationale for a sustained American military presence in the Middle East whose scope exceeded that of any previous empire. President George W. Bush put every nation on notice declaring that "you are either with us, or you are with the terrorists."[24] Students can usefully compare Bush's speech following 9/11 with earlier presidential statements about regional threats, including those previously cited by Truman, Eisenhower, and Carter. What continuities and discontinuities characterized US policy after 9/11? Following in Soviet footsteps, US forces invaded Afghanistan, where an Islamist government led by the Taliban harbored the group that planned 9/11. Osama bin Laden, a Saudi dissident, had opposed the presence of US troops in Saudi Arabia in 1991. Al-Qaʻida, his radical Islamist group, consisted of Afghan veterans and others opposed to the United States and its regional clients. Despite Bush's insistence that the United States was not at war with Islam, the presumed civilizational threat posed to the West by Islam served a similar purpose legitimizing US power in the Middle East as the ideological threat of Soviet communism had during the Cold War. The 9/11 attacks also strengthened the hand of those in the United States, including neoconservatives in Bush's administration, who had long advocated a more interventionist policy and closer alignment with Israel. Many Evangelical Christians also supported Bush and embraced Israel as fulfilling biblical prophecy. Falsely asserting that Saddam Hussein had nuclear, biological, and chemical weapons, as well as ties to al-Qaʻida, the Bush administration invaded Iraq, deposing Saddam and occupying the country. Resulting Iraqi deaths likely reached into the hundreds of thousands. The consequences are still unfolding, but it is clear that while the invasion destabilized Iraq and other states such as Syria, it also strengthened Iran and gave rise to new threats such as Daesh (or ISIS). A generation has come of age in the United States assuming that war is the country's normal state, and some of your students may well be or become veterans. Your class can explore veterans' accounts of their experiences recorded by the Library of Congress.[25] Consider, too, accounts by Iraqis who by 2003 had already experienced a generation of war.[26]

At the dawn of the twentieth century, Wilson had criticized British and French imperialism in the Middle East and called for "self-determination." One hundred years later, Americans presided over a regional empire of their own. In a self-perpetuating logic that would have been familiar to those earlier powers, the need to confront resistance to American interventions provided the rationale for ongoing and new interventions. Although Barack Obama campaigned on the basis of winding down the 9/11 wars, his policies as president followed this logic. Obama renewed the war in Afghanistan, pursued "regime change" in Libya, and expanded the use of special forces and armed drones that targeted "terrorists" while killing numerous civilians. Donald Trump, Obama's successor as president, claimed to oppose nation building of the sort attempted in Iraq, but Trump also vowed to defeat Daesh. The United States now has troops in dozens of countries across the Middle East, Africa, and beyond. Students can map the numbers of US military personnel in given countries over time using data provided by the Department of Defense.[27] In an echo of the Cold War, and a reminder of past imperial rivalries, Obama and Trump faced Russian intervention on behalf of Syria. What is especially striking, a century after Wilson went to Paris, is how thoroughly the United States has replaced Britain as the Middle East's leading imperial power. The US government has promoted billions of dollars in weapons sales to the Gulf monarchies not only for strategic reasons but also as a way of recovering a portion of the petrodollars earned by these exporters of oil and natural gas. The US Navy's Fifth Fleet is based at Bahrain, former site of Britain's imperial representative in the Gulf, and the United States maintains a major air base at al-Udeid in Qatar, another former British client. An imperial framework therefore situates the United States within the history of empires in the Middle East. This approach helps overcome student preconceptions that reduce the Middle East to cultural stereotypes and timeless religious conflicts. Studying American foreign policy in the context of empire also challenges claims that the United States plays an exceptional, democratic role in the world.

NOTES

1. See Douglas Little, *US versus Them: The United States, Radical Islam, and the Rise of the Green Threat* (Chapel Hill: University of North Carolina Press, 2016).

2. See Osamah F. Khalil, *America's Dream Palace: Middle East Expertise and the Rise of the National Security State* (Cambridge, MA: Harvard University Press, 2016), 1–3.

3. *The American Colony in Jerusalem*, https://www.loc.gov/exhibits/american colony/.

4. See point 12 of President Woodrow Wilson's Fourteen Points, Avalon Project, Yale Law School, http://avalon.law.yale.edu/20th_century/wilson14.asp.

5. Interactive Map, King-Crane Commission Digital Collection, http://www2.oberlin.edu/library/digital/king-crane/map.html; for instance, click on the port of Jaffa (#1) to reveal photos and documents.

6. George Antonius, *The Arab Awakening: The Story of the Arab National Movement* (Philadelphia: J. P. Lippincott, 1939), 443–58 (appendix H), copy available at the Internet Archive, https://archive.org/details/McGillLibrary-rbsc_isl_arab-awakening_DS636A461939-16015.

7. "Zionist Congresses: The Biltmore Conference (May 6–11, 1942)," Jewish Virtual Library, http://www.jewishvirtuallibrary.org/the-biltmore-conference-1942.

8. William A. Eddy, *F.D.R. Meets Ibn Saud* (Washington, DC: Amideast, 1954).

9. Harry S. Truman, "Special Message to the Congress on Greece and Turkey: The Truman Doctrine," March 12, 1947, https://www.presidency.ucsb.edu/documents/special-message-the-congress-greece-and-turkey-the-truman-doctrine.

10. See Kamal Abdel-Malik, ed., *America in an Arab Mirror: Images of America in Arabic Travel Literature; An Anthology, 1895–1995* (New York: St. Martin's Press, 2000).

11. Recognition of the State of Israel, Harry S. Truman Library and Museum, https://www.trumanlibrary.org/whistlestop/study_collections/israel/large/.

12. Yaacov Bar-Siman-Tov, "The United States and Israel since 1948: A 'Special Relationship'?," *Diplomatic History* 22 (April 1998): 231.

13. Malcolm Byrne, ed., *The Secret CIA History of the Iran Coup, 1953*, National Security Archive, Electronic Briefing Book no. 28, November 29, 2000, https://nsarchive2.gwu.edu/NSAEBB/NSAEBB28/.

14. "Gamal Abdel Nasser 1969 New York Interview in English," YouTube, August 2, 2015, https://www.youtube.com/watch?v=kYosYeesTYo.

15. Dwight D. Eisenhower, "Special Message to the Congress on the Situation in the Middle East," January 5, 1957, American Presidency Project, https://www.presidency.ucsb.edu/documents/special-message-the-congress-the-situation-the-middle-east.

16. See Douglas Little, "Mission Impossible: The CIA and the Cult of Covert Action in the Middle East," *Diplomatic History* 28 (November 2004): 663–701.

17. "Camp David Accords: Twenty-Five Documents after Twenty-Five Years," Jimmy Carter Presidential Library and Museum, https://www.jimmycarterlibrary.gov/research/twenty_five_documents_after_twenty_five_years.

18. Framework for Peace in the Middle East, September 17, 1978, https://peacemaker.un.org/sites/peacemaker.un.org/files/EG%20IL_780917_Framework%20for%20peace%20in%20the%20MiddleEast%20agreed%20at%20Camp%20David.pdf.

19. "Peace Treaty between Israel and Egypt," March 26, 1979, Israel Ministry of Foreign Affairs, http://www.mfa.gov.il/mfa/foreignpolicy/peace/guide/pages/israel-egypt%20peace%20treaty.aspx.

20. David Farber, *Taken Hostage: The Iran Hostage Crisis and America's First Encounter with Radical Islam* (Princeton, NJ: Princeton University Press, 2005).

21. Jimmy Carter, "The State of the Union Address Delivered before a Joint Session of the Congress," January 23, 1980, American Presidency Project, https://www.presidency.ucsb.edu/documents/the-state-the-union-address-delivered-before-joint-session-the-congress.

22. See "The Iran-Contra Affair 30 Years Later: A Milestone in Post-Truth Politics," National Security Archive, November 25, 2016, https://nsarchive.gwu.edu/briefing-book/iran/2016-11-25/iran-contra-affair-30-years-later-milestone-post-truth-politics.

23. See Kai Bird, *The Good Spy: The Life and Death of Robert Ames* (New York: Crown, 2014).

24. George W. Bush, "Address before a Joint Session of the Congress on the United States Response to the Terrorist Attacks of September 11," September 20, 2001, American Presidency Project, https://www.presidency.ucsb.edu/documents/address-before-joint-session-the-congress-the-united-states-response-the-terrorist-attacks.

25. "Experiencing War: Stories from the Veterans History Project," https://www.loc.gov/vets/stories/ex-war-afghanistaniraq.html.

26. See Dina Rizk Khoury, *Iraq in Wartime: Soldiering, Martyrdom, and Remembrance* (New York: Cambridge University Press, 2013).

27. See tables under "Military and Civilian Personnel by Service/Agency by State/Country," https://www.dmdc.osd.mil/appj/dwp/dwp_reports.jsp.

Key Resources

Gardner, Lloyd. *Three Kings: The Rise of an American Empire in the Middle East after World War II*. New York: New Press, 2009.

Khalil, Osamah F. *America's Dream Palace: Middle East Expertise and the Rise of the National Security State*. Cambridge, MA: Harvard University Press, 2016.

Laron, Guy. *The Six-Day War: The Breaking of the Middle East*. New Haven, CT: Yale University Press, 2017.

Little, Douglas. *American Orientalism: The United States and the Middle East since 1945*. 3rd ed. Chapel Hill: University of North Carolina Press, 2008.

Little, Douglas. *US versus Them: The United States, Radical Islam, and the Rise of the Green Threat*. Chapel Hill: University of North Carolina Press, 2016.

Makdisi, Ussama. *Faith Misplaced: The Broken Promise of US-Arab Relations, 1820–2001*. New York: PublicAffairs, 2010.

McAlister, Melani. *Epic Encounters: Culture, Media, and US Interests in the Middle East since 1945*. Rev. ed. Berkeley: University of California Press, 2005.

Patrick, Andrew. *America's Forgotten Middle East Initiative: The King-Crane Commission of 1919*. New York: I. B. Tauris, 2015.

Vitalis, Robert. *America's Kingdom: Mythmaking on the Saudi Oil Frontier*. Stanford, CA: Stanford University Press, 2007.

Yaqub, Salim. *Imperfect Strangers: Americans, Arabs, and US-Middle East Relations in the 1970s*. Ithaca, NY: Cornell University Press, 2016.

America, Oil, and War in the Middle East

TOBY CRAIG JONES

Middle Eastern oil has enchanted global powers and global capital since the early twentieth century. Its allure has been particularly powerful for the United States. Over the course of the twentieth century and the beginning of the twenty-first, preserving the security of allies in the Persian Gulf, most importantly Saudi Arabia, and of the flow of oil were among the United States' chief political-economic concerns.[1] The pursuit of American power in the Gulf has been fraught with peril, however, proving costly in both blood and treasure. Security, if that is measured by the absence of conflict, has been elusive. Since the late 1970s the Gulf has been rocked by revolution and almost permanent war. Securing the Persian Gulf and protecting its region's oil producers increasingly meant more direct forms of US intervention.

Making sense of why America has gone to war in the region can be challenging. Those who have officially advocated for war have done so in ways that appear to respond to urgent crises such as Iraq's invasion of Kuwait in 1990 or that strategically respond to generational struggles like the Cold War. At other moments, such as the American invasion of Iraq in 2003, the justifications for American war-making included fears about terrorism and Iraq's potential to use weapons of mass destruction. This chapter suggests a broader view and encourages teachers and students alike to reflect on one particular reason for so much American interest and military commitment to the Persian Gulf: oil. To understand oil's importance, however, it is necessary to reflect on how oil was connected to strategic thinking and foreign policy objectives. Protecting

Middle Eastern oil, the largest site of oil reserves in the world, has never been about protecting low prices—either of oil or the things it makes, such as gasoline for our daily consumption. The story is more complex.

This chapter encourages teachers to emphasize the political-economic aspects of oil and American policy. It narrates a longer history and argues that rather than seeing differences in Cold War policy compared to post–Cold War policy, teachers should look for connections between them. My thinking about how to approach this begins with President Jimmy Carter's State of the Union address in January 1980 in which he mapped out what would become the bedrock of American policy and war fighting for more than a generation in the Middle East. Better known later in life as an advocate for peace, Carter's comments in 1980 set a bellicose course for American policy in the Middle East. Teachers interested in framing discussion of later military interventions should encourage student readers to start with what has come to be known as the Carter Doctrine.

One risk in prioritizing strategic thinking and politics in our teaching is that economic concerns can fade away. To link politics and money, I also encourage teachers and students to think about the business of war in the Middle East and the potential for profit embedded in that region's destruction. Below, I take up the matter of arms sales by the United States to its partners in the Persian Gulf. Students can spend time tracing and making sense of the magnitude of weapons sales to places such as Saudi Arabia. Why sell so many weapons to a place that has not been able to defend itself? What kinds of weapons are sold and who benefits? These are questions worth exploring for students. It is the case that the drive to profit from war is routinely hidden in public discussions that stoke anxiety, fear, and potential calamity. But the business of war in the Middle East has long been hugely profitable for Western— American and European—arms dealers. These weapons sales may appear periodically in public discussion, usually at the moment agreements about them are made. It is important to establish that weapons sales are structural and permanent features of the regional order, and, that they make the United States a central actor rather than a peripheral one in regional affairs. Just as important, should teachers incorporate various sources such as the Stockholm International Peace Research Institute (SIPRI) or even US State Department data on weapons sales, it will be clear that the business of weapons is not a partisan one.

The Strategic Logic of Militarism

The United States is not the only Western power with a history of war in the oil rich Persian Gulf. In a rush to secure and expand their own supplies in the region, the British took control of Iraq in 1918, from which they projected power for several decades.[2] Unlike their predecessors, the United States did not wage war out of old-fashioned imperial calculation or ambition. America's oil wars were not about establishing direct control over oil fields. Nor were they about liberation or freedom. Instead, they have been primarily about protecting friendly oil producers. The objective was not necessarily to guarantee that Middle Eastern oil made its way to the United States, although meeting basic domestic energy needs remained a vital part of the broader calculation. Keeping prices stable (not low) and keeping friendly regimes in power were more important.

The pattern of militarism that began in the Persian Gulf in the 1970s has partly been the product of the deliberate militarization of and American support for brutal *and* vulnerable authoritarian regimes. Massive weapons sales to oil autocrats and the commitment to building a geopolitical military order in the Gulf that depended on them and empowered them resulted in a highly weaponized but also highly fragile balance of power. And from the 1970s, oil states have faced repeated internal and external threats. Using the SIPRI database, teachers and students alike can track the scale of weapons provided by the United States and others to help regional allies address these threats.

Oil producers have either been directly engaged in or faced the imminent prospect of domestic unrest, invasion, and regional or civil war. Domestic and regional conflict has had much to do, of course, with their particular internal political problems, only some of which were the result of outside intervention. The history of militarization that began in earnest under the watch of the United States exacerbated and accelerated these uncertainties and helped further destabilize them and the region. Rather than stability, the United States' efforts to assert its hegemony in the Persian Gulf, and the desire to shore up a geopolitical order that many believed would best serve US material interests, instead helped produce the opposite.

The United States' late twentieth-century approach to oil and the Persian Gulf was both a sign of its superpower status and of its limits. What began as an effort to build up and empower surrogates, clients in the Gulf who would do the bidding of the United States, proved instead to be the gateway for a more direct projection of American military power. Jimmy Carter warned during his 1980 State of the Union address that the United States would use "any means necessary, including military force" to safeguard its "vital interests" in the Gulf. This has clearly come to pass.

The late 1960s and early 1970s marked the transformative moment in the United States' approach to security and militarism in the Persian Gulf. In January 1968 the British government announced an end to its long-time imperial presence, finally withdrawing its forces in 1971. The move unsettled American policy makers who were anxious about a potential power vacuum. Other pressures began to mount around the same time. In the decade leading up to the British announcement, government officials in oil-producing countries had already begun to bristle against the neocolonial dominance and unfair practices of the major oil companies, which exercised monopolistic control over the means of production and pricing for much of the twentieth century. In 1960 several major oil producers established the Organization of Petroleum Exporting Countries (OPEC) in a gambit to drive prices higher. At its founding, OPEC achieved little. The assertiveness of the oil producers would grow by the 1970s, however, as the major producers began to nationalize the operations of the oil companies.

Contradictions in America's broader Middle East security strategy would challenge its efforts to maintain friendly relations with the region's oil producers. The United States struggled to balance its support for Israel with its support for the region's oil producers, who had long considered the United States' Israel-friendly foreign policy as an irritant. In 1973 their irritation transformed into outrage. During the 1973 October War, when Egypt launched a surprise attack on Israeli forces in an effort to recapture territory in the Sinai Peninsula, Gulf oil producers were infuriated when the United States helped reequip the beleaguered Israeli military in the course of battle. Led by Saudi Arabia, oil producers and oil companies orchestrated a weak embargo of the United States.[3] One outcome of this was the oil-producing countries finally seized direct control over production and pricing mechanisms from the giant Western oil conglomerates, leading to an increase in oil revenues. The embargo troubled American officials, who struggled to re-strengthen relations with oil-producing allies after the war. But the anxieties generated as a result of the contradictions of American policy on Israel and oil and during the course of the embargo did not lead to a reconsideration of regional security policy. Rather, the United States deepened its commitment to militarization.

Indeed, in subsequent years, US officials and weapons manufacturers would come to rely on the rising tide of oil revenues to construct a new geopolitical arrangement and new forms of American hegemony in the Persian Gulf. The waves of nationalization did help dismantle an older geopolitical framework that had served American oil interests in the past, a framework in which Western oil companies, allied cooperatively with their home governments, exercised direct control over Middle Eastern oil. Regional governments fought to achieve a modicum of equity in profit sharing from the sale of oil, but they remained almost entirely beholden to the companies for the extraction, refining, distribution, and sale of petroleum. It was an arrangement that enjoyed the full support of the US government. Companies such as Aramco that operated in Saudi Arabia not only cooperated closely with the US government but often had members of the American political and intelligence communities on its payroll.[4]

The convergence of corporate and political interests around oil had profound consequences on the character of political authority in the region. The United States had demonstrated its preference for autocrats in 1953, when the CIA orchestrated a coup to overthrow Mohammad Mossadegh, the democratically elected prime minister of Iran, in order to bring back the shah.[5] The oil companies did their part in strengthening authoritarians elsewhere in the region. During the 1950s and 1960s both US government officials and oil company executives feared the potential power of Arab nationalism, considering it a threat to American Cold War and material interests in the Persian Gulf.[6] Fears about Arab nationalists and the possibility that they might nationalize Arab oil and refuse to supplicate to American and Western interests were pervasive in the US government and in the board rooms of the oil companies.

Although direct politico-corporate control over Persian Gulf oil passed in the 1970s, the authoritarians remained. The United States government would seek to do new kinds of business with them, this time by arming them and positioning them as surrogates for American interests and power. Richard Nixon provided the impetus for the new militarization strategy in 1969. Under pressure to guide the United States out of the quagmire in Vietnam, the Nixon Doctrine called on American allies to bear a greater role in providing for their own defense.[7] US policy makers observed the doctrine in the Gulf by keeping American military forces "over the horizon." American energies focused primarily on strengthening the hands of Iran and Saudi Arabia, propping them up as the "twin pillars" of the United States' new regional geopolitical strategy. Between 1970 and 1979 the United States committed to over $22 billion in arms sales to Iran, accounting for roughly three-quarters of all of Iran's weapons purchased in the decade. Sales commitments to Saudi Arabia were more modest at just under $3.5 billion for the decade, but still a significant development considering the United States only started selling weapons to the kingdom in 1972.[8]

The Perils of Militarization

The consequences of the new militarization policy were considerable. Although they were not immediately destabilizing, they did help lay the foundation for an era of violence and insecurity that would follow. As militarization became a regional phenomenon, it also resulted in a growing boldness on the part of Gulf dictators, who became increasingly assertive and threatening to one another. Emerging threats in the Gulf were the result of complicated domestic and regional politics, only a few of which the United States would directly engage. However, both emboldened and embattled leaders sought security through the purchase of billions of dollars of weapons, which the American government and the American war industry were happy to provide. The result was a boom for the military-industrial complex and the massive militarization of the region. By the end of the decade the largest oil producers in the Gulf were taking part in a full-blown arms race. The Soviet Union pitched in by committing to sell over $10 billion in weapons to Iraq, its main client in the region and principal rival to Iran.[9] While the Soviet Union helped encourage regional militarization, the United States did the most to facilitate the pattern. Between 1975 and 1979 Iran, Iraq, and Saudi Arabia purchased 56 percent of all the weapons sold in the Middle East and almost one-quarter of global arms purchases.[10] Lee Hamilton, a leading Democratic congressman, warned in a 1973 statement on the floor of Congress about the potentially excessive nature of arms sales to the region. He remarked that "the net impression left . . . is that we are willing to sell just about everything these Persian Gulf states want and will buy."[11] And they did. Iran proved particularly keen to acquire as much high-tech military weaponry as possible. The shah purchased the newest weapons systems available from American manufacturers, including seventy-nine F-14 Tomcat fighter jets, the US Navy's premier fighter, in 1974.[12] By the middle of the 1970s, the American notion of security in the Persian Gulf was based almost on entirely on the ability of oil producers to purchase the machines of war.

The militarization of the Persian Gulf exacerbated existing instabilities and hastened an era of regional conflict. During the heyday of arms sales, some in the US government sensed a cause for alarm. Throughout the 1970s and into the following decade, American members of Congress convened regular meetings to flesh out the potential harm that could be produced through the massive militarization taking place. Much of the concern was directed toward the potential threat that newly armed Arab oil producers might pose to Israel. Some observers did express anxiety about the impact of the sales on the region. Hamilton cautioned that "the appropriate area for justifiable concerns is in the general policy of pouring lots of sophisticated arms in an extremely volatile portion of the Middle East, known not for exemplary regional cooperation, but instead for a plethora of territorial, ethnic, familial and political disputes over the last several hundred years."[13]

The expression of concern about the potential for instability within the oil-producing states and the various ways that their domestic political challenges could and would affect the region were dismissed by those responsible for overseeing the program. These should have been greater sources of concern. But few policy makers or arms manufacturers were inclined to question the stability of authoritarian regimes that had been longtime allies. Especially after the first oil boom, oil states in the Gulf seemed even more in command than before. Flush with billions of dollars of new oil revenues by the mid-1970s, the Gulf oil producers went on a decade-long domestic spending spree, throwing money at a range of social, economic, and potential political problems. Regional regimes committed billions of dollars to modernization and development programs and to the expansion of cradle-to-grave social services.[14]

The intent was to redistribute oil wealth as a means to stave off potential restiveness. And the potential was considerable. Most of the Gulf's autocrats came to power through conquest, through alliances with imperial powers, or both. The United States' preferred clients, the rulers of Iran and Saudi Arabia, used a combination of coercion and cooption to establish and then maintain themselves in power. But even after decades of rule, neither regime possessed much credibility or legitimacy in the eyes of their citizens. There were important domestic political fault lines. Although most Saudi Arabians and Iranians embraced the new wealth and the services it provided, many continued to bristle against their rulers for a broad range of reasons, from the social to the ideological. Both regimes assumed that the widespread redistribution of wealth would placate whatever simmering hostilities lurked beneath the surface of Saudi Arabian and Iranian society. Neither took steps to engage in any significant reform or allowed for a greater role for their citizens in government. Saudi Arabia, with a smaller population, became less coercive, although the threat of regime violence was omnipresent. In contrast, the shah in Iran remained a brutal and cruel tyrant. Martin Ennals, secretary general of Amnesty International, remarked in 1977 that Iran "has the highest rate of death penalties in the world, no valid system of civilian courts and a history of torture which is beyond belief. No country in the world has a worse record in human rights than Iran."[15] Leaders in both countries proceeded as though the spike in oil revenues and their new spending power had allowed them to renew autocracy at home. Their social programs were meant to offer a new deal with the governed, one in which the state redistributed wealth in exchange for complete political quiescence.

Yet in neither Saudi Arabia nor Iran did the bargain hold up. Rather than emerge from the oil boom stronger, both regimes proved vulnerable to significant domestic pressures by the end of the 1970s.[16] Saudi Arabia faced two episodes of unrest in November 1979. In the kingdom's Eastern Province, tens of thousands of Shi'ites rebelled against Saudi rule and especially against their status as second-class citizens.[17] Simultaneously, but in an unrelated event, hundreds of rebels seized and occupied the Mecca Mosque. The rebels, who denounced the Al-Sa'ud as illegitimate rulers, held the mosque for two weeks before being rooted out by a combination of Saudi and French special forces.[18]

It was in Iran that oil-fueled authoritarianism proved most vulnerable. Iranian revolutionaries tossed the shah from power in 1979.[19] The fall of the shah, considered unthinkable by American officials a few years before, also demolished the twin pillar policy. From the perspective of American policy makers, the outcome of the revolution radically transformed the balance of power in the region, turning Iran from a strategic ally to a menacing rival. Whatever the reality of Iran's new position in the region, the revolution brought to dramatic conclusion the United States' reliance on highly militarized local powers as defenders of the Gulf's regional order. While they would continue to encourage and oversee the militarization of Saudi Arabia and other Arab oil producers in the 1980s and beyond, American leaders lost faith that local surrogates possessed the political capacity to safeguard US interests. Anxieties that Middle Eastern oil was vulnerable to new developments in the Cold War also deepened shortly after the fall of the shah, and this too accelerated the transformation of how the United States would project its power in the region. In December 1979 the invasion of nearby Afghanistan by tens of thousands of Soviet troops prompted Carter to make clear the United States' deep attachment to the Persian Gulf and its willingness to engage there militarily if necessary to protect the flow of oil. Although Carter mapped out a new strategic/military vision for the region, it took a few years for it to be fully realized. Even so, it was here that the era of direct American intervention in the Persian Gulf got its start.

The Long War

The Iranian Revolution not only transformed the regional order and reshaped American policy; it also helped unleash many of the destructive forces that have plagued the Persian Gulf ever since. In September 1980, sensing weakness in Iran and concerned about potential domestic challenges to its power, Iraq launched an invasion against Iran. Fighting between Iran and Iraq persisted until 1988, with hundreds of thousands killed and wounded. American oil policy was not directly responsible for Iraq's decision to invade Iran. Saddam Hussein perceived himself to be beset by a number of domestic and regional challenges, challenges that he believed war would resolve.[20] Greg Gause maps many of these out in an essay students will find accessible and clear.

While the United States claimed to have been caught off guard by Iraq's invasion of Iran, many policy makers came to see continuing the war as a useful way to bog down two of the region's most highly militarized regimes. To this end, the United States supplied weapons, funding, and intelligence to both sides in the conflict, including acknowledging and condoning Iraq's use of chemical weapons on the battlefield and against its own citizens.[21] The decision to view the Iran-Iraq war as a useful conflict, one worth abetting as a means to contain the belligerents and therefore ensure security elsewhere in the Gulf, proved to be a

dangerous gambit. Ultimately, that decision would result in the reali-
zation of the Carter Doctrine and the entanglement of the United States
directly in regional conflict. And it was the threat to oil shipping that
finally brought the American military in to stay.

In 1986 Kuwait requested protection from both the United States
and the Soviet Union from Iranian attacks on its oil tankers. The following March the United States obliged by allowing Kuwaiti tankers to
fly the American flag, rendering attacks on them attacks on American
interests, and by dispatching a large naval fleet to provide direct protection. American and Iranian military forces exchanged fire on several
occasions in 1987. Hostilities escalated in 1988, with the United States
sinking several Iranian warships and damaging oil platforms. That summer the USS *Vincennes* shot down an Iranian passenger jet, killing all 290
civilians on board, a stunning blow to Iran, one that effectively sapped
its will to fight further.[22] That the United States became an active participant in the Iran-Iraq war, taking and causing casualties, is hardly a
secret. Fisher explores the American shooting down of Iran Air Flight
655 and its permanent military presence in the Gulf afterward in a long
essay in the *Washington Post* that should be accessible to students.[23] The
war intensified American and Arab anxieties about Iranian power and
ambition that the revolution first set in motion. Iran's status as one of
the region's principal bogeymen and "rogue states" has endured and
continues today to be one of the primary reasons for repeated injunc-
tions for a continued American military presence in the region.

American involvement in, and its efforts to protract, the war also
shaped future conflict with Iraq. Although it received substantial military, technical, and financial assistance from the United States and its
Arab neighbors during the war, Iraq emerged from the conflict deeply
in debt and deeply shaken. Although Iraq was encouraged by its allies
and its patrons to drag out the war, the reality was that Iraq could not
afford it. Saddam Hussein borrowed heavily from neighboring oil states
to fund his war machine. He urgently sought a remedy, for he understood that his grip on power was potentially imperiled if he proved
unable to steward Iraq back on the path of reasonable prosperity.[24]
Reestablishing its oil industry and resecuring a share of the global oil
market might have provided Iraq a way out of indebtedness. But Iraq's
oil-producing neighbors were not sympathetic. Arab lenders demanded
that Iraq repay its war debts. Meanwhile several of Iraq's neighbors,
including Kuwait, were dumping excess oil onto the market, which had

the effect of driving prices down, limiting Iraqi revenues, and constraining its potential recovery.[25]

The anxieties, traumas, and hyper-militarism that precipitated Iran's revolution, Iraq's invasion, and the escalation of regional insecurity in the 1980s have persisted ever since. After two years of pleading and saber rattling, Saddam Hussein once again pursued a military solution, invading Kuwait in August 1990 and precipitating an even more dramatic escalation of American military intervention in the Gulf. Much of the history of Desert Storm and the 1990s sanctions regime are well known. Alarmed by the potential fallout of Iraq being in possession of not only Kuwaiti oil but also Saudi Arabian oil led the United States to mobilize over five hundred thousand military in its largest war effort since Vietnam. In just a few days the American-led coalition drove Iraqi forces from Kuwait. In the decade that followed, the United States oversaw a devastating sanctions regime that eviscerated Iraq's society and economy. The official American position immediately after the war was a policy of containing both Iraq and Iran—keeping the region's "rogue states" from threatening the other oil producers. By the end of the 1990s, however, containment had given way to a policy of regime change, the high-water mark of direct American militarism in the region, in which the United States government began to actively pursue the overthrow of Saddam Hussein.[26] Even the sanctions regime, which was officially rationalized as a system designed to ensure that Iraq abandon its weapons of mass destruction program, functioned instead as an extension of the regime change policy.[27] Regime change was realized with the 2003 American invasion of Iraq.

Capturing oil and oil fields and establishing direct or imperial control over oil has not been a factor in American aggression or their strategic logic for war in the late twentieth century. But protecting oil, oil producers, and the flow of oil has been. This is a critical distinction. If oil and American oil policy, rather than the behavior of Saddam Hussein, the politics of the war on terrorism, or a handful of other political factors, is kept in focus, then it is arguable that this period constitutes not a series of wars, but a single long one—one in which pursuing regional security and protecting oil and American-friendly oil producers has been the principal strategic rationale. That the permanent shadow of war has settled in over the Persian Gulf in the last three decades is in large measure the direct outcome of the ways that oil has been tied to

American national security and the ways that American policy makers linked security to militarization.

An Elusive Security

It might be tempting to argue that the United States' escalating involvement, its history of militarism and military engagement in the region, has actually provided some kind of security for the region. After all, oil has continued to flow, the network of oil producers has remained the same, and thus the United States' primary interests in the region have been served. But three decades of war belie this argument. War is not tantamount to security, stability, or peace. Even in the periods between regional wars the violence carried out by regimes against their own subjects makes clear that peace is also not always peaceful. The cost has been high for the United States and especially for those who make their homes in the Middle East. In thirty years of war, hundreds of thousands have died excruciating and violent deaths. Poverty, environmental disaster, torture, and wretched living conditions haunt the lives of many in Iraq, Iran, and elsewhere in the region. Of course, the burden of death and destruction does not fall solely on the United States and its policy of militarization. The politics of war has primarily served the interests of regional leaders who, often out of a position of weakness, have exported violence in order to deflect internal challenges to their authority. And international political rivalry, particularly during the Cold War, meant the other global powers, most notably the Soviet Union, also helped facilitate insecurity and disorder in the Middle East.

The autocrats have also remained in power. As citizens in the Gulf began to challenge these regimes in early 2011 in Bahrain, Saudi Arabia, and Oman, three of the United States' closest allies in the region, it became clear that the regional governments are all too willing to turn the weapons of war, purchased mostly from the United States, on their own subjects. It is also clear that these regimes are hardly stable and that they are and will remain perennially vulnerable to domestic and regional shocks, a fact that poses a real dilemma for American policy. In addition to the human toll of war and the moral dilemmas it raises, the true price of oil in the United States must take into account the financial cost of maintaining a massive military presence in the region and the network of bases to house soldiers, marines, and sailors. Roger Stern estimates that between 1976 and 2007 the total cost of maintaining the US military in the Persian Gulf is around $7 trillion.[28]

The increasing willingness of the United States to use force and violence to shore up the flow of oil to global markets has not been a sign of American strength, but of its limits. Popular political discourse in this country often posits the United States, and Americans, as either unwitting victims of an unhealthy addiction or as duped by duplicitous oil producers to continue an unsustainable habit. It would certainly be wise to break the addiction to oil. But to do so requires coming to terms with the history of that addiction, how it came to be, and the multiple costs it entails. But it is hardly clear that any such reconsideration is happening. Instead, the United States appears set to continue along a familiar path. Crafting a set of relationships with oil and unstable oil producers and linking their fate to American national security have virtually ensured that while the United States is wrapping up the most recent oil war, its military and political strategists are already preparing for the next one.

NOTES

This chapter is a modified version of "America, Oil, and War in the Middle East," *Journal of American History* 99, no. 1 (2012): 208–18.

1. See Timothy Mitchell, "McJihad: Islam in the US Global Order," *Social Text* 73, 20, no. 4 (2002): 5.

2. For more on Iraq and the British role there see Charles Tripp, *A History of Iraq* (New York: Cambridge University Press, 2000); Hanna Batatu, *The Old Social Classes and the Revolutionary Movements of Iraq: A Study of Iraq's Old Landed and Commercial Classes and of Its Communists, Ba'thists, and Free Officers* (Princeton, NJ: Princeton University Press, 1978); Eric Davis, *Memories of State: Politics, History, and Collective Identity in Modern Iraq* (Berkeley: University of California Press, 2005); Toby Dodge, *Inventing Iraq: A History of Nation Building and a History Denied* (New York: Columbia University Press, 2005); and Priya Satia, *Spies in Arabia: The Great War and the Cultural Foundations of Britain's Covert Empire in the Middle East* (New York: Oxford University Press, 2009).

3. Joe Stork, *Middle East Oil and the Energy Crisis* (New York: Monthly Review Press, 1975). See also James Gelvin, *The Modern Middle East: A History*, 3rd ed. (New York: Oxford University Press, 2011).

4. Robert Vitalis, *America's Kingdom: Mythmaking on the Saudi Oil Frontier* (Palo Alto, CA: Stanford University Press, 2006). Aramco was the name for the

Arabian American Oil Company, a consortium of the US-based oil giants Chevron, Texaco, Exxon, and Mobil. Aramco operated under their ownership until 1980, when it was fully nationalized by Saudi Arabia.

5. Mark J. Gasiorowski, "The 1953 Coup d'Etat in Iran," *International Journal of Middle East Studies* 19, no. 3 (1987): 261–86.

6. Nathan Citino, *From Arab Nationalism to OPEC: Eisenhower, King Saʿud, and the Making of US-Saudi Relations* (Bloomington: Indiana University Press, 2002).

7. Douglas Little, *American Orientalism: The United States and the Middle East since 1945* (Chapel Hill: University of North Carolina Press, 2002).

8. These figures are drawn from SIPRI's online trend indicator values (TIV) at www.sipri.org. The dollar amounts are expressed in constant 1990 prices.

9. SIPRI Trend Indicator Values Database at www.sipri.org.

10. F. Gregory Gause III, *The International Relations of the Persian Gulf* (Cambridge: Cambridge University Press, 2009), 33.

11. Statement by Hon. Lee Hamilton on "Arms Policy in Persian Gulf Area," May 31, 1978, in *New Perspectives on the Persian Gulf*, Hearings before the Subcommittee on the Near East and South Asia of the Committee on Foreign Affairs, House of Representatives, Ninety-Third Congress, 1973 (Washington, DC: US Government Printing Office, 1978), 191.

12. SIPRI Arms Transfer Database, Trade Register Database available at www.sipri.org. The original sale was for eighty planes; seventy-nine were delivered between 1976 and 1978, with the United States quarantining one with the outbreak of the Iranian Revolution.

13. Lee Hamilton, "US Policy toward the Persian Gulf," in *New Perspectives on the Persian Gulf*, 192.

14. Steffen Hertog, *Princes, Brokers, and Bureaucrats: Oil and the State in Saudi Arabia* (Ithaca, NY: Cornell University Press, 2010); Daryl Champion, *The Paradoxical Kingdom: Saudi Arabia and the Momentum of Reform* (New York: Columbia University Press, 2005); Alexei Vassiliev, *The History of Saudi Arabia* (New York: New York University Press, 2000).

15. Noam Chomsky and Edward Hermann, *The Washington Connection and Third World Fascism: The Political Economy of Human Rights*, vol. 1 (Cambridge, MA: South End Press, 1979), 13.

16. This has been true in oil-producing states elsewhere as well. Terry Karl, *The Paradox of Plenty: Oil Booms and Petro-States* (Berkeley: University of California Press, 1997).

17. Toby Craig Jones, *Desert Kingdom: How Oil and Water Forged Modern Saudi Arabia* (Cambridge, MA: Harvard University Press, 2010), chapter 5.

18. Thomas Hegghammer and Stephane Lacroix, "Rejectionist Islam in Saudi Arabia: The Story of Juhayman al-ʿUtaybi Reconsidered," *International Journal of Middle East Studies* 39, no. 1 (2007): 103–22. See also Yaroslav Trofimov's

excellent book *The Siege of Mecca: The 1979 Uprising at Islam's Holiest Shrine* (New York: Doubleday, 2007).

19. Ervand Abrahamian, *Iran between Two Revolutions* (Princeton, NJ: Princeton University Press, 1982); Nikki Keddie, *Modern Iran: Roots and Results of Revolution* (New Haven, CT: Yale University Press, 2006).

20. F. Gregory Gause III, "Iraq's Decisions to Go to War, 1980 and 1990," *Middle East Journal* 56, no. 1 (Winter 2002): 47–70.

21. Joost Hiltermann, *A Poisonous Affair: America, Iraq, and the Gassing of Halabja* (New York: Cambridge University Press, 2007).

22. Gause, *International Relations of the Persian Gulf*, 81–85.

23. Max Fisher, "What Iran 655 Says about America's Role in the Middle East," *Washington Post*, October 17, 2013, https://www.washingtonpost.com/news/worldviews/wp/2013/10/17/what-iran-air-flight-655-says-about-americas-role-in-the-middle-east/?utm_term=.29e57625e1eb.

24. Tripp, *History of Iraq*, 248–53.

25. Their intent in dumping oil on global spot markets and exceeding OPEC quotas was not to harm Iraq directly. Kuwait and the UAE, the two states most responsible for overproducing oil, had economic reasons of their own to do so. Even so, Saddam Hussein saw their actions as acts of betrayal.

26. For more on exploring the history of regime change and how it came to be the objective of American policy, teachers might direct students to the Project for the New American Century (PNAC). PNAC's members included influential neoconservative intellectuals and policy makers who led the charge to overthrow Iraq's Saddam Hussein in the late 1990s and then took up positions of influence in the George W. Bush administration. See Library of Congress, Web Archives, http://webarchive.loc.gov/all/. While the website for the Project for the New American Century has been removed, there are thousands of site captures taken since October 17, 2001, available at https://web.archive.org/web/*/http://newamericancentury.org/.

27. In a sober and devastating account of the politics of the sanctions regime, see Joy Gordon, *Invisible War: The United States and the Iraq Sanctions* (Cambridge, MA: Harvard University Press, 2010). See also Sarah Graham Brown, *Sanctioning Saddam: The Politics of Intervention in Iraq* (New York: I. B. Tauris, 1999).

28. Roger J. Stern, "United States Cost of Military Force Projection in the Persian Gulf, 1976–2007," *Energy Policy* 38, no. 6 (2010): 2816–25.

KEY RESOURCES

Carter, Jimmy. "The State of the Union Address Delivered before a Joint Session of the Congress." January 23, 1980. American Presidency Project. https://www.presidency.ucsb.edu/documents/the-state-the-union-address-delivered-before-joint-session-the-congress.

Gause, F. Gregory, III. *The International Relations of the Persian Gulf.* Cambridge: Cambridge University Press, 2009.

Halliday, Fred. *Arabia without Sultans.* New York: Saqi Books, 2013.

Middle East Research and Information Project (MERIP). *Middle East Report.* www.merip.org.

Project for the New American Century. https://www.loc.gov/item/lcwa00010308/.

Stockholm International Peace Research Institute (SIPRI). SIPRI Arms Transfers Database. https://www.sipri.org/databases/armstransfers.

US Energy Information Administration. Petroleum & Other Liquids. https://www.eia.gov/petroleum/.

Teaching the
Global War on Terror

DARRYL LI

There are few debates that have generated as much heat and as little light in recent decades as those on the topic of "jihadism." From the September 2001 attacks in New York and Washington, DC, to the rise of the self-styled Islamic State in Iraq and Syria over a decade later, the specter of jihadism has served as a kind of universal enemy. Jihadism is something that apparently everyone can agree the United States must fight in a "war on terror" on behalf of humanity, civilization, and tolerance. But if the purpose of pedagogy is to instill critical thinking skills, then this idea of universal agreement should raise a red flag. Politics is in many ways fundamentally about *dis*agreement, about the existence of competing interests in the world that are sometimes negotiated and fought over.[1]

This chapter has two goals. The first is to show how jihadism is an empty and unhelpful concept that is often used to promote anti-Muslim racism.[2] The premise here is that Muslims have long had wide-ranging and rich debates under radically different historical circumstances over the practice of jihad—how it should be defined, understood, and carried out. Yet it is precisely because those debates are so open-ended that jihad*ism* as a category is neither useful nor benign, for several reasons: (1) The category of jihadism requires elevating some notions of jihad— often those most controversial among Muslims—over others. It thereby implicitly takes sides in debates among believers rooted in Islamic traditions, even as it claims the credibility of detached and objective social science; (2) Making some notions of jihad stand in for jihadism as a general phenomenon conflates and rips out of context very different

184

situations of political violence that happen to involve Muslims and artificially separates them from comparable situations of non-Muslims engaged in political violence; (3) Jihadism discourages critical thinking by reinforcing the idea that only violence meted out by Western states is presumptively legitimate; (4) Finally, jihadism purports to provide grounds for distinguishing between "good" and "bad" Muslims but, in practice, sets up a trap of toxic authenticity whereby Muslims are subjected to unending and insatiable demands to condemn and repudiate acts by other Muslims to prove that they are loyal or moderate.[3]

The second goal of this chapter is to provide some basic background on one specific subset of contemporary jihads: transnational groups that engage in armed confrontation against the United States of America in the name of a global Muslim community and without geographical constraints, the best known being al-Qaʿida. Such groups have a membership base, field of struggle, and goals that are not based in a single country; yet transnational groups must always be understood and taught in the context of both local and international (as in interstate) developments. What made al-Qaʿida distinctive was not that it opposed the United States, that it invoked Islam, or that it was willing to target civilians. Many other groups in history shared at least some of these characteristics but usually within the framework of a local or nationalist war, such as the Moro Rebellion in the Philippines or the Viet Cong. In contrast, al-Qaʿida's membership was multinational, it explicitly rejected a nationalist framework, and it envisioned a global battlefield that mirrored and challenged the global scope of American power, striking targets in places as far afield as Kenya, Tanzania, and Yemen, as well as within the US homeland. This chapter unpacks the dynamic of an asymmetric armed struggle between a global superpower and a dispersed transnational network that has come to be known as the Global War on Terror.

Jihad, Jihadism—From Meanings to Uses

There is jihad and then there is jihad*ism*. The Arabic term *jihād* comes from a root that connotes striving and the exertion of effort. The word "jihad" and its variants appear in the Qurʾan numerous times with both armed and unarmed connotations and accordingly, jihad is a concept that has a place in the divine law of Islam, also known as *sharīʿa*. There are extensive debates among Muslims on the peaceful versus the violent meanings of jihad.[4] For example, within mystical traditions in Islam (Sufism) the term "jihad of the soul" has been used to describe efforts to be a better human being, to overcome temptation, and to attain higher levels of piety and devotion (Sufis have also historically been engaged in more than their fair share of violent jihads).[5] It is important, however, to avoid falling into the trap of uncritically organizing discussions around the categories of violence versus nonviolence only or approaching the question of Muslims who engage in violence with defensiveness. Violence is central to politics and history across places and times, so treating "violent jihad" or "violent Muslims" as a category is underdescriptive and takes other forms of violence for granted. For example, the label of "violent Muslim" should logically encompass a Muslim working for the New York Police Department who believes their job to be consistent with their faith (a position that has plenty of support among religious scholars); but such a person would be largely overlooked in terms of how that category is most often thought. In other words, violence by Muslims only registers as a problem when it defies mainstream assumptions of the liberal state.

Within the jurisprudence of shari'a, or *fiqh*, jihad is generally understood as religiously justified combat against non-Muslims and is governed by various rules.[6] But a discussion of jihad cannot be reduced to juristic categories for several reasons. First, the vast majority of Muslims in the world today do not live under fiqh-based legal systems. To the extent these rules directly govern their lives, in many countries this is in the realm of family law. A few states, such as Saudi Arabia and Iran, have Islamic penal law, but even those states do not apply the classical fiqh of jihad in their military operations. Second, even when states decide to use certain parts of shari'a, they are applying them in a modern governmental structure where procedures, ways of weighing evidence, and forms of legal interpretation may not be part of these classical traditions. This is akin to using a new computer to run old software designed for a different era; it may work, but outcomes may be even less predictable and beyond what the original designers intended. In other words, today's "Islamic law" is a thoroughly modern phenomenon.[7] Third, there was likely *never* a time in the history of Muslim societies where rulers applied shari'a by itself; different forms of law, such as legislation and custom, always existed alongside and influenced shari'a, including in matters of jihad. Searching for a single scripturally correct definition of jihad does little to explain why some Muslims participate in activities that they call jihad. Muslims, like everyone else, make their decisions based on a wide variety of factors; they engage, cite, and wrestle with religious texts, but the texts themselves cannot automatically predict how people will act.

Thus, it is necessary to draw a distinction between jihad as a technical juristic term and jihad as it has been invoked by different Muslim authorities—be they rulers, jurists, mystics, political parties, or social movements. Throughout history up until the present, states have described their wars as jihads, with or without reference to the rules of fiqh: in recent decades, Pakistan, Iran, and Iraq are among the many states to have done so. Non-Muslim states also have a long history of supporting jihad: during World War I, the Ottoman Empire declared a jihad against the British, French, and Russian empires at the urging of its own ally, Germany.[8] Drawing more notoriety have been nonstate groups invoking jihad, but even these should be carefully distinguished. For example, many groups invoking jihad work within a roughly nationalist framework in terms of their membership and political framework: these include Hamas in Palestine or Hizb Allah in Lebanon, both originally founded to confront foreign occupiers. Others use the term jihad to describe rebellion against one's own rulers when deemed oppressive or corrupt, as with insurgencies in Egypt and Algeria in the 1990s.[9] Finally, there have been armed transnational solidarity movements that have invoked jihad, whereby volunteers join conflicts in other countries to fight alongside fellow Muslims: this occurred in Afghanistan, Bosnia-Herzegovina, Chechnya, Iraq, and other locales. Thus, any time one reads about a "jihadist" group, it is important to pay attention to their specific political goals.

As against all of these different types of jihad, jihad*ism* is a much more recent concept, and one primarily developed in the West. It is generally used to refer to contemporary nonstate groups who label their own use of violence as jihad. This category tends to leave out states that also claim the mantle of jihad. But putting aside such a glaring omission, the preceding paragraph should make clear that treating this panoply of nonstate groups as anything like a single ideology or movement is not analytically helpful for the simple reason that jihad itself can mean so many different things. We can further illustrate the problem with the following example. The Republican Party in the United States (also known as the GOP) and the Irish Republican Army (IRA) arguably share many things in common. Both have the word "republican" in their names, and their memberships are predominantly white and Christian. Both support violence under certain circumstances: the IRA pursued a decades-long armed struggle against Britain, and GOP-controlled governments have waged war on dozens of countries and support domestic police forces that routinely brutalize nonwhites, both citizen and noncitizen. The GOP and IRA belong to "Western civilization" and agree in endorsing republican systems of government over monarchies. They are linked by a set of sacred ideological texts, since members of both have assuredly read and quoted from the Bible as well as from Plato's *The Republic* at some point in their careers. They may even share some radicalized supporters: during the Spanish Civil War, Irish Republican foreign fighters joined the predominantly American Abraham Lincoln brigade, named after the first Republican US president. In my home city of Boston there are people who have given money to the IRA and have also voted for the GOP. One could, on the basis of all of the foregoing links, conceivably label them as part of a common and violent ideology and movement called "republicanism"—even if the resemblances and connections highlighted here between the GOP and IRA don't really shed much light on either group. Yet this kind of superficial, decontextualized, and tendentious thinking is precisely what occurs when diverse groups of Muslims engaged in political violence in the name of jihad are clustered together under the heading of "jihadism," a label that justifies and generates a field of study with its own experts, conferences, books, and research institutes.

In contrast to searching for a magically correct dictionary meaning of jihad that explains jihadism, it is more useful to think of jihad as a term used by some Muslims when they wish to endow a struggle with religious, and specifically Islamic, legitimacy.[10] Sometimes their arguments reference shariʻa jurisprudence; other times they do not. This distinction between fixed abstract meaning of words and their use in context is also helpful for thinking about "terrorism," a word often associated with jihad. An enormous amount of ink has been spilled debating definitions of terrorism and complaining about the lack of a single usable definition. What is reasonably clear, however, is that "terrorism" is a label applied to political violence that the speaker wishes to delegitimize. Studying and discussing the uses of the label can be more productive than arguing over whether someone really fits it or not.

Jihadism—Pedagogical Challenges

There are numerous challenges to teaching on this topic as part of a history class, not least of which is that many of the issues touch on current affairs and require a critical perspective on US state and society. It is worth highlighting three in particular.

The first challenge is a tendency to pronounce upon what is properly "Islamic" without the requisite authority to do so. While such statements may be appropriate for pedagogical contexts that are explicitly oriented toward believers, this chapter is not written with such lessons in mind. Rather, the idea is to help develop clearer ways for thinking and teaching on jihad regardless of whether students are believers or not. Such an approach, however, does not preclude making empirical observations, for example, that the vast majority of Muslims in a given context may share a particular interpretation or position or that most scholars condemn certain acts or groups.[11]

Second is the predicament of Muslim students, who are sometimes asked to speak for Islam, even though there are over one billion Muslims in the world who hold different opinions about multiple issues. This is especially disturbing when such students are made to feel that they must condemn violence described as jihad to demonstrate that they are "moderate" or "loyal." Important in this regard is the rise of "Countering Violent Extremism" (CVE) programs that attempt to use schools to prevent "radicalization" but also turn them into de facto instruments of state security policy, monitoring and surveilling student attitudes.[12] This challenge extends outside the classroom—even if a lesson is conducted with sensitivity and nuance, US students are often already exposed to an ambient level of anti-Muslim animus, such that teaching on this topic may trigger or justify harassment or bullying. Such attacks also affect those racialized as Muslim, including non-Muslim Blacks, Arabs, and South Asians.

Finally, any thoughtful discussion of jihadism is often hindered by the widespread taking for granted of state violence. Merely stressing that not all Muslims are violent or that groups invoking jihad do not represent all Muslims is not enough; a thorough exploration of the topic of contemporary meanings of jihad also requires a critical discussion of state policies, especially those of the US government. This can be challenging, as primary and secondary education often involves teaching students to accept and even revere institutions of state violence such as the military and the police. Even when schooling exposes students to critiques of state violence—such as structural violence against black people and other communities of color—it is often on terms that stress the process or procedures through which violence is exercised instead of structural issues. But when jihad is invoked to justify violence against the state, it is often by people who fundamentally reject the legitimacy of that state. In order to understand the motivations and contexts of such jihad groups, letting go of the presumption that state violence is legitimate (and that no other violence ever is) is also important.

Al-Qaʿida—Basics and Clarifications

The rest of this chapter focuses on providing the context for the Global War on Terror, especially the emergence of the group known as al-Qaʿida, which was widely blamed for the attacks in New York and Washington, DC, on September 11, 2001. When teaching about al-Qaʿida, it may help to keep in mind how this transnational armed group developed in relation to both the local context (Afghanistan) and to the international context (the Cold War and post–Cold War US hegemony).

Al-Qaʿida's leader, Osama bin Laden, first emerged into global prominence when he was accused of orchestrating simultaneous bombings of US embassies in Kenya and Tanzania in 1998 and attacking a US warship in Yemen in 2000. To this day, little is known about al-Qaʿida's origins, and commentators debate whether to think of it as a clearly defined organization, a loose network, an ideology that has been franchised to other groups, or something else.[13] At the time of the 9/11 attacks, al-Qaʿida appears to have numbered a few hundred people, mostly Arabs of diverse nationalities, operating in Afghanistan under the rule of a group called the Taliban. When teaching about al-Qaʿida, several major themes can be emphasized.

First, al-Qaʿida set forth a number of political goals whose desirability and feasibility can and should be debated in pedagogical contexts. As articulated by bin Laden in his public statements, these goals concerned ending US influence in the Muslim world, especially its military presence in Saudi Arabia (home of the holiest sites in Islam) and its support for dictatorships such as in Egypt and for the state of Israel. Al-Qaʿida's focus on the United States is sometimes referred to as the "far enemy" strategy, in opposition to the "near enemy" strategy of attacking regimes

in Muslim-majority countries that were deemed to be repressive and corrupt apostates. Many of those who joined al-Qaʿida had backgrounds
in other organizations that were focused on "near enemy" regimes,
especially the Egyptian state under Hosni Mubarak. The far enemy
approach was born from the argument that such regimes would never
be defeated without also attacking their sponsor, the United States.
Al-Qaʿida also had vaguer commitments, such as supporting the idea
of a "caliphate" that would unite the world's Muslims. As for the often-
cited notion that al-Qaʿida hates America because of its freedoms, bin
Laden ridiculed this argument, once asking sarcastically, "Tell us why
we did not attack Sweden, for example?"[14]

Second, al-Qaʿida emerged in the wake of decades of armed conflict in Afghanistan that claimed hundreds of thousands of lives and
was in significant part driven by external powers, including the United
States. From 1979 to 1989, the Soviet Union fought a war in Afghanistan in support of a local Marxist regime. The United States and Saudi
Arabia together spent some $6 billion to support a coalition of armed
anti-Soviet factions known as the *mujahideen* (the Arabic-origin term for
"those who are engaged in jihad"). Much of that aid was channeled
through Pakistan, which allowed the mujahideen factions to operate
bases along the border shared by the two countries, and which also
hosted millions of Afghan refugees. This is a reminder that non-Muslim
states such as the United States have also supported jihad when it was
in their interests to do so. US president Ronald Reagan publicly welcomed mujahideen leaders at the White House and referred to them
multiple times as "freedom fighters" — these speeches can be useful resources for teaching about different perspectives on jihad.[15] Analysts
have also criticized the United States, Saudi Arabia, and Pakistan for
putting their own narrow geopolitical interests over those of ordinary
Afghans. They effectively empowered mujahideen groups that were
less politically accountable, either because they were seen as more militarily effective or to keep the factions weak and dependent. As a result
of the way powerful state sponsors co-opted and divided the Afghan
mujahideen factions, they turned on each other after the fall of the Marxist regime in Kabul. This internecine fighting did much to discredit the
Afghan jihad with many Islamist groups around the world. It also set
the stage for the emergence of a new group called the Taliban. The term
"Taliban" refers to students in Islamic schools, many of them refugees
who grew up in Pakistan and who had been too young to fight against

the Soviets. They presented themselves as an alternative to the corruption and infighting of the mujahideen factions and promised to unify the country. They also enjoyed extensive support from Pakistan, which had tired of the infighting it had previously encouraged among the mujahideen. The Taliban captured Kabul in 1996 and ruled much of Afghanistan. The Taliban and mujahideen factions may both be classified as "Islamist" or "jihadist" by the outside world, but they were enemies—another reminder that quasi-religious labels can sometimes obscure the political conflicts at stake.[16]

Third, it is important to distinguish the various Afghan actors that fought for control of the country from the far smaller number of non-Afghan groups on the scene. During the war against the Soviets, thousands of foreign Muslims came and participated in fighting, relief work, and other forms of activism. These volunteers were mostly from Arab countries and were nicknamed the "Afghan Arabs." They had only a limited military impact; their value to the mujahideen was in raising awareness, sympathy, and funds from other majority-Muslim countries. The Afghan Arabs were not a unified force, and indeed, they were often plagued by the same factionalism that divided the Afghan mujahideen. The most prominent Afghan Arab was the Palestinian jurist ʿAbd Allah ʿAzzam, who mentored Osama bin Laden when the latter was still a relatively unknown son of a wealthy family in Saudi Arabia. During the 1980s there was no indication that Afghan Arabs were contemplating a jihad against the United States. Regarding bin Laden, it appears that he started to turn his attention to the United States only later in the 1990s after Saudi Arabia allowed a large contingent of US troops in the country as part of the buildup to the 1991 Gulf War against Iraq.

For the Afghan Arabs, the jihad in Afghanistan in the 1980s was about transnational solidarity to eject a non-Muslim invader from a predominantly Muslim country. The al-Qaʿida program, which came about a decade later, was about attacking a superpower anywhere in the world to combat its influence over majority Muslim countries. Joining the former did not necessarily mean signing up for the latter, and the distinction was far from theoretical: ʿAzzam's son, Hudhayfa, would later endorse jihad against the United States, but in the specific sense that he traveled to Iraq to fight US forces there, using the same logic as the Afghan jihad. At the same time, he criticized the 9/11 attacks and rejected the al-Qaʿida program.[17]

On the eve of 9/11, the Taliban ruled most of Afghanistan. Within its territory, it hosted many armed foreign Islamist organizations, of which al-Qaʿida was only one. From the later years of the anti-Soviet jihad through the civil war of the 1990s, these groups found Afghanistan to be a useful place to gain military experience and operate away from the scrutiny of their governments. Most were dedicated to seizing control in their home countries, especially Egyptians and Algerians. There were also groups devoted to providing training to people who wanted to participate in conflicts with non-Muslims elsewhere such as Bosnia-Herzegovina, Chechnya, and Kashmir.[18] The Taliban was still in the process of consolidating its control over these groups when the US invasion began. Indeed, al-Qaʿida's various provocations against the US were a continuous source of friction with elements of the Taliban leadership.

A Globalized Counterinsurgency

The term "Global War on Terror" (GWOT) has often been used to refer to a cluster of policies and initiatives undertaken by the US government and its allies in the name of fighting "jihadism" and its variants. GWOT is not only a war in the legal sense, but an entire outlook or logic for organizing governance. Addressing GWOT in all of its dimensions is beyond the scope of this chapter. The invasions of Afghanistan and Iraq, while certainly major parts of GWOT, occasioned a number of dilemmas and challenges around imperial governance and state-building. This section focuses instead on more specific campaigns to hunt down transnational armed groups outside of these two countries, where the "globalness" of GWOT was made much more manifest.

Although GWOT is often seen as a response to the 9/11 attacks, the United States has been waging a sort of globalized counterinsurgency against transnational armed Islamist groups since the mid-1990s. The 1993 bombing of the World Trade Center in New York was blamed on armed opposition groups in Egypt and can be seen as an early and relatively limited instance of the "far enemy" approach: attacking the United States for its support for Hosni Mubarak's regime in Egypt. Shortly after this incident we find the first reports of US and Egyptian intelligence agents teaming up to abduct Egyptian Islamists in countries such as Croatia, Albania, and Azerbaijan and to forcibly repatriate them to Egypt; some of these individuals were imprisoned, others simply disappeared.[19] US agencies referred to this practice as "extraordinary rendition" and treated it as a way to capture political opponents without assuming any legal responsibility for their treatment or fate. Extraordinary rendition is symptomatic of how US foreign policy generally operates: much of the violence perpetrated abroad is carried out by *other* governments at the behest of the United States and with its support.

After the 9/11 attacks, the United States developed a complex web of detention practices. It invaded Afghanistan but mostly relied on supporting a coalition of local militias that opposed the Taliban. These forces executed and mistreated prisoners; in at least one incident they locked detainees in shipping containers and left them to die in the desert.[20] The United States found itself in control of thousands of Afghan and non-Afghan captives. Many were sent to prisons run by either the US military or the CIA in Afghanistan; hundreds of those ended up in a US military prison at Guantánamo Bay in Cuba. An unknown number were shipped directly to US client states where they were imprisoned or disappeared. At the same time, US intelligence agencies and their partners continued to abduct suspects from around the world—Bosnia-Herzegovina, Mauritania, Italy, China (Hong Kong), Gambia, Macedonia, Sweden, and many other countries. Some were transferred to their home countries, others to CIA-run secret "black site" prisons located in countries such as Thailand, Poland, and Lithuania. US-aligned militias in places as diverse as Somalia, Syria, Iraq, and Yemen continue to do the bulk of detention and interrogation in the Global War on Terror, drawing far less scrutiny than Guantánamo.

In addition to the detention network, the United States resorted to various tactics to hunt individuals around the world, including the use of remotely piloted aircraft (drones), long-distance missile strikes, and commando missions in Libya, Pakistan, Yemen, Somalia, and numerous other sites. In 1998, the US fired missiles at alleged al-Qaʻida training camps in Afghanistan and a pharmaceutical factory in Sudan that they accused of involvement with al-Qaʻida. Under the administration of President Barack Obama (2008–2016), the United States dramatically escalated its use of drones outside of war zones, especially in the tribal areas of Pakistan along the border with Afghanistan.[21] Again, it is important to stress that even in these situations, the United States is frequently working with and depending on local regimes, be they states (such as the Pakistani government) or nonstate militias.

194

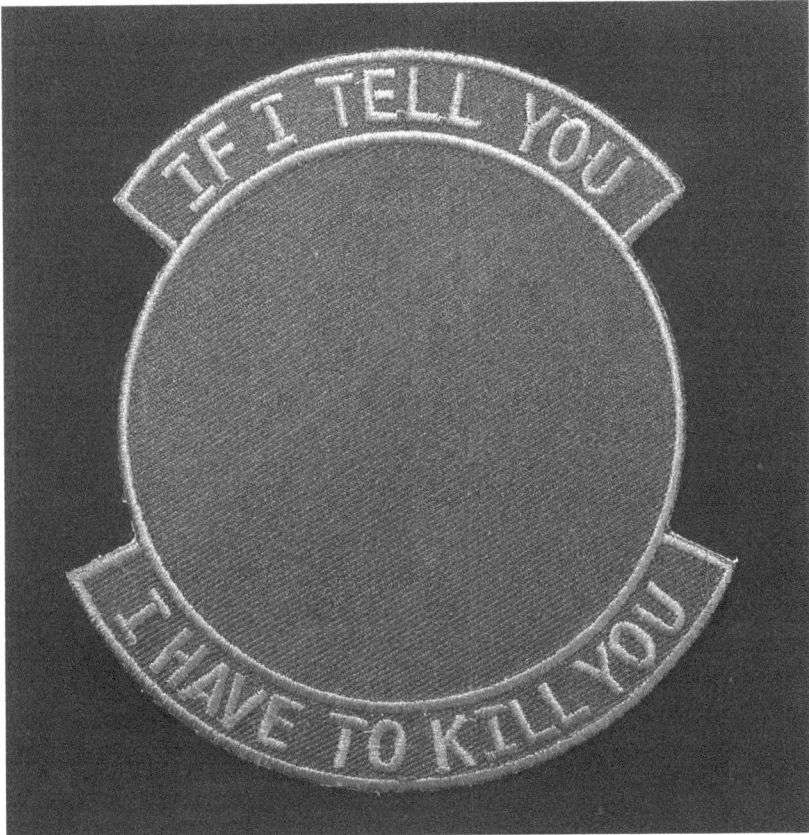

A colloquial translation of the Latin phrase "Si ego certiorem faciam . . . mihi tu delendus eris" (I could tell you, but then you would have to be destroyed by me), this US military patch denotes secret Pentagon "black projects" around the world. Trevor Paglen, detail of *Symbology*, volume 3, 2009. Courtesy of the artist and Altman Siegel, San Francisco.

Al-Qaʿida and Its Affiliates and Successors

As a result of the US invasion of Afghanistan, al-Qaʿida's members were dispersed and forced into hiding, mostly in Pakistan. The loss of the territorial haven provided by Taliban rule sharply curtailed al-Qaʿida's ability to operate, and the group largely reconfigured itself to provide inspiration, guidance, and advice to groups elsewhere rather than executing armed operations itself. In subsequent years, "franchise" organizations using the al-Qaʻida name emerged in various regions, such as al-Qaʻida in the Arabian Peninsula (Saudi Arabia and Yemen), al-Qaʻida in Mesopotamia (Iraq), al-Qaʻida in the Islamic Maghrib (Algeria). These groups appeared to have operated largely autonomously and in their own contexts but to have found utility in attaching themselves to the al-Qaʻida "brand." The most extreme form of fragmentation comes in the "lone wolf" attacks—acts of violence by individuals living in the West who may draw inspiration from groups such as al-Qaʻida but often lack any operational ties or even direct communication with such organizations. Lone wolves in the United States arguably have more in common with non-Muslim mass shooters than with individuals immersed in collective political action as represented by transnational or even nationally oriented armed groups.

The most important challenge to al-Qaʻida's reputation among transnational armed Islamists has been the crisis in Syria and the rise of the self-declared Islamic State in Iraq and Syria (ISIS). If al-Qaʻida's program was to attack the United States to facilitate the overthrow of the governing regimes in majority-Muslim countries, ISIS sought to set up its own territorial rule instead and to declare it to be an ideal Muslim state superior to all others. While there is still little reliable research on ISIS at this time beyond studies of its media output, it is safe to say that the group benefited from parallel armed conflicts that eroded centralized authority in the two neighboring states. In Iraq, the remnants of al-Qaʻida's local affiliate in coalition with army officers from the former Baʻth regime found new opportunities in the Syrian war to consolidate and expand authority. In Syria, fighting between the regime and rival armed groups supported by external powers such as the United States, Saudi Arabia, Qatar, and Turkey created a power vacuum in the east of the country. From 2014 to 2017, ISIS was able to exert governmental authority on both sides of the border.[22] While thousands of foreign Muslims joined ISIS or came to live under its rule, the organization's ability and commitment to launching armed operations abroad in Europe and the United States remained confined to encouraging spectacular attacks such as those in Paris in November 2015. ISIS is not strictly a transnational or a local entity—although it included many foreigners, most of its leadership appears to have been Iraqi or Syrian. While it rejected the Iraqi and Syrian nation-states and purported to erase the boundary between them, it was still resolutely focused on consolidating its territorial rule. ISIS and al-Qaʿida publicly feuded over many issues, but one fundamental strategic question set them apart from one another: whether to seek state-like authority. For al-Qaʿida, the ISIS path of statehood would only create unsustainable burdens and vulnerabilities[23]; for ISIS, al-Qaʿida's lack of a territorial base would doom it to impotence and empty symbolism. By 2018, ISIS had lost most of the territory under its control, raising the possibility of reverting to an underground guerrilla organization.

War on Terror Films: The So-So, the Bad, and the Ugly

There have been no great Hollywood films to emerge out of the War on Terror. This is true about the movies focusing on the US military and is even more so about those that attempt to depict Muslims engaged in jihad. A few have been mildly thought-provoking and are potentially useful for classroom teaching—perhaps as clips more than as whole films.

Body of Lies (2008, directed by Ridley Scott, starring Russell Crowe and Leonardo DiCaprio)—One of the few movies to show the extent of US reliance on client regimes, in this case by highlighting the fraught relationship between the CIA and the Jordanian secret police.

Four Lions (2010, directed by Chris Morris, starring Riz Ahmed)— Loosely based on the 2005 London bombings, this film follows the bumbling antics of a cell of British Muslims planning a bombing. Helpful for demonstrating how tangential religious motivations can be in such attacks, but in ridiculing lack of religious knowledge it also verges into classism and caricature.

The State (2017 Channel 4 UK series, directed by Peter Kosminsky)— Fictionalized account of Britons joining ISIS. Does a decent job of showing a range of possible scenarios and reactions for living under the regime, weakened by an extremely implausible and problematic subplot involving the sexual abuse of captive Yazidi women.

Timbuktu (2014, directed by Abderrahmane Sissako)—Fictionalized account of Ansar Dine's occupation of the Malian city of Timbuktu in 2012.

Notes

1. Political theorist Roxanne Euben has forcefully argued that jihad "is a form of political action in which . . . the pursuit of immortality is inextricably linked to a profoundly this-worldly endeavor—the founding or recreation of a just community on earth." Roxanne Euben, "Killing (for) Politics: Jihad, Martyrdom, and Political Action," *Political Theory* 30, no. 1 (2002): 9.

2. For further readings on anti-Muslim racism, see the #IslamophobiaIsRacism syllabus at https://islamophobiaisracism.wordpress.com (accessed April 4, 2020.)

3. For more on the distinction between "good Muslims," who are defined as those supporting US policies, and "bad Muslims," who do not, see Mahmood Mamdani, *Good Muslim, Bad Muslim: America, the Cold War, and the Roots of Terror* (New York: Pantheon, 2004).

4. These competing meanings of jihad stretch all the way back to the earliest periods of Islamic history. See, for example, Asma Afsaruddin, *Striving in the Path of God: Jihād and Martyrdom in Islamic Thought* (New York: Oxford University Press, 2013), 5. "The conceptualizations of *jihād* as *primarily* armed combat and of *shahāda* as *primarily* military martyrdom are relatively late and contested ones, and deviate considerably from the Qur'anic significations of these terms" (emphasis in original).

5. The phrase in Arabic is *jihād al-nafs*, also translated as "jihad of the self." This spiritual struggle is sometimes described as "greater" jihad, as distinct from the "lesser," armed jihad. "Many traditions claim that the true, 'greater' jihad is not a fight against physical, external enemies, but is rather a fight rather against the self (*nafs*)." Michael Bonner, *Jihad in Islamic History: Doctrines and Practice* (Princeton, NJ: Princeton University Press, [2004] 2006), 51.

6. Fiqh is the jurisprudence through which human believers interpret and develop the divinely inspired shari'a.

7. "Islamic law" is a modern and deeply contested category that may include shari'a and fiqh but can also include informal norms of certain nonstate communities as well as codes, institutions, and regimes that come from the modern nation-state but ground their legitimacy in an appeal to Islam. Iza Hussin, *The Politics of Islamic Law: Local Elites, Colonial Authority, and the Making of the Muslim State* (Chicago: University of Chicago Press, 2016), 3–16.

8. The response mostly fell on deaf ears, especially those of Muslim troops in the British and French colonial armies. Cemil Aydın, *The Idea of the Muslim World: A Global Intellectual History* (Cambridge, MA: Harvard University Press, 2017), 99–132.

9. In premodern times, such uprisings were more likely to be classified by fiqh scholars as *baghy* (rebellion), a further reminder that even within Islamic juristic traditions "jihad" and "violence" cannot be equated with one another.

Khaled Abou El Fadl, *Rebellion and Violence in Islamic Law* (Cambridge: Cambridge University Press, 2001).

10. As Fred Donner, a scholar of early Islamic history, put it: "It seems doubtful that one can fully understand the attitude of a particular civilization—in this case, Islamic civilization—toward a phenomenon as complex and as fundamental to human society as war merely by examining the juridical and theological definition of war and its status. To do so would be to strip it of most of its human significance, since what really matters in human terms is how the Muslims of a particular time and place dealt with the vital questions of war and peace. The juridical definition, of course, has been a major force shaping the reactions of Muslims toward war over the centuries, but it would be rash to assume that it has been the only one." Fred Donner, "The Sources of Islamic Conceptions of War," in *Just War and Jihad: Historical and Theoretical Perspectives on War and Peace in Western and Islamic Traditions,* ed. John Kelsay and James Turner Johnson (Westport, CT: Greenwood Press, 1991), 32.

11. For a useful explanation of the problems with claiming that jihad groups are "authentic" interpreters of Islamic traditions, see Caner Dağlı, "The Phony Islam of ISIS," *Atlantic,* February 27, 2015.

12. See Nicole Nguyen, *Suspect Communities: Anti-Muslim Racism and the Domestic War on Terror* (Minneapolis: University of Minnesota Press, 2019).

13. See Christina Hellmich, *Al-Qaeda: From Global Network to Local Franchise* (London: Zed Books, 2011).

14. Osama bin Laden, *Messages to the World: The Statements of Osama bin Laden* (London: Verso, 2005), 238. On bin Laden's rhetorical style, see Flagg Miller, *The Audacious Ascetic: What the bin Laden Tapes Reveal about al-Qaʾida* (London: Hurst, 2015).

15. See, for example, Reagan's "Statement on the Fourth Anniversary of the Soviet Invasion of Afghanistan," December 27, 1983, available at Ronald Reagan Presidential Library and Museum, https://www.reaganlibrary.gov/research/speeches/122783b.

16. On the development of the mujahideen factions and the Taliban before 2001, a useful introduction is Gilles Dorronsoro, *Revolution Unending: Afghanistan: 1979 to the Present,* trans. John King (New York: Columbia University Press, [2000] 2005).

17. See Nir Rosen, "Iraq's Jordanian Jihadis," *New York Times Magazine,* February 19, 2006.

18. The most useful account in English of al-Qaʾida's development in the latter half of the 1990s in the context of other transnational armed groups operating under Taliban rule is Anne Stenersen, *Al-Qaida in Afghanistan* (Cambridge: Cambridge University Press, 2017).

19. See Thomas Kellogg and Hossam El-Hamalawy, "Black Hole: The Fate of Islamists Rendered to Egypt" (New York: Human Rights Watch, 2005).

20. See Physicians for Human Rights, "Preliminary Assessment of Alleged Mass Gravesites in the Area of Mazar-i-Sharif, Afghanistan," amended December 2008.

21. For a rare ethnographically informed analysis of how drone warfare intersects with Pakistani state structures on the ground, see Madiha Tahir, "The Containment Zone," in *Life in the Age of Drone Warfare*, ed. Lisa Parks and Caren Kaplan (Durham, NC: Duke University Press, 2017).

22. ISIS's rule, especially its use of spectacular punishments, has generated much sensationalist commentary. The most careful and empirically grounded study of ISIS legal systems so far is probably Mara Revkin, "The Legal Foundations of the Islamic State" (Washington, DC: Brookings Institution, 2016).

23. Al-Qaʿida's Yemen affiliate did, however, rule over the eastern city of Mukalla between 2015 and 2016 before withdrawing in advance of an offensive by the UAE military.

KEY RESOURCES

Anas, Abdullah, and Tam Hussein. *To the Mountains: My Life in Jihad, from Algeria to Afghanistan*. London: Hurst, 2019. Memoir of a key figure in the Afghan Arab movement; parts of this will be of interest mainly to specialists, but some of the early chapters in particular give a flavor of the role and experiences of Arabs volunteers in the Afghan jihad.

Bin Laden, Osama. *Messages to the World: The Statements of Osama bin Laden*. London: Verso, 2005. Translations of the al-Qaʿida leader's major speeches.

Gerges, Fawaz. *The Far Enemy: Why Jihad Went Global*. Cambridge: Cambridge University Press, 2009. Among the books tracing the emergence of al-Qaʿida and other transnational jihad movements, this one probably does the best job of being readable while eschewing sensationalism. Most of the research is drawn from the Arabic-language press.

Kanji, Azeezah, and S. K. Hussan. "The Problem with Liberal Opposition to Islamophobia." *ROAR Magazine*, Spring 2017, 82–95. Very useful overview of dangers involved in discussing anti-Muslim racism.

Ould Mohamedou, Mohammad-Mahmoud. *Understanding Al Qaeda: The Transformation of War*. London: Pluto Press, 2007. The text is useful because it attempts to analyze al-Qaʿida by taking it seriously as an actor with a strategic logic.

Rosen, Nir. "Iraq's Jordanian Jihadis." *New York Times Magazine*, February 19, 2006. This article profiles jihad fighters who opposed the 9/11 attacks on the United States but also traveled to Iraq to fight the US-led invasion, giving a sense of the very different kinds of agendas that exist under the label of jihad.

Strick van Linschoten, Alex, and Felix Kuehn. *An Enemy We Created: The Myth of the Taliban-Al Qaeda Merger in Afghanistan*. London: Hurst, 2011. Helpful analysis of the Taliban and its conflicted relationship with al-Qaʿida.

Arab Uprisings in the Modern Middle East

A S E F   B A Y A T

On December 16, 2010, Mohammed Bouazizi, a poor street vendor, set himself on fire in the depressed Tunisian town of Sidi-Bouzid after the police abusively confiscated his scale and vegetables because he lacked a permit. The incident set the stage for the spectacular Arab uprisings that were to engulf the Arab region in a ferocity and scale unseen before. In Tunisia, the uprising involved mostly ordinary people—workers, educated unemployed youths, provincial populations, and later the middle-class professionals—as the street protests moved northward to the capital, Tunis. Within a month a long-standing dictator, Zein al-Abedine Ben Ali, was toppled after twenty-three years of authoritarian rule, opening the way for the formation of a democratic government. Egyptians were watching the events in Tunisia with great interest and enthusiasm. Within two weeks, they began their own uprising on January 25, when tens of thousands of protestors poured into Tahrir Square in Cairo from different parts of the city including the poor informal communities. The crowd, spearheaded by young activists, occupied the central Tahrir Square for the following days and nights, while massive street protests spread into other cities and towns. Unable to tackle the crowd, the police retreated from the public scene, giving way to the military to deploy its forces onto the streets, but the military signaled its neutrality. Within two weeks President Hosni Mubarak, who had ruled Egypt for some thirty years, was forced to step down. Egyptians were still relishing their revolutionary honeymoon when mass revolts overtook Libya, then Yemen, Syria, Bahrain, and other neighboring countries. In total nineteen Arab states went through popular protests—the key demands included "Bread, Freedom, Social Justice" and "The People Want the Downfall of the Regime." In the end, four dictators—Zein al-Abedine Ben Ali in Tunisia, Hosni Mubarak in Egypt, Muammar al-Qaddafi in Libya, and Ali Saleh in Yemen—were toppled, while the Syrian President Bashar al-Assad was brought to the brink. Even the affluent monarchies and sheikhdoms in the Persian Gulf such as Saudi Arabia, the United Arab Emirates, and Oman felt the shockwaves of the revolutions. Their response included appeasing their citizens through handouts or reforms, while attempting to sabotage the revolutions elsewhere in the region.

The Arab uprisings were remarkable in speed and spread, ones that conjured up the 1848 revolutions that overtook Europe in a fairly short span of time. But the uprisings were not the first revolutionary experience in the Arab region. Since Gamal Abdel Nasser's revolution of 1952 that ended the monarchy and British dominance in Egypt, the Middle East witnessed numerous revolutionary movements that took their ideological cues from both Nasserite anti-imperialism and Marxism-Leninism. The Algerian revolution threw the French colonists out of Algeria in 1962 in a dramatic war of liberation that became a model in the region. So, in Yemen, where Britain had forged a federal government run by the local amirs and sultans, a guerrilla group later called the National Liberation Front (NLF) began an insurgency, and by 1967 they established a secular socialist republic of South Yemen.[1] The new Yemen saw income equality improved, corruption reduced, and health and educational services expanded, while considerable efforts were made toward women's emancipation despite continuing conservative backlash. The victory of NLF in Yemen boosted the insurgency in the neighboring Sultanate of Oman, where the nationalist youths in Salala had already established the People's Front for the Liberation of Oman since the mid-1960s to free the southern province of Dhofar from the rule of Sultan Said Ibn Taimur and his British ally. Disenchanted by Nasser's defeat in the 1967 war and emboldened by the departure of Britain and the NLF victory in Yemen, the Dhofari liberation movement adopted Marxist-Leninist ideology and aimed to liberate "all of the Gulf from imperialism."[2] The legacy of these liberation movements, in particular that of the Palestinian movement to end the Israeli occupation, became part of the intellectual universe of many revolutionaries in the region, including those in Iran who ended the rule of the shah in 1979. The impact of the Iranian revolution far exceeded that of the previous experiences—it transformed Middle East politics and beyond on a new scale; it toppled the closest ally of the United States in the region, ended a 2,500-year-old monarchy, and established the first Islamic republic in recent history, thus prefiguring a wave of Islamist movements and religious politics that dominated the Muslim world for over three decades.

The Arab uprisings of 2011 came against this historical backdrop, but they propelled different types of revolutions—indeed, departing from the radical, ideological, and anti-imperialist traditions that marked the earlier experiences in the region. Enjoying a remarkable mobilization, the Arab uprisings remained mostly non-ideological and nonreligious and accompanied some significant changes in favor of democratic norms and egalitarian aspirations among the poor, women, youth, and social minorities. But they fell short of transforming the structure of state power. A history teacher should then ask why, against all expectations, the Arab revolutions did not take an Islamist turn? And why did Arab revolutionaries continue to aspire for democratic rule and social justice even after these monumental uprisings?

New Dawn and Old Demons

The revolutions and the downfall of dictators generated an extraordinary sense of hope and renewal among activists and the ordinary alike. But few could imagine what was to come at a later stage. In Tunisia, after the departure of President Ben Ali to Saudi Arabia, a provisional government took power. It included ministers from both the opposition groups and officials of the old regime. Profoundly outraged, revolutionaries waged daily protests to disband the agents of the old regime from the new government. Popular pressure also led to the release of political prisoners, the abolition of the old ruling party, and closure of political police. On October 23, 2011, Tunisians went to the polls to elect deputies for a Constituent Assembly to draft a new constitution. The Islamic al-Nahda Party, led by Rachid al-Ghannouchi, captured most of the seats, including forty-two women deputies. The new progressive constitution was ratified in January 2014 after months of debate, guiding Tunisia's path to a pluralist democracy and progressive gender policies.

The Tunisian revolution certainly eliminated many repressive legacies of Ben Ali's police state; it established free elections, speech, press, and organization. The right to protest was recognized, and the Truth and Dignity Commission promised to bring human rights violators of the ancien régime to justice. Significantly, the revolutionary moment and free climate bolstered an unprecedented wave of activism and initiatives at the grassroots level by youth, women, farmers, and intellectuals. Yet, a lot remained unaltered. The Ministry of Interior rebuffed the reforms that the revolutionaries had demanded and continued with arrests, torture, and even killing of the opposition.[3] "The networks of the old regime are all there," an activist recounted in July 2011.[4] The elites and economic mafias of the Ben Ali era, organized in some forty-seven political parties and supported by another seventy organizations, began to fight back and block the path to genuine social transformation. They retained their dense network of political factions, friendly media, and business organizations at their disposal.[5] Even though a national alliance of the Islamic, secular, liberal, and labor groups neutralized the initial move, the victory of the rightist Nidaa Tounes in the 2015 presidential elections consolidated the position of the old "parallel state" — the security sector, business elites, and local mafia that had served as the de facto authority before the revolution. In January 2016, Amnesty International reported that the prerevolution violation of human rights had fully returned to Tunisia. One could only expect the indignation of youths over the fate of their stalled revolution. "When young people took to the streets, they were asking for freedom, dignity and employment," stated a prominent activist, "but almost none of these objectives were fulfilled."[6]

In Egypt the democratic thrust of Tahrir movements symbolized the revolutionary dawn. Here in this iconic roundabout, over a period of eighteen days, mass rallies were held, stages were erected, large banners with revolutionary messages went up, and makeshift tents were set up to house those who spent their nights in the square. Soon after, medical teams, cleaning crews, and security groups were organized. In the headquarters around the square, multiple leaders took respite, discussed strategies, assigned tasks, and allocated resources—food, resting locations, communication tools, tract writings, and the like. Young men and women spent night time in the makeshift tents; Muslims and Christians assisted each other in their prayer services. As days passed and revolutionaries settled in their campsites, ordinary residents—men and women, children and elders—descended into the arena, turning the battlefield Tahrir into evenings of carnivalesque conviviality and fun. Travelers came from provincial towns to pay a visit to Tahrir, and young couples held their marriage ceremonies and spent their honeymoon in this square. Tahrir appeared as if it were the microcosm of an alternative order to which the revolutionaries seemed to aspire—democratic governance, horizontal organization, collective decision-making, self-help, and altruism. No wonder the idea of Tahrir traveled fast worldwide, finding resonance in the Occupy Movements in some five hundred cities around the globe including New York, Madrid, Tel Aviv, Bangkok, Sao Paulo, and Istanbul and continuing with Ukraine's Maidan Square and Hong Kong's arena of the "umbrella revolution."[7]

Tahrir represented a novel repertoire of contention—it embodied a desired model of governance while serving as a battle zone to fight for regime change. Tahrir protestors insisted that they would not go home before President Mubarak stepped down. The president did step down within two weeks but transferred power to the Supreme Council of Armed Forces (SCAF) to oversee transition to civilian rule within six months. However, it would take two turbulent years before a new elected government, led by Muhammad Morsi of the Muslim Brotherhood, took office in June 2012. The SCAF rule faced nonstop street protests caused by the delays in the transition timetable, SCAF's repression of dissent, "virginity tests" and state-sponsored sexual assaults

Angel-winged, young revolutionaries fight attacks from the police and teargas. Street art by Ammar Abo Bakr, Luxor, Egypt, January 2012. Courtesy of the artist.

on women in public spaces, and the acquittal of key political culprits during the Mubarak trial. Even Morsi's presidency, incidentally the most open political time after the revolution, failed to bring political calm. If anything, discord and discontent reached a new height during his short-cut tenure. Morsi's Islamist leanings, reflected in the new constitution, alarmed many liberals, leftists, and Coptic Christians who fearfully imagined Egypt adopting an Iranian-style Islamist regime. The "deep state" — the judiciary, intelligence agencies, and the military among others — remained defiant to Morsi and actively worked to subvert him, but President Morsi's incompetence in governance had already caused unprecedented social unrest. During 2012, Egyptians held 500 sit-ins, 581 local protests, 414 labor strikes (up from 335 during 2011), and 558 street demonstrations.[8] A year later, during Morsi's presidency, local protests reached a staggering 7,709, and street demonstrations and clashes rose to 5,821.[9]

The discontent grew further in the summer of 2013, when a nationwide movement, *tamarrod* (rebellion), launched a campaign reportedly collecting twenty-two million signatures of no confidence in order to dismiss President Morsi. The campaign culminated on June 30 in the largest street demonstration in Egypt's history. Even though, it was revealed later, Tamarrod leadership acted on behalf of the generals to undermine Morsi, the enormous popular dissent galvanized in the movement was undeniable. Watching the immense dissent without a powerful unified leadership, the military encouraged and jumped on the wave, inserting itself as the leader of the anti-Morsi "revolution." On July 3, 2013, General el-Sisi forcibly ousted the elected President Muhammad Morsi. The military annulled the constitution and installed an interim civilian government to undertake new elections for a new president, parliament, and constitution. In a violent crackdown on Muslim Brotherhood protestors on August 14, 2013, that left more than a thousand dead (including one hundred police), the generals began to quell the defiant Brotherhood. With the Muslim Brothers in retreat and the "liberal-secular" opposition in disarray, the Mubarakists rejoiced in ecstasy and went on the offensive in the media, in the streets, and in state institutions. An orgy of national chauvinism, misinformation, and self-indulgence fed their fantasy of restoring the ancien régime. President Mubarak and his son were set free before long, and the old guard — the security captains, intelligence bosses, big businessmen, and media chiefs — gained fresh blood. General Sisi stood for and won the elections for the presidency. Soon, state surveillance began to extend from the Muslim Brothers to hunt down any known figure deemed defying the new rule—including left, liberal, and revolutionary activists. Even Muhammad El-Baradei, the ex-vice president of the new government, was not spared. Stunned, the revolutionaries (those dispersed constituencies who initiated and carried through the uprising of January 25, 2011, for the cause of "bread, freedom, and social justice") watched the counterrevolution march on.

Key Questions

A history teacher would face three key questions to highlight and explain to students: How can we explain the emergence of these remarkable uprisings in societies that were deemed resistant to democratic transformation? Why did the revolutions, against all expectations, not take on a singular religious, Islamic ideology? Why did they mostly fail to bring the democratic rule and social justice to which the revolutionaries seemed to aspire?

It is commonly accepted that perhaps no one had anticipated this most important political earthquake in the region's postcolonial history. Intelligence agencies, political establishments, think tanks, academic circles, and even the protagonists themselves were taken by surprise. Even the US intelligence services seemed to be confident that the Mubarak regime was safe enough not to be crumbled by a handful of "usual" demonstrators who appeared in the streets of Cairo every so often.[10] Although all revolutions come as a surprise, there was something peculiar about the Arab uprisings. Teachers of history should particularly emphasize the fact that the Middle East in general and Arab societies in particular are often viewed from an exceptionalist lens by the media and some academic circles. This way of seeing the Middle East is widely discussed in terms of Orientalism, the idea that Middle East culture and religion, notably Islam, shape the mindset of societies that are resistant to change. So, a great deal of discourse is devoted to how authoritarian regimes manage to persist. If indeed change were to come, it would come either by strong leaders and military men, or by the powerful religious movements, as we saw in the Iranian Revolution of 1979 that entailed the establishment of an Islamic state.

The Arab uprisings, however, challenged such deep-seated assumptions about Arab societies and politics. Not only did the uprisings express popular desire for social justice, freedom from repression, and democracy, but they also held civil nonreligious language and nonviolent campaigns. Of course, most participants were pious Muslims who fought along with seculars, leftists, nationalists, and non-Muslims. Many protestors participated in religious practices (such as praying in streets and squares), utilizing religious times (Fridays) and places (such as mosques); but these religious practices are all part of the regular doings of all pious Muslims who perform them in everyday life, rather than signaling an intent to Islamize the uprisings. Even though Islamist activists such as the Muslim Brothers or al-Nahda were certainly present during the uprisings, they never unilaterally determined the direction of the movements—after all, there was hardly any central leadership in these uprisings. In Tunisia, supporters of the Islamic al-Nahda did take part in the revolution. But their leader, Rachid al-Ghannouchi, made it clear that his party did not want a Khomeini-type religious state; he favored a nonreligious and civil state.

These overwhelmingly civil and nonreligious revolts represented a sharp departure from the Arab politics of the mid-1980s and 1990s, when the political class was consumed by nationalist, anti-Zionist, and moral politics framed overwhelmingly in an Islamist paradigm. It was to take a decade or so for a turnaround to occur. Early signs in Egypt of a turnaround (a new political discourse and new ways of doing politics) seemed to appear in the early 2000s. They manifested themselves in the activities around the Popular Committee for Solidarity with the Palestinian and Iraqi People, but later and more notably in the episode of the Kifaya (Enough!) movement, which heralded the coming of a postnational (focusing more on democracy and human rights at home rather than external domination), post-ideological (overriding ideological lines, especially religious and secular divisions, leftists and nationalists), and post-Islamist politics that culminated in the revolution of January 25. In Tunisia, the prerevolution police state had restricted open expression of political ideologies whether Islamic or secular liberal. The limited activism during the late 2000s came largely from youth who espoused a more pragmatic politics around human rights, jobs, and income disparities.

Causes

This new political vision resulted from a combination of new actors, a new political environment, and novel means and manners of mobilization, all of which came to fruition in turn through a series of structural changes that Arab societies undertook in the 1990s. In a sense the authoritarian Arab states, affected by the forces of globalization, unintentionally created environments and actors that came to challenge the very essence of these states. To begin with, since the 1990s, Middle Eastern societies became more urban and globalized, with over 65 percent of the population currently living in cities. In the meantime, certain urban features (institutions, means of communication, and literacy) permeated into the countryside, bringing rural life into the national orbit. Urban life, in turn, generated desires, demands, and rights, chiefly the "right to the city" (such as paid jobs, decent shelters, optimum amenities, and respect) that these regimes failed to fulfill for a large portion of urban inhabitants. Cities then inculcated in the urban dwellers a sense of entitlement and citizenship. Secondly, a dramatic demographic shift made these societies excessively young, with an estimated 70 percent of the population under the age of thirty-five. Here in these overcrowded habitats, the young encountered tremendous constraints (economic deprivation, social control, and moral pressure) in fulfilling their youthful claims. And yet these very cities also offered them great opportunities to forge collective identities and to demand social inclusion—in street corner gatherings, tea shops, schools, and colleges, and recently in the virtual world and social media. It was in these cities that fragmented young persons turned into *youth*, as collective agents.

Significantly, these urbanizing and youthful societies became increasingly literate (over 90 percent of those fourteen to twenty-four years of age). With the explosion of higher education institutions (there were by 2010 more than 280 universities in the Arab world), thousands of graduates poured each year into the highly segmented labor markets, which had been aggressively neoliberalized by the policy of structural adjustment pushed by the World Bank and International Monetary Fund (IMF) since the early 1990s. In this new economic restructuring, well-connected elite groups in such globalized sectors as high-tech, entertainment, real estate development, communication, or import-export have thrived, while disproportionate numbers were pushed away from the economic outcomes that they expected to enjoy. It is no surprise that the MENA Region (Middle East and North Africa) just prior to the uprisings suffered from the highest rate of unemployment in particular among youth (over 25 percent) in the world. The diminishing subsidies, job insecurity, and deteriorating social provisions had caused massive urban riots in the major Arab cities in the 1980s and early 1990s. To off-set the destabilizing effects of social exclusion, most Arab states assigned since the 1990s a good portion of development and welfare tasks to the rapidly growing NGOs, religious charities, and microcredit projects. But these arrangements, often framed in neoliberal logic, failed to address welfare needs, not to mention a deep inequality that the end of social contracts and the diminishing role of the state in fostering economic prosperity for the masses had caused. Thus, the subaltern groups resorted either to the subsistent economy, self-help, and "quiet encroachment" such as building shelters without permits or waited for an opportunity to explode. When food prices increased in the late 2000s, a new series of urban riots broke out; labor strikes overtook industries subject to "ratio-nalization" and restructuring.

One outcome of such uneven development has been the growth of the "middle-class poor," a class that has played a key role in the Arab revolts of 2011. This paradoxical class enjoys college degrees, knows about the world, uses new media, and expects a middle-class lifestyle. But it is pushed by economic deprivation to live the life of the tradi-tional urban dispossessed in the shanty towns and slums and to under-take jobs in the largely precarious and low-status parallel economy—as taxi drivers, fruit sellers, street vendors, or boss boys. The middle-class poor constituted a segment of the 36 percent of Arabs who lived in slums and of the 40–50 percent who subsisted on the insecure informal economy just prior to the uprisings.

In the 1980s and 1990s, much of this stratum had merged into a political class absorbed by the nationalist and Islamist sentiments, even though in their quotidian existence, many members of the middle-class poor, just like the other discontented clusters, were involved in every-day struggles to advance their claims in often individualized and quiet fashion. The urban poor made sure to secure a shelter, consolidate their communities, and earn a living by devising work in the vast subsistent and street economy. Muslim women strove to assert their presence in public, go to college, and ensure justice in courts. And youths took every opportunity to affirm their autonomy, challenge social control, and plan for their future, even though many remained atomized and dreamed of migrating to the West. These quiet struggles, "nonmove-ments," immersed often in the ordinary practices of everyday life, carved off pieces of power and opportunity in favor of ordinary people who under repressive regimes were prevented from forging open and organized mobilization. When the political opportunity arrived at the end of the 2000s, these subaltern groups merged into political struggles that had now assumed a new life by transcending the exclusive confines of nationalist and Islamist politics.

Three developments since the early 2000s helped generate a new Arab public with a post-ideological and post-Islamist outlook. First, Islamist politics—experiments that sought to establish an exclusivist Islamic state based on shari'a law and moral codes—had begun to lose their hegemony in the post 9/11 Middle East. The Iranian model had already faced a deep crisis for its repression, misogyny, exclusionary attitudes, and unfulfilled promises. And al-Qa'ida's severe violence and extremism had caused a widespread Islamophobia from which largely ordinary Muslims suffered. Islamism encountered serious challenge from without and within—from seculars and the faithful alike who felt the deep scars that Islamists' disregard for human rights, tolerance, and pluralism had left on the body politics and religious life in the Muslim world.

Second, such ways of thinking permeated into the inner circles of Islamism, compelling activists and ideologues to rethink their exclusivist, nativist, and nondemocratic political project. Post-Islamism emerged as an alternative to imagine a religious polity that was more inclusive, pluralistic, and rights-based. It envisioned a nonreligious state to operate within a pious society. Muslims could now confidently remain Muslim, while imagining a democratic state. Turkey under the AKP (Justice and Development Party) stood as a workable model of post-Islamist polity during 2011, before Recep Tayyip Erdoğan pursued an authoritarian populist path.

And finally, in the Arab world, the expanding electronic media since the mid-2000s (satellite dishes, Al Jazeera, internet, websites, weblogs, and then Facebook and Twitter) offered an unprecedented public arena for activists to communicate and debate these ideas. In 2010, some 25 percent of Egyptians and 34 percent of Tunisians were linked to the internet. Personal and political views circulated through the virtual world, which at the time had remained fairly free from police surveillance. With the discontented actors, novel political thinking, and new channels of communication and exchange, Arab countries produced a new public—one marked by a largely postnational, post-ideological, and post-Islamist orientation. Arab revolutions embodied this new thinking. Even though the revolutions opened the space for the rise of both highly liberal and highly conservative religious ideas and groups, the mainstream continued to uphold a more moderate position. It is no surprise that a comprehensive survey by Pew Research Center in six Arab countries showed that 94–99 percent of the respondents opposed ISIS and what it stood for.

Outcome

The history teacher should raise the question and explain why these revolutions in the end faced such a dispiriting outcome. Who was responsible? And what happened to the revolutionary protagonists who initiated the uprisings? The Arab revolutions experienced such a disheartening aftermath that many began to question the very wisdom behind the making of those otherwise monumental movements. Syria sank into a civil war creating one of the most tragic (7.5 million) refugee crises since WWII; Bahrain's revolution was stalled by the intervention of Saudi Arabia; and little changed in the power structure in Yemen in favor of the ordinary people before it turned in 2015 into a front for a civil war between the Houthi rebels and the deposed president Ali Saleh, on the one side, and the Saudi regime that backed the central government, on the other. In Egypt, the release of ex-president Hosni Mubarak from prison on August 22, 2013, marked the return of the counterrevolution following the military ouster of President Morsi in July 2013. Even the most hopeful transition in Tunisia suffered setbacks. Despite the success in establishing a pluralist democracy, the official neglect of the key revolutionary demands—jobs, justice, and dignity—dispirited many ordinary Tunisians, prompting thousands of youths with Islamist inclinations to join ISIS.

Why did the Arab revolutions face such an unfortunate destiny? Most observers have pointed to domestic and regional counterrevolutionary intrigues and foreign meddling.[11] There is certainly truth in this. NATO forces used the Libyan revolution to crush Qaddafi's rule and to secure close ties to a post-Qaddafi government and access to its oil. Deeply apprehensive of the spread of the Arab Spring in its cities and the backyard, the Saudi regime rolled its tanks through the streets of Bahrain to obstruct the revolution in the Persian Gulf. Interventions by Iran, Russia, and Lebanese Hizballah to support Assad's rule, and of Turkey, Saudi Arabia, and the United States to topple the regime turned Syria into a war theater to settle geopolitical accounts. Qatar backed

Islamist groups in Libya and Egypt as well as ISIS, whereas the United Arab Emirates (UAE) led a campaign against them in support of the military regime in Egypt and anti-Islamist factions in Libya.[12] The Yemeni revolution not only fell victim to its own serious limitations, but it equally suffered from the geopolitical competition between Iran and Saudi Arabia that deployed military force to fight the Iran-backed Houthi rebels in support of the central government. In Tunisia, Egypt, and Yemen where the old-standing dictators were indeed toppled, foreign actors, in particular Saudi Arabia and UAE, pursued a strategy of destabilization, sectarianization, and influence through economic leverage.[13]

As the major counterrevolutionary power, the Saudi regime continued to subvert any democratic openings or footprints of Iran deemed jeopardizing to its hegemony. To this end, Riyadh supported extremist Salafis, provoked sectarian discord, backed an early ISIS, intervened militarily in Syria and Yemen in 2015, and used financial blackmail to dissuade Egypt's postcoup government from any reconciliation with the Brotherhood.[14] On its part, the United States simultaneously supported and sabotaged the revolutions, depending on which regimes and what interests they were threatening.[15] The United States and its Israeli ally were only happy to find the sectarian war in Syria benefiting the neighboring Jewish state, because it significantly weakened the regime of Bashar al-Assad.[16]

But counterrevolutionary sabotage is not particular to the Arab experience; all revolutions carry within them the germs of counterrevolution waiting for a chance to strike; yet they rarely succeed, primarily because they lack wide popular support. In the twentieth century, the internal intrigues and international wars against the revolutions in Russia, China, Cuba, and Iran all failed, even though they rendered these revolutions deeply security conscious and repressive. In the Philippines, the military's consecutive coup attempts against Cory Aquino's government, following the anti-Marcos "People's Revolution" in 1986, were all neutralized. Only in Nicaragua, a rare experience of democratic polity after the 1979 revolution, did the counterrevolution succeed through electoral means; the US-backed Contra war severely undermined the revolutionary Sandinista government, thus ensuring the electoral victory of the rightist Violeta Chamorro in 1990.

Thus, the crucial question the instructor of history may pose is: were the Arab revolutions "revolutionary enough" to offset the dangers of the counterrevolution? The Arab revolutions were particularly more vulnerable to a counterrevolutionary restoration because they failed to radically transform states—a step necessary to establish new social and political orders, that is, new institutions, policies, and modes of governance in line with the objectives of the revolutions. While the protagonists succeeded in creating such magic as the Tahrir mobilization, little changed in institutions of the old order. In Egypt, Yemen, and to a lesser extent in Tunisia, some of the key institutions of the old regimes—the security apparatus, the judiciary, the state media, political networks of powerful business circles, cultural organizations, and especially the military—remained largely unaltered.

Conclusion

Egypt, Tunisia, and Yemen undertook not revolutions in the twentieth-century sense that began with the rapid and radical overhaul of the state; rather they experienced "refo-lutions," "reformist revolutions," that wanted to push for reforms in and through the institutions of the incumbent states.[17] Thus, revolutionaries enjoyed massive popular support but lacked administrative power; they earned remarkable hegemony but did not actually rule, with the consequence that they had to rest on the institutions of the incumbent states (for instance, the existing ministries, judiciary, or the military) to change things. But it was unrealistic to expect such institutions with entrenched interests to alter, let alone undo, themselves. If anything, they remained defiant, continued to reinforce their positions, and waited for a chance to strike back. The protagonist revolutionaries remained outside the centers of power, because they were not planning to take governmental power; and when at the later stages they realized that they should, they lacked the resources—solid organizations, powerful leadership, a strategic vision, and some form of hard power—necessary to wrest power from the old regimes or the free riders. Thus, while the old state functionaries continued with their usual business, and the traditional religious parties mobilized in the villages, urban neighborhoods, and mosques, winning significant elections, the revolutionaries made themselves busy with the street protests against the new governments. It was largely the grassroots—the poor, marginalized women, youth, and social minorities—who through their daily campaign for housing, work, self-organization, and recognition gave a radical impulse to these non-radical revolutions. But this needs a separate treatment.[18]

NOTES

This chapter draws heavily on my book *Revolution without Revolutionaries: Making Sense of the Arab Spring* (Palo Alto: Stanford University Press, 2017) in information and analysis.

1. This section draws on Fred Halliday, *Arabia without Sultans* (London: Saqi Books, 2002), 153–226.

2. Halliday, *Arabia without Sultans*, 320–21; see also John Chalcraft, "Migration and Popular Protest in the Arabian Peninsula and the Gulf in the 1950s and 1960s," special issue, *International Labor and Working Class History* 79, no. 1 (Spring 2011): 28–47.

3. Interview with Tarek and Ghassam, Tunis, July 2011.

4. Interview with Tarek, a cyberactivist, Tunis, July 2011.

5. See Tunisian daily *Al-Sabah*, August 16, 2011, www.assabah.com.tn/article-56485.htoml.

6. Lina Ben Mhenni, "My Arab Spring: Tunisia's Revolution Was a Dream," Al Jazeera, December 17, 2015.

7. Asef Bayat, "Global Tahrir," in *Global Middle East: Into the Twenty-First Century*, ed. Asef Bayat and Linda Herrera (Oakland: University of California Press, 2020).

8. Reported by the Egyptian Center for Social and Economic Rights, 2013. The Egyptian Ministry of Manpower reported that during 2011 workers organized 335 strikes (including 135 sit-ins in the public sector and 123 in the private sector) and made 4,460 complaints to the ministry; *Al-Masry al-Youm*, January 17, 2012.

9. Office of President Morsi, published in a poster and distributed officially, June 2013.

10. Reported by Richard Norton-Taylor in the *Guardian*, February 1, 2011. See also Greg Gause, "Why Middle East Studies Missed the Arab Spring: The Myth of Authoritarian Stability," *Foreign Affairs* 90, no. 4 (July 2011).

11. See, for instance, Gilbert Achcar, *The People Want: A Radical Exploration of the Arab Uprising* (Berkeley: University of California Press, 2013); Jean-Pierre Filiu, *From Deep State to Islamic State: The Arab Counter-Revolution and Its Jihadi Legacy* (Oxford: Oxford University Press, 2015). These are against analyses such as those of Bernard Lewis that attribute the despairing Arab spring to the absence of democratic culture.

12. David Kirkpatrick, "Leaked Emirati Emails Could Threaten Peace Talks in Libya," *New York Times*, November 12, 2015.

13. Guido Steinberg, "Leading the Counter-Revolution: Saudi Arabia and the Arab Spring," SWP Research Paper, German Institute for International and Security Affairs, Berlin, June 2014. Recently, Saudi officials admitted that the regime has supported radical Islamism including Wahhabism since the 1960s

as a way to counter secular, socialist, or democratic ideas that threatened the Saudi regime; see Zalmay Khalilzad, "'We Misled You': How the Saudis Are Coming Clean on Funding Terrorism," *Politico Magazine*, September 1, 2016, http://www.politico.com/magazine/story/2016/09/saudi-arabia-terrorism-fund ing-214241.

14. This is according to the Egyptian journalist Fahmi Huwaidi in a May 2014 interview that aired on Al Jazeera. See "Huwaidi: Saudi and UAE Are Funding Media Attack on the Brotherhood," *Middle East Monitor*, May 4, 2014, https://www.middleeastmonitor.com/20140504-huwaidi-saudi-and-uae-are -funding-media-attack-on-the-brotherhood/.

15. According to Hugh Roberts ("The Hijackers," *London Review of Books* 37, no. 14 [2015]), it has been primarily the Western powers (United States, UK, France), the Arab Gulf States (Saudi Arabia, Qatar), and Turkey that have hijacked the Syrian revolution, because of insisting on regime change and thus sidelining the nonviolent opposition. Roberts cites a leaked document by the US Defense Intelligence Agency showing that as early as 2012, the United States anticipated ISIS and its establishment of a caliphate in Iraq and Syria but did nothing to prevent it because it served as a counterpoint to the Assad regime.

16. A WikiLeaks revelation of Hillary Clinton's emails suggest that the Israeli government believed that the escalating of civil war in neighboring Syria would undermine the regime and would keep Iran preoccupied with Syrian affairs; see email from Sidney Blumenthal to Hilary Clinton, July 24, 2012, https://wikileaks.org/clinton-emails/emailid/12171.

17. Asef Bayat, "Paradoxes of Arab Refo-lutions," *Jadaliyya*, March 3, 2011; Asef Bayat, "Revolutions in Bad Times," *New Left Review* 80 (March-April 2013).

18. For an elaboration see Asef Bayat, *Revolution without Revolutionaries*.

KEY RESOURCES

Bayat, Asef. *Revolution without Revolutionaries: Making Sense of the Arab Spring*. Stanford, CA: Stanford University Press, 2017.

Idle, Nadia, and Alex Nunns. *Tweets from Tahrir*. New York: OR Books, 2011.

Noujaim, Jehane, dir. *The Square*. Participant Media, 2013.

Pearlman, Wendy. *We Crossed a Bridge and It Trembled: Voices from Syria*. New York: Custom House, 2017.

Return to Homs. YouTube, 2014. https://www.youtube.com/user/returntohoms.

Al-Zubaidi, Lyla, and Matthew Cassel, eds. *Diaries of an Unfinished Revolution: Voices from Tunis to Damascus*. New York: Penguin Books, 2013.

Refugees in and from the Middle East

Teaching about Displacement in the Context of the International Refugee Regime

ROCHELLE DAVIS

According to international law, a refugee is someone who is no longer living in their home country and who either cannot return or is not allowed to return. Refugees exist today because we use political borders to delimit the countries to which people "belong," and when they flee that country, they are called refugees or "forced migrants." These political borders regulate human movement across geographical spaces. Within this nation-state system of political borders, people legally cross borders with passports. And other people regularly move across these political borders for safety, with or without passports and visas. Because they were forced to leave their countries due to wars, targeted killing, genocide, famines, environmental disasters, political oppression, and other forces beyond their control, there are provisions for these movements in refuge- and asylum-seeking practices and laws.[1] The term "forced migrants" also includes internally displaced people, who are not refugees, who are displaced but remain inside their country.

The news tells us that we are facing the largest numbers of forced migrants since World War II; numbers that in 2018 reached almost 75 million people as "Persons of Concern," which includes almost 25 million refugees, over 40 million internally displaced persons (IDPs),

5 million returnees, and 3 million each of stateless persons and asylum seekers. The Middle East and North Africa host 15 of these 75 million, or 20 percent of these Persons of Concern, and refugees from the Middle East and North Africa also contribute, in part, to those in Africa (26 million), Europe (11 million), and beyond.[2]

Teaching about displacement and refugees requires understanding three larger issues, which will be discussed throughout this chapter: the state-citizen model, the international refugee regime, and the discursive framing of refugees (in other words, the way we think and talk about displaced people). Some questions for teachers to address with students follow.

First, our contemporary political system is built on the Westphalian order of states, enshrined in the United Nations, in which each state has sovereignty over territory and citizens. But refugees, as citizens who have fled their states (and also stateless people), explicitly disrupt this political model, while international and national laws allow them the ability to reside legally in a country other than their own. Both history and the news can be usefully mined to find examples of how countries define and police their borders around the entry and existence of noncitizens, and of debates around international and national laws. And to understand this fully, we should always ask, how do refugees encounter and navigate borders and the laws of host countries and where do they find protection?

Second, an international refugee regime has developed in the twentieth century that aims to provide *humanitarian* solutions for refugees and the displaced; but forced migration is most often a result of *political* problems. So, in what ways do humanitarian solutions help those who are displaced, if they cannot return home? How does the continuation of conflicts and the absence of political solutions make refugee issues worse or prolong their situations? We find today millions of people still displaced from decades ago, and answering these questions helps us understand why.

Third, we commonly see the framing of refugees as "a crisis" or "problem," rather than the political and environmental forces that displace people as the problem. Worthy questions to ask and that can be tracked in primary sources include: When do refugees become a crisis? And who gets to define them that way?[3] Why do we often conceive and label people as the problem but so often fail to see structural issues or violence as problems?

In addressing these three larger issues, we can provide the bigger picture for students who want to learn about refugees because they have empathy for others or they want to work in fields that are related to humanitarian aid provision or social work. Having students ponder these questions and answers helps students understand that the context of refugee movements and experiences not only is situated in idealistic notions of aid and assistance, but also is framed by the political actions of states and nonstate actors.

Defining Displacement

Linguistically, the concept of having a "place" is embedded in the word "dis*place*ment." Displacement suggests that everyone has a "place" that they "should" be. The modern world frames a person's place in terms of citizenship, nationality, and belonging. Refugees, by definition, can only exist in a world that is defined by state sovereignty over borders, borders that allow some to pass while keeping others out.[4] Refugees are governed both by host country and international laws, which allow them certain rights including protection against forced return (*non refoulement* in international law). Internally displaced persons (IDPs) are those who have fled their homes but remain within their country. IDPs remain citizens of their countries and face different challenges, depending on their relationship with their government.[5] Because we know that that people often move multiple times internally before fleeing their country, it is common to use terms, such as "the displaced" or "forced migrants," which include both refugees and IDPs from a particular conflict.

Liisa Malkki and Shahram Khosravi argue that refugees may be perceived as symbolically dangerous because they are "out of place"— they hold citizenship in another country or it is feared that they bring the violence they fled with them. This perception of their symbolic danger can morph into also seeing them as physically dangerous to the "purity" of the host nation and its culture, values, and way of life.[6] The ways many contemporary political parties and countries' elected officials describe refugees is pregnant with the allegations of the symbolic and physical dangers that refugees pose. For example, Hungarian Prime Minister Viktor Orbán described migrants and refugees to Hungary as "poison" in 2016 and Muslim refugees as "invaders" in 2018.[7] American President Donald Trump tweeted in 2016: "Refugees from Syria over

10k plus more coming. Lots young males, poorly vetted."[8] This statement is inaccurate because no refugee entering the United States is "poorly vetted," but more specifically he insinuates that "young males" are dangerous and bring the violence Syria is experiencing with them.

Refugee Movements in the Middle East and North Africa

The discussion of refugee movements in the Middle East can be divided into three overlapping time periods and phases. The first period spans the end of the Ottoman Empire and the rise of nationalism and the nation-state system. The second period encompasses French, British, Italian, and Spanish colonialism in the Middle East and North Africa and postcolonial state formations. And the third period is the post–World War II rise of the international refugee regime and the various current conflicts.

Period I: End of Empire and the Rise of Nationalism and the Nation-State System

One way to understand the state-citizen-refugee framing is to study forced population movements prior to the rise of the nation-state system. Living within the Ottoman Empire at the end of the nineteenth century were many ethno-linguistic groups (Greeks, Turks, Arabs, Kurds, among others) and religious groups including Muslims, Christians, Jews, Yezidis, Mandaeans, and their respective sects. The work of historians today helps a modern student understand how governance was structured during this period that allowed for the centrality of this diversity.[9]

Displaced communities moving *into* the Ottoman Empire from Russia and Europe were often given special status.[10] Various legal codes and commissions were established by the Ottoman Empire to help settle these communities.[11] For example, the Charity Commission was set up in 1893 to "collect and distribute aid, provide health care, and find employment for both Muslims and Christians" seeking to reside in the Ottoman Empire.[12] People fleeing the Balkans and Caucasus were resettled in the southeastern frontier provinces of the empire (modern-day Syria and Jordan) to gain their loyalty and support against local tribes that were opposed to Ottoman rule.[13]

However, this period also witnessed efforts to force people *out* of the empire. Armenians and other communities in Anatolia were labeled as separatists and subsequently targeted, culminating in the Armenian genocide and forced marches of 1915–1917.[14] Survivors ended up in what is today Syria, Lebanon, Palestine, Jordan, and Egypt, and their descendants remain in parts of those nation-states today.[15]

Post–WWI Creation of Modern States

The post–World War I period in the Middle East and North Africa witnessed the establishment or entrenchment of French, British, Spanish, and Italian colonial enterprises. The emerging nation-states for which the populations fought usually included all those present and living in new states' borders.[16] People who were born and raised in Algeria or Syria, and who had moved to Egypt, Sudan, or Palestine, became citizens of the newly created states (both ruled by colonial powers and independent). These individuals and communities may have retained their ethnic or linguistic markers, but they have also been included as citizens of the state.

However, this was not true everywhere or in other parts of the world. The global post–World War I political impetus, led by the League of Nations, advocated for the idea of "nations" as an ethno-linguistic characteristic of the new world order of nation-states, which, as Dawn Chatty explains, meant that "each new state sought to unmix their nationalities as their minorities came to be regarded as obstacles to state building."[17] A striking example is the Greek-Turkish Population Exchange that took place in the Balkans in 1922. The Lausanne Treaty determined that Turkish and Greek nation-states should be created based on ethnic, linguistic, and religious identifiers. Thus, the League of Nations high commissioner for refugees Fridtjof Nansen brokered the forced movement ("exchange") of the Greek-speaking populations of Anatolia (modern-day Turkey) and the Turkish-speaking populations of Greece.[18] With this decision, half a million Muslims whose ancestors had resided, procreated, traded, and worshipped within the new borders of Greece were deemed to be Turks and were relocated to their "own" nation, the just-created Republic of Turkey, where many could not even speak the language. At the same time, some 1.5 million Greek Orthodox Christians—whose ancestors lived within the area now defined as Turkey from a period predating the Roman Empire—were now forcibly relocated to Greece. Ethnic, linguistic, and religious markers became national identity as families were uprooted, neighborhoods destroyed, and trade networks eradicated.[19]

Thus, with the League of Nations at the helm, two independent states, Greece (1830) and Turkey (1923), participated in a forced migration of people who were perceived as "others" in the places they had lived for generations and who had little to no connection to the places to which they were moved. This case is often cited as a marker in the increasing ethno-nationalist separation of the world, and as a failure of global vision and an imposed suffering on people.

As Turkey was created with the idea of "Turkishness" as central to the nation, the non-Turkish Kurdish, Syriac, and Armenian communities in Anatolia were targeted as not "natural" members of the nation, since they were not "Turkish."[20] Kurdish drives for inclusion in the state, and then also later for independence for a Kurdish state (given Kurdistan's spread across multiple new states in the Middle East), were often met with violence, and Kurdish political ambitions were repressed.[21] Subsequent years of repression of Kurds as independent political actors have been part of various governments in Turkey, Iran, Iraq, and Syria. Extending to the present, with the creation of the Kurdistan regional government of Iraq in the post-2003 US invasion of Iraq, the Kurdistan history of displacement is a useful case study that spans all three of these time periods and relates to issues around identity, modern state formation, international intervention in the Middle East, and refugee rights.[22]

Historians' work helps students answer questions relating to the motivations behind these state-building policies and practices, and the subsequent suffering of those who were impacted. In particular, something worth exploring is the reason behind the restrictive ethnic, linguistic, and religious character of newly independent Turkey and Greece, when compared to the more inclusive Ottoman Empire. Why did other new countries in the Middle East accept their diverse religious and ethnic new citizens? Local communities' acceptance and the absence of discourses about fear of outsiders and threats suggests empathy for the newcomers. And the states themselves saw an advantage to keeping these new citizens who had developed ties to the land, ran mercantile enterprises, and established institutions such as schools and newspapers.[23] A deeper look into the events of this period can be helpful in understanding policies and politics today, as well as providing analytical tools and perspectives for understanding other refugee movements rising out of ethno-nationalist identifications or violence.

Period 2: Colonial and Postcolonial Rule—North Africa

The nineteenth and twentieth centuries saw the deepening of French, Spanish, and Italian colonial rule over northern Africa. Although often not discussed within the context of refugee movements, millions of Algerians and Libyans who were accused of sympathizing with the rebel anticolonial movements were uprooted from their villages and homes and imprisoned in camps. In Libya during the Italian colonial period (1911–1943), at least half a million people (of a total population under 2 million) were killed or died, and another 250,000 were forced into exile as a result of colonial policies and enforced encampment.[24] In Algeria, the French settler-colonial movement brought in hundreds of thousands of French settlers. Yet when Algeria was annexed to France in 1870, its non-European residents were made subjects, not citizens, of the French state.[25] The declaration of an Algerian independence movement in 1954 resulted in a massive French response that sought to keep Algeria for France. Between 1954 and 1962, "about 3,525,000 Algerians were forced to leave their homes. 2,350,000 of them were resettled in camps created ex-nihilo by the French army and 1,175,000 of them were resettled in pre-existing villages near French military outposts. This practice of resettlement, euphemistically referred to as *regroupement* in the French official terminology, was an essential tool of the French military policy of pacification."[26]

These populations remain unrecognized as victims of forced displacement, because they were labeled either as terrorists or sympathizers and most remained within the state's borders. The situation of those internally displaced rarely see interventions by other states or international organizations beyond humanitarian aid because of the perceived need to respect the concept of state sovereignty.

A contemporary refugee issue tied to both colonialism and national independence movements is the territory of the Western Sahara. Spain was the colonial power ruling the "Spanish Sahara" (Western Sahara) until it withdrew in 1975 and divided the territory between Mauritania and Morocco. People living there formed the Polisario, a Sahrawi liberation movement that sought independence for the country and defied what they saw as recolonization.[27] In the post-1975 fighting, many fled across the border to a series of encampments in southwestern Algeria (in and around Tindouf) where they continue to live today. Mauritania withdrew its claims in 1979; Morocco, however, annexed the territory, settling Moroccan citizens there, mining its resources, and building a giant berm in the desert to reinforce its claim and marginalize the Polisario.[28] Morocco annexed the Western Sahara, and the United Nations Mission for the Referendum in Western Sahara (MINURSO) was established in 1991; but still there is no resolution to the issue.

An additional postcolonial holdover are two enclaves in Morocco (geographic North Africa) that are Spanish territory: Ceuta and Melilla. These enclaves have proven a magnet for refugee and asylum seekers who hope to reach Europe without embarking on a dangerous sea journey. Regularly reinforced with ever more advanced technology and higher walls, they form an impassable European border, albeit one not on the European continent.[29] These legacies of colonialism in North Africa continue to be part of global politics today, and learning these histories helps make sense of the suppressed past as well as the geography and politics of the present.

Period 3: Twentieth-Century Wars and Conflicts

The Middle East as Host to Europeans Fleeing World War II Violence

Those who have seen the movie *Casablanca* will know that French colonial rule also brought the Vichy regime, which was sympathetic to the Nazis, to control parts of Morocco and Algeria.[30] The rise of Nazi Germany and its spread across Europe not only resulted in a massive genocide (Holocaust) of Jews, Roma, and others but also forced millions of people to flee. The Middle East proved to be an area of safety for European refugees, especially Jewish refugees.[31] Camps were set up in Palestine, Iran, Syria, and Egypt for tens of thousands of forced migrants. These camps were operated "in a collaborative effort by national governments, military officials and domestic and international aid organizations."[32] Most refugees returned home or moved on to third countries following the war, and this history of the Middle East as a place hosting European refugees is largely forgotten. We tend to think of refugees as coming to Europe from conflicts in the Middle East. But in the mid-twentieth century, Europeans found the Middle East to be a place of refuge to escape from their home conflicts and oppression. In addition,

European colonialism caused more displacement proportionally than what we are seeing today. So how do we think about migration and refugee perceptions today, compared to the mid-twentieth century?

Post–World War II Refugees

In 1945, the global community established the United Nations (UN) to address issues of global governance as well as the refugees who were often the result of the failures of such governance. The widespread refugee movements that resulted from World War II led the UN initially to establish institutions that could address those who remained displaced following the war. Liisa Malkki describes how "principle elements of international refugee law and related legal instruments grew largely out of the aftermath of the war in Europe."[33] At the same time, other conflicts were causing additional refugee movements, including the partition of India in 1947 and the partition of Palestine/creation of Israel in 1948.

The UN General Assembly decision to partition Palestine between Arab and Jewish states in November 1947 resulted in two years of fighting, the displacement of half of the non-Jewish population (what the British Mandate government labeled the population), and the creation of Israel on lands apportioned to both the Jewish and Arab states. Following the 1949 armistice agreements, Palestinians did not gain a state and Israel controlled the majority of what had been historic Palestine, while the West Bank was annexed by Jordan and the Gaza Strip came under Egyptian administration. With this scenario in front of it, and 750,000 mostly destitute refugees in the area, the UN voted to create the United Nations Relief and Works Agency for Palestine Refugees (UNRWA) in late 1949.[34]

UNRWA began its operations in May 1950, taking over from a variety of international groups, governments, and local efforts that had been providing aid in Lebanon, Syria, the West Bank, Jordan, and the Gaza Strip.[35] Other options existed, including that of the return of the refugees, which Israel refused to accept. "It is often forgotten that the General Assembly had previously established the Conciliation Commission for Palestine to implement all of the previous UN resolutions, including Resolution 194 (December 1948) which asserts the right of refugees to return to their homes and property."[36] With the passage of time, UNRWA became the key provider of health, education, and social services to Palestinian refugees in Lebanon, Syria, the Gaza Strip, Jordan, and the West Bank and established itself as a semi-parallel system to governmental services.[37] Around 30 percent of Palestinian refugees still live in refugee camps today, which are no longer "camps" but, rather, have become densely packed neighborhoods within cities and towns. Despite the seventy-plus years since their initial displacement, many Palestinians' only official identity documents define them as refugees. Others who have gained citizenships still define themselves as refugees, because they assert that they were never given their rights to return or compensation. Students often ask, "Why do Palestinians hold on to this identity?" It is worth discussing how we as humans self-identify as well as defy others, more powerful than us, who want us to change, as well as the presumptions behind asking that of someone else.[38]

The International Refugee Regime

Two early UN institutions addressing refugees are still extant today: the previously described UNRWA and the United Nations High Commissioner for Refugees (UNHCR—established in 1951).[39] UNHCR comes from the UN Convention Relating to the Status of Refugees, signed in 1951, that today guides how signatory countries address refugees.

> A person who is outside his/her country of nationality or habitual residence; has a well-founded fear of persecution because of his/her race, religion, nationality, membership in a particular social group or political opinion; and is unable or unwilling to avail himself/herself of the protection of that country, or to return there, for fear of persecution.[40]

In addition, the Convention details that a refugee has rights, including to the freedom of religion and movement, as well as to work, be educated, and obtain travel documents. A refugee has obligations to the host government to obey laws. The Convention also stipulates that host countries should not force refugees to return to a country where they fear persecution.[41] The 1951 Convention definition does not include environmental or climate change refugees, people who are forced to move because lakes dry up or because of natural disasters, because the definition is limited to those subject to "persecution." This issue is one increasingly facing the globe, and yet it is unlikely that any amendments to the Convention to expand the definition of refugees will happen given the large numbers of those displaced as well as increasing xenophobia worldwide.

What made the 1951 Convention different from earlier refugee frameworks, according to Peter Gatrell, was that this UN definition was framed in terms of an individual's relationship to the country and his or her "well-founded fear of persecution." This definition "represented a departure from the pre-war doctrine whereby protection was offered to specific groups."[42] This definition has not changed, but with the passage of time, the UN deemed the need for a protocol in 1967 to lift the geographic restrictions in the 1951 Convention, which focused on refugees displaced in Europe during World War II.

While the 1951 Convention Articles provide details on how states should treat refugees within their borders, no state comes close to meeting these provisions.[43] In the Middle East, the signatories to either the 1951 Convention or the 1967 Protocol are Algeria, Egypt, Iran, Israel, Morocco, Sudan, Tunisia, and Turkey. Even countries that are signatories to one or both of the documents may have internal policies that address refugees (Turkey, which hosts the largest number of Syrian refugees at 3 million people, for example, does not allow UNHCR to register or be responsible for these refugees). Other countries that are not signatories have devised policies toward refugees through Memorandums of Understanding (MoU) with UNHCR (Jordan, for example) that ensure protection for refugees and aid provision.

The main role of UNHCR is to provide protection to refugees. "Protection" in this sense is not necessarily physical safety, but rather the responsibility to work with host governments to prevent their *non-refoulement* (forcible return). Refugees need this protection as they are often seen as illegal entities because they enter or reside in a country without valid visas.[44] "Protection" also means UNHCR issues refugee status documentation, which is particularly useful for people who fled without identity cards or passports or whose national documents have expired. In addition to the protection mandate, UNHCR offers to assist the host country with the establishment of refugee camps and emergency aid in the form of food, shelter, and cash assistance. These actions require the host government's consent and are often in cooperation and coordination with other UN agencies, governments, and nongovernmental organizations.

Refugees around the world are the mandate of UNHCR, with one exception: Palestine refugees. As mentioned previously, they are the responsibility of UNRWA. This is because UNRWA was founded prior to UNHCR and the 1951 Refugee Convention, and there cannot be dual mandates. The resolution was uniquely designed to provide aid (the "works and relief" in its title) to Palestine refugees, rather than protection.[45] Thus, Palestinian refugees are often discussed as falling into a protection gap because unlike UNHCR, UNRWA has no protection mandate.[46] The Trump administration's recent decision to rescind its funding for any UNRWA activities and defund all USAID and other projects providing aid to Palestinians has deeply impacted the ability of UNRWA and other organizations to provide schools, health care, and services to Palestinian refugees.[47]

Twenty-First-Century Conflicts and Forced Population Movements

The largest refugee movement today in the Middle East is Syrians, who, following the 2011 uprising, fled the violence of the subsequent war. Syrian refugees are estimated by the UN to be 5.5 million (out of a total population of 22 million), with 3.5 million (65 percent of total) hosted in Turkey and the remaining divided between Lebanon, Jordan, Iraq, and Egypt.[48] In 2014, hundreds of thousands also began fleeing to Europe, as they saw no future or feared remaining in Syria. This was particularly true for young men whose families encouraged them to flee from conscription into the Syrian army.[49] Syria has long been a host to Palestinian and Iraqi refugees, and once the conflict broke out, they too faced the uncertainties of new displacement.[50] Teaching students about Syrian refugees benefits from media exercises and multimedia sources because Syrians have produced so much meaningful material about their displacement.[51]

Another continuing displacement is in Iraq. Iraqis have experienced multiple waves of displacement beginning with Saddam Hussein's Arabization policies and sectarian favoritism that were part of a calculated marginalization of ethnic and religious minorities, and that displaced over 1 million Kurds and Shi'a.[52] The 2003 US invasion of Iraq did not immediately cause a large amount of displacement. However, the occupation's policies, and resulting instability, led to sectarian violence. This violence, coupled with the failures of governance and security and with Iraqi political parties seeking to fill power vacuums, all caused repeated waves of displacement, both internal and external, beginning in 2006.[53] By 2008, 2.8 million Iraqis had become refugees and the same number were internally displaced.[54] Chatty and Mansour argue that Iraqi refugees do not fit the Western understanding of the refugee regime because their migration is circular: while they are living outside the country, Iraqi refugees return to Iraq to check on family members, pick up pension checks, and conduct routine business. They characterize this mobility as the "result of a strategy to manage life risks by dispersal of family members along pre-established social networks whenever possible."[55] The violent takeover by the Islamic State of Iraq and Syria (ISIS) of parts of northern and central Iraq (and parts of Syria) in 2013 led to a massive internal displacement crisis.[56] By July 2017, the number of IDPs stood at over 3 million,[57] but throughout this period, IDPs continued to flee if they could. With the cessation of violence, as of December 2018, many began to return and the number of returnees was 4.1 million, with 1.8 million people still counted as IDPs.[58] Understanding the massive displacement of Iraqis and Syrians in the twenty-first century necessitates understanding the political forces and international interests that have been part of these conflicts, which brings refugee studies to consider the causes of refugee movements and what are seen as solutions to refugee issues.

Durable Solutions

The UN and humanitarian aid systems use a variety of concepts to talk about and provide programming for refugees. The most important concept to consider is "durable solutions," which are defined as (1) return to home country; (2) resettlement to third country; or (3) integration into the host country/society.[59] These three solutions to displacement provide a tool to avoid discussing the political issues that caused or perpetuate the displacement. In doing so, these solutions protect the sovereignty of countries involved in the conflicts or disasters because no solution can be achieved without explicit government approval.[60] Some examples are discussed below.

Return

Thousands of Sudanese returned to Sudan and South Sudan when the latter was created in 2008 (some only to flee South Sudan again when fighting broke out in 2013). Palestinians want to return and UN Resolution 194 provides for it, but Israel does not allow them to return.

Resettlement

Since the late 1990s, there has been an active program via UNHCR and resettlement agencies to resettle Somali refugees in parts of Europe and the United States. Syrians who fled to Turkey, Jordan, and Lebanon also have been part of limited resettlement programs. It usually takes three or more years for resettlement to happen, after someone is accepted for resettlement. In the twenty-first century, governments have restricted refugee movements; the response by refugees was to enter Europe on their own, as events from 2014 onward show.

Integration

Jordan annexed the West Bank post 1948 and offered Jordanian citizenship to all Palestinian refugees living within Jordan and the West Bank. De facto integration would have included Palestinian refugees in Syria between 1948 and 2011. By the 1970s, Palestinians living in Syria could attend universities, hold government jobs, own limited property, and receive health care; they could not vote in elections. But how Palestinians will fare in a postwar Syria is unknown.

Despite these three solutions, the vast majority of refugees in the Middle East, and the world, live in limbo, accessing none of the solutions and living without rights (human, labor, health, etc.). But neither are they, for the most part, forced to return. Somalis fled to Kenya as a result of the 1991 collapse of the Siad Barre regime in Somalia and the ensuing civil war. Now almost thirty years later, they continue to live in refugee camps in Kenya, without the right to work, constrained by limited education for their children, and facing a future of yet another generation born in Kenya. Likewise, the Sahrawi refugees from the Moroccan occupation of the Western Sahara, mentioned previously, continue to live in refugee camps in southern Algeria, completely dependent on aid and solidarity, and are pawns to the political forces fighting for and against Saharawi liberation from Morocco. Palestinian refugees from the 1948 and 1967 Wars remain refugees without a political settlement or implementation of UN resolutions for their right of return. Palestinians in Lebanon, Iraq, and Syria in recent wars have been yet again displaced. These are all situations of "protracted displacement," the label for refugee situations that exist for five or more years.

What gets lost amid all of the discussion of humanitarian solutions to aid people is that preventing or ending the conflicts that caused their displacement in the first place is the preferred solution for refugees. The refugees are often labeled as the crisis, and are always labeled as the problem when they stay for long periods in host countries. Keeping the focus on the actions and interests of the political actors, whether local, national, or international, who continue the political violence that caused the refugees, or who prevent return, is crucial to finding solutions to refugee crises.

Conclusion: Humanitarian Solutions to Political Problems

With the continuance of the nation-state system and its codification within the United Nations, the issue of how to address those displaced from their "nation-state" remains. States are at the center of the causes of displacement, they are at the center of humanitarian aid provision, and thus they should also be at the center of efforts to seek solutions. Without a shift in addressing the underlying causes of forced migration crises, we will continue to provide humanitarian solutions to political problems.

When only portrayed as humanitarian problems, refugees and the issues they face are depoliticized, resulting in particular framings that allow powerful governments and others to avoid any responsibility for their roles in supporting violence through geopolitics and the global arms trade. Such framings cast refugees as the "problem," when in actuality the problem is either the situations that created them or the host country's and the international community's responses to them. Such framings leave unchanged the rigidity of states and the borders that circumscribe refugees' lives. Finally, such framings fail to consider how refugees actively navigate their situations and make decisions about their futures. Aihwa Ong describes how "in official and public domains refugees become subjects of norms, rules and systems, but they also modify practices and agendas while nimbly deflecting control and interjecting critique."[61] Likewise, Hoffman comments on how "the cornerstones of this portrayal are that refugees are a burden on host societies and a potential security problem. Both aspects are crucial for mobilizing donors. But this framing also means that humanitarian measures have become increasingly entangled with state security measures that oppress refugees."[62]

Most refugees were once citizens. They have endured the sudden upheaval of losing their rights and homes. And yet, their ability to adapt to their new situations is rarely seen as a strength or an asset. Many who write about refugees and displaced persons note, as Gatrell does, that humanitarianism "is an essential component of fashioning the modern refugee as a passive and 'traumatized' object of intervention as compared to the active, purposeful and much-travelled relief worker, a distinction that was not altered by the so-called shift from relief-based to rights-based humanitarianism."[63] Teaching about refugees in ways that present them as we ourselves would want to be portrayed in similar situations—as people, citizens, who have been subjected to terrible violence or persecution—will better prepare students to understand how governmental and media discourse frames refugees in certain places and times. Such framings can then help students learn more about the politicization of aid money, the idealism of humanitarian aid careers (which are constrained by the political structures that fail to change and adapt), and the Sisyphean task of providing humanitarian solutions to political problems.

NOTES

1. For more on how international law and organizations address refugees, see the Refugees and Migrants website of the United Nations, http://refugees migrants.un.org.

2. United Nations High Commissioner for Refugees, "Populations," http://reporting.unhcr.org/population (accessed March 24, 2020).

3. Peter Gatrell, *The Making of the Modern Refugee* (Oxford: Oxford University Press, 2013), 5. "We also need to consider how the modern refugee came to be construed as a 'problem' amenable to a 'solution.'"

4. Michael Barnett, "Humanitarianism with a Sovereign Face: UNHCR in the Global Undertow," *International Migration Review* 35, no. 1 (Spring 2001): 251.

5. Dawn Chatty, *Displacement and Dispossession in the Modern Middle East* (Cambridge: Cambridge University Press, 2010). Chapter 1 has a comprehensive historical and theoretical discussion of displacement as a topic, as does Gatrell, *Making of the Modern Refugee*. A fact sheet by the International Rescue Committee helps define terms as well: "Migrants, Asylum Seekers, Refugees and Immigrants: What's the Difference?," June 22, 2018, updated December 11, 2018, https://www.rescue.org/article/migrants-asylum-seekers-refugees-and-im migrants-whats-difference.

6. See Liisa Malkki, "Refugees and Exile: From 'Refugee Studies' to the National Order of Things," in *Annual Review of Anthropology* (1995); Shahram Khosravi, *'Illegal' Traveller: An Auto-Ethnography of Borders* (New York: Palgrave Macmillan, 2010); and Shahram Khosravi, "The 'Illegal' Traveller: An Auto-Ethnography of Borders," *Social Anthropology* 15, no. 3 (2007): 321–34.

7. "Hungarian Prime Minister Says Migrants Are 'Poison' and 'Not Needed,'" *The Guardian*, July 26, 2016, https://www.theguardian.com/world/2016/jul/26/hungarian-prime-minister-viktor-orban-praises-donald-trump; Orla Barry, "In Orbán's Hungary, Refugees Are Unwelcome—So Are Those Who Try to Help," *PRI*, February 11, 2019, https://www.pri.org/stories/2019-02-11/orban-s-hungary-refugees-are-unwelcome-so-are-those-who-try-help.

8. Donald J. Trump, Twitter post, September 19, 2016, 8:27 a.m., https://twitter.com/realDonaldTrump/status/777846568741441536?s=20.

9. See, for example, Michelle Campos, *Ottoman Brothers: Muslims, Christians, and Jews in Early Twentieth-Century Palestine* (Stanford, CA: Stanford University Press, 2010); Resat Kasaba, *A Moveable Empire: Ottoman Nomads, Migrants, and Refugees* (Seattle: University of Washington Press, 2011); Melanie Tanielian, "Politics of Wartime Relief in Ottoman Beirut (1914–1918)," *First World War Studies* 5, no. 1 (2014): 69–82; Ryan Gingeras, *Sorrowful Shores: Violence, Ethnicity, and the End of the Ottoman Empire, 1912–1923* (Oxford: Oxford University Press, 2009).

10. Dawn Chatty, "Refugees, Exiles, and Other Forced Migrants in the Late Ottoman Empire," *Refugee Survey Quarterly* 32, no. 2 (2013): 44. While individual movement was not uncommon and is harder to analyze collectively due to limited historical sources, large forced migrations are easier to understand, given that the Ottoman administration endeavored to manage them. We know that various groups moving into the empire were granted tax exemptions on land, recruited to act as gendarmes to quell conflict with local tribes, and given minimal humanitarian support.

11. The Ottoman Refugee Code (Immigrant Law) of 1857 and the Immigration Commission of 1860 (following the Crimean War) and another Immigration Commission of 1877–1878 following the Ottoman-Russian wars formed the legal response of the empire. Chatty, *Displacement and Dispossession*, 97–98. This law provided land grants, free of taxation, to immigrant families, in addition to protecting their religious freedom and exempting them from conscription. See also Norman Lewis, *Nomads and Settlers in Syria and Jordan, 1800–1980* (Cambridge: Cambridge University Press, 1987), 96.

12. Chatty, "Refugees, Exiles, and Other Forced Migrants," 44.

13. The first Circassian community settled in Amman (in what is now Jordan) in 1878 on land granted to them by the Ottoman authorities. In 1914, the General Directorate of Tribes and Immigrants was created to manage the increased influx of refugees moving east from the Balkan Wars in 1912–13. Chatty,

"Refugees, Exiles, and Other Forced Migrants," 44; Lewis, *Nomads and Settlers*, 107; Chatty, *Displacement and Dispossession*, 116.

14. See Chatty, *Displacement and Dispossession*, 163; Ronald Grigor Suny, Fatma Müge Göçek, and Norman M. Naimark, *A Question of Genocide: Armenians and Turks at the End of the Ottoman Empire* (Oxford: Oxford University Press, 2011), 260–84; Hannibal Travis, "The Assyrian Genocide: A Tale of Oblivion and Denial," in *Forgotten Genocides: Oblivion, Denial and Memory*, ed. René Lemarchand (Philadelphia: University of Pennsylvania Press, 2011), 123–36.

15. See Ani Derderian-Aghajanian, "Armenians' Dual Identity in Jordan," *International Education Studies* 2, no. 3 (2009).

16. Rochelle Davis, Grace Benton, Will Todman, and Emma Murphy, "Hosting Guests, Creating Citizens: Models of Refugee Administration in Jordan and Egypt," *Refugee Studies Quarterly* 36, no. 2 (2017).

17. Chatty, *Displacement and Dispossession*, 289.

18. Sarah Shields, "The Greek-Turkish Population Exchange: Internationally Administered Ethnic Cleansing," *Middle East Report* 267 (2013). Shields describes how, supervised through "the reciprocal emigration of the racial minorities of the two countries," religious groups became "racialized."

19. Shields, "Greek-Turkish Population Exchange," 5.

20. Robert Olson, *The Emergence of Kurdish Nationalism and the Sheikh Said Rebellion, 1880–1925* (Austin: University of Texas Press, 2013).

21. Martin van Bruinessen, *Transnational Aspects of the Kurdish Question*, working paper, Robert Schuman Centre for Advanced Studies, European University Institute, Florence, 2000, https://dspace.library.uu.nl/handle/1874/20511.

22. David McDowall, *Modern History of the Kurds* (London: I. B. Tauris, 2003).

23. Stacy Fahrenthold, "Transnational Modes and Media: The Syrian Press in the Mahjar and Emigrant Activism during World War I," *Mashriq and Mahjar* 1, no. 1 (2013): 30–54; Marjorie Stevens, "Mapping Women Writers in the Mahjar," https://www.arcgis.com/apps/MapJournal/index.html?appid=1e09d680f93 144dc8cb10e42abffbf79.

24. Ali Ahmida, *Forgotten Voices: Power and Agency in Colonial and Postcolonial Libya* (London: Routledge: 2005), 35–54.

25. Eugene Rogan, *The Arabs: A History* (London: Allen Lane, 2009), 119.

26. Dorothee Kellou, "A Microhistory of the Forced Resettlement of the Algerian Muslim Population during the Algerian War of Independence (1954–1962): Mansourah, Kabylia" (MA thesis, Georgetown University, 2012), iii.

27. Alice Wilson, *Sovereignty in Exile: A Saharan Liberation Movement Governs* (Philadelphia: University of Pennsylvania Press, 2016).

28. Stephen Zunes and Jacob Mundy, *Western Sahara: War, Nationalism and Conflict Irresolution*, Syracuse Studies on Peace and Conflict Resolution (Syracuse, NY: Syracuse University Press, 2010); and Anouar Boukhars and Jacques

Roussellier, eds., *Perspectives on Western Sahara: Myths, Nationalism, and Geopolitics* (Lanham, MD: Rowman Littlefield, 2014).

29. Said Saddiki, "Ceuta and Melilla Fences: An EU Multidimensional Border," in *The 82nd Annual Conference of the Canadian Political Science Association*, vol. 3, 2010.

30. The Moroccan king protected the Jews living in Morocco. Mohammed Kenbib, "Moroccan Jews and the Vichy Regime, 1940–42," *Journal of North African Studies* 19, no. 4 (2014): 540–53.

31. J. N. Byler, "Middle East Relief and Refugee Administration," *Global Anabaptist Mennonite Encyclopedia Online*, 1957, http://gameo.org/index.php?title=Middle_East_Relief_and_Refugee_Administration&oldid=89942 (accessed September 20, 2016).

32. Evan Taparata and Kuang Keng Kuek Ser, "During WWII, European Refugees Fled to Syria. Here's What the Camps Were Like," Public Radio International, April 26, 2016, http://www.pri.org/stories/2016-04-26/what-it-s-inside-refugee-camp-europeans-who-fled-syria-egypt-and-palestine-during (accessed September 14, 2016). See also Rym Ghazal, "When a Refugee Fled in the Other Direction," *National*, August 17, 2016, http://www.thenational.ae/world/middle-east/when-a-refugee-fled-in-the-other-direction (accessed September 14, 2016).

33. Malkki, "Refugees and Exile," 500.

34. Riccardo Bocco, "UNRWA and the Palestinian Refugees: A History within History," *Refugee Survey Quarterly* 28, no. 2–3 (2009): 229.

35. Oroub El Abed, "Palestinian Refugees in Jordan," *Forced Migration Online*, February 2004, https://www.academia.edu/206913/Palestinian_refugees_in_Jordan (accessed April 10, 2020). "While the AFSC, the Quakers' organization, had been active mainly in Gaza, the [International Committee of the Red Cross] and the [League of the Red Cross Societies] had been catering to the needs of the displaced in the West Bank, Jordan, Syria and Lebanon."

36. Davis et al., "Hosting Guests, Creating Citizens." See also L. Takkenberg, "UNRWA and the Palestinian Refugees after Sixty Years: Some Reflections," *Refugee Survey Quarterly* 28, no. 2–3 (2009): 227–83. See the Conciliation Commission Resolution at "A Decade of American Foreign Policy, 1941–1949: Creation of a Conciliation Commission for Palestine," http://avalon.law.yale.edu/20th_century/decad171.asp (last accessed March 13, 2017).

37. Ilana Feldman, *Life Lived in Relief: Humanitarian Predicaments and Palestinian Refugee Politics* (Oakland: University of California Press, 2018).

38. A useful essay to read and discuss on this power to define is Anaheed Al-Hardan, "Decolonizing Research on Palestinians: Towards Critical Epistemologies and Research Practices," *Qualitative Inquiry* 20, no. 1 (January 2014): 61–71.

39. More on each institution is available at UNHCR.org and UNRWA.org. Other bodies that address issues related to displacement include the International Organization for Migration (established in 1951) that was included in the

UN in 2016 and the Organization of African Unity (now the Organization of African States).

40. It is useful to have students read the Convention in order to introduce them to UN documents and to the idea of a rights-based approach. See United Nations, "Convention and Protocol Relating to the Status of Refugees," 1951, https://www.unhcr.org/4ae57b489.pdf.

41. *Refugee Magazine* 2, no. 123 (2001): 16.

42. Gatrell, *Making of the Modern Refugee*, 6. "It made implicit reference to Nazism but had Soviet totalitarianism even more in its sights."

43. Certain states offer such provisions as access to employment while seeking asylum; Uganda.

44. States "shall not impose penalties, on account of their illegal entry or presence, on refugees." Article 31, UN Convention on Refugees 1951. "Host governments are primarily responsible for protecting refugees and the 140 parties to the Convention and/or the Protocol are obliged to carry out its provisions. UNHCR maintains a 'watching brief,' intervening if necessary to ensure bona fide refugees are granted asylum and are not forcibly returned to countries where their lives may be in danger." UNHCR FAQ, https://www.unhcr.org/news/stories/2001/6/3b4c06578/frequently-asked-questions-1951-refugee-convention.html.

45. Feldman, *Life Lived in Relief*, 41–49.

46. B. Goddard, "UNHCR and the International Protection of Palestinian Refugees," *Refugee Survey Quarterly* 28, no. 2–3 (2009): 475–510.

47. Francesca Albanese, "UNRWA and Palestinian Refugees under Attack: When Politics Trump Law and History," October 2018, https://www.jadaliyya.com/Details/38006/UNRWA-and-Palestinian-Refugees-Under-Attack-When-Politics-Trump-Law-and-History.

48. As of March 2020. The most recent UNHCR statistics are on their data portal. See UNHCR, "United Nations Operational Portal Refugee Situations," April 2020, https://data2.unhcr.org/en/situations/syria.

49. Rochelle Davis, "Gendered Vulnerability and Forced Conscription in the War in Syria," in *The Long-Term Challenges of Forced Migration: Perspectives from Lebanon, Jordan and Iraq*, London School of Economics Middle East Centre Collected Papers, September 2016.

50. Mohamed Kamel Doraï, "Palestinian and Iraqi Refugees and Urban Change in Lebanon and Syria." *Middle East Institute*, April 19, 2010, https://www.mei.edu/publications/palestinian-and-iraqi-refugees-and-urban-change-lebanon-and-syria; Mai Abu Moghli, Nael Bitarie, and Nell Gabiam, "Palestinian Refugees from Syria: Stranded on the Margins of Law," *Al-Shabaka*, October 19, 2015.

51. Some graphic novels: "The Graphic Novels and Cartoons That Capture the Complexities of Life as a Refugee," Arts&Culture, March 18, 2019, https://

www.thenational.ae/arts-culture/art/the-graphic-novels-and-cartoons-that
-capture-the-complexities-of-life-as-a-refugee-1.838615; and Kristyn Dorfman,
"Graphic Novels Involving the Refugee Experience," *School Library Journal*,
November 19, 2018, http://www.teenlibrariantoolbox.com/2018/11/graphic-nov
els-involving-the-refugee-experience-a-guest-post-by-kristyn-dorfman/. Some
videos are here: Lauren Parater, "7 Videos Guaranteed to Change the Way You
See Refugees," United Nations High Commissioner for Refugees, June 26, 2015,
https://www.unhcr.org/innovation/7-videos-guaranteed-to-change-the-way
-you-see-refugees/; Nick Vivarelli, "Five Films That Depicted Europe's Migrant
Crisis in 2016," *Variety*, December 23, 2016, https://variety.com/2016/film/news/
movies-europe-refugee-crisis-2016-syria-1201947838/; and Patrice Taddonio, "As
the Global Refugee Crisis Intensifies, 6 Docs to Watch," *Frontline*, PBS, June
19, 2018, https://www.pbs.org/wgbh/frontline/article/as-the-global-refugee-crisis
-intensifies-6-docs-to-watch/.

52. Joseph Sassoon, *The Iraqi Refugees: The New Crisis in the Middle East* (London: I. B. Tauris, 2009), 9; see also Geraldine Chatelard, "What Visibility Con-
ceals: Re-embedding Refugee Migration from Iraq," and Nabil al-Takriti, "There
Go the Neighbourhoods: Policy Effects vis-à-vis Iraqi Forced Migration," both
chapters in *Dispossession and Displacement: Forced Migration in the Middle East
and North Africa*, ed. Dawn Chatty and Bill Finlayson (Oxford: Oxford University Press, 2010).

53. Dawn Chatty and Nisrine Mansour, "Unlocking Protracted Displacement: An Iraqi Case Study," *Refugee Survey Quarterly* 30 (2011): 52, http://rsq
.oxfordjournals.org/content/30/4/50.full.pdf+html; Geraldine Chatelard, "Iraqi
Refugee and IDPs: From Humanitarian Intervention to Durable Solutions,"
Middle East Institute and Fondation Pour La Recherche Strategique, June 9, 2011.

54. Sassoon, *Iraqi Refugees*, 13. See also Geraldine Chatelard, *Jordan as a Transit Country: Semi-Protectionist Immigration Policies and Their Effects on Iraqi Forced
Migrants*, New Issues in Refugee Research, 61 (Geneva: UNHCR, 2002); IOM
"Review of Displacement and Return in Iraq, February 2011," https://reliefweb.
int/report/iraq/iom-iraq-report-5-years-post-samarra-displacement.

55. Chatty and Mansour, "Unlocking Protracted Displacement."

56. IOM, *Displacement Tracking Matrix-Iraq Mission*, Round 30, October 2015,
4–7.

57. IOM, *Displacement Tracking Matrix-Iraq Mission*, Round 70, April 2017, 1.
For a snapshot of 2014–19, see Displacement Tracking Matrix, International
Organization for Migration, http://iraqdtm.iom.int/IDPsML.aspx.

58. Displacement Tracking Matrix, Iraq-IOM, http://iraqdtm.iom.int/ (accessed January 10, 2018).

59. See the UNHCR discussion: "Solutions," UNHCR, https://www.unhcr
.org/solutions.html.

60. "Questions arose about the appropriate 'durable solution' to pursue in each case—whether repatriation, resettlement or local integration—and how this might square with the interests of host states and countries of prospective immigration. Inevitably decisions reflected not the wishes of UNHCR, but the interests of member states, each of which affirmed its sovereignty in respect of decisions over asylum." Gatrell, *Making of the Modern Refugee*, 200.

61. Aihwa Ong, *Buddha Is Hiding: Refugees, Citizenship, the New America* (Berkeley: University of California Press, 2003), xvii, as quoted in Gatrell, *Making of the Modern Refugee*, 9.

62. Sophia Hoffman, "Refugee Rights Hit the Wall," *MERIP* 286 (Spring 2018): 37, https://merip.org/2018/10/refugee-rights-hit-the-wall/.

63. Gatrell, *Making of the Modern Refugee*, 8.

KEY RESOURCES

Two very good background books (one on refugees generally, one on the Middle East specifically) can help an instructor take on these questions and framings in courses where students may not have time to do a lot of pages of reading: Peter Gatrell, *The Making of the Modern Refugee* (Oxford, 2013); Dawn Chatty, *Displacement and Dispossession in the Modern Middle East* (Cambridge, 2010).

For larger issues about what being a refugee means to the persons who are displaced, this is a very readable and compelling article version of a longer book by a professor of anthropology who reflects on his experiences being displaced: Shahram Khosravi, "The 'Illegal' Traveller: An Auto-Ethnography of Borders," *Social Anthropology* 15, no. 3 (2007).

Other accounts that center the voices and perspectives of refugees and are very readable: Wendy Pearlman, *We Crossed a Bridge and It Trembled: Voices from Syria* (New York: Custom House, 2017), and *Meet the Somalis*, a collection of fourteen illustrated stories depicting the real-life experiences of Somalis in seven cities in Europe (2013), https://www.opensocietyfoundations.org/multimedia/meet-the-somalis#all.

For forced displacement issues over time (displacement, refugee-ness, resettlement) and an excellent chapter on American policy toward refugees: Catherine Besteman, *Making Refuge: Somali Bantu Refugees and Lewiston, Maine* (Durham, NC: Duke University Press, 2016).

Understanding the UNRWA mandate, its differences from UNHCR, and what this means for Palestinian refugees is well done in two different articles: Ilana Feldman, "Difficult Distinctions: Refugee Law, Humanitarian Practice, and Political Identification in Gaza," *Cultural Anthropology* 22, no. 1 (2007): 129–70; Lex Takkenberg, "UNRWA and the Palestinian Refugees after Sixty Years: Some Reflections," *Refugee Survey Quarterly* 28, no. 2–3 (2010).

How does the UN write about its work? How does it chart a policy shift from camp-based services to the reality on the ground that most refugees are non-camp, and urban, residents? To see how the UN writes for itself, see Jeff Crisp, Jane Janz, José Riera, and Shahira Samy, "Surviving in the City: A Review of UNHCR's Operation for Iraqi Refugees in Urban Areas of Jordan, Lebanon and Syria," July 2009, http://www.unhcr.org/en-us/research/evalreports/4a69ad639/surviving-city-review-unhcrs-operation-iraqi-refugees-urban-areas-jordan.html.

PART FOUR

Methods and Sources

Literature as a Source for Teaching Modern Middle East History

ELLIOTT COLLA

Works of literature are frequently used in the classroom to offset or correct the third-person, omniscient perspective of grand history. Novels are especially useful in this regard since they can give a sense of the "structures of feeling" of a particular time and place.[1] Literary works routinely present the experience of family and social life, of the everyday, of hopes and fears, of the critical (yet banal) details that make up life as it is lived.

Yet, to think of literature as a source "to be used" for teaching history is to risk making literature into something it is not. A literary text is a ready-made historical source in that it always *bears witness* to actual human events and experiences, aspirations and fears. Yet *how* it does this is not always obvious, since what distinguishes literary modes of communication from nonliterary ones is usually their mediated quality of presentation and their sometimes oblique relation to the empirical world. A literary work—even a realist novel—is always a crafted representation that converses (and often breaks) with established aesthetic conventions. In the Middle East as elsewhere, high-prestige literary works often earn their status through ambiguous (rather than unequivocal) and latent (rather than direct) modes of expression. In other words, to grapple with high-status literary works entails grappling with their mediated quality and their place within canons.

A second issue has to do with what we mean by "literature." Colloquially, the word *literature* suggests an object that is universal and transhistorical. However, for literary scholars, "literature" entails the study of practices, institutions, and texts called "literary" (by various names, in various languages), as they evolve across time and geographic space. These various things are neither reducible to a single thing, nor are they all approached in the same way. Thus, few of us speak of "Middle Eastern Literature," since it is unclear whether that term names a real-world object.

In fact, it is difficult even to speak coherently of *modern Arabic literature* as a single object of study. Part of this is due to the fact that the Arabic literary tradition contains 1,500 years of poetry and prose, whose classical and postclassical traditions survive as vital presences in modern and contemporary writing. Part of this is also due to the huge range of linguistic registers, conventions, practices, and institutions of the modern Arab world. To take an example from a single country: in Egypt, "literature" includes both Naguib Mahfouz's *Palace Walk,* written in Modern Standard Arabic (MSA) for literate audiences across the Arab world (and beyond), and also the poetry of Ahmed Fouad Negm, composed in Egyptian colloquial Arabic for performance as popular chant and song. Mahfouz's novels engage with daily life in Cairo and also with Sufism and Western philosophy; Negm's poems employ premodern local genres of poetry as well as emancipatory discourses drawn from the non-Aligned Movement of the 1960s. These same splits—between the various vernaculars of Arabic and the MSA, between literature of the page and literature of the stage—characterize literary production from Morocco to Iraq. With so much variation there is effectively no consensus about an Arabic canon for the modern period. At most, there are canons of national literature for the various states of the Arab world, but even these are characterized by divisions, exclusions, and ongoing debates. All of this makes it difficult to make broad claims about modern Arabic literature.

How the various literary traditions of the Arab world speak to those of other languages and traditions in the region is even more vexing, since each of the "major" modern literary traditions—Arabic, Hebrew, Persian, and Turkish—operate with little regard for one another. They interact even less with the "minor" traditions of the region—from Francophone North African writing to Armenian and Kurdish writing—all of which embrace different languages and engage different audiences spread from homelands to diasporas. Another more recent development is the increasing share of what is marketed as "contemporary Middle

244

Eastern literature," written and published in postcolonial exile, with titles in English, French, German, Spanish, and Italian, whose readership often outstrips those of regional languages.

Questions of Form

Despite all the problems with the term *Middle Eastern literature*, by focusing analysis on literary works (in the plural) rather than literature (in the abstract) we can nevertheless see many points of intersection, resonance, and conversation. Comparisons are eminently possible.

This brings us to the questions raised when grappling with a particular literary text: what *kind* of text is it, what is its *form*? To answer this question is to explore how a text speaks to the context in which it was created, and the context in which we read it. Traditionally, many scholars have conceived of this relation in terms of reflection, though this raises as many questions as it answers. For instance, if literary texts "reflect" the world, they do so in mediated, crafted ways, which might be ironic or sincere, symbolic or metaphoric, realist or surrealist, and so on. So to speak of reflection compels us to ask other questions: what kind of mirror—the kind that hangs above the bathroom sink, or the kind found in a funhouse?

First, the question of form entails an interrogation of the literary and rhetorical dynamics of works that present narrative, argument, and image by way of fiction and trope. To use literary texts as sources for writing history, we must acknowledge that not only are they not presented as objective or scientific, but they also commonly exaggerate, distort, and speak in an otherwise fashion. This is obvious in highly metaphorical works, such as the poetry of Mahmoud Darwish, which often employ *linguistic* strain—the impossibility to say in words what one wants to say—to illustrate the *ontological* strain of speaking about Palestinian presence in the face of its erasure. Similarly, the poetry of Ahmed Fouad Negm contains nonce and nonsense words and rests heavily on sounds that signify, though without connotative meaning. Straightforward memoirs, such as Karnig Panian's account of the Armenian genocide are no less mediated or composed: attentive readers will notice the way Panian frames his lived experience in terms of biblical figures and stories, especially those of Exodus. This is not to say that Panian's testimonial account deserves to be read as fiction, but rather to note how much it depends on fictional modes to tell truths that may not be told in another fashion.

Second, conceiving of literary texts as mere "sources" from events obscures the ways in which they sometimes participate in the shaping of events. Many of Darwish's poems were composed to inspire and move audiences to political action—and they did that. Similarly, many of Negm's poems were meant to mobilize activist audiences. Indeed, both poets were arrested because their poetry was understood to be more than words. Literary texts move audiences in other ways as well. Some narratives bear witness to incidents long repressed in official histories or can cause people to remember forgotten episodes. In this capacity, Abderrahman Munif's novel *Cities of Salt* told the history of labor struggles in the oil fields of Saudi Arabia long before there was any "history" of them. Similarly, in Assia Djebar's *Fantasia*—a genre-defying work mixing history with fiction—the author digs through the canons of colonial documentation in order to recover actual stories of brutal violence, which, while based in fact, are nonetheless presented in the speculative voice of fiction. Such works have inspired readers in the region to do things they could not do without the texts they hold in their hands (or minds). In this sense, literary texts might be treated as *actants* within a broader network of human agency shaping events.[2] Indeed, some literary texts are best conceived of not as sources depicting events but as events in their own right.

Third, treating a literary text as a source compels us to ask about its status as a source. Some literary texts might appear to be *primary* sources in that they make direct claims about worldly events. Panian's memoir, for instance, is presented as witness testimony to make a moral case about crimes against humanity. A different kind of testimony is at work in *Human Landscapes*, Nazim Hikmet's epic poem of cataclysmic changes that attended the end of the Ottoman Empire and the birth of the Turkish Republic. But in Hikmet's account, as in Panian's, the lens is that of an actor participating within events. However, most literary texts are more removed from lived history than this. For example, as a young boy, Naguib Mahfouz witnessed the 1919 Revolution in Egypt. But while writing his novel of the revolution, *Palace Walk*, he relied on an array of primary and secondary sources—eyewitness testimony, media accounts, published histories, or more ephemeral aspects of collective memory. A collage aesthetic is evident throughout Mahfouz's novel, with different styles of writing and different forms of sourcing—from thick descriptions of particular places to journalistic precision with times and dates, from newspaper reportage to snippets of popular song—working together to create an overarching sense of historical realism.

Fourth, the meaning of literary texts is never wholly determined by the circumstances of textual production for the simple reason that writers never have the final say on the interpretation of their work. On the contrary, texts do not signify anything without audiences who consume them and discuss them in different, often evolving, ways. Thus, to speak of literary reception also involves recognizing the historically contingent institutional processes that grant prestige to some literary texts and arrange groups of texts into hierarchical canons of taste and authority. For much of the twentieth century, Arab critics disdained prose genres—short stories and novels—in favor of poetry and focused solely on works written in MSA, while ignoring works composed in the colloquial. Thus, MSA poets (such as Mahmoud Darwish and Adonis) have enjoyed a higher cultural status than most novelists or colloquial poets, such as Negm. In recent years, the balance has shifted in the other direction, with novels now supported by regional competitions, such as the IPAF (or Arab Booker). Thus a novel with once marginal status— Mohammad Choukri's *For Bread Alone*—has come to hold a much higher place now than it once did. These dynamics are by no means secondary to the life of literary texts, since part of what they mean is tied to the tastes and preferences of audiences for whom they have meaning. In this regard, we might consider Tayeb Salih's novel, *Season of Migration to the North*, long regarded by Arab critics (and others) as one of very best works in the Arabic canon. In a 2018 poll conducted by *Banipal*, Arab critics confirmed this reputation by voting it top Arabic novel of all time. Yet, recent archival research has shown that the novel was commissioned by American intelligence agents, for publication in a literary journal that was covertly funded and run by the CIA, all with the knowledge and approval of the author. As news of the novel's hidden history spreads, it is hard to imagine these discoveries will not impact its status. In sum, because literary texts do not exist outside particular habits and traditions of reading, those traditions become part of (or inescapably adjacent to) the text itself. Thus reception, along with these other questions of form, poses a complication to consider when engaging literary texts as sources.

Structural Components

At the outset of *Metahistory*, Hayden White declares that his method is formalist, and that he seeks "to identify the structural components of . . . accounts."[3] While White's call is for a method of historiography—for reading the accounts of historians as if they were literary compositions—it applies just as well for reading literature as history. A basic list of the structural components includes form, genre, frame, perspective, and voice, each of which raises its own set of questions that should be familiar to any historian.

By *form*, we are asking: what kind of text is this? Djebar's *Fantasia* compels this question from the outset, and it is pertinent to remember that the author was an academic historian who turned toward literary methods precisely because of the limitations of her discipline. Indeed, when we consider that Djebar's goal as a historian was to recover the experience of Algerian women—essentially erased from the historical record of the colonial period—we can better appreciate why she was driven toward speculative forms of writing, including fiction, in the attempt to represent empirical history. But not every work of women's literature is so formally experimental: Latifa al-Zayyat's novel *The Open Door*, for instance, does not break so completely from the patriarchal, heteronormative form of national romance popularized by Mahfouz but rather employs it and adapts its tropes to feminist ends.

Similarly, it is useful to think of the differences between poetry and prose. In this way, it is productive to consider why Darwish writes poetry while Kanafani writes prose, when both writers were involved in the same national liberation struggle, albeit from different positions. By the same token, it is fruitful to look for narrative elements in nonnarrative forms (such as poetry), or poetic features (such as metaphor and voice) within narrative forms. Questions of orality and register are paramount for colloquial texts (such as Negm's), many of which were not composed for the page, nor even "published" in the traditional sense of the word: they circulated, often on cassette tapes, among leftist circles in Egypt and the Levant. Asking questions about form is thus to inquire about how something was composed, for whom, and for what purpose. These questions tell us how texts circulate and how they have been received.

By *genre*, we are asking more particular questions about form: Is this novel a tragedy or comedy? It is quite striking, for instance, to observe that most Arabic novels have a tragic structure. For all the differences between Egypt, Palestine, and Saudi Arabia, what causes Mahfouz, Kanafani, and Munif to write such bleak stories about the possibility of change? Similarly, a cursory reading of Darwish and Negm indicates that there is real variation in tone and genre in poetry, with invective, elegy, or panegyric all thriving in the modern period. The answers to these questions will tell us quite a bit about the *expectations* of audiences, their *stances* toward the texts, and possibly the ways in which audiences are *moved* rhetorically by texts.

By *frame*, we ask about the shape of the text as a closed and finite work: Where does the text begin its story? Where does it end? Is there a middle or end? What is the nature of the relation between events within a narrative? Djebar's *Fantasia* is very concerned with these questions — since, for her, the ability to tell a coherent tale is a condition of existence. Are the events narrated in an episodic and merely sequential way, or are their relation causal, dialectical, or cyclical? Djebar's answer to these questions is to develop the figure of the *fantasia*, a North African cavalry ritual whose back-and-forth movements embody, for her, the movement of history itself. The answers to these questions will reveal something about a text's philosophy (or notion) of time, history, and human agency.

To inquire into *perspective* is to ask: Who is the narrator? Is the protagonist also the narrator? Is the presentation in the first or second or third person? Who are the antagonists? Are there characters who are more objects than subjects? Which characters are granted a depth of interiority, memory, and a past? Which characters remain underdeveloped? Himket's epic hinges on these very questions: it begins as a rail journey from Ottoman Istanbul to the new republican capital of Ankara and explores the experience and memories of first- and third-class passengers. Sometime, as characters watch the passing landscape from fogged windows, the point of view suddenly shifts to that of peasants watching as the train speeds by. Hikmet's epic explores all sorts of characters, including from the privileged to the most abject — and compels his reader to watch on the margins of action and speech, and in the gaps where we might expect characters. Paying attention to these perspectival dynamics of the text leads us to discover which kinds of human experience are foregrounded, which are backgrounded, and which are wholly absent.

By *voice*, we ask a different question: How does the text engage with linguistic style? Is it composed in a vernacular or formal register? Is the work monologic or dialogic in nature; in other words, does it present one voice or stage a conversation—or debate—between many? In this regard, Hikmet's epic presents tableaux of many voices, speaking with, against, and past each other. In another way, Kanafani's short novella, *Men in the Sun*, uses voice (and perspective) to explore how different characters caught in the same predicament nonetheless live divergent lives. Does it stage—like some of Negm's poems—the kinds of linguistic conflicts that exist in Middle Eastern societies, such as those between spoken-colloquial and prestige-written registers? Or does it exclude register altogether to create an artifice of linguistic unity? The answers to these questions are foundational, since diglossia—the existence of sharply distinct forms of spoken and written languages—pervades many Middle Eastern societies. Just as illiteracy rates vary in the region, one cannot assume that audiences whose mother tongue is in a language will necessarily have linguistic competence in all of its registers.

To tackle these questions is to engage with the formal elements of a given text: how it presents information; how it argues; how it speaks, to whom it speaks and from which angle; which audiences are included, which are excluded, and so on. It is at that point we can make grounded observations about the specific rhetorical features of literary works that attempt to *witness* and *document* past events, articulate a *critique of* or *claims on* the present, and express *aspirations* for the future. In this way, we trace what literary works *do* in history—how they move audiences and in what ways. How they present readers with the opportunity of vicarious experience and serve as critical sources for the kinds of aspects—such as the structures of feeling—absent from other kinds of sources.

Themes

With all these qualifications and questions in mind, we can consider how literary texts might be used for exploring topics such as migration and national identity. The lists below refer to works available in English translation, which represent just a fraction of the total amount of literary works on the subjects.

Migration

Throughout the modern period, the Mashriq has been the site of massive forced migrations, ethnic cleansings, genocides, and programs of forcible resettlement. For the Maghreb, mass migration has been no less pronounced, though it is relatively newer (post-WWII) and driven by a different set of dynamics, including longstanding economic dependencies that stem from the colonial period. These migrations have been one of the central facts of modern Middle Eastern history, and literature has been one of the main platforms for migrants and refugees to express and reflect upon the experience. Salih's *Season of Migration to the North* is more than just a tale of Sudanese men navigating the colonial metropole; it also engages deeply and creatively with prestige titles of British literature, including Shakespeare's *Othello* and Joseph Conrad's *Heart of Darkness*.

The student of forced migration in the Middle East faces a number of difficulties, including the scale, frequency, and specificity of these events. Literary texts can help immensely in this regard: memoirs and novels narrate these histories through the perspective of individual lives and thus put a "human face" onto phenomena that are otherwise difficult to grasp. Panian's memoir of his experience of the Armenian genocide certainly does this, as does Ghassan Kanafani's novella, *Men in the Sun*, which tells the story of Palestinian laborers attempting to smuggle themselves into Kuwait. From the Maghreb, we find this theme also at work in Choukri's novel, which traces the experiences of a Moroccan boy driven from the countryside to the city by famine, and in Laila Lalami's English-language novel, which narrates the motivations of a boat full of Moroccans desperately fleeing across the Straits of Gibraltar. Similarly, while each group of refugees sees its experience of migration as sui generis and local, a comparative study of literary texts composed by refugees reveals shared patterns across the region. Finally, while it is easy to imagine migration as the end of a story, literary accounts remind us that for migrants, it may be just the beginning of another story. There is a long history of migration epics from this world, as the classical accounts of Exodus, the *Aeneid*, and the *Sirat Bani Hilal* remind us.

National Identity

Benedict Anderson's model connecting print culture and imagined national community finds purchase for the Middle East, even if there are significant challenges—such as diglossia—to his broader theses.[4] Mahfouz's *Palace Walk*, in this regard, is exemplary for how it (like many of his novels) allegorizes a moment of national history—the 1919 Revolution—from the perspective of the urban *effendiyya* class. Likewise, Negm's poetry articulates a very clear vision of nationalist identity, although, in contrast to Mahfouz, his nation has a pronounced working-class and peasant center of gravity. Latifa al-Zayyat's novel *The Open Door* also fits within the paradigms of Egyptian national romance, but it does so by exploring the gaps between masculinist discourses of the nation and the lived experience of women. Given its roman à clef form, which presents real-life figures from Saudi Arabia's founding as a petrol state in the form of literary characters, Munif's *Cities of Salt* is an even clearer example of national allegory. In a different vein, many Palestinian literary works—like those of Darwish, al-Qasim, and Kanafani—are consumed by the question of national identity. Given the contested, unfulfilled nature of Palestinian nationhood, the nationalist theme is arguably even more urgent in such works. The same theme of national belonging pervades Israeli literature to a similar degree, though for different reasons. A. B. Yehoshua's *Mr. Mani* develops this theme through a figure of an autochthonous Jewish man—at times Sephardic, at times Mizrahi, at times Ashkenazi—who recurs at various historical moments in the region. Despite the many guises of Yehoshua's character, his identity remains rooted and authentic. Finally, we might bring up Djebar's richly satisfying *Fantasia* once again, for in its own idiosyncratic way, it too insists on a very complicated and dialectical accounting of Algerian identity in the aftermath of French colonization. For Djebar, national "identity" is far less fixed than for other authors mentioned here, because it is always a product of difference and struggle, of movement between colonizer and colonized, between men and women, between Arabic and French (and Berber), between Africa and Europe, between the historical past and the historical present.

NOTES

1. The phrase "structure of feeling" is from Raymond Williams, *Marxism and Literature* (Oxford: Oxford University Press, 1977), 128–35.

2. Borrowed from the fields of semiotics and narratology, the concept of the *actant* allows us to see how human agency is always embedded in wider networks of people, things, and concepts. See Bruno Latour, *Reassembling the Social: An Introduction to Actor-Network-Theory* (Oxford: Oxford University Press, 2005).

3. Hayden White, *Metahistory: The Historical Imagination in Nineteenth-Century Europe* (Baltimore: Johns Hopkins University Press, 1973), 3–4.

4. Benedict Anderson, *Imagined Communities: Reflections on the Origins and Spread of Nationalism* (London: Verso, 2006).

KEY RESOURCES

Choukri, Muhammad. *For Bread Alone*. London: Telegram Books, 2007.

Darwish, Mahmoud, Samih al-Qasim, and Adonis. *Victims of a Map: A Bilingual Anthology of Arabic Poetry*. London: Saqi Books, 2008.

Djebar, Assia. *Fantasia: An Algerian Cavalcade*. Portsmouth, NH: Heineman, 2003.

Hikmet, Nazim. *Human Landscapes from My Country: An Epic Novel in Verse*. New York: Persea Books, 2009.

Kanafani, Ghassan. *Men in the Sun*. Boulder, CO: Lynne Reiner Books, 1999.

Lalami, Laila. *Hope and Other Dangerous Pursuits*. New York: Algonquin Books, 2005.

Mahfouz, Naguib. *Palace Walk*. New York: Doubleday Books, 1990.

Munif, Abdelrahman. *Cities of Salt*. New York: Vintage Books, 1989.

Negm, Ahmed Fouad. *I Say My Words Out Loud*. Amsterdam: Prince Klaus Fund, 2013.

Panian, Karnig. *Goodbye Antoura*. Stanford, CA: Stanford University Press, 2015.

Salih, Tayyib. *Season of Migration to the North*. New York: New York Review Books, 2009.

Yehoshua, A. B. *Mr. Mani*. New York: Harvest Books, 1993.

Al-Zayyat, Latifa. *The Open Door*. Cairo: Hoopoe Books, 2017.

Cinema as a Source for Teaching Modern Middle East History

KAMRAN RASTEGAR

This chapter outlines resources drawn from cinema for the teaching of modern Middle Eastern history. To explore this topic, it will be important to first outline briefly some qualities of the film cultures of the Middle East region, as well as to address the history of interest in the Middle East as a setting for films produced by US or Western European filmmakers. Then we may outline a set of exemplary film texts that may be useful in the teaching of the history of region, with a better understanding of contexts for their production and circulation. The reason for this approach is to dissuade colleagues from the teaching of cinema works as mere "illustrations" of historical or social events, but rather to use films in history classes as a product of discrete cultural and historical conditions that must inform our understanding of their content and reception—to develop a critical literacy around films as historical documents. As the authors of a recent volume on using cinema to teach history in high schools have argued, "Historical film literacy revolves around empowering young people to recognize, describe, question, and analyze a film's purposes and themes. Why is a history movie telling a story about an era or event in a particular way? Why are certain perspectives emphasized and others de-emphasized or ignored? Whom does the movie want the audience to cheer for or against? What perspectives on the past does the movie encourage the audience to empathize with and why? What moral reactions about the past does the movie aim to evoke, or provoke, in viewers?"[1]

When pertaining to teaching the history of the Middle East in a Western classroom, these questions take on a particular valence, framed by the complexities not only of the history of the Middle East itself but also by the ways by which the region is currently generally understood and represented in the West.

What I argue is that to use cinema in the teaching of history requires moving beyond the truth claims that a film text may make. *Battle of Algiers* is sometimes—perhaps often—taught as a (near-)documentary representation of the first years of the Algerian war of independence, with little attention given to the context for its own production and circulation as a product of anticolonial internationalist Marxism, much less as a work of aesthetic complexity that also speaks to the changing ideals of using cinema as a vehicle for an emotional and affective experience. To this end, it will be useful for this chapter to offer some means for the contextualization of films that may be used in the history classroom. First, I provide a brief overview of Western filmmaking about the Middle East and then move to a discussion of filmmaking by filmmakers in the region who are part of the region's own indigenous film cultures. I address documentary cinema in a further separate section.

A Brief History of Western Filmmaking Set in the Middle East

To teach Middle Eastern history using Hollywood films—a label I use to describe a style and model of filmmaking that goes beyond the formal institutions of the studios that were and to some extent still are based in Hollywood, California—requires an understanding of the legacy of the region as one of the central nodes in the early cinematic imagination of the West. Beginning in the 1890s with some of the first experiments carried out by the Lumière Brothers—the inventor/entrepreneurs more often credited with the "invention" of cinema—the Middle East has served as an enduring setting for the cinematic imagination of Western European and North American filmmakers. The Lumières produced many short one-reel films of a number of locations in the region: 35 films in Egypt, 33 films in Algeria, 18 films in Tunisia, 16 films in Palestine, 4 films in Ottoman Turkey (Istanbul), 2 films in Syria, and 2 films in Lebanon (https://catalogue-lumiere.com). British and French colonial interests in the Middle East were primary engines of this interest, and three other production companies sent crews to the region to make "actuality" films—the Edison Company, Pathé, and Kalem.[2] Cinema, therefore, generally simply picked up where prior popular media had already established a semiotic system for representing the Middle East. Whether in the visual approaches that framed the genre of what is usually termed Orientalist painting, to early photographic representations of the region (often staged imaginatively), to the long history of literary works in the genre of the Oriental Tale, one may discern two separate modes of representation: one that makes claims of verisimilitude (however specious these claims may be to a historian) and another that is self-consciously imaginative and fantastic.

In its early stage Hollywood cinema took on the themes and motifs of these prior cultural forms and incorporated them into what were usually imaginative works. Egyptomania served as the engine for the early Fox Studio extravaganza *Cleopatra* (1917), which was already the fourth commercial film of that title produced.[3] *The Thief of Baghdad* (1924) and *The Sheik* (1921) made Douglas Fairbanks and Rudolph Valentino among the first "stars" of Hollywood. But early Hollywood also included examples of films that purported to be "true" or "historical"—usually these were films on colonial topics. British, French, and American directors contributed significant efforts to the establishment of a particular genre that has been termed either *colonial cinema* or *empire cinema*. Colonially themed films such as John Ford's *The Black Watch* (1929) and Harry Hathaway's *The Lives of a Bengal Lancer* (1935)—although set in South Asian rather than Middle Eastern settings—were foundational to the commercial success of early Hollywood and the emergence of such major stars such as Myrna Loy, Gary Cooper, and John Wayne. In France, *Cinema Coloniale* was also a popular genre with its own stars. In these ways, filmmaking about the Middle East has been constitutive of the history of narrative cinema and the development of Hollywood as a commercial film industry more generally.

The lineage of these two categories of Western filmmaking on the Middle East—"imaginative" versus "colonial-historical"—continues more or less unabated through the present day, with the latter category perhaps now better being thought of as "imperialist-historical." With the early signs of the decline of British empire, a number of classic films such as the Korda Brothers' *The Four Feathers* (1939) sought to redeem the virtues of empire, even if these efforts sought to redirect colonial discourses of British supremacy into the field of battle that constituted

World War II. So, one may choose to screen *The Four Feathers* as part of a discussion on British colonial interests in Egypt and Sudan in the 1880s, but it is equally telling of British anxieties as a new Great War loomed in Europe, and British control of colonial dominions was increasingly less certain. By the early 1960s, with the loss of most colonial holdings in the region—most significantly, the loss of Egypt and outcome of the Suez crisis of 1956—British and American films tended to adopt a nostalgic if somewhat critical vantage in renewed entries in the colonial film genre. Perhaps no better example of this may be considered than *Lawrence of Arabia* (1963), which in anthropologist Steven Caton's view is "an anti-imperialist, Orientalist epic."[4]

From the 1970s through the 2000s, the majority of films made by Hollywood about the Middle East have tended to be action thrillers. Most of these films have depended on facile, two-dimensional representations of the region as a violent, primitive region, where religious fanaticism has sought to confront Western rationality and modernity. After the attacks of September 11, 2001, these kinds of representations have proliferated, but also some attempts have been made to offer a more complex view of the region—with mixed results. David O. Russell's *Three Kings* (1999) offered a critical view of US militarism in a story set in the first Gulf War (1991)—a historical setting also used by *Jarhead* (2005), which likewise presented a critique of the culture of militarism surrounding that war.

More recently, the 2003 invasion of Iraq has resulted in further attempts to examine US militarism abroad, although some of the more successful of these films have tended to valorize the wars of the region or have primarily focused on US soldiers as victims of the conflict, ignoring or overlooking the much greater degree of loss experienced by Iraqis and others in the region. Kathryn Bigelow's two major films *Hurt Locker* (2008) and *Zero Dark Thirty* (2012) both exemplify this trend: *Hurt Locker* attends to the harm experienced by US military personnel in the course of the war, almost to the exclusion of Iraqis, while *Zero Dark Thirty* represents its American protagonists as professionals who make a sacrifice in conducting torture of suspected terrorists, rather than as war criminals. More recently, Clint Eastwood's *American Sniper* (2014) takes this same theme and raises it to the level of hagiography, while again omitting any analysis of why the United States is waging war in Iraq and whether or not it is a legitimate commitment. Clearly, I do not recommend the use of these prior films as illustrative of the history of the war, but I have taught them all as examples of US public discourse on the war. More critical views on the occupation of Iraq are supplied by the thriller *Green Zone* (2010) and the battlefield dramas *The Battle for Haditha* (2007) and *Redacted* (2007). The latter two films focus on documented atrocities committed by US soldiers, while the former exposes the hubris and lies upon which the entire war venture was based.

A Brief History of Filmmaking in the Middle East

Given the diversity of experiences with cinema across the region, it is difficult and perhaps dangerous for one to generalize too much (which, for the purposes of our discussion, will include North Africa as well as what is more commonly known as the "Middle East"). Nonetheless it may be helpful to identify at least four distinct types when speaking of the different kinds of film industries that have emerged across the Middle East.

Principal Regional Cinemas

These are the most productive and historically consequential countries in which the roots of a cinema culture may be identified from an early period. Specifically, in Egypt, Turkey, and Iran, we may find robust social and historical factors that supported the establishment of a popular as well as artistic cinema culture by the mid-twentieth century. This, despite the fact that even among these three countries there are wide variances in experience: Egypt's cinema industry has its origins in the 1920s and 1930s, and at its heights (1940–1960s) Egyptian cinema found enthusiastic audiences across the Arab world, beyond its own national borders. By comparison, in both Iran and Turkey, for the most part the popular cinema cultures were limited to their own national borders, and the appearance of what we might call a cinema industry dates rather later, to the 1950s and 1960s, rising in productivity and influence after the 1980s. In terms of quantity of films produced, and the rise of indigenous institutions for filmmaking and film distribution, Egypt, Iran, and Turkey far outpace any other national cinema context in the region. Israel may later be included in this category, although in numerical terms it lags somewhat behind the other three countries: UNESCO

258

reported that during the years 1988–1999, Israel produced an average of 14-feature length films per year, while Egypt produced 72 and Turkey and Iran produced 63 and 62, respectively. Unsurprisingly, these numbers have since fluctuated—in part due to social and political factors such as the aftermath of the Egyptian revolution of 2011. For example, in 2015 UNESCO reported that Turkey produced 137 feature films, Iran produced 85, Egypt 34, and Israel 32. (By comparison, India—the largest film-producing country in the world—produced over 2,000 films in 2015). In recent decades, Morocco may be seen as entering this category even though its industry is yet smaller than any of those listed above. However, given that its film industry has quite a long history and has, at least in more recent decades, been professionalized and produces a consistent number of films (usually 15–20) per year, it must be seen as one of the more durable settings for a film culture in the region. Finally, since the 1960s Lebanon has had a small but increasingly robust film industry, and in the last two decades has also consistently produced 7–15 films per year.

Socialist State-Sponsored Cinemas

The second category would encompass a number of regional cinemas that arose largely out of the socialist policies of postcolonial states that established a state-sponsored cinema industry to promote the ideological and social aims of the newly independent nation-states. These would include, in part, countries such as Syria, Algeria, Iraq, and, to some extent, Tunisia. In some of these contexts state sponsorship resulted in the establishment of fairly robust cinema industries with small but consistent numbers of quality feature-length films produced each year, especially in the 1960s and 1970s; by the 1980s, however, state sponsorship began to come under increasing economic pressure and eventually all but collapsed in each of these contexts—resulting in very small numbers of filmmakers having to more independently sustain a film culture in these countries. Of these only Tunisia has enjoyed a more recent rebound in its film industry, by embracing the neoliberal model of co-productions (films that are produced by entities located in more than one national context), usually with French co-producers. In Iraq, film production has grown in the post-2003 period, but again on a model that relies on international financing rather than national state funding.

Nationless Cinemas

The third category of Middle Eastern filmmaking would include non-"national" cinemas—cinemas that operate either outside of a national system as part of a national liberation struggle, or as part of a minority social group not subject to representation in the national cinemas of the regions. These would include Palestinian, Kurdish, and Amazigh (Berber) filmmakers, among others. In these contexts, filmmakers have often had to navigate complex identities and fraught political and cultural landscapes in the aim of producing films that have some basis in the culture, language, and historical experience of their oppressed communities. For example, although Palestinian filmmakers can be traced in the region's history back to the 1920s (e.g., the Lama brothers, who were silent filmmakers of Palestinian origin, but who were based in Egypt), what is now generally viewed as Palestinian cinema originates in the cultural organs of national liberation organizations under the umbrella of the Palestine Liberation Organization (PLO). These efforts originated in the late 1960s, often bolstered by internationalist support of the Palestinian cause by European or other filmmakers. By the 1980s, in addition, a number of filmmakers arose from the community of Palestinians who are citizens of the state of Israel, articulating a cultural vision that was less beholden to the strictures of the PLO's politics, but that was no less political. In the 1990s and early 2000s, a number of new voices arose from the Palestinian diaspora, which includes the Palestinians who were made into refugees after the 1948 and 1967 wars. From these various locations, which include the Palestinian-occupied territories of the West Bank and Gaza and Palestinians living inside the borders of Israel "proper" (inside the "Green Line") to diverse diasporic locations from Lebanese refugee camps to Parisian second-generation Palestinians, to Palestinian American filmmakers from the US Midwest, one may discern certain commonalities of intention and voice that make coherent the idea of a Palestinian cinema, despite the absence of a Palestinian nation-state. Kurds and Amazigh share some characteristics in terms of identity and history with Palestinians, but each differ in various ways in terms of their relationships to the recognized nation-states of the region and the modes of oppression that are deployed against them. For example, the experience of Kurdish filmmakers in Turkey is historically quite distinct from that of Iranian Kurds, or of Iraqi Kurds (especially in the aftermath of the 1991 Gulf War). Regardless, each of these communities has produced a cinema culture—diverse and multi-farious as it may be—that represents both a core adherence to a marginalized identity as well as the historical fragmentation and division of their communities by various national and international actors.

Nascent Cinemas

Finally, the fourth category would include countries in which no appreciable film culture or industry may be spoken of—at least until very recently. Largely this category would include the monarchies of the Persian Gulf and Arabian Peninsula, joined by Libya and Yemen as well. In these countries, for various reasons, the development of a cinema culture or cinema industry has been stymied—often despite plentiful resources, in particular among petrostates such as Kuwait, Saudi Arabia, or Libya. In some cases, these countries have begun to support local cinema industries very recently, leading to some remarkable new voices being added to what we may term as Middle Eastern cinema—for example, Saudi Arabian women filmmakers or young filmmakers from the United Arab Emirates. Regardless of these new developments in some countries, in others, especially those that have been the setting of post–Arab Spring wars and internal instability—Libya and Yemen, in particular—the establishment of any cinema industry remains very much an impossibility for the near future at least.

Teaching History with Fiction Films from the Middle East

Given the outline provided above, it should be clear to any teacher of Middle Eastern history that until the mid-twentieth century, examples of narrative films that may be useful for illustrating aspects of the history of the region would come primarily from Egypt. When looking at Egypt's pre-1952 film industry, there is a great deal that may be of interest in illustrating aspects of the historical and social considerations of the period, but there are few films that make "history" their central concern. Beyond this, the most popular genres of Egyptian popular cinema were variants on the light comedy, the musical (usually romantic), or the upper-class parlor drama—none of which merit much interest for historical teaching, despite the fact that each genre may be full of social detail that could be interesting for students seeking to learn about the region.

So, for example, Ahmad Badrakhan's film *Fatma* (1947) serves as an example of a social drama with elements of musical and romance, in telling the story of a lower-class woman in Cairo whose career as a nurse takes her out of her inherited social circumstances and eventually leads to her marriage to the son of an aristocrat. The film takes a tragic turn when the son disavows his marriage under pressure by his family, which leads to a courtroom climax in which he finally embraces his wife and their child and acknowledges them publicly before following her to her lower-middle-class neighborhood and to the warm embrace of her family and neighbors. While the film does not address broader political issues, it does keenly illustrate shifting ideals around class, education, and women's social status. When adding to this the fact that the film stars Umm Kulthum, who is a nearly transcendent figure of Arabic music and the greatest star across the region in the twentieth century, one can also fold into the discussion her particular social persona and her later political commitments. Umm Kulthum came to be a stalwart of the revolutionary project of Gamal Abdel Nasser and became a transnational ambassador to his vision of pan-Arabism.

As noted above, the changes in Egypt after 1952, and more broadly across the region over the course of the 1950s and 1960s, result in new forms of cinema that often were more realist in their form and more directly political in their content. In Egypt a number of films across the late 1950s and early 1960s directly addressed colonialism, the anticolonial struggle, and postcolonial events such as the 1956 Suez War. In *I Am Free* (1958), an example of the turn to "neorealism" in Egyptian cinema, a young woman growing up in the prerevolutionary period finds meaning in her life once she dedicates herself to the revolutionary struggle. In *A Man in Our House* (1961), director Henri Barakat explores the politicization of a middle-class Cairo family sheltering a young militant who has assassinated an Egyptian politician. Outside of Egypt, films such as the Syrian-produced *The Dupes* (1972), directed by Tawfiq Salih (and based on the Palestinian novella *Men in the Sun* by Ghassan Kanafani), focus on the Palestinian predicament in telling the story of three Palestinian workers who attempt to be smuggled across the Iraqi desert into Kuwait. The film implicitly critiques Arab rulers for abandoning the Palestinians, even as it also represents the plight of Palestinian refugees more generally.

Each of these films could work well in teaching themes of anticolonial resistance, but the film that surpasses any other in this role would have to be *The Battle of Algiers* (1966). While the director of *Battle*, Gillo Pontecorvo, is not from the Middle East (he is Italian), the film is a hybrid work of internationalist commitment that viewed the Algerian war of independence as not just a local anticolonial struggle but as a bellwether event of global significance. The stylistic mastery of the film allows it to retain a certain vitality and vigor that renders it "relatable" to students of varied ages and backgrounds. The treatment of social prejudice and police tactics also resonates with the experiences of many American students (especially students of color), and allows for the transnational aspirations of the film to continue to chart connections to other contexts and struggles.

By the 1980s and 1990s, much of the filmmaking in the region takes an increasingly critical view of the oppressive forms of government that ruled in most countries of the region. For example, Yilmaz Güney's *Yol* (1982), which was directed remotely from a prison cell, gained accolades for its brave depiction of Turkey as a society smothered by different forms of repression—political authoritarianism, ethnic repression, in particular against Kurds, and patriarchal repression of women. In Tunisia, Moufida Tlatli's *Silences of the Palace* (1993) explores the history of the end of colonialism, but through the eyes of female domestic workers in an aristocratic palace. Though the film is deeply critical of the forms of oppression governing prerevolutionary Tunisian society, it also critiques postcolonial Tunisia for having failed to deliver on the promise of liberation for all Tunisians.

For teaching post-1979 Iran, various films give a critical view of Iran after the revolution. Bahram Bayza'i's beautiful film *Bashu, The Little Stranger* (1985—released in 1987) critiqued the state view on the Iran-Iraq War through the story of a boy who escapes the devastation of the war's front and finds refuge in a distant northern Iranian village where the residents do not even speak the same language as he does. By the 1990s, Iranian films come to be more directly critical of the revolutionary order, with films such as Mohsen Makhmalbaf's *A Moment of Innocence* (1996), which explores the legacy of the revolution by restaging a militant revolutionary act carried out by the director in his youth and then poses questions about the ethics of violence around that act. By the 2000s, Iranian films are even more openly critical, such as Ja'far Panahi's *The Circle* (2000), which gives a blistering attack on state-sponsored patriarchy, or his *Crimson Gold* (2003), which tells the story of an Iran-Iraq War veteran who has been neglected by the state and who is pushed to

Poster from the film *The Battle of Algiers*, directed by Gillo Pontecorvo (Italy, Algeria: Casbah Film and Igor Film, 1966). Courtesy of Janus Films.

extreme measures by his circumstances. However, the criticism mounted by Panahi in almost all of his films since 2000 is less commonly found in other films from Iran, which tend to focus on questions of social inequity or an aspiration to change in more oblique or sometimes melodramatic ways—the award-winning films of Asghar Farhadi, and in particular his drama *A Separation* (2011), offer rich social texts that also explore ethical concerns, but they may be less effective for teaching postrevolutionary Iranian history.

A number of feature films address the lead-up to and aftermath of the revolutions of the last decade—a period I would begin with the Iranian "Green Movement" of 2009, followed by the Tahrir Square revolution of 2011 and the outbreak of the Syrian revolution (*cum* civil war), through the Gezi Square protests in Turkey in 2013. This set of regional events interlock youth-led revolutionary eruptions that sought alternatives to the corrupt and nepotistic regimes in each setting. Films on youth cultures in the region can serve as a useful entry point to teaching these events: semi-documentary/semi-fictional films such as *No One Knows about Persian Cats* (2009), about underground musicians in Iran attempting to find a way to leave the country, or *Microphone* (2010), about Egyptian underground musicians attempting to set up a concert in Alexandria. Both films weave in a fictional narrative with acting alongside musical vignettes featuring real bands and musicians in each setting. The aftermath of these failed revolutions remains fertile ground for unsanctioned underground music, which is at the heart of *Yallah! Underground* (2015) or the field of television dreams that is the setting of *The Idol* (2015), which tells the true story of a man from Gaza who won the pan-Arab *Arab Idol* contest.

Documentary Films on the Middle East

Most of the discussion above has pertained most directly to fictional narrative feature filmmaking, although the discussion of the earliest "actuality" films by the Lumière Brothers may lend itself more to the genre of documentary than to fiction. The Middle East has long been a site for documentary filmmaking—initially by Western filmmakers, but then increasingly by filmmakers from the region. In the last twenty years, documentary filmmaking by filmmakers in the Middle East has come to eclipse fiction filmmaking, with nearly every major event in the region now subject to one or often many documentaries—often of varied quality, and of varied impact in terms of reaching broad audiences.

Looking beyond the so-called actuality films of the 1890s and 1900s, in the first decades of the twentieth century a small but important set of documentary films remains extant from the region and may be useful for teaching purposes. These would include the Iranian court films of Mozaffar al-Din Shah's court photographer from the 1920s, who recorded scenes of urban life in Tehran, and the footage of the Ottoman Sultan Mehmet VI's ascent to the throne—these are reasonably easily accessible on the internet. But these short films produced for courtly or official state use were a far cry from the more fully formed genre of documentary as it began to emerge in the "ethnographic" cinema of the 1920s and 1930s. A large number of these films are now available on the web archive Colonial Film UK (www.colonialfilm.org.uk) and when taught critically may be of great value for teaching about colonial ideology and administration.

The reportage documentary has origins in the newsreel genre—the short films that were screened before feature films in cinemas and that addressed the news of the day. These works are easily accessible online via the Pathé archive (https://www.britishpathe.com/); they are highly illustrative of the ideological framing of colonial practice in the region and are wonderful complements to the teaching of how Britain wished for its colonial projects, including those in the Middle East, to be seen by its subjects. But as formal and de facto forms of colonialism began ending in the region in the mid-twentieth century, documentary cinema slowly came to play a productive role as a form of resistance to colonialism. In the 1960s and 1970s filmmakers such as Kamran Shirdel in Iran and Omar Amiralay in Syria had realized the power of documentary filmmaking to make films that are socially critical even in repressive political settings. Shirdel's works such as *Women's Prison* (1965) or *Tehran Is the Capital of Iran* (1966) exposed social injustice and forms of poverty that belied the Iranian regime's propaganda around its projects of modernization and westernization. Amiralay's film *Everyday Life in a Syrian Village* (1974) explores the devastation that a major dam project brings to the lives of marginalized Syrian villagers, in a criticism of the Ba'thist socialist project in Syria that also fetishized modernization with little concern for the effects on the poor.

By the early 1980s in both Lebanese and Israeli/Palestinian contexts documentary came to play a significant role in visual cultural interventions into the Lebanese civil war and the Israeli-Palestinian conflict, respectively. In Lebanon, the filmmakers Mai Masri and Jean Chamoun co-directed a series of films including *Under the Rubble* (1983), *Wild Flowers* (1986), and *War Generation: Beirut* (1989) that took on the sectarian politics and international geopolitical considerations that provided the engine for the civil war and as a whole provide some of the best visual materials for teaching that conflict. It is somewhat fitting that Mai Masri is Palestinian, while her partner Jean Chamoun was Lebanese, in that the Palestinian and Lebanese contexts are deeply intertwined. During the period in which the PLO was headquartered in Lebanon (1970–1982) Palestinian filmmakers such as Mustafa Abu Ali worked through the cultural organs of PLO factions to make films that addressed Palestinian refugee experiences and those of the emerging militants, who idealized liberation through guerrilla means. Films of his, such as *They Do Not Exist* (1974) or *Palestine in the Eye* (1977), use vérité documentary style and judicious use of avant-garde montage to produce films that are both wonderful documents of the "real" experiences of Palestinians living in refugee camps, but that also sought to act as a form of agitprop, provoking viewers to action. But Palestinian documentary cinema took other forms as well: in 1980, Michel Khleifi, a Palestinian citizen of Israel, launched his career as a filmmaker with the celebrated film *Fertile Memory*. Focusing on forms of resistance by two very different Palestinian women—a working-class factory worker living in Israel who seeks the return of lands of hers appropriated by the Israeli state, and a divorced novelist living under occupation in the West Bank—*Fertile Memory* includes representations of Palestinian experience that could not be encompassed by the PLO filmmakers, in particular by focusing on women as the primary characters of the film.

Since the 1980s, Palestinian and Israel documentarians have produced an incredibly rich and varied portfolio of films exploring the conflict from a variety of angles. Amos Gitai's *Field Diary* (1982) explores the realities of military occupation in the West Bank from the perspective of Israeli soldiers. By the 2000s, films such as Juliano Mer Khamis's *Arna's Children* (2003)—a personal documentary looking at a theater program for Palestinian refugees run by his mother, an Israeli Jewish woman, in the West Bank—charted the progression of resistance to the occupation up through the violence that characterized the second intifada. In 2012, *5 Broken Cameras,* a film shot by a Palestinian farmer with little background in filmmaking, and then edited by an Israeli Jewish activist, broke through with international acclaim, even garnering an Academy Award nomination. *5 Broken Cameras* traced yet another stage in Palestinian experience under occupation in the West Bank, chronicling nonviolent resistance by Palestinian villagers to the Israeli separation wall that would dispossess them of their agricultural lands. All of these films—and many others—can be excellent tools for teaching the history of the region.

I end with a few words about documentary in the post–Arab Spring moment. In this last decade, documentary in the region has often focused on social movements for change and the effects they have had. Iranian director Rakhshan Bani-Etemad addresses the mounting groundswell of a desire for change in Iran with her masterful documentary *Our Times* (2002), which chronicles the experiences of a number of young Iranians—primarily women—in the election campaign of 2001. Her film sets the groundwork for understanding the eruptions of the next decade, in which societies from Iran to Egypt to Turkey have all found their burgeoning youth to be impatient with economic stagnation, cultural and social restrictions, and a political system that is largely unresponsive to their needs and dreams.

Since 2011 and the fact that most of these movements would have to be considered as failing in achieving their objectives, a great deal of documentary work has been made by amateur or semi-amateur filmmakers endeavoring to simply act as a witness to the political and social changes around them. These works tend to be found in online archives: in Egypt, the Mosireen Collective (works archived on https://858.ma) accumulated many dozens of films about the 2011 revolution and the tumultuous years afterward, while the Syrian "Abou Naddara" collective (abounaddara.com) have similarly used documentary to offer myriad short snapshots of the evolution of the Syrian conflict. Both of these archives are unique and excellent examples of film material as primary texts and can be invaluable for use in the classroom. A smaller selective set of high-end professional documentaries offer a more crafted analysis of recent history. In particular, Jehane Noujaim's *The Square* represents a compelling attempt to filter the inchoate energies of the Tahrir

Square sit-ins in Cairo of 2011 into a coherent narrative. It provides a clear and condensed understanding of those events that is very useful as a teaching tool.

Conclusion

This chapter seeks to offer some useful thoughts regarding the use of cinema as a tool for teaching the history of the region by nonspecialists in the study of cinema. As I argue, it is important for such nonspecialists to have a general overview of the phenomenon of filmmaking both about and from the Middle East. The reason for this is that cinematic works are foremost artifacts of a particular cultural history, and that they often say as much if not more about the time and context of their production than they serve to "illustrate" the history of the events related in the film's narrative. Equipped with a knowledge of cinema as an important part of the cultural histories of both the Middle East and West, the history teacher can introduce works of cinema as multifarious texts that are rich sources for understanding both historical events, but then also the contestations that frame the representation of such events, and how they are remembered often far after their occurrence.

Perhaps a useful end point is to recognize that many important historical episodes in the region are very poorly represented by cinematic works—for different reasons in each case, but often because they are simply too complex, or the interpretations of them are too contested, for a single film to be able to address them. For example, there are only a small number of relatively modest attempts to tackle the Palestinian *Nakba*—specifically, the dispossession of Palestinians in 1947–1949—in a cinematic manner. Or the Iranian Revolution of 1979, which is often viewed as one of the most important events of the region in the second half of the century, is almost completely absent as a topic or even a backdrop for narrative filmmaking. Additionally, other events may be addressed in certain film works, but sometimes these exceptional films cannot be easily found in the available catalogs of films available to teachers. So, it is necessary for us to also acknowledge the limitations that teachers may face in finding materials that work well for them and that address various specific historical topics.

NOTES

1. Alan S. Marcus, Scott Alan Metzger, Richard J. Paxton, and Jeremy D. Stoddard, *Teaching History with Film: Strategies for Secondary Social Studies* (New York: Routledge, 2010), 7.

2. Antonia Lant, "The Curse of the Pharaoh, or How Cinema Contracted Egyptomania," *October* 59 (1992): 87–112, 101.

3. Lant, "Curse of the Pharaoh," 102.

4. Steven C. Caton, *Lawrence of Arabia: A Film's Anthropology* (Berkeley: University of California Press, 1999), 172.

KEY RESOURCES

Armes, Roy. *Arab Filmmakers of the Middle East: A Dictionary*. Bloomington: Indiana University Press, 2010.

Arsalan, Savas. *Cinema in Turkey: A New Critical History*. New York: Oxford University Press, 2010.

Dönmez-Colin, Gönül. *The Cinema of North Africa and the Middle East*. London: Wallflower Press, 2007.

Hillauer, Rebecca. *Encyclopedia of Arab Women Filmmakers*. Cairo: American University in Cairo Press, 2005.

Naficy, Hamid. *A Social History of Iranian Cinema*. Vols. 1–4. Durham, NC: Duke University Press, 2011.

Rastegar, Kamran. *Surviving Images: Cinema, War, and Cultural Memory in the Middle East*. Oxford: Oxford University Press, 2015.

Shafik, Viola. *Arab Cinema: History and Cultural Identity*. Cairo: American University in Cairo Press, 1998.

Shohat, Ella. *Israeli Cinema: East/West and the Politics of Representation*. Rev. ed. London: I. B. Tauris, 2010.

Yaqub, Nadia. *Palestinian Cinema in the Days of Revolution*. Austin: University of Texas Press, 2018.

Gender and Sexuality

Sources and Methods

H A N A N H A M M A D

At every first meeting of my History of Women in the Middle East class, I ask students what they are interested to learn. Students' answers have been consistent over the years, mostly around this line: why Middle Eastern culture has been rigid and shackling toward women. Students' words underscore their presumptions that women in the Middle East have never experienced progress, that gender relations and the social construction of sexuality in the Middle East have been static throughout history, that culture has been the only decisive factor in informing gender and sexuality, and that religion (i.e., Islam) defines culture. Enabling students in American classrooms to understand that gender and sexuality in Muslim communities, as everywhere else, result from historical, religious, cultural, social, economic, and political processes requires critical thinking and empathy, as well as close readings of primary sources. The ever-growing number of published anthologies and source books has made it possible to utilize primary sources from the Middle East in English translation in order to examine authoritative texts such as the Qur'an and hadith on gender and sexuality, and to learn the broad social contexts in which gender and sexuality formed and are re-formed.[1]

A Muslim Theology of Birth Control

The question of the permissibility of birth control has generated various opinions among Muslim scholars, providing a good example to examine authoritative texts, discuss Islamic interpretations of the scripture, and explore the gap between religious ideals and practices in the predominantly Muslim Middle East. The teaching of Abu Hamid al-Ghazali, one of the most prominent and influential jurists, theologians, and mystics from the medieval classical Islamic age, can be a useful way to engage students directly with a primary authoritative text.[2] Al-Ghazali (450–505 AH/1058–1111 AD) discussed questions relevant to the daily life of ordinary Muslims; thus, his writings can invigorate a discussion on the body and on sexuality. I employ his writings on birth control to facilitate and foster empathy among young American students without further amplifying the incorrect assumption that the Middle East and Islamic cultures have been static. Andrew Rippin and Jan Knappert's *Textual Sources for the Study of Islam* gives an accessible translated excerpt of al-Ghazali's document.[3] In that excerpt, al-Ghazali provides his interpretation of what he thinks Islam decreed about *'azl*, coitus interruptus, as a method for birth control, acknowledging that the Qur'an does not address this question in any clear verse. He bases his opinion on legal analogy from the Qur'an. Analogy, or *qiyas* in Arabic, refers to a form of legal reasoning Muslim scholars often use to generate a rule when there is no clear Qur'anic verse regarding the matter.

Al-Ghazali's document on birth control gives texture to illuminate the intellectual openness in the Islamic scholarly debate on sexuality. Al-Ghazali acknowledges the differences among the learned class concerning *'azl*; as one group says *'azl* is lawful in all circumstances, a second group says it is unlawful in all circumstances, a third group says it is lawful with the consent of one's wife, and a fourth group says it is lawful in the case of female slaves but not in the case of free women. Those various opinions offer an opportunity to teach the importance of interpretation of the Qur'an and hadith and how the interpretation is not only a product of Qur'anic or prophetic statements; rather, it is an intellectual exercise whose outcome relies on a multiplicity of factors including the gender of the scholar. It gives a point of entry to evaluate the role of authoritative texts and how textual statements take on different lives based on interpretation. Some opinions are more permissible while others are rigid and banning. Some scholars consider wifely consent while others ignore it.

Al-Ghazali states his position that *'azl* is permissible, but not commendable, and there is no sin if semen and a female egg are not allowed to mix. He concludes that *'azl* as a birth control method is lawful when the aims are to preserve the beauty and health of one's wife and to prevent the birth of too many children since maintaining too many children is difficult and since it is no sin to protect one's wealth and properties. Meanwhile, avoiding pregnancy for fear of the birth of daughters is unlawful. He cites the Qur'anic prohibition on the pre-Islamic custom of burying daughters alive and fearing the birth of females. 'Azl is also unlawful if it is to protect the honor of a woman, to keep her neat and clean, and to save her from maintaining children.[4]

Al-Ghazali's religious opinion provides a teaching moment; he speaks as a man, keeping in mind his male audience. He decides that birth control is lawful when it aims at achieving a man's interests in protecting woman's beauty and health so that her man can enjoy her always. Al-Ghazali also allows birth control so that the man could keep his wealth and does not have to face financial burdens due to having many children. On the other hand, al-Ghazali decides birth control is unlawful when it is beneficial for the woman as to protect her honor, to keep herself neat and clean, or to save her from maintaining children. Explicitly patriarchal discourse can teach students more than the religious opinion of an important scholar. Students must learn to read between the lines, read against the grain, and understand the historical contexts so that they can examine the gap between the sacred scripture—the Qur'an— and the Qur'anic interpretation as dominated by men throughout most of Islamic history. Trained as professional scholars in almost exclusively male domains, male interpreters speak for their gender biases, particularly whenever there was not a clear statement in the scripture.

Muslim feminist scholars, such as Fatima Mernissi, Amina Wadud, and Asma Barlas, have challenged the patriarchal interpretation of the Qur'an during the last few decades.[5] Historical analysis of religious authority and knowledge has revealed the patriarchal biases of Muslim male scholars. More importantly, a critical reading of al-Ghazali's document helps students examine the gap between the actual practices of Muslims and religious ideals, whether these ideals are patriarchal or otherwise. Students learn that people actually practice 'azl for various reasons, regardless of al-Ghazali's opinion. They also learn that people participate in a variety of social and sexual practices that are explicitly prohibited in Qur'anic statements. Avoiding pregnancy to save a women's honor means illicit sexual contact takes place and, in some cases, leads to unwanted pregnancy despite the religious ban on zina (adultery). Likewise, avoiding pregnancy out of fear of producing daughters exposes the fact that avoiding having daughters has continued after Islam despite the straightforward and explicit Qur'anic statements. Students learn to be good historians and to evaluate the position of Islam in Middle Eastern culture and to evaluate culture as one among many other factors in deciding people's choices and practices. Individual sexual practices and social notions of sexuality in Middle Eastern history and cultures are a product of a wide range of social, economic, and cultural factors, not only religion (i.e., Islam).

Students become well equipped to learn about and to question the broader socio-economic circumstances in which gender and sexuality formed and were reformed in the modern Middle East. Religious opinions express, as well as affect, the socio-cultural milieu. Thus, students realize that sexuality and gender in the Middle East and in Islamic cultures have been changeable, malleable, and influential, rather than fixed categories. We must consider the sociocultural factors in which scholars lived and worked, in addition to their gender biases. My lectures on the importance of interpretation and its role in forming and informing gender in Islamic thoughts are grounded in the scholarly literature on intellectual Islamic history and gender in Islam. Leila Ahmad's *Women and Gender in Islam: Historical Roots of a Modern Debate* and Denise Spellberg's *Politics, Gender, and the Islamic Past: The Legacy of 'A'isha Bint Abi Bakr* are still classics in both fields.[6] For shorter readings sufficient to equip students with knowledge and analysis of the subject, students read two book chapters: Ahmad's "Early Islam and the Position of Women: The Problem of Interpretation" and Spellberg's "Political Action and Public Example: 'Aisha and the Battle of the Camel."[7]

Al-Ghazali's document further serves as a basis for the discussion of reproductive health and women's control over their bodies and sexuality, important issues in the modern Middle East as well as in all modern societies as indicated by the vigorous debates surrounding birth control in contemporary Catholic contexts. Al-Ghazali's answer to the birth control question is human rather than sacred and as practical as it is ideologically motivated. He speaks of what he considers good for Muslim individuals and for the Muslim society. Yet, it is a male-biased opinion that expresses a patriarchal ideology of favoring male control over the reproductive process and controlling women's sexuality. His answer constrains women's control over their bodies. Reproductive health and birth control have been part of postcolonial Middle Eastern states' policies and societal debates. These issues always intersect with religious beliefs and sociocultural customs as much as with the goals and plans for socioeconomic development. For example, the state of Iran made contraceptives available in the 1960s as part of the Pahlavi regime's state-sponsored feminism. The Iranian Revolution overthrew the repressive Pahlavi regime in 1979 and spawned the Islamic Republic of Iran (IRI) under the leadership of Ayatollah Khomeini. The IRI reversed the state's reproductive health policies, making contraceptives less accessible in 1980s as part of the regime's so-called Islamic Cultural Revolution. The Iranian state under both regimes, the Pahlavi Monarchy and the Islamic Republic, encouraged or discouraged reproduction, respectively, to serve the regime's vision of national interests.

Employing Khomeini's religious interpretation, the IRI initially urged Iranians to reproduce, discouraged the use of contraceptives, and lowered the marriage age. The regime used an overtly religious discourse to serve Khomeini's notion of creating an abundant pious Islamic society. The annual population growth rate was as high as 3.34 percent in 1978, one year before the collapse of the Pahlavi regime, and then jumped to 4.21 percent in 1983, three years after Khomeini came to power. Ten years later, the annual population growth sharply declined to 1.25 percent in 1993 shortly after the same Islamic regime in Iran advocated birth control and small-sized families. The Iranian regime had to quickly reverse its reproduction policies in the wake of countering the challenges of rapid over population, particularly after the end of the war with Iraq that lasted from 1980 to 1988. Rhetorical advocacy of small but strong and well-off families replaced the rhetoric of the virtue of an abundant Islamic society in the Iranian public discourse. Coupling textual sources with statistics energizes the discussion.

A publicly accessible interactive set of demographic statistics generated from the World Bank's data is available online and accessible for our classroom use.[8] That source makes it easy for students to compare annual population growth rates since 1960 in the Middle East region and its individual countries. Despite all the problems of demographic statistics, the source is a useful tool for students to pair with textual sources, so that students can evaluate the position of religion, ideology, and culture in formulating decisions about birth control in Middle Eastern societies. Students can compare annual population growth in Iran with each Middle East country and with the region as whole. Statistics show that the Islamic Republic of Iran has one of the lowest population growth rates in the Middle East during the last two decades.

Statistics also show the continuing decline in the annual rate of population growth across the Middle East region after 1990. Of course, there are many reasons to explain the decline in the annual population growth rate in Iran and in the entire region, but this is the point. Religious culture is not the only decisive factor, and the culture is changeable depending on the socioeconomic and political contexts. In Middle Eastern societies, as in all societies, more often than not, sociocultures could be fluid and changeable.

The interpretations of Islamic texts are open to many different conclusions. Different, even conflicting, rules could be claimed to be consistent with social and religious cultures. Ideologies sometimes determine social policies and vice versa. Discussing birth control in relation to gender and sexuality in the Middle East inevitably evokes parallel debates in American societies. Students often voluntarily cite the parallel difficulties American women face when male lawmakers dominate the discussion about women's reproductive health and sexuality. The parallel expands the discussion to the role of the state in empowering and/or disempowering women through allocating resources. Questions about the state's role to support or deprive women of quality reproductive health and birth control and about whether the state could be a feminist force for gender equality are relevant to all modern societies. Bringing the discussion back to modern Middle East history, students can think critically about the achievements and the shortcomings of experiences of Middle Eastern feminisms, including the experiences of state feminism when several postcolonial Middle Eastern states championed universal health care, free education, and equal employment opportunities in state bureaucracy and state-owned economic establishments.

In-class debates are the assignment that I find suitable to evaluate students' effort to think through the above-mentioned open-ended questions. Examples of debate topics include these questions: Are women in Islam in good or bad positions? Are women's roles crucial or minimal in shaping Islamic history? Did state feminism liberate or shackle women and feminist movements in the modern Middle East? Students receive the debate question beforehand, and I urge them to think about supporting points such as these: women in the Qur'an and in Islamic law; women before and after the rise of Islam and the establishment of the Muslim state; problems in writing the history of women; who writes history for what purpose; women in politics; the history of women's movements; and continuity, change, and diversity in Muslim societies.

The homework is careful reading of the class material and critical thought about the subject matter. Students can bring all their annotated readings to the class and use them during the debate. On the debate day, I assign each student to serve on one of the debating teams or on the judging team. That team assignment is spontaneous, and students do not pick a team of personal preference or intellectual inclination. I do that because one of the debate goals is to test students' knowledge about the opposing arguments and get them to appreciate different views. This random choice also adds a great deal of energy and humor to the debate as well as sharpening students' critical thinking and intellectual empathy. For example, a Muslim student wearing a hijab excelled in arguing how Islamic culture undermines women, despite her known personal opinion against that argument; a male student was vigilant to stop a casual misogynist remark.

The evaluation of the performance of debating students is based on each student's ability to articulate a well-informed argument and counterargument and to engage the opposite team in critical questions. I evaluate students on the judging team based on their ability to make a well-informed decision, to correct any factual mistake, and to act as an active bystander to correct any behavioral or verbal violation. I am always impressed when students stand up to any misogynist, homophobic, or ethnically biased expressions. The debate exercise always makes for the best class meetings; it relies on students' participation and gives them a safe space to practice freethinking and appreciate their role as ethical active learners. The debate about parallels and comparisons among Middle Eastern societies and between the Middle East and American societies enhances empathy as a pedagogical approach. That approach encourages students in an American classroom to relate to the experiences of people living in the Middle East, a region that seems distant and different. Students study the region as ever-changing, containing complex human experiences. They critically and consistently examine gender and sexuality as debatable issues in the modern Middle East, just as they are in American society.

History of Homosexuality in the Modern Middle East

Teaching gender and sexuality in the broader sociocultural and political contexts of modern Middle East history makes the critical history of homosexuality particularly important. Akram Fouad

Khater's *Sources in the History of the Modern Middle East* provides a good collection of important primary sources produced between the nineteenth century and the present time.[9] The source book privileges the issue of women's emancipation and education as debated among male and female feminists, Muslims and non-Muslim Middle Easterners. In addition to an excerpt by the famous Egyptian feminist Qasim Amin (1863–1908), there are articles from the Egyptian, Iranian, and North African press during late nineteenth and early twentieth centuries.[10] Those documents collectively introduce students to Middle Eastern modernist and Islamic enlightenment discourses. They show how Middle Eastern feminists developed both religious and secular arguments for gender equality.

Khater's collection is not as rich with primary sources discussing sexuality, however. Two documents that are particularly useful for class discussion on the history of homosexuality are Lilian Liang's "Hiding Themselves in the Crowd," published in *Middle East Times* in 1999, and an excerpt from Rifaʿa Rafiʾ al-Tahtawi's *The Extrication of Gold in Summarizing Paris* (1834).[11] In a reversed chronological order, students first read Liang's piece, which discusses the contemporary social taboo around homosexuality, the prosecution of gay men, and the psychological trauma some Egyptian homosexuals face due to police harassment and social marginalization. The report is easy to read and resonates with students' perceived notion about "rigid and intolerant" Middle Eastern societies. Questioning when Middle Eastern society began rigidly favoring heteronormativity and being intolerant toward homosexuality allows the leap from contemporary society back to the beginning of the nineteenth century, when the contacts between peoples from the Middle East and the West intensified. To answer the question, students read short passages from *Takhlis al-Ibriz fi Talkhis Bariz*, or *The Extrication of Gold in Summarizing Paris, also known as A Paris Profile* (1834) by educator Shaykh Rifaʿa Rafiʾ al-Tahtawi (1801–1873).[12] The entire book is an account of al-Tahtawi's visit to Paris between 1826 and 1830, the first in-depth Arabic account of a visit to Western Europe by a Muslim from the Near East. The excerpt offers al-Tahtawi's comparisons between the French and the Egyptians and Arabs pertaining to social and sexual habits. Al-Tahtawi reports that among the French's characteristics is

> their disinclination toward homosexuality and the love of young men, for this is something that is odd with their nature and moral sense. In

their speech and poetry, they do not mention the homosexual love. It is not proper in the French language to say that a man fell in love with a boy, for such a relationship is considered taboo. If a Frenchman translated one of our books, he would alter the text to say that "I fell in love with a girl," as opposed to a boy as in the original. The French consider homosexuality as a fallen state of being.[13]

Regardless of how accurate al-Tahtawi's depiction of Parisian sociosexual norms is, the document informs students that homosexuality was anything but a taboo in early nineteenth-century Arabic writings and, perhaps, in ordinary life. The fact that al-Tahtawi noticed the disinclination of the French toward homosexuality speaks of the opposite attitude in al-Tahtawi's home society and culture. Al-Tahtawi's mentor Shaykh Hassan al-'Attar (1766–1835) wrote poetry about his love of young males; thus the society at the time did not see a contradiction between an inclination to homosexuality and one's merit to become one of the top religious scholars and famous poets. Writing about homosexuality was not a taboo that devalued intellectual production. More importantly, al-Tahtawi's document provides a good start to discuss the notion of seeing oneself in the mirror of the other and "othering" those who are different. Homo- and heterosexuality have been an important issue in informing the perception of self and other since early encounters between the Middle East and the West. These encounters took place when global power shifted toward the West, and while the West pursued its colonial imperialism, the Middle East struggled for modernization and self-defense. Rigid heteronormativity spilled from the colonizing West to the colonized Middle East. Sexuality in the Middle East, as everywhere, is a social construct that is always changeable, and the mirror of the West—both in the past and present times—has informed that change.

The misperceptions of gender and sexuality in the Middle East invites a discussion of Orientalism as Western misperceptions of the entire region were documented in the writings of travelers, artists, colonial personnel, orientalist scholars, and mass media. Edward Said's scholarship becomes very relevant to the discussion. To make that intellectually challenging scholarship accessible to students, some online sources are available for use in classrooms. Students watch the Media Education Foundation's production "Edward Said on Orientalism," available on YouTube. It provides a condensed but sufficient and accessible version of Said's ideas in his own words along with brief commentaries by a scholar.[14] In that documentary, Said's easy spoken language helps students grasp the concepts while they watch visual examples in support of Said's argument.

Women's Voices Breaking Taboos

Gender-based violence is an important theme that a discussion on gender and sexuality can neither avoid nor escape. Questions about honor killing in some societies can become a teaching moment about how to deconstruct the Middle East into various social experiences that are important to understanding their differences. Intersectionality is a crucial concept, particularly in studying women's experiences. Women's experiences in rural areas are different from those in urban or Bedouin settings, and different from one social class to another. Scholarship employing court cases shows various responses to women violating principles of sexual chastity, for example, men got married to repentant sex workers and mothers covered up unmarried daughters' lost virginity or pregnancy. Unfortunately, we do not have an accessible source for court records from the Middle East or any another source that captures the voice of victims of violence. The Permanent Arab Court to Resist Violence Against Women in Beirut posted several testimonies of women from different Arab societies in the mid-1990s. Unfortunately, the website of the informal Arab Women Court that carried these testimonies (http://www.arabwomencourt.org/) has disappeared; Khater's source book preserved few testimonies. Anthropologist Jessica Winegar's provocative article "Not So Far Away: Why US Domestic Violence Is Akin to Honor Crimes" helps in deepening empathy and sharpening students' ability to understand the experiences of Middle Eastern women in global perspective.[15] The piece encourages critical thinking and removes the mask of different names for the same violent practices, labeled as passion crimes, in American society. Though short, that article is well documented and has many hyperlinks that help students think of gender-based violence in the Middle East and the United States in the same terms. One of the most valuable sources that the article links readers to is the Centers for Disease Control and Prevention.[16] Drawing parallels between patterns of violence against women in the Middle East and in the United States provokes students to think about a wider range of sociocultural reasons that produce and perpetuate gender-based violence. Discussing similarities and differences of discrete experiences of women in and out the Middle East and the United States fosters empathy and critical thinking. Students can appreciate similarities in gender-based violence despite the seeming religious and sociocultural differences between US and Middle Eastern societies. More importantly, students understand that Middle Eastern societies vary among themselves in their social culture, even when most of their population follow the same religion. Rather than approaching the entire region as one cultural unit, students become better equipped to critically think and look for variations in practices and ideals.

NOTES

1. *Hadith* are a collection of traditions containing the words, actions, and the silent approval of the prophet Muhammad, which, with accounts of his daily practice (known as the *Sunna*), constitutes the major source of religious law and moral guidance for Muslims apart from the Qur'an.

2. The Ghazali organization (https://www.ghazali.org/) is a good online source of the work of al-Ghazali and of the scholarly works on him.

3. Andrew Rippin and Jan Knappert, eds., *Textual Sources for the Study of Islam* (Chicago: University of Chicago Press, 1986), 108–9.

4. The translated excerpt uses "women's honor" here, which might not be the best translation. Al-Ghazali might have meant woman's reputation, as in the case of illicit sexual intercourse.

5. "Islam Belongs to All Its Believers," interview with Amina Wadud by Abderrahmane Ammar, Qantara, 2013, https://en.qantara.de/content/interview -with-amina-wadud-islam-belongs-to-all-its-believers.

6. Leila Ahmad, *Women and Gender in Islam: Historical Roots of a Modern Debate* (New Haven, CT: Yale University Press, 1992); Denise Spellberg, *Politics, Gender, and the Islamic Past: The Legacy of 'A'isha Bint Abi Bakr* (New York: Columbia University Press, 1996).

7. Leila Ahmad, "Early Islam and the Position of Women: The Problem of Interpretation," in *Women in Middle Eastern History: Shifting Boundaries in Sex and Gender*, ed. Nikki R. Keddie and Beth Baron (New Haven, CT: Yale University Press, 2008), 58–73; Denise A. Spellberg, "Political Action and Public Example: 'Aisha and the Battle of the Camel," in Keddie and Baron, *Women in Middle Eastern History*, 45–57.

8. World Bank, Public Data, https://data.worldbank.org/country.

9. Akram Fouad Khater, *Sources in the History of the Modern Middle East* (Boston, MA: Cengage Learning, 2010).

10. For a complete translation of Qasim Amin's two famous feminist books, see Qasim Amin, *The Liberation of Women and The New Woman: Two Documents in the History of Egyptian Feminism*, trans. Samiha Sidhom Peterson (Cairo: American University in Cairo Press, 2000).

281

11. Khater, *Sources in the History of the Modern Middle East*, 324–27, 58–61.

12. Khater, *Sources in the History of the Modern Middle East*, 324–27 and 58–61. For the complete English translation of the book, see Rifaʻa Rafiʻ al-Tahtawi, *An Imam in Paris: Account of a Stay in France by an Egyptian Cleric (1826–1831)*, trans. and intro. Daniel L. Newman (London: Saqi, 2004).

13. Rifaʻa Rafiʻ al-Tahtawi, *Takhlis al-Ibriz fi Talkhis Bariz* (first published in 1834), here from Khater, *Sources in the History of the Modern Middle East*, 58–61.

14. "Edward Said on Orientalism," YouTube, October 28, 2012, https://www.youtube.com/watch?v=fVC8EYd_Z_g.

15. Jessica Winegar, "Not So Far Away: Why U.S. Domestic Violence Is Akin to Honor Crimes," Women's Enews, April 7, 2016, https://womensenews.org/2016/04/not-so-far-away-why-u-s-domestic-violence-is-akin-to-honor-crimes/.

16. Matthew J. Breiding et al., "Prevalence and Characteristics of Sexual Violence, Stalking, and Intimate Partner Violence Victimization—National Intimate Partner and Sexual Violence Survey, United States, 2011," Morbidity and Mortality Weekly Report, September 5, 2014, 63 (SS08): 1–18, Centers for Disease Control and Prevention, https://www.cdc.gov/mmwr/preview/mmwrhtml/ss6308a1.htm.

KEY RESOURCES

Abu-Lughod, Lila. *Remaking Women: Feminism and Modernity in the Middle East.* Princeton, NJ: Princeton University Press, 1998.

Ahmed, Leila. *Women and Gender in Islam: Historical Roots of a Modern Debate.* New Haven, CT: Yale University Press, 1992.

Barlas, Asma. *Believing Women in Islam: Unreading Patriarchal Interpretations of the Qurʼan.* Austin: University of Texas Press, 2009.

Keddie, Nikki R. *Women in the Middle East: Past and Present.* Princeton, NJ: Princeton University Press, 2012.

Keddie, Nikkie R., and Beth Baron, eds. *Women in Middle Eastern History: Shifting Boundaries in Sex and Gender.* New Haven, CT: Yale University Press, 2008.

Meriwether, Margaret Lee. *A Social History of Women and Gender in the Modern Middle East.* 2nd ed. New York: Routledge, 2018.

Mernissi, Fatima. *The Veil and the Male Elite: A Feminist Interpretation of Women's Rights in Islam.* Trans. Mary Jo Lakeland. Cambridge, MA: Perseus Books, 1991.

Moghadam, Valentine M. *Modernizing Women: Gender and Social Change in the Middle East.* 3rd ed. Boulder, CO: Lynne Rienner, 2013.

Spellberg, Denise. *Politics, Gender, and the Islamic Past: The Legacy of ʻAʼisha Bint Abi Bakr.* New York: Columbia University Press, 1996.

Wadud, Amina. *Qurʼan and Woman: Rereading the Sacred Text from a Woman's Perspective.* New York: Oxford University Press, 1999.

Nuancing the Narrative

Teaching the Jewish Modern Middle East

Alma Rachel Heckman

Jews are one of the few (indeed, if not the only) minorities that historically extended across the entire Middle East and North Africa (MENA) region, from Morocco to Iran, and everywhere in between. Until relatively recently, the trend in both Jewish and MENA historiographical circles was to segment Jews from Muslims (not to mention other minorities), reproducing colonial political strategy in narrative form. One cannot simply "add Jews and stir" to the narrative of the Middle East, just as one cannot "add women and stir" or any other population (incorrectly) deemed ancillary to major story lines and themes. As with any majority or minority population, it is imperative to emphasize that Jews were not and are not homogenous across this wide expanse of territory, languages, customs, histories, and more between Morocco and Iran (and everywhere in between). Judaism and daily Jewish practice differed dramatically between even relatively small units of space and time (for example, eighteenth-century southern rural and northern urban Morocco), as did languages, sartorial custom, and everything else that one might consider for categorization of a people and watching it change over time. Indeed, defining "Jewishness," always a thorny subject, need not depend at all on religious practice — there were (and are) plenty of non-observant Jews across the region, particularly during the second half of the twentieth century and into the twenty-first.

To teach Jewish history in the MENA region is to teach the history of the MENA region itself, and vice-versa. To do right by Jewish history, and by MENA history, is to embrace diversity, fluidity, and contingency. In this piece, I first present a set of terminology and assumptions to combat when teaching Jewish history in the MENA. Second, I unpack the meaning of "modernity" in Jewish history of the Modern Middle East. As I demonstrate, an examination of Jews sheds light on the particular as well as the whole. Third, I present available sources for teachers seeking to incorporate Jewish history of the MENA into their syllabi.

Assumptions, Terms, and Strategies

When teaching about Jews in the Modern Middle East, it is critical to consider students' assumptions and backgrounds on the topic. In the United States, if students are familiar with Jewish history at all, it is likely that of Ashkenazi Jews, and not with Sephardi and Mizrahi Jews (although, students are often surprised to learn, the first Jews in the Americas, including North America, were Sephardim). Before diving any further, it is important to clarify these terms. Each of these three terms is problematic in its own way, and each has its own fraught history.

Without going too much in depth on this subtopic, Ashkenazi (adjective and noun, pl. Ashkenazim) refers to Jews whose ethnic origin and/or cultural heritage stretch back to the territorial unit of "Ashkenaz," the Hebrew term for the Rhineland region in medieval Central Europe and whither the Ashkenazim spread (largely Central and Eastern Europe, expelled in the medieval period from Western Europe). This is the group identified with the Yiddish language, or Judeo-German written in Hebrew letters, with its own vast differences across the Ashkenazi historical terrain. Ashkenazim were the dominant Jewish population of most of Europe as well as eventually the United States.

Sephardi (adjective and noun, pl. Sephardim) refers to Jews whose ethnic origin and/or cultural heritage extend to the territorial unit of "Sepharad," "Spain" in Hebrew, and whither the Sephardim spread, particularly after the end of the Reconquista of the Spanish Catholic monarchs of the Iberian Peninsula from Muslim rule (extending roughly from 711–1492 with varying degrees of territorial control over the peninsula) and the expulsion of the Jews in 1492. Sephardim historically spoke Arabic as well as Ladino (which also goes by Judezmo or Judeo-Spanish, in North Africa as Haketía, although Haketía is distinct from most other forms of Judeo-Spanish). After the 1492 expulsion, the vast majority of Sephardim migrated to North Africa and to lands controlled by the Ottoman Empire. Others made their way to the Italian states, Portugal, the Netherlands, England, southern France, and the Americas; many traveled a circuitous route across several of these territories, often finding a terminus in the vast domains of the Ottoman Empire. The Ottoman Sultan Bayezid II (r. 1481–1512) is apocryphally attributed with crowing: "You call Ferdinand a wise king, he who impoverishes his country and enriches our own!"[1]

Mizrahi (adjective and noun, pl. Mizrahim) literally translates to "eastern" or "oriental" in Hebrew. Between the three broad categories of Ashkenazi, Sephardi, and Mizrahi, Mizrahi is perhaps the most problematic and fraught. Mizrahi is often used as a catch-all category for those Jews who are neither of Ashkenazi nor Sephardi ethnic background. The term began its life in the mouths of Ashkenazim to describe these "unfamiliar" Jews and is best understood at its origin as the product of ignorance (Morocco is, after all, far to the west of Poland). However, the term has since been reclaimed by Mizrahi populations themselves, particularly in Israel after the mass migrations of Jews from the MENA region to Israel in the 1950s and 1960s. Since then, "Mizrahi" has become a term of empowerment, cultural affinity, and political difference in addition to a very nonspecific descriptive term that can mean Persian Jews, Central Asian Jews, and Amazigh (Berber) Jews and is often applied to Sephardim. Other categories important to Jewish history in the MENA are the Romaniote, or the Judeo-Greek-speaking Jews of the Byzantine empire; the Amazigh (Berber) Jews, inhabiting North Africa before the Arab-Muslim conquests speaking Judeo-Tamazight dialects; Iraqi Arab Jews, speaking Judeo-Arabic; Kurdish Jews, in northern Iraq speaking neo-Aramaic; and Persian Jews, mapping onto today's Iran speaking Judeo-Farsi and Farsi. Thus, when introducing students to the Jewish populations of the MENA region, introducing the main three categories of Ashkenazi, Sephardi, and Mizrahi is helpful as this will be the most common set of terminology they will encounter in published texts, alongside a recurring discussion throughout the term regarding the utility, history, and diversity within each of these terms as well as their politicization. Further, it is important to emphasize that as with Jews in the broader MENA, Jews of different backgrounds interacted across the above-listed categories, and that the categories themselves are fluid and entangled.

In addition to terminological clarification, it is important to get a sense of student background on the topic and the assumptions they may hold. As I previously indicated, if students are familiar with Jewish history at all, it is typically with Ashkenazi history. This raises a problem within the field of teaching Jewish history, which, until recently, often neglected MENA Jews, seeing them as ancillary to the "main events" of Jewish history, which, apart from the ancient and medieval Spanish–North African interludes, were assumed to take place in Europe. Thankfully, the broader Jewish historical community now accepts MENA Jews as intrinsically important to Jewish history, from the very ancient to the very current periods. It has taken longer, however, to integrate MENA Jews at the classroom level, in standard surveys of Jewish history as well as surveys of MENA history. This too is changing and sheds light on the connective tissue MENA Jews provide between MENA history and European history. Jews, like other minorities in the region, often served as diplomatic and commercial intermediaries for the Middle East and Europe. In the medieval era and accelerating during the early modern period, Jews often had kinship networks around the Mediterranean and beyond, including the Americas and East Asia into the modern period. In other words, teaching MENA Jewish history underscores the circulation of populations, goods, and ideas across periods, globalizing the Middle East in the classroom; it also provides a different point of entry for teaching world history.

As with any history class, students may approach the history of MENA Jews with anachronistic assumptions. It is important to remind students not to impose what they may know about the MENA region today onto the past. For many students, the Middle East may be synonymous with the Israeli-Palestinian and Israeli-Arab conflicts. Teaching the history of Jews in the Middle East and North Africa offers the opportunity to decenter such myopic understandings of the region's history and explore the long, diverse, and rich history of Jews across the entire region. Further, courses on the Israeli-Palestinian and Israeli-Arab conflicts often privilege "Ashkenormativity"[2] without discussions of Jews from the broader region, intra-Jewish conflict in modern Israel, as well as those Sephardi Jews long present in Ottoman Palestine and earlier political formations of the territory.

Early on in all of my courses I teach my students the word "teleology" and give examples of teleological readings of Jewish history in the MENA. The word "teleology" derives from the Greek *telos* meaning "end" or "goal." A teleological reading of history would use the "end" result to overdetermine a historical narrative leading up to that end, when the people of earlier centuries could not possibly have known what would happen in the future. In the case of Jewish history in the MENA, this would mean reading the ultimate exodus of most Jews from the region during the 1950s and 1960s into the past, when, for example, Spanish Jews fleeing post-Reconquista Spain in 1492 went to Morocco or the Ottoman Empire for safe harbor. Yes, by the 1960s the vast majority of MENA Jews had emigrated from their home countries elsewhere, often to Israel but very often as well to other lands. However, this knowledge of major demographic upheavals in the 1960s should not be read backward and projected onto an understanding of Jews in the Babylonian Talmudic academies of Sura and Pumbedita, medieval Fustat or Fez, the Tanzimat period of the Ottoman Empire, or even a period as proximate to the 1960s as that of World War II.

Periodization and syllabus organization present another challenge and opportunity for reframing narratives of the Jewish Middle Eastern and North African past. When does Jewish history of the MENA begin? While modern Jewish history in the region is fraught with its own overdetermination surrounding events in Palestine and Israel, the ancient past is likewise heavily politicized, as work on archeology in the region has demonstrated.[3] Further, how can one address the Bible and the history of Jews, or stories such as that of Queen Esther of Persia, whose tomb sits in today's Iran? Each period—ancient, medieval, early modern, modern, and the contemporary—presents its narrative and controversial touchstones. While the content may differ, methodologically speaking, teaching about Jews in the MENA faces similar challenges as other subjects. These challenges represent opportunities to highlight contingency, mindfulness of historical context, examination of narrative frames and themes as well as aberrations. Recognizing that most teachers will not have the opportunity to teach classes entirely dedicated to Jewish history in the MENA, what follows are a few suggestions for where to position Jews of the Modern Middle East in terms of thematic and temporal scope for broader classes as well as a few notes on available resources for teaching.

Modernity and the Jewish MENA

It is important to unpack the concept of "modernity" when teaching the history of the Modern Middle East. In Jewish history, the "modern" begins, historiographically speaking, around the

time of the French Revolution of 1789. This is due to the political emancipations of Jews in France in 1790 and 1791, turning Jews from subjects into citizens. The French Revolution, and the emancipations of the
Jews that attended it, emerged from the Enlightenment. The Ottoman
Empire, long engaged in Enlightenment exchanges, implemented a plan
of state-sponsored reforms called the "Tanzimat" — "reorganization" in
Ottoman Turkish—including legislation extending from 1839 until 1876.
The intellectual discourse that allowed Jews to become Frenchmen also
allowed Jews and other minorities to become Ottomans. Such reforms
eventually led to constitutionalism in the MENA, notably in the Ottoman Empire and in Qajar Iran, which engaged minorities in national
state-building political projects. Modernity in the MENA also includes
colonialism. French, British, and Italian colonial officials active in the
MENA justified colonialism as a *mission civilisatrice*—"civilizing mission" in French. Jews were a fundamental component of this mission
and its practical implications in the MENA.

During the Napoleonic wars, France ordered vast quantities of grain
via Jewish merchants in Algeria—the Baqri and Bushnaq families—to
fuel the war effort. However, France refused to pay. The Baqri and Bushnaq families were in turn indebted to the Algerian Dey and stated they
could not pay what they owed to the state until France paid them for
the wheat. This escalated into a diplomatic conflict, resulting in the
Ottoman Dey of Algiers hitting a French diplomat in the face with a
flyswatter, giving France its pretext for invading Algeria in 1830, inau-
gurating 132 years of settler colonial rule.[4] Meanwhile, prominent Jewish philanthropic figures, notably Adolphe Crémieux of France and Sir
Moses Montefiore of England, became deeply interested and involved
in the affairs of Jews of the MENA and, in turn, MENA affairs of state.
French and British interests in the MENA coincided with such Jewish
philanthropic efforts, leading to one of the most consequential organizations in MENA Jewish history: the Alliance Israélite Universelle.

The Alliance Israélite Universelle (hereafter simply referred to as
the Alliance) was a French Jewish philanthropic educational network
founded in 1860 to help Jews of the Middle East and North Africa,
as well as European Ottoman lands, "regenerate." "Regeneration" was
one byword for the *mission civilisatrice*—the idea was, according to pre-
vailing European Orientalist and colonial logic, that the peoples of the
MENA had somehow "stalled" or gone "backward" while Europe had
"progressed"—the goal now was to "regenerate" the MENA subject

into an *évolué*—an "evolved" subject, at least according to French whims and standards. The Alliance was born out of the partnership of Adolphe Crémieux, an esteemed lawyer and French Jew of the earliest emancipated generation after the French Revolution, and Moses Montefiore, a prominent British political figure, in tackling two major events: the Blood Libel crisis of Damascus in 1840 and the kidnapping and baptism of an Italian Jewish boy by the name of Edgardo Mortara in 1858. The two men were of a generation of recently emancipated Jews who embraced citizenship and participation in the nation-state with tremendous zeal, seeking to extend these construed universal benefits to their blighted coreligionists abroad. For Crémieux, the best way to achieve the goal of "regenerating" the "backward" Jews of the MENA was through French education. In many ways, the Alliance shared a degree of contextual and aspirational similarity to European Catholic and Protestant missionary intervention in the region.

The Alliance established its first school in the northern Moroccan city of Tetuan in 1862; by 1895, the Alliance boasted seventy schools and nearly 17,000 students from Morocco to Iran and everywhere in between. The Alliance encouraged the formation of new Jewish subjectivities and, inevitably, politicized identities. "Regeneration" often also meant deracination. In the process of becoming *évolués*, in speaking and thinking in French, in becoming entrenched in Francophone history, geography, and a sprinkling of Jewish studies, students became divorced from their home language and home customs.[5] Alliance pupils often found themselves, in the words of Albert Memmi, "à cheval entre deux civilisations"—straddling two worlds, unable to be fully of the home community of their non-Alliance-educated parents or their Muslim neighbors, nor accepted as fully French or European.[6] In a cruel twist of irony, the very organization that was motivated by the zeal of citizenship and emancipation in France made it much more difficult for MENA Jews to be ultimately embraced as local, "authentic" citizens as movements for national independence developed.

Events of the twentieth century magnified these challenges of state and citizenship formation not only for Jews in the MENA, but for the MENA as a whole. For example, during World War II the region served at once as a place of safe harbor and a place of anti-Semitic legislation and violence. The Allied victory would be critical for changes in a new postwar world order that would facilitate and embolden national liberation movements. Jewish diversity in this time period in the MENA means not only Jews from the MENA region, but also the European Jewish refugees who fled to many locations in the MENA, most often in the hopes of securing transit visas to the Americas. European Jewish refugees streamed through the MENA, including Turkey, Iran, Iraq, Egypt, Morocco, Algeria, and more. In French North Africa in particular, local Jews were subject to anti-Semitic legislation by the Vichy regime established in the summer of 1940 upon France's loss to Nazi Germany. Political refugees, including antifascist activists, Spanish Civil War fighters, as well as politically "undesirable" European Jews were placed in forced labor and punishment camps across North Africa, subject to torture, wretched living conditions, and arbitrary death from overseers, disease, or exhaustion. In Iraq, the incident of the Farhud (June 1–2, 1941) was an infamous moment of violence against Jews, resulting from a complicated mixture of colonial politics in post–British Mandate Iraq, the influence of fascism within nationalism, and suspicions of the Jew as a disloyal, colonial agent. In Egypt, Jews feared the advance of Nazi and Italian Fascist forces fighting on the border area between Libya and Egypt. In the Italian colony of Libya, some Libyan Jews, particularly those with British citizenship, were placed in forced labor and concentration camps, with a small fraction deported to Bergen-Belsen in Germany. In Tunisia, Jews were subject to direct Nazi occupation and forced labor as well as heavy communal fines. In Algeria, Jews who had been granted French citizenship by dint of the 1870 Crémieux decree had their citizenship revoked. Across French North Africa, quotas on Jews in state institutions and a number of professions were enforced. Sephardi and Romaniote Jews of the formerly Ottoman Balkans were in the direct path of genocide. For example, the once thriving community of Salonica was utterly decimated under Nazi occupation, with most Salonican Jews murdered at Auschwitz-Birkenau following mass deportation and ghettoization.

The American army's presence in the MENA grew dramatically as a result of World War II and set the stage for the region's position in the coming Cold War. For MENA Jews, the existential dread of the period prompted them to question their relationship to colonial powers, to national liberation politics and their home countries, and to Zionism. The mass exodus of Jews from the MENA region during the 1950s and 1960s to Israel, a number of European countries, and the Americas fits into a number of twentieth-century subjects and complicates understandings of the world wars, economic fluctuations, nationalisms, the Cold War, wars of decolonization, and postcolonial nation and citizen formation.

Sources for Teaching

The challenge for American undergraduate or high school students is having sources that are available in English. Thankfully, there are several primary source collections, and scholars are constantly producing new translations and collections based on their primary research work. Most of these readers, notably those from Norman Stillman, Aron Rodrigue, Julia Phillips Cohen, and Sarah Abrevaya Stein, include contextualizing essays. Aron Rodrigue's source book of documents from the Alliance Israélite Universelle has a strong set of documents regarding gender as the Alliance held that "regeneration" of society would take place most effectively in "civilizing" women and, in turn, their families. In addition to such readers, there are a number of excellent translated novels and memoirs from Jews in the MENA. Lia Brozgal and Sarah Abrevaya Stein's edited translation of Alliance teacher and school director Vitalis Danon's *Ninette of Sin Street* illustrates the *mission civilisatrice* in action. In it, the title character Ninette, a downtrodden Tunisian Jewish prostitute, seeks only to improve the life of her son through the opportunities of an Alliance education. The protagonist in Albert Memmi's semi-autobiographical memoir *The Pillar of Salt* in many ways demonstrates the deracination that Ninette's son might have eventually suffered, caught in the crosshairs of French colonialism, Tunisian nationalism, and Zionism.

There are a number of engaging films that discuss Jews in the MENA. These films include *Where Are You Going, Moshe?* (Hassan Benjelloun, 2007), addressing the mass migration of Moroccan Jews to Israel during the 1950s and 1950s; *A Summer in La Goulette* (Férid Boughedir, 1996), presenting three teenage female friends (a Muslim, a Christian, and a Jew) living in the seaside town of La Goulette in Tunisia just before the outbreak of the 1967 Six-Day War; *Free Men* (Ismael Ferroukhi, 2011), exploring the story of an Algerian Muslim in Paris during World War II working with the Great Mosque of Paris to help Jews evade Nazi capture, including Algerian Jewish popstar Salim Hilali; and *Wedding Song* (Karin Albou, 2008), showing the friendship of two young women—a Muslim and a Jew—under Nazi-occupied Tunisia while each prepares for her wedding. The documentary *Forget Baghdad: Jews and Arabs — The Iraqi Connection* (Samir, 2003) presents the mass departure of Iraqi Jews in the early 1950s within a context of deep Iraqi patriotism and identity among that Jewish population; the trauma of arrival in Ashkenazi-dominated Israel; and the political responses of Iraqi Jews in Israel of the 1960s and 1970s in organizations such as HaPaterim HaSchorim — the Israel Black Panthers, a name the group adopted from the US Black Panthers to express racial grievances as Mizrahim in Israel.

Finally, music also serves as a helpful entry point for discussion, particularly for contemporary Mizrahi culture in Israel. The group A-WA, for example, is composed of three Jewish Israeli sisters of Yemeni background, singing in Yemeni Arabic and Judeo-Arabic; Neta Elkayam, a Jewish Israeli of Moroccan descent, and her band play the traditional repertoire of Jewish Morocco as well as twentieth-century hits from such Moroccan Jewish pop stars as Zohra El Fassia (1905 Sefrou, Morocco — 1994 Ashkelon, Israel). In the musical category, I would be remiss not to include Leila Mourad (1918–1995, in Cairo, Egypt), an Egyptian Jew who later converted to Islam and was at the top of the charts in her own day performing in Egyptian Arabic. I have listed several other excellent source readers, novels, memoirs, and overview texts under "Key Resources" — it is only a selection and is by no means a definitive accounting of all the available sources in the field.

Conclusion

Jewish history and MENA history are inextricable. Introducing students to the many subjects of modern MENA Jewish history gives the teacher and the students the opportunity to historicize the politicized, and properly contextualized, Jewish lives in Muslim majority lands. Further, following such an approach allows students to appreciate the diversity of the MENA and its varied populations, languages, religious practices, and political and social organizations for a nuanced narrative of MENA, Jewish, and world history.

NOTES

1. Quoted in Jane S. Gerber, *The Jews of Spain: A History of the Sephardic Experience* (New York: Free Press, 1992), 151.
2. Jonathan Katz, "Learning to Undo 'Ashkenormativity,'" *Forward*, November 5, 2014, https://forward.com/opinion/208473/learning-to-undo-ashkenorma

tivity/ (accessed August 2, 2018). This article first appeared on the website New Voices: News and Views of Campus Jews as "Learning to Undo Ashke-normativity—A Jew in the Motherland," October 22, 2014, http://newvoices.org/2014/10/22/learning-to-undo-ashke-normativity-a-jew-in-the-motherland/ (accessed August 2, 2018).

3. See, for example, Nadia Abu El-Haj's *Facts on the Ground: Archaeological Practice and Territorial Self-Fashioning in Israeli Society* (Chicago: University of Chicago Press, 2001) and the public controversy surrounding it, as well as Yael Zerubavel's *Recovered Roots: Collective Memory and the Making of an Israeli National Tradition* (Chicago: University of Chicago Press, 1995).

4. For a thorough account of this incident, see Jamil M. Abun-Nasr, *A History of the Maghrib in the Islamic Period* (Cambridge: Cambridge University Press, 1987), 249–50. For long-term implications for Algerian Jews, see Joshua Schreier's *Arabs of the Jewish Faith: The Civilizing Mission in Colonial Algeria* (New Brunswick, NJ: Rutgers University Press, 2010).

5. There is a rich body of literature on this topic. See, for example, Aron Rodrigue, *French Jews, Turkish Jews: The Alliance Israélite Universelle and the Politics of Jewish Schooling in Turkey, 1860–1925* (Bloomington: Indiana University Press, 1990); Esther Benbassa and Aron Rodrigue, *Sephardi Jewry: A History of the Judeo-Spanish Community* (Berkeley: University of California Press, 2000). Aron Rodrigue's groundbreaking and field-shaping research has led to further critical works in the field authored by his former students, including Sarah Abrevaya Stein, Julia Phillips Cohen, Michelle Campos, Devin Naar, and others.

6. Albert Memmi, *La Statue de Sel* (Paris: Folio, 2002 [Gallimard, 1966]), 123.

KEY RESOURCES

Aciman, André. *Out of Egypt: A Memoir*. New York: Picador, 1994.
Behar, Moshe, and Zvi Ben-Dor, eds. *Modern Middle Eastern Jewish Thought: Writings on Identity, Politics and Culture, 1893–1958*. Waltham, MA: Brandeis University Press, 2013.
Brozgal, Lia, and Sarah Abrevaya Stein, eds. *Ninette of Sin Street: A Novella by Vitalis Danon*. Stanford, CA: Stanford University Press, 2017.
Cohen, Julia Phillips, and Sarah Abrevaya Stein, eds. *Sephardi Lives: A Documentary History, 1700–1950*. Stanford, CA: Stanford University Press, 2014.
Hakakian, Roya. *Journey from the Land of No: A Girlhood Caught in Revolutionary Iran*. New York: Broadway Books, 2005.
Lagnado, Lucette. *The Man in the White Sharkskin Suit: A Jewish Family's Exodus from Old Cairo to the New World*. New York: Harper Perennial, 2008.
Memmi, Albert. *The Pillar of Salt*. Boston: Beacon Press, 1992.
Mendes-Flohr, Paul, and Jehuda Reinharz, eds. *The Jew in the Modern World: A Documentary History*. 3rd ed. Oxford: Oxford University Press, 2010.

Rodrigue, Aron. *Jews and Muslims: Images of Sephardi and Eastern Jewry in Modern Times*. Seattle: University of Washington Press, 2003.

Simon, Reeva Spector, Michael Menachem Laskier, and Sara Reguer, eds. *The Jews of the Middle East and North Africa in Modern Times*. New York: Columbia University Press, 2003.

Somekh, Sasson. *Baghdad, Yesterday: The Making of an Arab Jew*. Jerusalem: Ibis Editions, 2007.

Stillman, Norman. *The Jews of Arab Lands: A History and Source Book*. Philadelphia: Jewish Publication Society, 1979.

Stillman, Norman. *The Jews of Arab Lands in Modern Times*. Philadelphia: Jewish Publication Society, 1991.

Tsabari, Ayelet. *The Best Place on Earth*. New York: Random House, 2016.

The Armenian Genocide and the Politics of Knowledge

CHRISTINE PHILLIOU

In the centennial year (2015) since the Armenian Genocide, countless conferences, meetings, and commemorations were underway across the globe. While they were all peaceful,
they come at the end of a century of violence. I refer not just to the
events of 1915–1917, but also the waves of violence spurred by memory, recognition, and denial ever since. First came the killings, at the
hands of individual Armenians, of two of the leading perpetrators of
the violence, Talaat and Cemal Pashas in Berlin and Tiflis, respectively,
in the 1920s. Then came the nearly fifty people, many of them Turkish
diplomats, killed and the hundreds more injured across the globe by
the Armenian organization ASALA (Armenian Secret Army for the Liberation of Armenia) in the 1970s to protest Turkey's continuing refusal
to recognize the genocide. More recently, in 2005, death threats were
leveled against the Nobel Prize–winning Turkish writer Orhan Pamuk
for merely referring in an interview to the mass violence against Armenians and Kurds, forcing him to leave the country. And there was perhaps the most tragic turn of events in 2007, when Armenian-Turkish
intellectual Hrant Dink was assassinated for his role in organizing a
conference in Turkey to discuss the genocide.

But the violence around the "Armenian Issue" has long penetrated
academia, within and far beyond Turkey, too: many of us remember as
recently as the late 1990s finding, in major research libraries in the United
States, pertinent pages ripped out of library books, books vanishing off
the shelves, and historians hired (or not hired) based on their views on
the question of genocide and their willingness to use the word. Given

the mortal danger inherent in merely discussing the events of 1915 in Turkey, and the professional hazards of doing so even in the United States, it stands to reason that scholars would approach the issue of the genocide with great trepidation, if at all. Scholarship on the Ottoman past had evolved such that nearly any kind of research regarding Ottoman involvement in World War I would be off-limits, certainly within Turkey, but also in the field at large, even in North America and Europe. Erik-Jan Zürcher, who blazed the trail of looking into the continuities between the late Ottoman and early Republican Turkish state in his 1984 work, *The Unionist Factor*, points out in a recent book that the Ottoman state archives for the period between 1914 and 1922 were opened only in the late 1980s, and even then access was given sparingly. But the fear of having the Ottoman state's role in mass killings of Armenians exposed to scholarly scrutiny extended far beyond the secreting away of sources from that period; indeed, even research into the social, economic, or political role of Armenians in earlier periods of the empire's history was off-limits, or at least highly suspect. Norman Itzkowitz, a professor at Princeton, used to relate to his students a story from the 1960s about being prohibited access to documents about the day-to-day workings of the eighteenth-century Ottoman postal system in Anatolia, only to find out it was due to the fact that Armenians had monopolized the postal system at the time.

Recognition of the genocide is not only the central taboo at the heart of the modern Turkish nation-state, it is also a kind of Gordian knot of Ottoman studies, and the two problems have worked to reinforce each other until recently. Ronald Grigor Suny's *"They Can Live in the Desert but Nowhere Else": A History of the Armenian Genocide* is a work of synthesis that carries a significance far beyond its contributions to our understanding of the genocide; it also marks a turning point in scholarship and is the fruit of fifteen years of collaborative research regarding the events of 1915. The book is a necessary watershed for the fields of Armenian history and genocide studies, but also for the changing relationships between official history, public history, and the academic study of the Ottoman past in Turkey and abroad. The importance of this book will be lost, however, on those who do not understand not only the long-term setting of discussions of this issue but especially the events of the last fifteen years.

There has been a proliferation in sound, archivally based scholarship regarding the events of 1915–1917 in the last decade and a half, in

Turkey as well as in Europe and North America. It should be noted that Suny himself has played a major role in fostering this new wealth of scholarship on the genocide, even if from the adjacent fields of Russian/ Soviet, Georgian, and Armenian history. In 2000, a collaborative project housed at the University of Michigan, the Workshop on Armenian and Turkish Scholarship (WATS), was initiated by Suny, Fatma Müge Göçek, and Gerard Libaridian. Through a series of workshops and conferences and an ongoing listserv discussion, the stated aim of the project was to "investigate the causes, circumstances, and consequences of the Armenian Genocide of 1915, overcoming the politics of recognition and denial."[1] The seven conferences, held between 2000 and 2011, involved scores of scholars from fields such as Ottoman, Armenian, German, Jewish, Habsburg, and Russian history and yielded several important monographs and one collected volume, *A Question of Genocide: Armenians and Turks at the End of the Ottoman Empire* (2011). The result has indeed been a kind of overcoming of the politics of recognition and denial, such that a scholarly consensus has been achieved, recognizing that the mass killings of Armenians by the Ottoman state in 1915 did in fact constitute a genocide (this is not to say that there is no longer a "denialist" camp, but that camp has become marginal to the discussion). This consensus has become a starting point for far more interesting (to scholars, if not lawyers) questions regarding the context, causes, and consequences of the genocide and the relationships between these events and the larger arc of Ottoman (and Armenian, and Russian, and Greek, and Kurdish) history.

During the 2000s, as the conferences were being held, massive changes were happening in Turkey that directly affected the politics of remembering the Armenian Genocide; changes in which Turkish academics played a crucial role. In the course of Turkey's accession talks with the European Union (EU), specific indexes of democratization and transparency were set as goals, and among those were the open discussion of history, specifically regarding the mass killings of Armenians in 1915, known in Turkish at the time and since as *tehcir ve taktil* (massacres and deportations). The Justice and Development Party (AKP) was elected for the first time in the fall of 2002, setting a tone (for the first two terms of President Erdoğan's administration, if not the third) of opening the historical archives, finding the "truth" regarding 1915, and exposing the past crimes of the secularists (going back to the Young Turks) that AKP saw as their opponents. Several Turkish intellectuals and scholars, some employed at North American and European universities and many working in Turkish universities, took it upon themselves to organize a conference for Turkish citizens only, in Istanbul, in September 2005, entitled "Ottoman Armenians in the Era of the Empire's Collapse: Scholarly Responsibility and Questions of Democracy." The conference volume was published, in Turkish, in 2011, the same year as *A Question of Genocide* from the WATS group.

While the starting point of the discussion in Turkey was not that the events of 1915 constituted a "genocide" per se (partly because some of the scholars involved did not share that view for various reasons, and partly because the organizers did not feel it productive to make that the central issue of the meeting), the word "genocide" (*soykırım*) was used by several scholars in their papers, and the question of genocide recognition was tied explicitly to questions of democratization in contemporary Turkey, as is clear from the title of the conference. The conference was prevented at the last minute from happening at its initial venue—the premier state university of Turkey, Bosphorus University—only to be reconvened and held at a private university in Istanbul. At roughly the same time, Orhan Pamuk was forced to flee Turkey after giving an interview to a Swiss newspaper in which he spoke about the mass slaughter of Armenians in 1915 (and, more recently, of Kurds in Anatolia). Then Hrant Dink, the Armenian-Turkish intellectual and newspaper editor who was one of the organizers of the 2005 Istanbul conference (and the only Armenian on the organizing board), was gunned down outside of his office in Istanbul in January 2007, an event that galvanized many in Turkey to take a more critical stance toward their government's official line denying the genocide and to inquire into their own history in new ways. While the official Turkish government line may not (yet) have changed to acknowledge the genocide, popular understandings of the past have become far more critical and nuanced, and the use of the word "genocide" has now become all but commonplace (or is, at least, no longer grounds for jail or exile). This is an achievement of scholars and intellectuals in Turkey and abroad, who have chipped away with great courage at the politics of denial with research and open discussion of a very complex recent past.

Were it not for the politics and context, Suny's book would merely be a solid historical narrative, accessible to the non-academic public, but not earth-shattering in its approach, methodology, or conclusions. That is to say, if it were a history of the Holocaust, it would be added

without fanfare to the long list of works that narrate the event and place it in a larger historical context. But it is not a history of the Holocaust. Precisely because of the politics of remembering and denying, because of the lack of consensus between states, publics, and the academic community, and because of the historical context of the book, it is not just an accessible work of historical synthesis but a bold political move, an important and necessary turning point in the production of knowledge and memory of the genocide and, perhaps, of the Ottoman past more broadly.

This book marks a turning point among so many other scholarly works on the topic because it is the first to put together an authoritative narrative that takes as given that the events of 1915 did constitute a genocide, and that this genocide has a *history* of its own. This is an important distinction. The book is not written as a polemical, emotional case expressly to prove that it was a genocide, although it does implicitly demonstrate that the criteria for genocide were met. Nor is it simply about using the intricate context in which the genocide happened to explain away the deep questions of culpability and responsibility (the tactic historically employed by denialists), although Suny's treatment is highly sensitive to the political, social, and even psycho-emotional motivations of the Young Turk perpetrators.

There are, of course, drawbacks to framing a history as an authoritative account (even if its title only claims it to be "a" history and not "the" history) of the Armenian Genocide. On one level, to do so is to assume that the genocide can be separated as a historical event from World War I and the larger collapse of the Ottoman Empire. Of course, we also separate the nearly contemporaneous Russian Revolution from World War I and the larger crisis of the Tsarist Empire, even though these threads are probably inseparable, and we routinely cordon off the Holocaust from the horrific larger goings-on at the Eastern Front of World War II, even though this is probably just as artificial a division.

The fact that this is still an uncomfortable separation, between the Armenian Genocide and the rest of late Ottoman history (whereas cordoning off the Russian Revolution and the Holocaust is not), is testament to the state of the field of Ottoman studies. The collaborative WATS project to unpack the causes, course, and consequences of the genocide has become a subfield of its own, for better and worse, and one that is not necessarily engaged by historians of the late Ottoman Empire who are not already convinced of the genocide. As a field of knowledge, then, it overlaps in significant ways with, but is not yet integrated fully into the mainstream of, scholarship on the late Ottoman Empire. In order for this integration to happen, students of Ottoman history "proper" need to think about the deeper causes and contingencies that brought about the impulses and the policies of the leaders of the Committee of Union and Progress that led to the annihilation of the Armenian population living within Ottoman borders. Not only that—they need to address directly the question of sovereignty in the final decade of the empire's existence: which individuals, representing which institutions and communities, were responsible for the murder of so many Armenians? Was it the so-called triumvirate of CUP (Young Turk Committee for Union and Progress) Pashas, or the CUP as an organization-turned-party, which hijacked many institutions of government and state between 1909 and 1914? Was it the Ottoman government as a whole, even if it had been taken over by the CUP? Or was it the "Turkish nation," the concept of which had not yet formally gelled into a basis for sovereignty for the Ottoman sultanate or the CUP? These, of course, are central questions that permeate, if implicitly, the way the genocide is remembered and its memory suppressed in Turkey today. And it is the difficulty in answering these questions—for historians, let alone lawyers and politicians—that makes the politics of memory of the genocide so dangerous today.

The Hunt for Sources

A major problem with framing the Armenian Genocide as an event with its own history—and a major stumbling block for the movement for official recognition—is that we still lack the evidence to trace each step of the actual deportations and killings themselves—the core, that is, of what constituted the genocide. Debates between the "Armenian" and "Turkish" sides of the "genocide question" in past decades have focused compulsively around the veracity of the sources cited by Armenians, who, prohibited access to the Ottoman archives, gravitated to memoirs such as that of American ambassador Henry Morgenthau, eyewitness accounts of Armenian survivors as well as European and American missionaries and other civilians who happened to have been in the area, and even German missionaries and officials, who despite their interest in defending the Ottoman state as a German ally in the war nevertheless reported and often protested the atrocities going on around them. The Turkish side in the debate over sources would accept the authority of only Ottoman state documents and thus had an easy time claiming that there was no "smoking gun" showing the top-down, intentional character of the killings, since the Turkish state authorities would control access to those documents and ensure that no smoking gun would be found.

After decades of back-and-forth, and now a decade and a half of more systematic research based also on Ottoman state documents, the specific chain of command, the operations of paramilitaries and other informal mechanisms such as the quasi-official "responsible secretaries" sent to the provinces to check up on orders issued from the center, and other specifics of the big picture are all clearer than ever, but still ungraspable in their entirety. And this is not by chance, as Taner Akçam points out in *The Young Turks' Crime against Humanity: Armenian Genocide and Ethnic Cleansing in the Ottoman Empire*, his 2012 work on which Suny draws in large part for his narrative. Akçam, using, for the first time hundreds of Ottoman state documents, explains that there were two tracks of violence: one was the "legal" track, involving agreements with other states to exchange populations and official decrees to deport Armenian populations, and the other was the "unofficial" track, including "forced evacuations, killing orders, and massacres." Akçam claims that "maximum effort was expended to create the impression that none of these actions by agents of the CUP were ever connected to the state."[2] "Triumvir" Talaat Pasha, the interior minister at the time and the figure known as the mastermind of the genocide, was said to have "directed the deportations from outside official channels by sending personal orders to the regional offices from a private telegraph in his home." It is clear that the Ottoman state with the CUP Triumvirate at the helm was savvy enough about modern record keeping and the legalities of culpability to distinguish between orders to be written, orders to be given verbally, and orders to be written, sent, and then destroyed.

As far as official documentation that may exist but is not accessible to researchers, papers from the Cipher Office of the Interior Ministry are among the most significant. These were short cables sent from the imperial capital to its branches in the provinces, but the files do not contain responses to these cables from the provinces. Some responses were scattered in the First, Second, and Third Departments of the General Security Directorate, but most are missing. "It should be mentioned that among these provincial responses, direct information on the Armenian deportations is as good as nonexistent." In the course of the deportation, "special notebooks and registries, which reported how many Armenians had been deported, how many still remained, and so on, were sent to the capital. The fate of the documents that contained such information remains one of the great outstanding questions on this subject."[3]

The other major official Ottoman source base for these questions was generated after the fact: the transcripts from the postwar court martial trials, between 1919 and 1921. These we can see as a kind of transitional justice, imposed by British occupying authorities, which was never completed, in part because this, along with the larger occupation of Ottoman lands, was itself a major catalyst for the Turkish national movement itself. The actual archive of the Istanbul Court-Martial and Commission to Investigate (Wartime) Crimes "ha[s] disappeared without a trace, and there is no solid knowledge as to [its] possible fate."[4] Akçam supposes that when the Turkish nationalists took Istanbul in November 1922 these files would have been transferred to the Turkish General Staff (Genelkurmay Başkanlığı); the archives of the General Staff's Directorate for Military History and Strategic Studies (Genelkurmay Askeri Tarih ve Stratejik Etüt ve Denetleme Başkanlığı, ATASE) are as good as closed to civilian or foreign researchers. According to Akçam, these archives contain over 3.5 million documents on World War I and at least 40,000 on the Teşkilat-i Mahsusa (Special Organization), the elite security force that played a special role in the genocide.

Twelve of the sixty-three court-martial cases were transcribed in the official Ottoman newspaper, *Takvim-i Vekayi*, and have been published in book form, in Turkish in 2007 and more recently in English, edited by Akçam and Vahakn N. Dadrian, as *Judgment at Istanbul: The Armenian Genocide Trials* (2011), but the evidence in them surely pales in comparison to what is or was contained in the archive of the court itself. Another important after-the-fact set of sources that we do have are the records of the *"Emval-ı Metruke,"* the euphemistically named "Abandoned Properties" Registry. The registry recorded the properties left behind by deported and murdered Armenians, to be cataloged and disbursed to deserving Ottoman/Turkish Muslims, often those who had been recently expelled from the Balkans. These records were the materials for Uğur Ümit Üngör and Mehmet Polatel's valuable 2011 book, *Confiscation and Destruction: The Young Turk Seizure of Armenian Property*, as well as Akçam and Ümit Kurt's *Kanunların Ruhu*, or *Spirit of the Laws*, from 2012, released in English in 2015).

Many other invaluable sources seem to be lost forever, however, permanently compromising any effort at complete documentation of the genocide. Papers of the CUP Central Committee, likely a goldmine of information about the goings-on in 1915, were smuggled out by notorious Central Committee member Dr. Nazim. Talaat Pasha, for his part, is said to have incinerated the Interior Ministry documents he deemed incriminating in the basement of a friend's seaside villa in the Bosphorus neighborhood of Arnavutköy before fleeing Istanbul for Berlin in 1918. Further complicating the question of direct sources is that orders in 1915 "regarding the killing of the deportees were sent via courier to the various provincial governors, and that after being read, the original message was to be given back to the courier." The upshot of this discussion and unearthing of sources, even for Akçam, who is seen as the historian who has come the closest to finding a "smoking gun," is that the strongest claim he can make in his book is "to show that the information in the Prime Ministerial Ottoman Archive clearly points in the direction of a deliberate Ottoman government policy to annihilate its Armenian population."[5]

This problem of sources, and therefore comprehensive evidence, becomes very clear in the core section of Suny's treatment, in the chapter entitled "Genocide," which remains surprisingly vague given that the book is framed as a history of this event, and points only to a few localized examples for which we have archival evidence. He depends on the recent work of Üngör for his most vivid local case study, of the city of Diyarbakir, and on the not undisputed scholarship of Taner Akçam, referred to above, for much of his other direct evidence. Supplemental sources are culled from German, Russian, and American memoirs and official correspondence, and the memoirs of stray mercenaries such as Spaniard de Nogales. This dearth of sources is the crux of the matter, lying at the heart of the dispute between those who claim it was an incidental and unfortunate series of events and those who frame it as a deliberate genocidal act. We have mainly circumstantial evidence, and even the direct evidence that has been unearthed by scholars such as Akçam and Üngör hardly provides us with a full, detailed picture of how, where, and by whom these acts were carried out. We know that it was horrific—who could possibly look at photograph after photograph of mangled bodies and starving, orphaned children, death marches and destroyed villages and neighborhoods, and doubt that these events occurred? We have enough evidence to be convinced that there was a definite pattern to the "deportations and killings," and that they add up to a conscious policy on the part of Talaat Pasha and several others in the leadership, at a minimum. This is not to say that the evidence does not make for a convincing case, and given the vehemence with which most Turks have consistently denied past wrongdoing the chances are good that wrongdoing did happen. WATS co-organizer Fatma Müge Göçek's recent book, the product of years of painstaking research into hundreds of memoirs of CUP members and others, *Denial of Violence* (2014), even pinpoints many instances of former CUP members bragging about past efforts to eliminate the Armenian population of the empire.

Suny makes a nuanced attempt, availing himself of the latest scholarship, to account for the causes—political and psychological—that led to the genocide: longstanding structural inequalities between Muslims and non-Muslims in Ottoman society; medium-term paranoia that Armenian civilians would constitute a fifth column for Russian interests in Eastern Anatolia to put the final nail in the coffin of Ottoman imperial control of the region and perhaps of the empire itself; and short-term responses to terrorist attacks by the Armenian Revolutionary Federation in 1896, the violent expulsion of Muslims from the Balkans in the first Balkan War of 1912, and the Ottoman military loss in the Battle of Sarıkamış that furthered the cycle of scapegoating and collective punishment. By Suny's account (and those of most other serious historians), the genocide was not predestined from centuries before, and yet that is when Suny's narrative history of the Armenian Genocide begins, implying that it was not an event of pure momentary contingency either. He rightly tries to differentiate between the localized massacres of Armenians in the 1890s and Adana in 1909, and the full-scale project to wipe out Armenians as a political entity (if not down to the last man, woman, and child) in 1915. And yet he constructs the narrative such that there is an "Ottoman" history and an "Armenian" national, or proto-national history, and a "Great Power" history, divided into different chapters. It all comes crashing together in the chapters "War," "Removal," and "Genocide." Students of Ottoman history reading this are prompted also to ask at what point, and in which cases, does Ottoman history have to also be Armenian history, and at what point were the Armenian subject populations doomed to this mass suffering? Was there, in fact, a kind of Ottoman/Turkish Sonderweg, and if so, how far back do we and should we trace it?

Ottoman History beyond Genocide

Suny has put together the most solid, readable, plausible narrative history of the Armenian Genocide to date. He took the trouble to learn Modern Turkish and read up, as an outsider to the field of Ottoman history, on the wealth of scholarship being produced on a wide range of topics within and beyond Ottoman history in order to construct his narrative. He deserves praise for transcending the emotional while still giving place to the emotions of suffering and trauma (of both Turks, driven from the Balkans, and Armenians) at the time and since. The book is as much a mark of collective accomplishment for the scholars of the past decade and a half as it is a signal that there is still much work to be done to flesh out the gory details of the genocide, and of the Ottoman experience in World War I more broadly, which, despite research that is now in progress, is still a terra incognita.

Until very recently Ottoman historians have been complicit, often inadvertently and out of well-founded fear, in accepting the divisions of Ottoman history that excise Armenians from Ottoman state and society, explain away or just avoid the Armenian Genocide and World War I more generally, and steer clear of questions regarding the politics of transition and continuity between the Ottoman and Republican Turkish states, at the core of which lie questions of culpability for the Armenian Genocide. When the centennial conferences and commemorations unfolded in 2015, it was interesting to see how remembrance of the genocide, like the recent scholarship on it, has become its own affair, amounting to a circuit of discussions for those who are already convinced of what happened and who is or was to blame. One can only hope that those who are not convinced will not close themselves off further from exploration into that dark past, if the aim of the commemorations is ultimately a consensus about what happened in 1915–1917. Turkish leaders, for their part, seem to be pursuing a number of policies, none of which involves formal recognition of the genocide. These range from punitive, albeit symbolic measures against states that have acknowledged the genocide, to an effort to deflect attention from commemoration of the genocide's centenary by celebrating instead the centennial of the Ottoman victory at Gallipoli in 1915. A Turkish NGO even staged dance performances, such as the one in Times Square a few days before the centennial, aimed at promoting peace between Turkey and Armenia. Many Ottoman historians have tried to square the centennial of the genocide with that of the Ottoman victory at Gallipoli, in order to understand more not just about the genocide as a separate event, but also its relationship to the vast and complex whole of Ottoman history.

Sources and Teaching

In addition to the Suny book discussed at length above, I refer readers below to texts and films that can be effective when teaching about the genocide. In general, it helps to give a sense of what society looked like before the genocide, to prompt students to think about all actors involved as human beings with their own historical and social experiences. They then need to understand the context in which the genocide occurred—including the longer-term devolution of the Ottoman Empire and the place of non-Muslim minorities, caught between the Ottoman state and European colonial powers; the expulsions of Balkan Muslims in 1912–1913 and the ways that experience informed the wartime leadership in Istanbul once World War I began in earnest; the Eastern Front between the Ottoman and Russian Empires and the ongoing rivalry between those states; and the highly ambiguous nature of Ottoman sovereignty and Young Turk involvement in the state, the war, and the mass killings. Students need to understand that the polarization that has traditionally accompanied the production of knowledge about the genocide involves on both "sides" some assumptions that to delve into the historical context and to understand the reasons that the genocide took place is tantamount to "apologizing" or denying that this was a genocide. Instead, as historians, our job is to understand the context and the perspective of multiple sides, without relativizing or explaining away the genocidal nature of the violence. In reading Fethiye Çetin's *My Grandmother* (listed below), students gain a visceral understanding of how deeply entangled Armenians and Turks were in the early twentieth century, and how deeply embedded the genocide is, not only in Armenian communities in the diaspora but in Turkish society itself. If I were to assign one book on the genocide, it would be *My Grandmother*.

NOTES

This chapter was originally published as "The Armenian Genocide and the Politics of Knowledge," *Public Books*, May 1, 2015, https://www.publicbooks.org/

the-armenian-genocide-and-the-politics-of-knowledge/, and republished in *Jada-liyya*, May 22, 2015, http://www.jadaliyya.com/Details/32113.

1. Ronald Grigor Suny, Fatma Müge Göçek, and Norman M. Naimark, *A Question of Genocide: Armenians and Turks at the End of the Ottoman Empire* (New York: Oxford University Press, 2011).

2. Taner Akçam, *The Young Turks' Crime against Humanity: The Armenian Genocide and Ethnic Cleansing in the Ottoman Empire* (Princeton, NJ: Princeton University Press, 2012).

3. Akçam, *The Young Turks' Crime against Humanity.*

4. Akçam, *The Young Turks' Crime against Humanity.*

5. Vahakn N. Dadrian and Taner Akçam, *Judgment at Istanbul: The Armenian Genocide Trials* (New York: Berghahn Books, 2011).

KEY RESOURCES

Akçam, Taner. *The Young Turks' Crime against Humanity: The Armenian Genocide and Ethnic Cleansing in the Ottoman Empire.* Princeton, NJ: Princeton University Press, 2012.

Akçam, Taner, and Ümit Kurt. *Spirit of the Laws: The Plunder of Wealth in the Armenian Genocide.* New York: Berghahn Books, 2015. Originally published as *Kanunların Ruhu.*

Çetin, Fethiye. *My Grandmother.* Melbourne: Spinifex Press, 2013. A gripping and poignant memoir by a prominent Turkish lawyer who discovers, as an adult, that her own grandmother was an Armenian survivor of the genocide.

Dadrian, Vahakn N., and Taner Akçam. *Judgment at Istanbul: The Armenian Genocide Trials.* New York: Berghahn Books, 2011.

Göçek, Fatma Müge. *Denial of Violence: Ottoman Past, Turkish Present, and Collective Violence against the Armenians, 1789–2009.* New York: Oxford University Press, 2015.

Halo, Thea. *Not Even My Name: A True Story of Genocide and Survival.* Athens: Govostis, 2011. A memoir by the (American) granddaughter of an Assyrian survivor of the genocide who immigrated to America.

Kevorkian, Raymond. *The Armenian Genocide: A Complete History.* London: I. B. Tauris, 2011.

Morgenthau, Henry. *Ambassador Morgenthau's Story.* Charleston, SC: Nabu Press, 2010. The memoirs of the American ambassador to the Ottoman Empire during World War I.

The Ottoman Lieutenant. Joseph Ruben, dir. 2017.

The Promise. Terry George, dir. 2016.

Suny, Ronald Grigor. *"They Can Live in the Desert but Nowhere Else": A History of the Armenian Genocide.* Princeton, NJ: Princeton University Press, 2015.

Suny, Ronald Grigor, Fatma Müge Göçek, and Norman M. Naimark. *A Question of Genocide: Armenians and Turks at the End of the Ottoman Empire*. New York: Oxford University Press, 2011.

Üngör, Uğur Ümit, and Mehmet Polatel. *Confiscation and Destruction: The Young Turk Seizure of Armenian Property*. London: Continuum, 2011.

Watenpaugh, Keith. *Bread from Stones: The Middle East and the Making of Modern Humanitarianism*. Berkeley: University of California Press, 2015.

Using Primary Source Documents to Teach Nationalization and Imperialism in the Modern Middle East

KIT ADAM WAINER

In 1951 the Iranian Majlis (parliament) voted to nationalize Iran's petroleum industry. This particularly impacted
the Anglo-Iranian Oil Company, which owned numerous oil refineries
in Iran. This led to two years of tumult and conflict between Prime Minister Mohammad Mossadegh's nationalist regime, on the one hand,
and the AIOC, the British and US governments, and Muhammad Reza
Shah Pahlavi, on the other. In 1953 the US Central Intelligence Agency
and the British Secret Intelligence Service, in collaboration with conservative Iranian military officers, the royal family, some factions of the
clergy, and criminal enterprises, orchestrated a successful coup d'état.
Mossadegh was deposed and imprisoned. What followed was twenty-
six years of dictatorial rule that gave way to the revolution of 1979.

In 1956 Egyptian president Gamal Abdel Nasser announced the
nationalization of the Suez Canal, a critical passageway for global oil
shipments that had been under Anglo-French control since the late nineteenth century. Fearing the loss of oil revenues and their eroding imperial power, London and Paris collaborated with the Israelis to attack
Egypt in October 1956 in what is known as the Tripartite Aggression.
Although Egypt was nominally an independent state, the British had

not yet removed their troops from their former colony, and the French blamed Nasser's pan-Arabism for the independence movement in Algeria. However, in part due to Washington's opposition, the Anglo-French-Israeli invaders withdrew after an initially successful assault on the canal zone. Nasser emerged the victor and became an inspiration to Arab nationalists in the region.

Both Mossadegh and Nasser were part of a larger wave of Third World nationalists who wanted to utilize their natural resources to spur economic development. Although both were anticommunist, they nonetheless believed that economic nationalization was critical to their nations' success. Both ran afoul of the great imperial powers, leading to violent confrontations. Nasser's project survived while Mossadegh's did not. The reasons for the different outcomes would make for an excellent class discussion.

Part of the larger context for the outcome of these two stories is the complicated relationship between the United States and Great Britain. Close World War II allies, they were nonetheless directly competing for global influence and economic advantage in the postwar world. While they collaborated to overthrow Mossadegh, they opposed each other on the question of how to handle the Suez crisis. The events of 1956 thus contributed to the decline of traditional European colonialism. Ironically, although neither Washington nor London could tolerate oil nationalization in 1953, a decade later they had no choice but to accept it in numerous countries.

The rise of independence movements in Asia and Africa after World War II was also part of the context. These movements took many forms and were driven by various ideologies. Some were communist, others were simply nationalist and favored a mixed economy. Some came to power through popular uprisings. Others, such as the Egyptian Free Officers, led military coups. Mossadegh was among a few who followed a parliamentary path to power.

Instructors may use the Iranian and Egyptian cases as illustrative examples in the larger dramas of postwar nationalism and inter-imperial rivalries. By analyzing the accompanying documents, students at various levels should be able to piece together a story of movements for meaningful national independence set against the backdrop of the Cold War. Instructors could choose to focus on any of a number of specific issues. First, these experiences could be a springboard to a comparative discussion of state-directed economic development among less-industrialized countries after World War II. While the defeat of nationalization and the 1953 coup in Iran led to privatization and corruption, Egypt's nationalization program accelerated after the Suez Crisis. State planning and state ownership were the hallmarks of communist regimes but were also favored, if administered less completely, by nationalist governments in Latin America and the Middle East. Students might be encouraged to discuss why state planning figured so heavily in Third World development strategies in the 1950s and 1960s but was so thoroughly out of favor among government leaders by the 1990s.

Alternatively, students might consider why Washington and London were so hostile to nationalist projects after World War II. Was the Cold War–era fear of Soviet influence merely a pretext for preserving Anglo-American political and economic power? Or were US and British leaders so taken with Cold War ideology that they could not distinguish between nationalist governments with whom they could have negotiated and communist regimes that would have inevitably joined the Soviet bloc? Along those lines students might discuss the moral dimensions of US and British foreign policies in the twentieth and twenty-first centuries. Woodrow Wilson's Fourteen Points, the Atlantic Charter, and the United Nations "Declaration on the Granting of Independence to Colonial Countries and Peoples" all articulated support for the concept of national self-determination. Yet the Western powers intervened repeatedly in the internal affairs of Third World countries. Students might be asked whether the United States should have the right to overthrow other governments. If so, is this a universal right or one only the US government possesses? In other words, should other governments also have the right to invade and occupy the United States when it is in their interests to do so? This lesson can be taught at the high school or college level in classes on modern world history. It could fit within one of several teaching units. The instructor who prefers a regional approach might teach it as part of a series of lessons on the modern Middle East. Alternatively, the Iranian and Egyptian episodes would make good exemplars of the complexities of Cold War geopolitics. Another approach might utilize this lesson as part of a series of discussions of postwar nationalist movements.

Instructors can focus a lesson on one or two of the documents discussed below and provide guiding questions. Alternatively, they might have students work in groups with the documents and identify relationships between them. College students might be able to create their own overarching theme and arrange the documents to support a particular thesis. High school students will likely need a guiding question. Student groups, at all levels, can design charts in which documents are arranged thematically. By doing so students are effectively preparing an outline for an essay and learning to utilize primary sources to support an argument. They can learn argumentation skills and historical content simultaneously.

This chapter consists of primary documents followed by notes for the instructor. These notes elaborate possible interpretations of the documents and suggest how they can be used in conjunction with other documents. They also offer questions students can be asked to discuss, should the instructor wish to delve more deeply.

Document One

Secret cable from United Kingdom prime minister Winston Churchill to US president Franklin D. Roosevelt, March 4, 1944.[1] Churchill was responding to a cable from Roosevelt in which the latter had promised that the United States had no intention of taking advantage of Britain's troubles during World War II by attempting to seize British oil assets in Iran and Iraq.

> Thank you very much for your assurances about no sheep's eyes at our oil fields at Iran and Iraq. Let me reciprocate by giving you the fullest assurance that we have no thought of trying to horn in upon your interests or property in Saudi Arabia. My position on this, as in all matters, is that Great Britain seeks no advantage, territorial or otherwise, as the result of the war. On the other hand she will not be deprived of anything which rightly belongs to her after having given her best services to the good cause—at least not so long as your humble servant is entrusted with the conduct of her affairs.

Notes on Document One

Professor Harvey Goldberg, to whom this series is dedicated, first introduced this quotation to me and I have found it to be an exceptionally rich and useful teaching tool. Throughout World War II President Franklin D. Roosevelt and Prime Minister Winston Churchill exchanged hundreds of top-secret cables discussing war strategy and plans for the postwar world. These cables provide invaluable insights into the degree of collaboration between the two world leaders but also the extent to which the two allies were in conflict with each other. Students should consider the significance of the format of cables such as the one excerpted in document one. These were not meant for public consumption. In fact, they were encrypted and sent over secure lines to guarantee secrecy. Consequently, they are free from the usual platitudes that often accompany official statements and represent the thinking of the two world leaders, at least to the extent to which they were candid with each other.

In this excerpt, Churchill uses careful and friendly language to soften what was likely intended as a threat. The prime minister begins by thanking the president for not looking with "sheep's eyes" at British oil fields in Iran and Iraq. Some students may not recognize the biblical reference to a sermon by Jesus (Matthew 7:15) to beware of false prophets who arrive wearing "sheep's clothing, but inwardly they are ravening wolves." Churchill wrote this in response to a cable from Roosevelt that assured the former that the United States did not intend to take advantage of Britain's wartime crises to dislodge British interests from Iran and Iraq. However, the president also pointed out that his State Department was studying all matters pertaining to oil in the postwar world. In fact, on February 22 the Interdivisional Petroleum Committee of the State Department issued a first draft of its policy document that committed the US to supporting the "equal access" provision of the Atlantic Charter with regard to petroleum. This sentiment, formalized in an IPC memorandum on April 11, 1944,[2] could have been interpreted as a threat to British imperial interests because of its implied opposition to British monopolistic power over petroleum assets anywhere. The text implies that Churchill, for one, likely interpreted Washington's intent that way. That interpretation made sense given the overall US commitment to free trade and open markets after the war. In the second sentence the prime minister "reciprocate[s]" by promising not to interfere with US oil interests in Saudi Arabia. This was likely intended as a threat: if the US made a move on Iranian oil, the British would respond in Saudi Arabia.

Students should be encouraged to ask why Churchill masked angry and threatening sentiments with thankful and cooperative phrasing. They should recognize that London had a deep interest in maintaining its alliance with Washington, not the least because it depended upon the latter for financial assistance. Students should also critically examine Churchill's claims that Britain sought "no advantage, territorial or otherwise." This is one of many cables in which Churchill made clear that preserving the British Empire, with all of its advantages, territorial and otherwise, was in fact a critical British war goal. Churchill was undoubtedly referring both to the British colonial empire and to British economic interests in Iran and Egypt when referring to that which "rightly belongs to her." Although written nine years before the Iranian coup d'état of 1953 and twelve years prior to the Suez Canal Crisis of 1956, this cable betrays British imperial attitudes. Churchill remained committed to the preservation of British colonies and Britain's access to Middle Eastern oil. For London, World War II was an imperial contest. Neither Churchill nor his Labor Party opponents considered the idea that the peoples of the Middle East might have a claim on their own assets, even though they had sacrificed far more for the "good cause" than the British had. Document one also foreshadows some of the complexities of the Anglo-American alliance. The United States collaborated with Great Britain to oppose nationalization of Iranian oil and to overthrow Iran's nationalist prime minister in 1953. However, Washington parted company with London over its handling of the Suez Canal crisis three years later, dealing an important blow to British power in the Middle East.

Document Two

Manucher Farmanfarmaian writing on the conditions in Abadan, site of a crucial Iranian oil refinery owned by the Anglo-Iranian Oil Company, 1949.[3] In April 1949 Farmanfarmaian, who had been educated in Great Britain, became Iran's director general of Petroleum, Concessions, and Mines.

> Wages were fifty cents a day. There was no vacation pay, no sick leave, no disability compensation. The workers lived in a shanty town . . . without running water or electricity, let alone luxuries [such] as ice boxes or fans. In winter the earth flooded and became a flat, perspiring lake. The mud in town was knee-deep, and . . . when the rains subsided, clouds of nipping, small-winged flies rose from the stagnant water to fill the nostrils. . . .
>
> Summer was worse. . . . The dwellings, . . . cobbled from rusted oil drums hammered flat, turned into sweltering ovens. . . .

To the management of AIOC in their pressed ecru shirts and air-conditioned offices, the workers were faceless drones. . . . In the British section of Abadan there were lawns, rose beds, tennis courts, swimming pools and clubs, in [the workers' section] there was nothing—not a tea shop, not a bath, not a single tree. . . . The unpaved alleyways were emporiums for rats. The man in the grocery store sold his wares while sitting in a barrel of water to avoid the heat.

Notes on Document Two

The Abadan oil refinery was the largest in the world and, production there more than doubled between 1944 and 1950. Top management was entirely British and lived in conditions Farmanfarmaian described. Skilled jobs were given to trained foreigners, mostly South Asians and Palestinians. Iranians were hired for the least skilled and lowest-paid positions. A 1946 refinery workers' strike forced AIOC to rescind its decision to cancel Friday pay. Oil workers' horrific living conditions caused numerous strikes throughout the country after the second World War, some of which elicited violent responses from the British military. Oil workers' strikes helped build resentment toward the AIOC and helped create the political conditions within which Mossadegh nationalized Iranian oil in 1951. Farmanfarmaian had direct access to observe both the living and working conditions. Farmanfarmaian was British educated, became an Iranian military officer after college, and was a high-ranking government official when he wrote these lines. He did not live under any of the conditions he described and probably could have ignored them. He may have shared the anger of well-educated Iranians and well-off bazaar merchants who were frustrated by Iran's underdevelopment at a time when foreign oil companies were extracting so much wealth. Mossadegh's Iran Party attracted European-educated professionals like that. In 1949, his party spearheaded the National Front with Islamic and left-wing parties. The Front demanded that oil profits be used for national development and social welfare.

Document Three

June 1951 speech by Iranian prime minister Mohammad Mossadegh to the World Court in The Hague, Netherlands.[4] The

Anglo-American Oil Company had sued Iran over its decision to nationalize Iranian oil in 1951.

> Our long years of negotiations with foreign countries . . . have yielded no results . . . With the oil revenues we could meet our entire budget and combat poverty, disease, and backwardness. . . . Another important consideration is that by the elimination of the power of the British company, we would also eliminate corruption and intrigue, by means of which the internal affairs of our country have been influenced. Once this tutelage has ceased, Iran will have achieved its economic and political independence.

Notes on Document Three

In March 1951 the Majlis nationalized Iranian oil following the growth of nationalist sentiments and the growing popularity of Mossadegh's National Front. The Majlis named Mossadegh as prime minister on April 28. Ervand Abrahamian argues the Majlis's actions were partially a result of a March 1951 general strike in the oil industry. That month the AIOC announced cuts to workers' housing allowances and thousands of layoffs. According to Abrahamian, Mossadegh believed that nationalization would allow the Iranian state to alleviate the conditions that led to labor unrest and halt the growth of the pro-Soviet Tudeh Party.[5] The AIOC, however, would not accept a compromise on the issue of oil nationalization. And the British government, dependent on Iranian oil to fuel the Royal Navy, was equally intransigent. The AIOC sued Iran before the International Court of Justice in The Hague. Mossadegh's response emphasized the nationalist conception of foreign influence as a corrupting force. He referred to Iranians as the "rightful owners" of Iranian oil. He also promised to utilize oil revenues to help develop his nation and combat poverty. In July 1952 the World Court dismissed the case.[6] Students may regard Mossadegh's statement as an example of a common nationalist view that nations have a right to their own natural resources. Instructors may also encourage students to place this document in global context. Indian prime minister Jawaharlal Nehru publicly congratulated Mossadegh, implying a comparison between nationalization and national independence. Former Mexican president Lázaro Cárdenas, who had famously nationalized his nation's oil industry, was similarly congratulatory. The British

Cabinet, by contrast, began planning military measures to oust Mossa-degh. Students, therefore, may contextualize this document by recognizing that Mossadegh's speech was one short episode in a longer saga of imperialism and decolonization after World War II.

Document Four

Iranian prime minister Mohammad Mossadegh to US president Dwight Eisenhower, May 28, 1953.[7]

> The standard of living of the Iranian people has been very low as a result of century-old imperialistic policies, and it will be impossible to raise it without extensive programs of development and rehabilitation.
>
> The Iranian nation hopes that with the help and assistance of the American Government the obstacles placed in the way of sale of Iranian oil can be removed.

Notes on Document Four

This private letter was neither encrypted nor top secret. Mossadegh likely knew that President Eisenhower would share it with top foreign policy advisers, such as Secretary of State John Foster Dulles. Perhaps the prime minister hoped to exploit divisions between Washington and London. Mossadegh possibly thought that Eisenhower would agree to provide aid if he believed that the United States would benefit from economic relations with Iran. London certainly feared that.[8] Historians have attempted to trace the extent to which Washington and London concurred during this period. While the two powers maintained a united posture in public, they did not always agree. During the Truman presidency, which ended in January 1953, the White House attempted to convince the AIOC to compromise and was suspicious about London's plans for military action. Nonetheless, the CIA collaborated with British actions to undermine Mossadegh.[9] By the time this letter arrived, Eisenhower had already determined to support British plans. In a provocative essay H. W. Brands argues that the 1952 Free Officers' coup in Egypt heightened British fears of oil nationalization and pushed the United States in the same direction. The British were alarmed at the possibility that the Egyptians would refuse to renew the British lease over the Suez Canal, set to expire in 1956. Iranian oil nationalization, London thought, might serve as a dangerous example to Cairo. In May 1953 Secretary Dulles toured the Middle East to put together an anti-Soviet alliance. Gamal Abdel Nasser refused to participate, leading Dulles to conclude that Iran would have to anchor any anticommunist bloc. Mossadegh seemed unlikely to lead such an alliance. Thus, US policy began to align more closely with Britain's. Mossadegh may not have known about this. His anti-imperial rhetoric also seems odd in a letter to a US president. Most likely, he was appealing to US leaders' self-image as champions of decolonization. Students may discern an element of desperation in Mossadegh's communiqué. Although he was immensely popular at home, he was isolated on the world's stage. In that context it is understandable that he would solicit international support.

Document Five

Excerpt from "Summary of Preliminary Plan Prepared by SIS (British Secret Intelligence Service, also known as Military Intelligence Section 6 or MI6) and CIA Representatives in Cyprus," a joint secret plan drawn up by US and British intelligence services, June 1, 1953.[10]

a. *Presentation to the Shah*
(1) Both governments consider oil question secondary.
(2) Major issue is to maintain independence Iran and keep from the Soviet orbit. To do this Mossadeq must be removed.
(5) Mossadeq must go.
(7) Acceptable oil settlement will be offered but successor government will not be rushed into it.
b. *Demands on the Shah*
(4) Who do you want to head successor government? (Try and maneuver Shah into naming Zahedi.)

II. *Arrangement with Zahedi*
B. .... Quasi-legal method to be tried first. If successful at least part of machinery for military coup will be brought into action. If it fails, military coup will follow in matter of hours.

III. *Relations with Majlis* [parliament]
A. Basic aim is to secure 41 votes against Mossadeq . . . (SIS considers 20 deputies now not controlled must be purchased).

Notes on Document Five

This document was top secret, and its contents would not be revealed for years. After the August 1953 coup d'état that restored the shah's power, both Washington and London denied involvement. They insisted that the coup was the product of internal conflicts and its antagonists were all Iranian. This document shows that the coup was carefully planned and orchestrated by the US and British intelligence services. The authors casually claim the right to depose an elected prime minister and choose his successor. Students may debate whether governments should have the right to depose foreign leaders whenever they deem it in their interest to do so. If so, does Iran have the right to orchestrate a coup d'état in the United States if it determines that the US government poses an imminent threat?

Document Six

Photograph of a Tehran resident cleaning graffiti from a city street one day after the coup d'état that ousted Mossadegh.[11] Newly installed prime minister Fazlollah Zahedi had ordered that all political graffiti be removed in the capital. August 21, 1953.

Notes on Document Six

This photograph provides a hint of the tragic consequences about to unfold. Students can use this image as evidence of the ways in which regimes try to control memory and eliminate records of an inconvenient past. The August 1953 coup led to the fall, trial, and imprisonment of Mossadegh. The Pahlavi dynasty was reinvigorated, and the shah eventually became an absolute monarch, backed by a notorious secret police force, the SAVAK. The new regime attempted to erase the memory of Iranian nationalism or any hope of utilizing oil revenues for national development. Students should ask whether it is possible to clean away popular sentiments with bleach and a scrub brush. In later decades the Iranian labor movement continued to organize clandestinely, much as it does today. Iranian students in the United States protested the shah's dictatorship, although they did so with their faces covered in order to protect their relatives. Ultimately, the 1979 revolution united oil workers and students in opposition to the shah. Anger over the 1953 coup fueled

A resident of Tehran washes "Yankee Go Home" graffiti from a wall in the capital city of Iran, August 21, 1953. The newly installed prime minister Fazlollah Zahedi requested the cleanup after the coup d'etat that restored the shah of Iran to power. Image courtesy of the Associated Press.

anti-Americanism, which the Islamic clerics successfully exploited. The US hostage crisis of 1979–1981 blinded many in the United States to the suffering of so many Iranians under the shah's rule and the ways in which US and European powers had taken advantage of Iranian petroleum after Mossadegh's ouster. Professor Goldberg frequently quipped that the US public's attention span is a mere twenty seconds. He complained that often US news consumers first become aware of other nations when they take actions the United States deems hostile. This photograph should help students see a longer view of US-Iranian relations. Hostility toward the United States hardened after the coup, and no amount of street cleaning could wipe that away.

Document Seven

Egyptian president Gamal Abdel Nasser, "Decree of the President of the Republic of Egypt on the Nationalization of the Suez Canal Company, Cairo, July 26, 1956."[12]

Article I
The Universal Company of the Suez Maritime Canal (Egyptian joint-stock company) is hereby nationalized. All its assets, rights and obligations are transferred to the Nation and all the organizations and committees that now operate its management are hereby dissolved.

Stockholders and holders of founders shares shall be compensated . . . in accordance with the value of the shares shown in the closing quotations of the Paris Stock Exchange.

Notes on Document Seven

Gamal Abdel Nasser came to power as a leader of the Free Officers Movement that organized a coup d'état and ousted the monarchy in 1952. The Free Officers were a mixed group ideologically. Some considered themselves Marxist while others had ties to the Muslim Brotherhood. Nasser, who had little ideology beyond Egyptian nationalism, became president in 1954. He had hoped to secure British and US aid to develop the Aswan High Dam, which would generate hydroelectric power and spur industrial development. Washington and London had indicated a willingness to finance the dam in return for Nasser's cooperation in the Cold War and his help with the Arab-Israeli conflict. Israel's 1955 invasion of Gaza, however, made it impossible for Nasser to maintain a pan-Arabist image while also brokering peace with Israel. Nasser attempted to remain nonaligned. He continued talks with the United States and Great Britain but also recognized Communist China and negotiated an arms deal with Czechoslovakia. Eisenhower and British prime minister Anthony Eden then canceled their aid offers. Nasser nationalized the Suez Canal in order to fund the dam. Income from the canal, a key passageway for the global energy trade, could have greatly boosted

Egyptian economic development. Nasser's July 1956 announcement cata-
pulted him to the leadership of Arab nationalism and the movement for
decolonization. The language of Article 1 reveals important aspects of
Nasser's decision. Not only was ownership of the company transferred
to "the Nation," but its management would be turned over to Egyptians. Students should recognize a similarity between this and Iranian
demands that Iranians be employed in managerial positions within
AIOC. The decree also specified that stockholders would be compensated according to the market price of their shares. In short, this was not
a communist-style expropriation. Like Mossadegh, Nasser emphasized
a strong role for the state in promoting economic development and re-
distributionist policies to alleviate poverty. Nasser would describe his
policies as "socialist." Although there is little room for this development model in the modern neoliberal order, it was popular in the Third
World from the 1950s through the 1980s. Students should discuss why
Third World nationalists relied so heavily on the state and had little
confidence in the free market as a tool for economic development.[13]

Document Eight

President Nasser, announcing the nationalization of the
Suez Canal to a cheering crowd in Alexandria, Egypt. July 26, 1956.[14]

Notes on Document Eight

Egyptian crowds jubilantly cheered. It seemed that Egypt finally had a
leader who placed Egyptian interests ahead of those of foreign investors.
Unlike Mossadegh, Nasser's commitment to democracy was thin. Soon
after coming to power in 1952 the Free Officers' government violently
suppressed strikes at the Misr Fine Spinning and Weaving factory in
Kafr al-Dawwar. In 1954 the regime persecuted the Muslim Brotherhood. However, Nasser's populist nationalism was far more than merely
rhetorical. In September 1952 the Free Officers promulgated the first
of several land reform measures. The government expropriated royal
property and instituted a minimum wage. By nationalizing the canal
Nasser seemed to be making good on his promise to fund the Aswan
High Dam and substantially improve the lives of Egyptian laborers
and the rural poor. However, although they were unable to secure US
cooperation to retake the Suez Canal, Great Britain, France, and Israel

Gamal Abdel Nasser cheered by supporters in Cairo, 1956.

agreed to manufacture a crisis and militarily seize the canal zone.[15] Britain relied on the canal for petroleum shipments. France blamed Nasser for the growing independence movement in Algeria. And Israel feared the growth of Arab nationalism, particularly because of its potential to ignite a Palestinian resistance movement. Eisenhower, however, reacted angrily. He brought the matter to the United Nations and threatened to cut off aid to Israel. He further warned Israeli prime minister David Ben-Gurion that he would not oppose Soviet military action against Israel. In a panic, Ben-Gurion agreed to withdraw on November 9, 1956, and Nasser's stature soared.

NOTES

1. Francis L. Loewenheim, Harold D. Langley, and Manfred Jonas, eds., *Roosevelt and Churchill: Their Secret Wartime Correspondence* (New York: Saturday Review Press, 1975), 459.
2. "Memorandum by the Inter-Divisional Petroleum Committee of the Department of State," Foreign Relations of the United States, Diplomatic Papers,

April 11, 1944, Office of the Historian, Department of State, 811.6363/4-1144, https://history.state.gov/historicaldocuments/frus1944v05/d21.

3. Quoted in D. R. Collier, *Democracy and the Nature of American Influence in Iran, 1941–1979* (Syracuse, NY: Syracuse University Press, 2017), 84.

4. "After 65 Years: Mossadegh's Speech at The Hague (June 1951)," *Iran Review*, June 8, 2016, http://www.iranreview.org/content/Documents/Mosaddegh -s-Speech-at-The-Hague-June-1951-.htm.

5. Ervand Abrahamian, *The Coup: 1953, the CIA, and the Roots of Modern US-Iranian Relations* (New York: The New Press, 2015), 68–77.

6. Mostafa Elm, *Oil, Power, and Principle: Iran's Oil Nationalization and Its Aftermath* (Syracuse, NY: Syracuse University Press, 1992), 208–14.

7. Yonah Alexander and Allan Nanes, eds. *The United States and Iran: A Documentary History* (Frederick, MD: Aletheia Books, 1980), 233.

8. Quoted in H. W. Brands, "The Cairo-Tehran Connection in Anglo-American Rivalry in the Middle East, 1951–1953," *International History Review* 11, no. 3 (August 1989): 439.

9. Elm, *Oil, Power, and Principle*, 155–67; Collier, *Democracy and the Nature of American Influence*, 91–103.

10. Donald R. Wilber, "Clandestine Service History: Overthrow of Premier Mossadeq of Iran, November 1952–1953," written March 1954, National Security Archives, 1969, https://nsarchive2.gwu.edu/NSAEBB/ciacase/EXL.pdf, n.p.

11. Dan Merica and Jason Hanna, "In Declassified Document, CIA Acknowledges Role in '53 Iran Coup," CNN online, August 19, 2013, http://www.cnn .com/2013/08/19/politics/cia-iran-1953-coup/index.html.

12. "Decree of the President of the Republic of Egypt on the Nationalization of the Suez Canal Company, Cairo, July 26, 1956," CVCE, University of Luxembourg, https://www.cvce.eu/content/publication/2001/10/9/50e44f1f-78d5-4aab -a0ae-8689874d12e6/publishable_en.pdf.

13. For a brief summary of the Free Officers' political philosophy see Peter Mansfield, "Nasser and Nasserism," *International Journal* 28, no. 4 (1973): 670–88; see also Omnia El Shakry, "Etatism: Theorizing Egypt's 1952 Revolution," in *The Great Social Laboratory: Subjects of Knowledge in Colonial and Post-Colonial Egypt* (Stanford, CA: Stanford University Press, 2007).

14. "The 1952 Revolution and Alexandria," Historical Eras, Alexandria, http://www.alexandria.gov.eg/Alex/english/julyrevolution.html.

15. Useful maps of troop movements during the Suez Canal crisis can be found at "The Suez Crisis: Key Maps," BBC News, July 21, 2006, http://news .bbc.co.uk/2/hi/middle_east/5195068.stm (accessed July 21, 2019).

KEY RESOURCES

Alexander, Yonah, and Allan S. Nanes, eds. *The United States and Iran: A Documentary History*. Frederick, MD: Alethia Books, 1980.

Chaqueri, Cosroe, ed. *The Left in Iran, 1941–1957*. Revolutionary History Series. London: Socialist Platform/Merlin Press, 2011.

Cleveland, William. *A History of the Modern Middle East*. Boulder, CO: Westview Press, 2013.

Elm, Mostafa. *Oil, Power, and Principle: Iran's Oil Nationalization and Its After-math*. Syracuse, NY: Syracuse University Press, 1992.

El Shakry, Omnia. "Egypt's Three Revolutions: The Force of History behind This Popular Uprising." In *The Dawn of the Arab Uprisings: End of an Old Order?*, ed. Bassam Haddad, Rosie Bsheer, and Ziad Abu-Rish. London: Pluto Press, 2012.

Hangen, Welles. "Mossadegh Gets 3-Year Jail Term." *New York Times*, December 22, 1953.

Katouzian, Homa. *The Political Economy of Modern Iran, 1926–1979*. New York: New York University Press, 1981.

Nasser, Gamal Abdel. "Denouncement of the Proposal for a Canal User's Association, 1956." Fordham University, Modern History Sourcebook. https://sourcebooks.fordham.edu/halsall/mod/1956Nasser-suez1.html (accessed July 21, 2019).

Keeping Current

*Contemporary Engagement When
Teaching Modern Middle East History*

Z I A D A B U - R I S H

Three sets of challenges confront the instructor in
the classroom: institutional, curricular, and contemporary.[1] Institutional challenges pivot around declining enrollments,
shifting educational priorities, and new modes of administrative governance. Public debate about the teaching of history has emphasized such
issues. Curricular challenges involve the temporal scope of the course,
the appropriate balance between emphasizing events versus processes,
and the uneven nature of available survey-level readings. Previous chapters in the present volume identify such challenges and strategies for
overcoming them. There is, however, a third set of challenges. Many
teachers seek to create a history course in which the events of the past
can be instructive in thinking about contemporary debates about the
Middle East. Yet keeping current is a formidable challenge we all face.
This chapter outlines several strategies for overcoming this challenge.

The most immediate way to address the challenge of contemporary
relevance is to draw on specific historical events or developments in
the region to shed light on current discussions that students may mis-
takenly assume are fundamentally unprecedented or uncalled for. The
modern history of the Middle East provides a diverse array of content
to make use of in such a manner. For example, there is a current debate
on whether criticisms of Israeli policies or Zionism as a principle for
political organization is a legitimate talking point, research agenda,

pedagogical approach, or discussion prompt. Drawing on the history of the Zionist movement, from its founding in 1881 through the establishment of the State of Israel in 1948, reveals several junctures in which external and internal critique was both central to its development and recognized by most protagonists as legitimate. Zionism was one of several European Jewish responses to anti-Semitism, including assimilationist, socialist, and emigrationist movements. There was an intense debate and rivalry between these competing types of movements within the European Jewish community as well as debates between various strains of Zionism. Such a history helps students better understand the political sociology behind what makes some movements successful and others not so. It highlights that history is contingent and that ideological dominance is forged through complex intellectual debate and contentious political struggle.[2]

Alternatively, consider the claim by many journalists and analysts that the series of mass protests that erupted across the Middle East in 2010–2011 was an unprecedented display of citizens' political agency. But these uprisings are not exceptional. There is a long history of political mobilizations, protests, and rebellions in the Middle East and North Africa.[3] These include the constitutional movements of the early twentieth century, the myriad political movements pursuing their particular model of representation, accountability, and justice in the aftermath of World War I, and the repeated attempts to challenge and subvert authoritarian rule from the 1950s onward. These examples challenge ahistorical narratives of the Arab uprisings. They allow students to locate the 2010–2011 mass protests in the continuities and ruptures of modern Middle East history.[4]

A final example is the debate that emerged after the US invasion and occupation of Iraq in 2003. Does the United States constitute an imperial power in the Middle East region? Some historians date the start of European imperialism in the Middle East at 1798. The subsequent two centuries provide numerous examples for understanding the undergirding dynamics of empire in both its formal and informal manifestations.[5] Teachers can measure the historical or contemporary record of US foreign policy in the region relative to those dynamics.[6] Students are often more willing to acknowledge European military, political, and economic imperialism. However, using comparative history to think critically about definitions of empire and its varied manifestations can serve as an important pedagogical approach to both understanding imperialism more generally as well as critiquing US foreign policy in the region.

The above examples highlight how teachers can draw on specific historical dynamics to shed light on current discussions. Yet a qualification is in order. If history teaches us anything, it is that context matters. In this sense, engaging such parallels and lessons requires that we also discuss with our students the differences between the context of the contemporary moment and that of the historical dynamics we are drawing on.

Practical Activities and Assignments

Many teachers face a classroom reality in which students are frequently more interested in the current moment and eager to make sense of the now rather than the past. This is especially so when a course might be the first or only opportunity for students to learn about the Middle East. To this end, teachers can frame student expectations at the outset of the course. Doing so involves providing an overview of where the course begins and ends in terms of chronology, the rationale for such choices, and an explicit discussion of the relationship of the course design to helping students make sense of the current moment. For example, does the course start with World War I, or earlier, and why? Similarly, does the course cover the post–Cold War period, and if so to what extent and why does it end where it does? Explicitly explaining such choices facilitates a more transparent relationship with students about the assumptions and approaches of the teacher, which in turn sets the stage for other strategies discussed in this chapter.

We as teachers need to resist and challenge the idea that productive history is only that which informs the immediate moment, whether defined by on-the-ground realities or the present news cycle. At the same time, we should acknowledge the desire of students to process the current moment and for their Middle East history course to be a resource in doing so. This, however, requires constructing the course in such a manner so as to engage this desire on the part of the students.

One method of doing so is to create a regular time during class meetings (weekly, biweekly, or otherwise) where students are encouraged to share what current news headlines or on-the-ground developments they are aware of. They could also be encouraged to ask questions during that time seeking to make sense of such news or developments.

Doing so accomplishes two pedagogical goals. First, these discussions establish the course as a place where students can obtain the necessary empirical knowledge or analytic skills to help them shed light on such topics. The discussions encourage students to think about how a history course can be just as relevant to understanding the contemporary moment as an anthropology or political science course would—even if in a different way. Second, these discussions can alternatively underscore the specificity of places, persons, and issues. The complexities of places, figures, and events that went into the making of a particular contemporary juncture give students a glimpse into the depth of Middle East history. All too often, students approach the Middle East expecting that any and all questions have a simple answer and that someone who teaches about the region is someone who can speak to any and all issues of the region. Creating a space where students can verbalize their questions and the teacher can highlight some of the needed information but also acknowledge that further information requires a different type of expertise or course focus reinforces the premise of the Middle East being a region deserving of careful and in-depth study (like any other).

Teachers can deploy other strategies to further encourage the historical engagement of contemporary events and processes. Students can ground what they are learning in the course with ongoing developments outside of the classroom (and inside the region). Three possible sets of activities follow.

Social Media Engagement

Most high school and college students are active on one or more social media platforms, including Facebook, Twitter, and Instagram, but others as well. With some advanced preparation and networking, teachers can develop a listing of social media accounts for students to "follow." Thinking carefully about what types of social media accounts students follow can facilitate the integration of those accounts, the personalities behind them, and their Middle East–related content into students' everyday lives.[7] Teachers or students can craft lists based on specific figures or vocations: scholars, analysts, activists, journalists, commentators, or information-sharing clearinghouses. They may choose to organize their lists geographically. Teachers can identify social media accounts related to specific countries or cities in the region and either supervise the students or allow them to choose from a variety of options. Social media engagement exposes students to daily developments in the Middle East and the debates around the region.

Conducting Supplementary Reading

An alternative set of activities involves identifying specific electronic publications (i.e., e-zines or blogs, but not news outlets) for students to read regularly throughout the semester.[8] Teachers can ask students to monitor the coverage of a particular online publication that comments on and analyzes developments in the Middle East, at a regional, national, or local level. Teachers can organize such a listing of online publications in relation to their geographic coverage, topical focus, or (in the case of multilingual students) publication language. This exposes students to the topics and developments animating people who produce knowledge on the Middle East. It also gives them a broad range of expertise that is available.

Following Country-Specific News

In any given broad survey of Middle East history, it is difficult to sustain a chronological and deep narrative of events in a given part of the region. Having students keep up with an English-language news platform of a particular country can be productive. In this case, the available options are far more limited than those of social media accounts and online platforms of analysis. While English-language sources are more limited, this activity affords students the opportunity to follow developments in a given country throughout the entirety of a school term. Teachers should, however, be cognizant of the uneven availability of English-language sources and the political alignments of those that do exist.[9] Doing so allows students to take particular note of topics or developments that are episodic in nature or coverage as well as those that have a longer-term presence in the news outlet.[10]

Selecting appropriate social media accounts, online supplementary readings, or region-based news stories is an especially difficult task for teachers unfamiliar with the region. It is hoped that some of the examples provided can allay some of the concerns arising from that difficulty. However, there is no substitute for due diligence. The case of *A Gay Girl in Damascus* demonstrates this well.[11] The blog and associated social media accounts professed to belong to a Syrian American named Amina

Abdallah Arraf. The character identified herself as lesbian and living in Damascus during the Syrian uprising. Journalists later revealed Amina to be a hoax persona created and maintained by Tom MacMaster, a US graduate student in Edinburgh, Scotland. The revelations raised important questions about anonymity, authenticity, and how different categories of voices carry different social and political weight in Western media.[12] While a cautionary tale, it can also serve as a useful entry point to discuss responsible social media engagement more generally. One strategy for being diligent about sources for supplementary activities is for teachers to reach out throughout their own networks. Another strategy is to request recommendations from editors at the online platforms cited in this chapter. Teachers can also make use of a number of pedagogical resources, including Programs, Experts, and Resources in Middle East Studies (PERMES)[13] at the Middle East Studies Association and the Middle East Pedagogy Initiative (MESPI)[14] at the Arab Studies Institute.

It is important to integrate these activities into the course as a central component, just as one would do with textbook readings, lecture attendance, quizzes, exams, and papers. Weekly journal assignments documenting these engagements is productive. Teachers should provide clear guidelines to students for the content and format of their entries. Some may emphasize social media. Others may require keeping up with online analysis or local news. A particularly useful component of this exercise is to ask students to identify how history is invoked in one or more of these sources.[15] This affords both the instructor and the students space to assess and critique the uses and abuses of the historical in any given contemporary reflection.

Case Studies in How History Matters

Many teachers seek to create a course whose cumulative takeaway is greater than the sum total of events and processes they cover through readings and lectures. Part of this goal can be accomplished by the above-described strategies of variously creating space and time in the course for students to critically engage with contemporary events and developments relative to the coursework. Yet there remains the matter of teaching the historical content itself in a manner that at times can be directly relevant to the current moment. Certainly, this is not possible with all course material covered in a modern history survey. However, there is much course material with which it is possible.

The guiding principle in doing so is to approach the students with the following orientation: history is necessary to make sense of the present; it does not explain the present in a causal way, but it helps us understand it. Put differently, history is necessary, even if not sufficient on its own, to understand current issues. Teachers can address contemporary dynamics as part of the syllabus in one of two ways. First, there can be specified sessions dealing with variously identified contemporary issues whereby a "necessary, but not sufficient" approach is adopted. Therein, teachers can identify a contemporary topic, provide its basic contours, and proceed to draw on previously covered historical material to shed light on the topic. Second, teachers can work to always include a "contemporary relevance" component to any reading or lecture topic. In this approach, emphasis is placed on the historical legacies of covered developments: how a particular historical dynamic would later impinge on a contemporary phenomenon. The following two case studies of the Arab uprisings and political Islam provide examples of how to link contemporary topics of interest to historical material covered in the course.

Historical Legacies and the Differential Trajectories of the Arab Uprisings

Few contemporary developments occupy the curiosity of the current generation of students as the Arab uprisings do. One challenge for history teachers in discussing the Arab uprisings is to demonstrate how history can be brought to bear on developing explanations for the different trajectories of the uprisings. Certainly, explanations of whichever differences selected can be competing and not mutually exclusive. The purpose here is not to adjudicate between different explanations and their merits, but rather to bring history to bear on debates about the uprisings' trajectories.

One important aspect of how the uprisings manifested relates to the institutions of the armed forces, and their collective response to the pressures of mass protests and the desire of the top echelons of their respective regimes to deploy them to suppress and disperse protesters. For example, the armed forces in Tunisia and Egypt demonstrated a capacity for disciplined and coordinated collective action. In both cases, at least during the period between the eruption of protests and fall of the head of state, the armed forces in Tunisia and Egypt refused to effectively deploy against civilians and—according to some accounts—precipitated the final blow to the head of state. This was not the case in Syria and Yemen. Therein, the armed forces—or some parts thereof—attacked civilian protesters, fragmented, or did some combination of both. In Syria, defections were relatively minimal, occurring at lower levels of the armed forces' organizational structure and primarily taking the form of desertion. Furthermore, many analysts have repeatedly pointed to the fact that the regime of Bashar al-Assad never deployed certain components of the armed forces, weary of its fracturing in a manner more detrimental to the regime's cause. In the case of Yemen, the armed forces splintered at the top levels of the organizational hierarchy, some siding with the regime and others siding with the opposition.

Teachers can discuss how these disparate dynamics vis-à-vis the armed forces reflect differential histories of military institution building across the four case studies. In Tunisia and Egypt, precolonial state elites established the core of the existing armed forces during the nineteenth century.[16] Colonial powers and successive post-independence regimes further advanced the fate of the armed forces, facilitating by 2011 what was almost two hundred years of continuous military institution building.[17] This in turn produced a degree of cohesive corporate identity and command structure that went to the heart of how the armed forces in either Tunisia and Egypt was able to conduct itself as an institution. In contrast, Syria and Yemen featured a much shorter history of military institution building.[18] In the case of Syria, this history is nonexistent prior to 1920, when the French Mandate initiated a process of creating a series of states in parts of the Levant that it would later amalgamate into the Syrian state. Furthermore, this particular history of military institution building can be said to have begun in earnest in the aftermath of 1946, when Syria became independent and state elites began to build its national armed forces on its share of French-created Special Troops of the Levant. In the case of Yemen, the elements that compromised the national armed forces of 2011 only came together in the aftermath of the 1990 unification between the Yemen Arab Republic and the People's Democratic Republic of Yemen. Prior to that date, there were multiple military institutions whose histories varied depending on in which part of present-day Yemen they were created.

Related to the issue of continuous military institution building is the relative balance of power between the armed forces and security services within each state.[19] In all four cases of Tunisia, Egypt, Syria, and Yemen, post-independence authoritarian regimes ultimately but-tressed their rule through creating various and multiple security ser-vices. However, the relative power of these services vis-à-vis the armed forces differed greatly in 2011 and thus impinged on the trajectory of the uprisings. Histories of authoritarian state building in general and of regimes in these countries in particular have paid special attention to the shifting balance of power between the two sets of institutions and the historical forces that led to that particular balance.[20] In Egypt, for example, the shift to an emphasis and preference for security services during the presidency of Hosni Mubarak was offset by Egypt's peace treaty with Israel and its concomitant relationship with the United States. The latter was anchored in a series of military aid packages that continued to fund the armed forces, thus allowing it to retain a level of corporate identity, hierarchy, and discipline central to the role it played in opting to dispatch Mubarak rather than militarily engage the pro-testers demanding his resignation. In Syria, for contrast, several factors motivated the shift to an emphasis on and preference for security ser-vices during the reign of Hafiz al-Assad. On the one hand, Assad's inter-nal coup within the Baʿth regime's leadership was in part a repudiation of the more radical wing's aspirations vis-à-vis a confrontation with Israel in 1967 and the three years immediately following it. On the other hand, Syria's history of multiple military coups incentivized Assad to politically neutralize the armed forces precisely at the expense of its capacity for independent collective action. Unlike Egypt, there were no other dynamics at play that could offset this policy and maintain the institutional capacities of the Syrian armed forces.

Historicizing Political Islam

Political Islam is another contemporary topic on which a history course can help shed light.[21] Critical scholarship and pedagogy in Middle East history have rightly sought to complicate previous trends of overem-phasizing Islam and Islamism. They have also demonstrated the ways in which the history of the region features several junctures that help explain the particular contours of political Islam. Before exploring these junctures, it is worth identifying what is meant by students' curiosity of political Islam. The standard narrative, which many students assume, runs something like this: In the Middle East, Islamist movements dom-inate the political field. They hold stronger sway over state policies, political parties, and popular views than any of their non-Islamist competitors. The conventional narrative also claims that Islamist movements oppose "secularism" or "modernity." Instead, we are told, Islamists view "Islam" as the only (or primary) legitimate guide for political ideas and public policies. In this sense, Islamist movements are variously deemed antimodern, traditionalist, or otherwise holding on to centuries-old ideas and practices.

There are some elements of this standard narrative that are accurate. Yet there is much else that is historically inaccurate and analytically flawed. A history course therefore offers several ways to critically engage this narrative. One approach is to identify those flaws, complicate the narrative, and unpack its underlying assumptions. Yet another approach is to historicize its elements, demonstrating how historical developments contributed to the making of contemporary political Islam.

One important aspect of historicizing political Islam is highlighting its complicity in the experience of modernity. Historians have analyzed the ways in which religious institutions, interpretations, and practices advocated by Islamists represent a break with the centuries prior to the nineteenth century, rather than some unchanging adherence to "traditional" religion. They variously do so by advancing a combination of arguments. Some historians demonstrate that the principles, organizations, and tactics of Islamist movements are circumscribed within the political framework of the nation-state model.[22] Other historians analyze how the nineteenth century was a critical period in which Islam was "ideologized."[23] It is therefore impossible to understand the fundamental premise of most Islamist movements without also understanding the ways Islamic institutions and practices featured an unprecedented transformation beginning in the nineteenth century. Concomitantly, the idea, meaning, and function of religion—including Islam—radically changed during this process. These transformations pivoted around efforts by state officials, religious figures, and colonial powers to standardize Islamic institutions, ideas, and practices, codify Islamic law, and spread them.[24] Such efforts primarily took two forms. First, particular schools of interpretation—or instances therein—were privileged at the expense of others that prior to the nineteenth century would have been viewed as equally valid.[25] Second, the interpretive jurisdiction of Islamic law was expanded to cover domains of life not necessarily the long-standing purview of Islamic jurisprudence.[26] In combination with these two efforts, state officials, religious figures, and colonial powers rendered "Islam" as a marker of the nation.

This is not to deny the specificity of different Islamist movements and the need to attend to the immediate historical context of their formation and operation. It is, however, to draw the attention of students to two historical facts: the very premise of these movements is dependent on a fundamental break with pre-nineteenth-century patterns; this break was concomitant with the integration of the Middle East into the world economy and increasing internalization of its population of the nation-state model of political organization.

Another important aspect of historicizing political Islam is explaining its alleged contemporary dominance. Doing so requires a commitment to exploring the nature of political movements throughout the history covered in the history course. This allows students to understand the existence and competition between a variety of political movements throughout the modern history of the region—including variations of liberal, conservative, socialist, communist, anarchist, fascist, and other movements.[27] It also provides the opportunity to highlight the reality that in the 1950s and 1960s, Islamist movements represented a marginal grouping relative to the dominance of leftist movements. Factors that reversed this power relation between these competing camps of political movements include state policies, regime repression, strategic adjustments of Islamist activists, failures of leftist movements, and foreign interventions.[28] Exploring these factors speaks to a central assumption in the conventional narrative students have about political Islam and its assumed naturalness as the region's dominant form of political ideology and organization.

Conclusion

The teaching of modern Middle East history has always had a built-in set of challenges, some related to the historical discipline and others related to the Middle East region. Compounding such challenges are the overall decline in college-level enrollments for history courses and majors, and the near totalizing shift within high schools to prioritizing subject matters and study skills that pertain to standardized testing. Yet teachers of Middle East history are today charged with unique responsibilities. On the one hand, the digital age—for better or worse—offers important ways to make connections between our students and the region. On the other hand, the contemporary concern with the Middle East as an object of scholarly inquiry, journalist coverage, or policy prescription makes possible the highlighting of just how important history is, both as a source of warning but also as a source of insight into making sense of the current moment.

NOTES

I would like to express my appreciation to Omnia El Shakry for her encouragement, comments, and edits as well as to Rosie Bsheer, Hesham Sallam, and Sherene Seikaly for their feedback on earlier drafts of this chapter.

1. By "contemporary," I refer to the premise of the present chapter: keeping current. For a discussion of institutional and curricular challenges that are beyond the scope of this chapter and volume, see Ziad Abu-Rish, "The Middle East Survey Course: Challenges and Opportunities," *Review of Middle East Studies* 51, no. 1 (2017): 27–30.

2. For an engaging article in this vein, see Molly Crabapple, "My Great-Grandfather the Bundist," *New York Review of Books*, October 6, 2018, https://www.nybooks.com/daily/2018/10/06/my-great-grandfather-the-bundist/.

3. Omnia El Shakry does so with respect to Egypt in an article she published in the midst of the eighteen-day uprising that forced the resignation of Egyptian president Hosni Mubarak in 2011. Joel Beinin, John Chalcraft, and Elizabeth Thompson provide three different approaches to narrating the broader history of popular politics and mobilizations in the region. Beinin provides a synthetic regional history textbook focusing on the experiences of peasants and workers, including their mobilizations. Chalcraft provides a series of essays, varying in lengths, on specific episodes of popular mobilizations. Thompson adopts a biographical approach, moving across the modern period while focusing on the role of specific individuals in their respective movements and countries. See Omnia El Shakry, "Egypt's Three Revolutions: The Force of History behind This Popular Uprising," in *The Dawn of the Arab Uprisings: End of an Old Order?*, ed. Bassam Haddad, Rosie Bsheer, and Ziad Abu-Rish (London: Pluto Press, 2012), 97–103; Joel Beinin, *Workers and Peasants in the Modern Middle East* (Cambridge: Cambridge University Press, 2001); John Chalcraft, *Popular Politics and the Making of the Modern Middle East* (Cambridge: Cambridge University Press, 2016); Elizabeth Thompson, *Justice Interrupted: The Struggle for Constitutional Government in the Middle East* (Cambridge, MA: Harvard University Press, 2013).

4. For example, see Rashid Khalidi, "Preliminary Historical Observations on the Arab Revolutions of 2011," in Haddad, Bsheer, and Abu-Rish, *Dawn of the Arab Uprisings*, 9–16.

5. For one approach to what constitutes modern imperialism in world history and how European interventions in the Middle East prior to World War I fit into that framework, see James L. Gelvin, *The Modern Middle East: A History* (Oxford: Oxford University Press, 2015), 90–105.

6. The lack of a synthetic account of US policy in the region since World War II makes this somewhat difficult. Yet teachers could use specific instances of the US record in the region. See the chapter by Nathan J. Citino in this volume for a broad overview as well as relevant references to secondary literature.

7. It is impossible to provide a comprehensive list, and any identified account may—in due course—become outdated. Examples of potential individual accounts include Maryam Alkhawaja (@maryamdalkhawaja, Bahraini human rights activist), Zenobia (@Zeinobia, Egyptian blogger and journalist), Souhail Karam (@Massinissa1973, journalist based in Rabat, Morocco), @ibra himhamidi (Ibrahim Hamidi, journalist covering Syria), and @fgeerdink (Frederike Geerdink, journalist based in Suleymaniyya, Iraq). There are also the Twitter accounts of various Middle East–related publications. See notes 8 and 9 for examples.

8. While some publications cover the region as a whole, others are more specialized. Here, again, a comprehensive list is not possible; however, any list should include +972 *Magazine* (https://972mag.com), *7iber* (https://www.7iber.com/category/english-content/), *Informed Comment* (https://www.juancole.com), *Jadaliyya* (http://www.jadaliyya.com), and *Middle East Report* (https://merip.org).

9. Here again, a comprehensive list is not possible; however, any list should include Egypt's *Mada Masr* (https://madamasr.com/en), Iraq's *Niqash* (http://www.niqash.org), and Lebanon's *Beirut Report* (http://www.beirutreport.com). In some countries, there is only one English-language news outlet. See, for example, *Libya Herald* (https://www.libyaherald.com/). In other countries, the only available English-language news outlet is closely aligned with—if not owned by—the government. See, for example, *The Jordan Times* (http://www.jordantimes.com/).

10. Students can also keep track of major developments related to a specific country through *Jadaliyya*'s series of media roundups, including region- or country-specific roundups (i.e., Arabian Peninsula, Egypt, Maghreb, Palestine, and Syria) and topical roundups (e.g., Cities, Migrants and Refugees, and Critical Currents in Islam). A different resource is Mideast Wire (www.mideastwire.com), which offers a daily digest of translated news articles and opinion pieces originally published in the Middle East in languages other than English. However, this service requires a paid subscription.

11. Brian Whitaker, "Gay Girl in Damascus Was an Arrogant Fantasy," *Guardian*, June 12, 2011, https://www.theguardian.com/commentisfree/2011/jun/13/gay-girl-in-damascus-hoax-blog.

12. Amira Jarmakani, *An Imperialist Love Story: Desert Romances and the War on Terror* (New York: New York University Press, 2015), xii–xiii. I thank Andrea Lea Miller for this reference and her broader encouragement to use *Gay Girl in Damascus* as a specific example of some of the pitfalls of uncritically engaging social media and the broader politics of representation.

13. PERMES, Middle East Studies Association, https://mesana.org/permes/.

14. MESPI, Arab Studies Institute, https://mespi.org.

15. For a model to which students can aspire based on historians doing the same, see Muriam Haleh Davis, "Quick Thoughts: Historical Memory in Algeria's Current Protests," *Jadaliyya*, March 7, 2019, https://www.jadaliyya.com/Details/38442/Quick-Thoughts-Historical-Memory-in-Algeria's-Current-Protests-38442.

16. Gelvin provides one synthesis of existing scholarship on this topic, comparing the cases of Khedival Egypt, Beylicate Tunisia, the Ottoman Empire, and Qajar Empire. Lisa Anderson explores how these dynamics manifested in Tunisia. Khaled Fahmy explores the Egyptian case. See Gelvin, *Modern Middle East*, 72–89; Lisa Anderson, *The State and Social Transformation in Tunisia and Libya, 1830–1980* (Princeton, NJ: Princeton University Press, 1986), 57–95; Khaled Fahmy, *All the Pasha's Men: Mehmed Ali, His Army and the Making of Modern Egypt* (Cairo: American University of Cairo Press, 2002), 41–78, 211–50.

17. On the Tunisian case, see Anderson, *State and Social Transformation*, 135–78, 223–50; Risa A. Brooks, "The Tunisian Military and Democratic Control of the Armed Forces," in *Armies and Insurgencies in the Arab Spring*, ed. Holger Albrecht, Aurel Coissant, and Fred H. Lawson (Philadelphia: University of Pennsylvania Press, 2016), 203–24. On the Egyptian case, see Zeinab Abul-Magd, *Militarizing the Nation: The Army, Business, and Revolution in Egypt* (New York: Columbia University Press, 2018); Imad Harb, "The Egyptian Military in Politics: Disengagement or Accommodation," *Middle East Journal* 57, no. 2 (2003), 269–90.

18. This helps account for the relatively sparse scholarship on the armed forces of Syria and Yemen. However, the commonly accepted political history of both states points to the plausibility of such differences with the cases of Tunisia and Egypt.

19. The scholarship on the issue of balance of power is uneven across case studies. Even in existing studies, it is difficult to ascertain the exact nature and balance of power. Conducting such research also poses a high risk to the researcher and their interlocutors.

20. For general comparative analyses and how the Arab uprisings affected them, see Fred H. Lawson, "Armed Forces, Internal Security Services, and Popular Contention in the Middle East and North Africa," in *Armies and Insurgencies in the Arab Spring*, ed. Holger Albrecht, Aurel Coissant, and Fred H. Lawson

(Philadelphia: University of Pennsylvania Press, 2016), 54–70. For a case-specific analysis of the balance of power between the armed forces and intelligence services, see Hazem Kandil, *Soldiers, Spies, and Statesmen: Egypt's Road to Revolt* (London: Verso, 2013).

21. See Joel Beinin and Joe Stork, "On the Modernity, Historical Specificity, and International Context of Political Islam," in *Political Islam: Essays from Middle East Report*, ed. Beinin and Stork (Berkeley: University of California Press, 1997), 3–28.

22. See, for example, Beinin and Stork, *Political Islam*; Sami Zubaida, "The Nation State in the Middle East," in *Islam, the People, and the State: Political Ideas and Movements in the Middle East* (London: I. B. Tauris, 1993): 121–82.

23. James Gelvin, "Secularism and Religion in the Arab Middle East: Reinventing Islam in a World of Nation-States," in *The Invention of Religion: Rethinking Belief in Politics and History*, ed. Derek R. Peterson and Darren Walhof (New Brunswick, NJ: Rutgers University Press, 2002).

24. On such transformations in the late Ottoman Empire, see Selim Deringil, *The Well-Protected Domains: Ideology and the Legitimation of Power in the Ottoman Empire, 1876–1909* (London: I. B. Tauris, 1998); Kemal H. Karpat, *The Politicization of Islam: Reconstructing Identity, State Authority, and Community in the Late Ottoman Empire* (Oxford: Oxford University Press, 2002).

25. The changing nature of how Islamic jurisprudence adjudicates gender relations is both an empirically and pedagogically illustrative example of this process. See Judith Tucker, *Women, Family, and Islamic Law* (Cambridge: Cambridge University Press, 2008).

26. See, for example, Khaled Fahmy, *In Quest of Justice: Islamic Law and Forensic Medicine in Modern Egypt* (Berkeley: University of California Press, 2018).

27. Scholars have produced a copious body of literature on specific movements as well as the broader political field it constituted. For an introductory course, Thompson's *Justice Interrupted* can serve as a useful snapshot of that diversity across space and time.

28. Scholarship on these dynamics is well developed. Yet a particularly useful text to excerpt from for an introductory course deals with students in particular: Abdullah al-Arian, *Answering the Call: Popular Islamic Activism in Sadat's Egypt* (Oxford: Oxford University Press, 2014).

KEY RESOURCES

TEXTBOOKS AND PRIMARY SOURCES

Anderson, Betty S. *A History of the Modern Middle East: Rulers, Rebels, and Rogues.* Stanford, CA: Stanford University Press, 2016.

Gelvin, James L. *The Modern Middle East: A History*. New York: Oxford University Press, 2015.

Khater, Akram Fouad. *Sources in the History of the Modern Middle East*. 2nd ed. New York: Cengage Learning, 2010.

PEDAGOGY-FOCUSED SOURCES

Checkered History. Home of the Political Uses of the Past Project. http://history checked.com.

Middle East Studies Pedagogy Initiative (MESPI). Arab Studies Institute. https:// mespi.org.

"Pedagogy." Special issue, *JADMAG* 7, no. 2 (2019).

MULTIMEDIA SOURCES

Ottoman History Podcast. http://www.ottomanhistorypodcast.com.

Status Audio Magazine. http://www.statushour.com.

Contributors

ZIAD ABU-RISH is codirector of the MA program in Human Rights and the Arts and a visiting associate professor at Bard College. He was previously assistant professor in the History Department and founding director of the Middle East and North Africa Studies Certificate program at Ohio University. Abu-Rish is codirector of the Middle East Studies Pedagogy Initiative and serves as coeditor of *Arab Studies Journal* and *Jadaliyya* e-zine.

OVAMIR ANJUM is a professor and the Imam Khattab Endowed Chair of Islamic Studies in the Department of Philosophy and Religious Studies at the University of Toledo. He is an intellectual historian and philosopher whose work focuses on the nexus of theology, politics, and epistemology in classical and modern Islam. He is the author of *Politics, Law, and Community in Islamic Thought: The Taymiyyan Moment* (2012). He is also near completing a decade-long project to translate a popular Islamic spiritual and theological classic, *Madarij al-Salikin* (Ranks of Divine Seekers) by Ibn al-Qayyim (d. 1351), whose first two (of four) volumes are due in 2020 from Brill Publishers. He is currently working on a number of projects, including a history of Islam in the caliphal period (first three centuries) and another on Islamic political thought.

ASEF BAYAT is the Catherine and Bruce Bastian Professor of Global and Transnational Studies in the Department of Sociology, University of Illinois, Urbana-Champaign. Before joining Illinois, Bayat taught at the American University in Cairo for many years and served as the director of the International Institute for the Study of Islam in the Modern World (ISIM), holding the Chair of Society and Culture of the Modern Middle East at Leiden University, Netherlands. His current research concerns an understanding of the Arab revolutions—historically, comparatively, and sociologically. He is the author of many books including, most recently, *Revolution without Revolutionaries: Making Sense of the Arab Spring* (2017), *Life as Politics: How Ordinary People Change the Middle East* (2nd ed., 2013), and *Post-Islamism: The Changing Face of Political Islam* (2013).

NATHAN J. CITINO is Barbara Kirkland Chiles Professor of History at Rice University. He is the author of *From Arab Nationalism to OPEC: Eisenhower, King Sa'ud, and the Making of US-Saudi Relations* (2002) and *Envisioning the Arab Future: Modernization in US-Arab Relations, 1945–1967* (2017; winner of the 2018 SHAFR Robert H. Ferrell Book Prize), as well as articles published in *Diplomacy and Statecraft, International Journal of Middle East Studies, Business History Review, Arab Studies Journal,* and *Cold War History.* From 2001 to 2014 he was associate editor of *Diplomatic History.* His current research examines the US empire in the Middle East and beyond. Citino teaches undergraduate and graduate courses in the history of the US and the world and in modern US history.

ELLIOTT COLLA is an associate professor of Arabic and Islamic studies at Georgetown University. His current research centers on modern Egyptian literary production in the context of social movement theory and performance studies. He is the author of *Conflicted Antiquities: Egyptology, Egyptomania, Egyptian Modernity* (2007) and many essays on modern Arab literature, culture, and politics. He has translated novels, short stories, and poems by authors from Libya, Syria, Egypt, and Palestine—including Ibrahim Aslan's *The Heron* (2005), Idris Ali's *Poor* (2007), Ibrahim al-Koni's *Gold Dust* (2008), and Raba'i al-Madhoun's *The Lady from Tel Aviv* (2014).

MURIAM HALEH DAVIS is an assistant professor of history at the University of California, Santa Cruz. Her research interests focus on development, decolonization, and race in Algeria. In addition to publishing articles in *Journal of Contemporary History, Journal of French and Francophone Philosophy,* and *Journal of European Integration History,* she recently coedited a volume entitled *North Africa and the Making of Europe: Governance, Institutions and Culture* (2018).

ROCHELLE DAVIS is an associate professor of cultural anthropology and outgoing director of the Center for Contemporary Arab Studies at Georgetown University's Edmund A. Walsh School of Foreign Service. Her main research is on forced migration, war, and conflict, particularly Palestinian, Syrian, and Iraqi refugees and internally displaced persons. Her first book, *Palestinian Village Histories: Geographies of the Displaced* (2011; co-winner of the Albert Hourani Book Award), addresses how Palestinian refugees today write histories of their villages that were destroyed in the 1948 war and the stories and commemorations of village life that are circulated in the diaspora. She is currently writing a book on the role of culture in the US wars in Iraq and Afghanistan. Davis is also the lead qualitative researcher on a five-year longitudinal study of four thousand Iraqi families displaced by ISIS. She has published articles and reports on displaced Syrians and on Sudanese and Somali refugees in Jordan, and she is working on issues related to gender and vulnerability. Her teaching interests include narrative theory and culture, refugees, migrants and immigrants in and out of the Arab World, and war and conflict.

OMNIA EL SHAKRY is a professor of history at the University of California, Davis. She specializes in the intellectual and cultural history of the modern Middle East, with a particular emphasis on the history of the human and religious sciences in modern Egypt. She is the author of *The Arabic Freud: Psychoanalysis and Islam in Modern Egypt* (2017) and *The Great Social Laboratory: Subjects of Knowledge in Colonial and Postcolonial Egypt* (2007) and the editor of *Gender and Sexuality in Islam* (2016). Her current book project traces the emergence of a vibrant movement of intellectual and religious exchange between Muslim and Catholic scholars in twentieth-century Egypt. El Shakry teaches undergraduate and graduate courses in modern Middle East history and world history and was the recipient of the Distinguished Graduate and Postdoctoral Mentoring Award at UC Davis in 2017.

MICHAEL GASPER is an associate professor of history at Occidental College in Los Angeles. He is the author of *The Power of Representation: Publics, Peasants and Islam in Egypt* (2009) and (with Michael Bonine and Abbas Amanat) coedited *Is There a Middle East? The Evolution of a Geopolitical Concept* (2011). His current book project, based on oral histories collected between 2008 and 2017, is tentatively entitled "Everyday Life during the Lebanese Civil War, 1975–1990."

ARIELLE GORDON is a PhD student at the University of Michigan in history and women's studies. She received her BA in history and Islamic and Middle Eastern studies from Brandeis University in 2016. Her research focuses on gender, protest, and visual culture in the twentieth-century Middle East and Latin America. She was awarded highest honors for her thesis, "The Woman with a Gun: A History of the Iranian Revolution's Most Famous Icon," and was the 2014 recipient of the Jane's Essay Prize in Latin American Studies at Brandeis University.

HANAN HAMMAD is an associate professor and the director of Middle East studies at Texas Christian University. She is the author of *Industrial Sexuality: Gender, Urbanization, and Social Transformation in Egypt* (2016; winner of the Sara A. Whaley Book Prize, Middle East Political Economy Project Book Award, and the AMEWS Book Award). Her work has appeared in *Arab*

Studies Journal, Alif: Journal of Comparative Poetics, International Review of Social History, Journal of International Women's Studies, Journal of Social History, and *Radical History Review.* She is currently working on her second book project, *Layla Murad: Popular Culture, Gender, and the Politics of Egyptianness.* She teaches introductory courses on Islamic civilization and the modern Middle East, as well as advanced and graduate courses on modern Egypt, revolutionary Iran, global history of prostitution, and women in the Middle East. In 2015 she was awarded the Jean Giles-Sims Wise Woman Award and received fellowships from Berlin-Brandenburg Academy of Sciences (2010–11), Woolf Institute (Cambridge, 2014–15), and Crown Center of Middle East Studies at Brandeis University (2018–19).

ALMA RACHEL HECKMAN is the Neufeld-Levin Chair of Holocaust Studies and an assistant professor of history and Jewish studies at the University of California, Santa Cruz. She specializes in modern Jewish history of North Africa and the Middle East with an interest in citizenship, political transformations, transnationalism, and empire. Her first book, *The Sultan's Communists: Moroccan Jews and the Politics of Belonging,* will be published in 2020. Additionally, she is working on a coedited volume examining Jews in radical politics in a comparative framework. She has held fellowships with Fulbright, the United States Holocaust Memorial Museum, and the Katz Center for Advanced Judaic Studies at the University of Pennsylvania and has published her work in a number of journals and edited volumes.

TOBY CRAIG JONES is an associate professor in the Department of History at Rutgers University and the director of the MA program in global and comparative history. He is the author of *Desert Kingdom: How Oil and Water Forged Modern Saudi Arabia* (2010) and *Running Dry: Essays on Energy, Water, and Environmental Crisis* (2015). He is currently working on a book about the shooting down of an Iranian passenger jet by the US Navy in 1988. He has written for the *International Journal of Middle East Studies, Journal of American History, Middle East Report, Raritan Quarterly Review, The Nation, The Atlantic, London Review of Books, New York Times,* and elsewhere. He teaches courses on global environmental history, energy, and the modern Middle East. In 2015 Jones was recognized as a Rutgers Chancellor's Scholar for distinguished scholarship.

DARRYL LI is an assistant professor of anthropology and a lecturer in law at the University of Chicago. He is the author of *The Universal Enemy: Jihad, Empire, and the Challenge of Solidarity* (2020) and an attorney who has litigated or provided expert testimony in cases arising from the Global War on Terror.

Ussama Makdisi is a professor of history and the first holder of the Arab-American Educational Foundation Chair of Arab Studies at Rice University. He is the author of *Age of Coexistence: The Ecumenical Frame and the Making of the Modern Arab World* (2019) and *Faith Misplaced: The Broken Promise of US-Arab Relations, 1820–2001* (2010). His previous books include *Artillery of Heaven: American Missionaries and the Failed Conversion of the Middle East* (2008; winner of the Albert Hourani Book Award and the John Hope Franklin Prize) and *The Culture of Sectarianism: Community, History, and Violence in Nineteenth Century Ottoman Lebanon* (2000). His articles have appeared in the *Journal of American History, American Historical Review, Diplomatic History, International Journal of Middle East Studies*, and *Comparative Studies in Society and History*. He is the recipient of numerous fellowships and awards and has previously held fellowships from the American Academy of Berlin, the Wissenschaftskolleg zu Berlin (Institute for Advanced Study, Berlin), and the American Council of Learned Societies. The Carnegie Corporation named Makdisi a 2009 Carnegie Scholar as part of its effort to promote original scholarship regarding Muslim societies and communities.

Christine Philliou is an associate professor of history at the University of California, Berkeley, where she specializes in the political and social history of the Ottoman Empire and modern Turkey and Greece as parts of the post-Ottoman world. Her book *Biography of an Empire: Governing Ottomans in an Age of Revolution* (2011) examines the changes in Ottoman governance leading up to the Tanzimat reforms of the mid-nineteenth century. Her second book, *Turkey: A Past against History* (2021), takes up the political and cultural concept of *muhalefet*, or opposition, in the course of transition from Ottoman to Republican Turkish regimes. Her interests and other publications focus on comparative empires across Eurasia, various levels of transitions from an "Ottoman" to a "post-Ottoman" world in the nineteenth and twentieth centuries, and political and cultural interfaces in the eastern Mediterranean, Middle East, and Balkans in the early modern and modern eras.

Sara Pursley is an assistant professor in the departments of history and Middle Eastern and Islamic studies at New York University. She is the author of *Familiar Futures: Time, Selfhood, and Sovereignty in Iraq, 1920–63* (2019), and her articles have appeared in *International Journal of Middle East Studies, History of the Present, Psychoanalysis and History, Journal of Middle East Women's Studies*, and *Jadaliyya*. Pursley was a Cotsen postdoctoral fellow at the Society of Fellows, Princeton University, from 2014 to 2016 and served as associate editor of *International Journal of Middle East Studies* from 2009 to 2014.

KAMRAN RASTEGAR is a professor of comparative literature in the Department of International Literary and Cultural Studies at Tufts University, where he also directs the Center for the Humanities at Tufts. He is the author of the books *Surviving Images: Cinema, War and Cultural Memory in the Middle East* (2015) and *Literary Modernity between the Middle East and Europe* (2007) and edited the special issue *Authoring the Nahda: Writing the Arabic Nineteenth Century* for the journal *Middle Eastern Literatures* (2013).

SHERENE SEIKALY is an associate professor of history at the University of California, Santa Barbara. Seikaly's *Men of Capital: Scarcity and Economy in Mandate Palestine* (2016) explores how Palestinian capitalists and British colonial officials used economy to shape territory, nationalism, the home, and the body. Her second book, *From Baltimore to Beirut: On the Question of Palestine* (forthcoming), focuses on a Palestinian man who was at once a colonial officer and a colonized subject, an enslaver and a refugee. His trajectory from nineteenth-century mobility across Baltimore and Sudan to twentieth-century immobility in Lebanon places the question of Palestine in a global history of race, capital, slavery, and dispossession. Seikaly is the recipient of the Distinguished Teaching Award from the Academic Senate, the University of California, Santa Barbara; the Harold J. Plous Award at UCSB; and the UC President's Faculty Research Fellowship. She currently serves as coeditor of *Journal of Palestine Studies* and is cofounder and coeditor of *Jadaliyya*.

NAGHMEH SOHRABI is the Charles (Corky) Goodman Professor of Middle East History and the Director for Research at the Crown Center for Middle East Studies at Brandeis University. She is the author of *Taken for Wonder: Nineteenth Century Travel Accounts from Iran to Europe* (2012) and numerous articles on Iranian history and politics. Her current book project is on the experience of the 1979 revolution in Iran for which she has received fellowships from the Andrew W. Mellon Foundation, the American Council for Learned Societies, and the American Academy in Berlin.

KIT ADAM WAINER teaches social studies at Leon M. Goldstein High School in Brooklyn, New York. He has been a New York City school teacher for more than thirty years and teaches primarily advanced placement world history and global history and geography. He is an AP World History Exam Table Leader and a College Board Workshop Consultant. He is the author of *Strive for a Five: Preparing for the AP World History Exam* (2019) and a contributor to Robert W. Strayer and Erik W. Nelson, *Ways of the World: A Global History with Sources* (4th ed., 2019).

Index

The Harvey Goldberg Series
for Understanding and Teaching History

www.ingramcontent.com/pod-product-compliance
Lightning Source LLC
Chambersburg PA
CBHW070403100426
42812CB00005B/1625